Perspectives on Ecosystem Management for the Great Lakes

SUNY Series in *Environmental Public Policy*
Lester W. Milbrath, Editor

PERSPECTIVES ON ECOSYSTEM MANAGEMENT FOR THE GREAT LAKES

A Reader

Lynton K. Caldwell, Editor

State University of New York Press

Published by
State University of New York Press, Albany

© 1988 State University of New York

All rights reserved

Printed in the United States of America

No part of this book may be used or reproduced
in any manner whatsoever without written permission
except in the case of brief quotations embodied in
critical articles and reviews.

For information, address State University of New York
Press, State University Plaza, Albany, N.Y., 12246

Library of Congress Cataloging in Publication Data

Library of Congress Cataloging-in-Publication Data
Perspectives on ecosystem management for the Great Lakes : a reader / Lynton K. Caldwell, editor.
    p. cm.—(SUNY series in environmental public policy)
    "This collection of papers grew out of a Canadian-United States inter-university seminar that was carried on for several years"—Pref.
    Includes index.
    ISBN 0-88706-765-4. ISBN 0-88706-766-2 (pbk.)
    1. Water resources development—Law and legislation—Great Lakes Region. 2. Water resources development—Great Lakes Region. I. Caldwell, Lynton Keith, 1913- . II. Series.
KDZ640.Z7P47 1988
346.7704'691—dc19
[347.7064691]   87-24497
         CIP

10 9 8 7 6 5 4 3 2 1

CONTENTS

Preface   vii

Acknowledgements   ix

Introduction: Implementing an Ecological Systems Approach to Basinwide Management
    Lynton K. Caldwell   1

1. The Ecosystems Approach: A Strategy for the Management of Renewable Resources in the Great Lakes Basin
    R. L. Thomas, J. R. Vallentyne, K. Ogilvie, and J. D. Kingham   31

2. The Great Lakes: 1955–1985
    Leonard B. Dworsky   59

3. Institutional Arrangements for Great Lakes Management
    Michael J. Donahue   115

4. A Governance Structure Designed to Learn Would Better Protect the Great Lakes Ecosystem
    Lester W. Milbrath   141

5. Remediation and Rehabilitation of the Great Lakes
    Henry Regier, with the assistance of Lee Botts and John E. Gannon   169

6. Biodancing: The 1-2-3 of Great Lakes Monitoring
    Bruce L. Bandurski   191

7. The Great Lakes as a Water Resource

   A. Questions of Ownership and Control
   Julia R. Wilder 243

   B. Great Lakes Diversions:
   A Conflict Assessment
   Sally Cole-Misch 287

8. Toward a More Accountable Process: The Royal Society–National Research Council Report
   Don Munton 299

9. Great Lakes Governance and the Ecosystem Approach: Where Next?
   George R. Francis 319

Appendices

   A. Treaty between the United States and Great Britain (1909) 345

   B. Agreement on Great Lakes Water Quality (1978) 355

   C. The Great Lakes Charter, adopted by Governors and Premiers (1985) 359

Contributors 363

PREFACE

This collection of papers grew out of a Canadian–United States interuniversity seminar that was held over several years and that was assisted by the Donner Foundation with incremental support by participating universities and the Johnson Foundation. The seminar produced two realizations that became the motivation for this book. First was the recognition of the need for a reader—a general interpretative set of papers—explaining and describing the need for a basinwide ecological approach to the implementation of the international agreements for the environmental protection and restoration of the Great Lakes. Second was the desirability of sharing the articles prepared for the seminar.

No general treatment of management for the lakes or set of relevant papers has appeared since 1974, when *The Great Lakes of the United States and Canada—A Reader on Management Improvement Strategies* was prepared at Cornell University for the Office of Water Resources Research, U.S. Corps of Engineers, under the direction of Dr. Leonard Dworsky, one of the contributors to this volume. But the 1978 Water Quality Agreement and its implementation make a new treatment of Great Lakes management timely.

The project title, *Perspectives on Ecosystem Management for the Great Lakes,* was chosen to reflect the following reasoning. With relatively few exceptions, the lakes themselves are not directly managed. There are, of course, specific instances of direct management—such as the regulation of water levels or the manipulation of biota (for example, species of fish). But the greater task of environmental protection for the lakes involves managing certain activities of people. The greater body of law and policy is directed toward those human activities that affect the lakes and their quality. The governments of Canada and the United States have made certain management commitments for the lakes, and this volume contains the professional reflections of those who have observed how those commitments have been implemented.

The nine chapters following this introduction relate to the common theme—the implementation of existing binational agreements—but more specifically to the actualization of an ecosystems approach as called for initially in the 1978 report of a special committee to the Great Lakes Research (now Science) Advisory Board of the International Joint Commission. Individual chapters, however, focus on differing aspects of the managerial problem and on the limits and possibilities of binational cooperation. Each paper represents the particular viewpoint of its author or authors. No attempt has been made to force their findings, interpretations, or styles of expression into a common mold. Variations in capitalization, references, and citations are not results of careless editing; rather they reflect the stylistic preferences of the contributors which the editors regarded as not unreasonable. Consistency and coherence in detail have not been sought; rather, the intent has been to explore various routes to a common goal.

The authors have not presumed to instruct the governments or peoples of Canada and the United States regarding specific policies or actions pursuant to agreements for the protection of the lakes. Their purpose, and hence the purpose of the book, is to stimulate public interest, to provide information regarding the ways in which the lakes are being (or might be better) protected, and to assist the growth of public understanding on both sides of the boundary waters regarding the common interest in safeguarding the valuable but vulnerable asset that this great freshwater system represents. In addition to the essays, the book contains (in chapter 2) a chronology of major events pertaining to international management for the lakes and essential portions of major agreements (such as the Boundary Waters Treaty of 1909 and the Water Quality Agreements of 1978). Copies of these basic documents are also provided in an appendix.

Public understanding of what is required to achieve a basinwide ecological approach to management for the lakes is possibly the greatest present need for putting into action what governments have agreed in principle to do. International Joint Commission reports and governmental and scientific documents relative to the lakes are not distributed with the breadth that public exposure requires; nor are they always written or packaged to give the public a convenient overview of management for the lakes. This volume seeks to meet a need not presently being met elsewhere.

Lynton K. Caldwell

ACKNOWLEDGEMENTS

The authors and editor gratefully acknowledge permissions granted by the following journals to reprint all or portions of the following chapters: *Natural Resource Journal,* chapter 2, by Leonard B. Dworsky; *Indiana Law Journal,* chapter 7A, by Julia R. Wilder; *The Environmental Professional,* chapter 7B by Sally Cole-Misch; *Alternatives,* chapter 9 by George R. Francis. Assistance from the Great Lakes Regional Office of the International Joint Commission should also be acknowledged. Individual authors have indicated personal appreciation for funding and other assistance to their particular contributions.

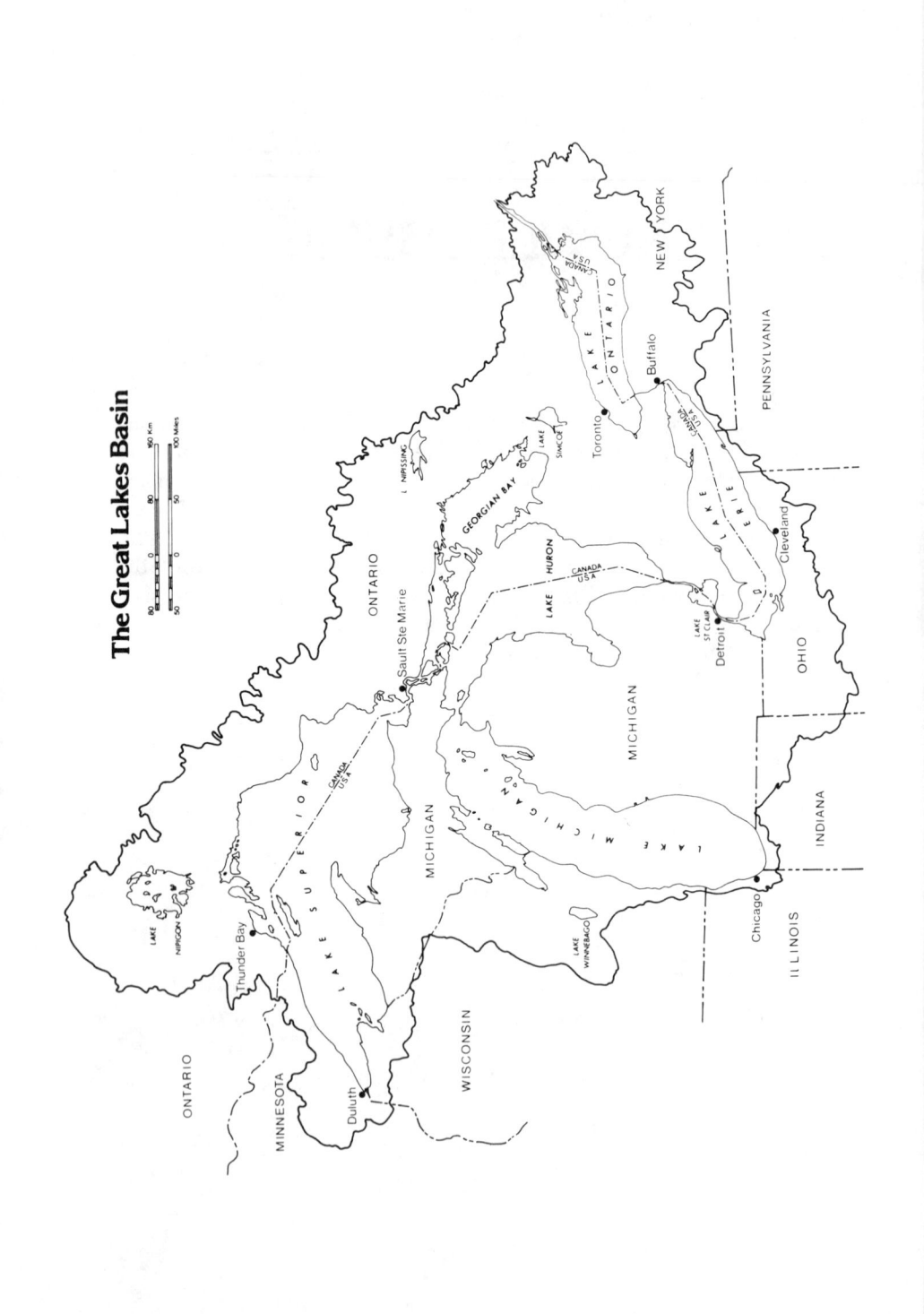

The Great Lakes Basin

LYNTON K. CALDWELL

INTRODUCTION: IMPLEMENTING AN ECOLOGICAL SYSTEMS APPROACH TO BASINWIDE MANAGEMENT

This book brings together the perspectives of a group of scholars, Canadian and American, who over a period of years have given thoughtful attention to public and international responsibility for the Great Lakes. The impact of humans on the lakes and their hinterlands has created adverse conditions that require human management to control or correct. Seldom are the lakes themselves "managed," and then indirectly through control over human action. Inadvertent change (for example, the introduction of lamprey eels) is not management, but often leads to consequences that require management.

Since the early twentieth century, man's impacts on the lakes have reached levels of complexity and severity that threaten their life support capabilities and that have in many places already greatly impaired their quality. Especially during the past decade, management for the lakes has acquired a new urgency. There is widespread agreement among informed people that more positive and coherent measures must be taken to arrest deterioration of the Great Lakes and to restore some of their former quality.

Several major studies and reports, presently to be cited, have addressed the problem of how to provide more effective management for the lakes. This introduction provides a background for the essays to follow by reviewing the principal concept that has emerged from these documents—the basinwide ecosystem approach. Four of the documents important to the definition and development of the ecosystem approach are referenced at the conclusion of this introduction. There is much greater agreement that a basinwide ecosystem approach is needed than there is on how to achieve it. Constructive thinking needs to be based on understanding how the present arrangements work and where experience has indicated that they fail to implement a basinwide ecosystem approach.

Each of the contributors to this volume looks at the institutional structure of governance for the Great Lakes from a personal point of view. All are professionally qualified to do so. There are differences as well as similarities in their perspectives. Implicit in most and explicit in some is a belief that the major deterrent to the implementation of an ecosystem approach is conceptual. This opinion was shared by members of the International Joint Commission Science Advisory Board for the Great Lakes in a nominal group process (opinion poll) exercise in November 1986. The group identified the following five principal barriers to achieving the basinwide ecosystem approach to a Great Lakes policy advocated by the board since 1978:

Concepts. Within this category the following specific problems were identifed: (1) lack of understanding of the ecosystem concepts, (2) lack of a biospheric or ecological perspective, and (3) a difference in opinion regarding the implications of an ecosystem approach.

Values. The following value problems were identified: (1) lack of an environmental ethic, (2) a religious orientation lacking an ecological or stewardship obligation, (3) an ego-centered rather than an eco-centered outlook on life, and (4) dominant materialistic or material use-centered values.

Priorities. Participants saw a widespread tendency to place economic (marketplace) considerations above ecological or environmental considerations. Some saw this problem as a result of ego-centered parochial perspectives and local or occupational biases.

Responsibilities. Closely related to values and priorities were opinions that local, self-centered, and short-range considerations obstructed the implementation of a more socially oriented, longer-range perspective on appropriate public action.

Institutions. An inadequate institutional structure, notably in government, was one of the problems frequently identified as obstructive. Failures included inertia in the present system, fractionalized jurisdiction, and lack of interdisciplinary cooperation (in science and government) that frustrated a holistic attack upon basinwide ecosystem problems.

Some participants saw the lack of monitoring and of reliable means for measuring progress toward objectives as problematic. But this deficiency did not show up in all of the rounds of responses. Inability to forecast was indicated as problematic (by three) but was not among the five top issues, perhaps because it was perceived as "operational" rather than substantive.

WHAT IS AN ECOSYSTEM APPROACH?

By formal agreement between Canada and the United States of America, policies directed toward the restoration and enhancement of water quality in the Great Lakes are to be based upon a basinwide ecosystemic view of the field of action. Article I(g) of the Great Lakes Water Quality Agreement of 1978 defines the Great Lakes ecosystem as: "the interacting components of air, land, water, and living organisms, including man, within the drainage basin of the St. Lawrence River at or upstream from the point at which this river becomes the international boundary between Canada and the United States." The agreement declares that "restoration and enhancement of the boundary waters cannot be achieved independently of other parts of the Great Lakes Basin Ecosystem with which these waters interact." An ecosystem approach means, therefore, that action affecting the lakes, taken or authorized by the governments, shall proceed on the understanding that the bounded field of policy is no less than the basinwide watershed of the Great Lakes and the multifarious relationships interacting within and intruding from without.

Article II of the Agreement—Purpose—reaffirms the commitment to an ecosystem approach to policy and action:

> The purpose of the Parties is to restore and maintain the chemical, physical, and biological integrity of the waters of the Great Lakes Basin Ecosystem. In order to achieve this purpose, the Parties agree to make a maximum effort to develop programs, practices and technology necessary for a better understanding of the Great Lakes Basin Ecosystem and to eliminate or reduce to the maximum extent practicable the discharge of pollutants into the Great Lakes System.

The history of the steps leading to adoption of the ecosystem approach by the International Joint Commission (IJC) may be found in a special report to the commission by the Great Lakes Research (now science) Advisory Board presented in July 1978. This document, entitled *The Ecosystem Approach,* was in response to a request from the IJC "for further advice on the scope and implications of the ecosystem approach in problem identification, research, and management in the Great Lakes Basin, advocated by the Board in its 1977 Annual Report." The 1978 special report to the IJC was prepared by an ad hoc committee of the Research Advisory Board chaired by Dr. Jack Vallentyne, and its recommendations for revising the 1972 Water Quality Agreement provided the basis for the ecosystem approach commitment in the 1978 agreement. The committee recognized that full implementation of the concept would be a long process, that new legislative and institutional arrangements would ultimately be needed, and that public understanding of the ecosystem concept was important to its implementation.

The adoption of a basinwide ecosystem approach to management for the lakes is a decision of major international importance. In its *Second Biennial Report* (December 31, 1984), the IJC, charged with special responsibilities and functions relating to the 1978 Great Lakes Water Quality Agreement made the following statement regarding ecosystem approaches and their implications. Because it is the most complete official interpretation of the concept by the IJC, the statement is cited here in full.

> The Great Lakes Water Quality Agreement is a milestone document, one of the first international statements that technical, diplomatic, and administrative approaches to resource management need to be considered in terms of holistic ecological concepts. Land, water, air and biota interact and are mutually influenced. Existing resource management approaches which partition the environment into separate components of land, water and air with associated biota are recognized as inadequate since management of a resource component in isolation from adjacent or interacting components would likely produce short-sighted strategies to protect one component of the environment at the expense of another. Because existing environmental and resource programs are separated, compartmentalized and spread throughout various bureaus, agencies, ministries and departments, the new approach requiring a holistic overview entails, at the very least, a reorganization of thinking, and perhaps a reorganization of institutional arrangements.
>
> A seemingly unrecognized dimension is the extent to which institutional arrangements limit the ability of scientists and scientific institutions to focus on relevant research leading to the technical resolution of environmental problems. Compartmentalization is often associated with rigid interpretations of "missions" or "mandates" as expressed by legislation or regulations which authorize programs.

Implementing an Ecological Systems Approach

The restrictions of the "mandate" or regulation are then translated into limitations on the style of technical solutions. This approach has led to considerable frustration on the part of individuals who have recognized the importance of holistic approaches to solving environmental problems.

The first recommendation in the Commission's first biennial report contained the following statement: "The Commission recommends therefore that: 1. Parties, Jurisdictions and others foster and encourage policies, programs and institutions that (a) help develop and maintain a long-term ecosystem perspective with respect to the pursuit of their other legitimate goals and to be more anticipatory in their actions." The Commission continues to encourage stronger activities in support of this recommendation to enable our environmental scientists to focus their attention on more long-term, ecologically important considerations.

The Commission believes an ecosystem approach will produce greater appreciation for the overall impacts of environmental management decisions and man's activities generally. It may also lead to changes in existing methods of analysis and actions which are currently constrained by geographical, disciplinary, functional, institutional or jurisdictional compartmentalizations. Adopting an ecosystem approach would catalyze changes in the practice of ecosystem science, with less emphasis being given to discrete, well-defined but often less important problems, and more emphasis being directed to the more complex and important problems which confront us today. An ecosystem approach is being taken by work groups of the Water Quality Board to develop surveillance plans for the Great Lakes and their connecting channels, including some co-ordination of air and water monitoring.

Viewed retrospectively from the future, this binational commitment, reiterated and reinforced, may be seen as not less significant than the Boundary Waters Treaty of 1909 upon which it has been based. In the perspective of international law, the agreement of 1978 may be of even greater significance. The treaty of 1909 was largely within the customary and conventional arrangements of international law. Many binational and multinational treaties establishing rights and obligations in boundary waters have been consummated before and since. The mutual obligation in the treaty of 1909 to prevent water pollution that could impair health or property across the international boundary reaffirmed a principle already asserted by authorities on international law—that no state should permit the use of its territory in ways harmful to its neighbors.

The important innovation in the 1909 treaty was the International Joint Commission (IJC)—a binational body that was to oversee the implementation of the treaty, that was authorized to act in an integrative, unifying manner, and that provided a means through which policy for the boundary waters could evolve. The history of the IJC has been evolutionary, and its responsibility and authority have expanded in response to changing conditions affecting the boundary waters and especially the Great Lakes. The governments have acceded to this expansion reluctantly, as sometimes have the commissioners. But expansion has nonetheless occurred because the alternatives appeared less feasible.

The Great Lakes Water Quality Agreement of 1978 has opened the way to a new and challenging phase in the implementation of the Boundary Waters Treaty. By declaration and purpose, the Agreement of 1978 moves far beyond its specific detailed objectives. These specific objectives are largely extensions and elaborations of the Water Quality Agreement of 1972, their focus is on water and abatement of its pollution. The purpose and general objectives of the agreement of 1978, however, clearly require an ecosystem approach to policies for the Great Lakes, an approach which is far more inclusive.

The implications of this approach to policy have been addressed by the Royal Society of Canada and the National Research Council of the United States in a joint review entitled *The Great Lakes Water Quality Agreement: An Evolving Instrument for Ecosystem Management* (1985). The conclusion of this report is, in effect, that we have the commitment to a basinwide ecosystem approach, but that the approach has yet to be undertaken. There has been a giant step in concept and principle, but implementation is as yet in the exploratory state, chiefly regarding efforts to obtain the information base (mapping and monitoring) upon which ecosystemic strategies depend.

In practice an ecosystem approach means much more than is stated in its more restrictive, scientific definitions.[1] It means that management for the lakes should evolve in response to a growth in understanding of the factors that influence the quality of the environment within the Great Lakes Basin and determine the quality of the waters that unify the ecosystem and define its boundaries. Regardless of the legal, political, or institutional arrangements by which an ecosystem approach is undertaken, its *tasks* include many of those associated with general governance. Amongst these tasks are many that traditionally fall within the jurisdiction of local governments and have been considered strictly domestic. A broad range of "domestic" activities affecting land use, air quality, and economic development may become matters of binational concern under an ecosystem approach; filling of wetlands, coastal lagoons, and marshes for economic development or waste disposal are examples.

The governments of Canada and the United States have agreed that a basinwide ecosystem approach is necessary for the restoration and enhancement of the Great Lakes. An ecosystem approach, however, implies more than the governments are now doing or may be prepared to do in the near future. Although such an *approach* has been declared, time will be required to realize its objectives. There are indications, however, that an occasion for the first practical steps toward implementation may have arrived.

WHY AN ECOLOGICAL APPROACH NOW?

There is a simple explanation for why an ecological approach now? It is the increase and dissemination of information regarding the danger to the lakes and the possibilities for remedial action that have created a public constituency in Canada and the United States in favor of treating the lakes as a basinwide endangered ecosystem. This information and its impact upon public attitudes and political systems have been relatively recent; the effects revealed are complex, and the scientific reasons for an ecological approach are far from simple. If one accepts the scientific findings on the conditions and prospects for the Great Lakes, there is ample justification for initiating an ecosystems approach now. To move from intent to action may require progressive stages.

From the Boundary Waters Treaty of 1909 to the Great Lakes Charter adopted by Great Lakes governors and premiers in 1984, there has been a slow incremental development toward more coherent and unified policies of management for the lakes. This integrative trend has been impelled by practical considerations in response to problems affecting all political jurisdictions on the lakes, notably (a) water quality and pollution, (b) decimation of fisheries by exotic intruders (lampreys and alewives), (c) problems relating to navigation (seaway maintenance and winter navigation), (d) diversion or interbasin transfer of Great Lakes water, and (e) water levels and shoreline development. Issues like these in oversimplified form reach the desks of responsible public officials, commanding their attention. But assigning priorities to these issues is complicated by their interconnections. To resolve one problem, others must be considered; and Great Lakes policymakers are pushed, sometimes reluctantly, toward a more comprehensive, integrative view of their tasks. From this more inclusive viewpoint, they discover that the legal and institutional structures through which they must address the problems are inadequate to their broadened understanding of what remedial actions are required. There is a more fundamental reason, however, for viewing the Great Lakes as a total system within a basinwide ecological context. The reason is that scientific investigation increasingly describes and explains the lakes in ecological systemic terms, and informed people have come to accept this comprehensive perspective as the context for Great Lakes policies.

As often happens with environmental or ecological changes, deterioration of the Great Lakes was far advanced before its dangers were generally recognized or scientifically evaluated. As threats to the lakes became evident, the problems they presented were differently perceived by different users. Commercial and sports fishing interests experienced one set of problems, whereas users of beaches encountered others, and municipalities using the lakes for their water supply encountered still others. Public concern in both Canada and the United States regarding the condition of the lakes caused governments, universities, and research institutes to initiate remedial studies, many of which were undertaken under sponsorship of the IJC, its boards, and committees. These studies identified possible causes for the deterioration of the lakes; and findings and recommendations were published to which governments might reasonably be expected to respond. Then followed a new problem for responsible governments—how to respond? The problems were more readily identified than the solutions.

The governments—federal, state, and provincial—have not been accustomed to cooperating in a unified manner on matters requiring continuing management. Yet on Great Lakes issues converging interests from both sides of the international boundary have argued the need for continuing coordinative study of the problems and of mutually consistent courses of action. The implementing processes here are planning, management, and, unavoidably, finance. But implementing these processes through political action presents a formidable challenge. Because of disciplinary and academic introversion and the undependability of funding, cooperative research has not been easy. Failure to develop and maintain a corps of scientific workers with special competence in Great Lakes problems handicaps scientific implementation of an ecosystem approach and may do so for years to come.

An Ecosystem Approach Workshop held at Hiram, Ohio, in 1983 and sponsored by several binational organizations identified the obstacles to the ecosystem approach from five perspectives: personal, industrial (economic), voluntary, governmental, and finally, everyone's obstacles.[2] These were consistent with the Science Advisory Board opinions summarized at the beginning of this introduction. Notably, they included an inability to comprehend the reasons for an ecosystem approach, fear of loss of personal rights (such as property), resistance to public planning and to restraints on free enterprise, localized and bureaucratic jurisdictional jealousies, and most of all lack of a holistic perspective on the Great Lakes region.

National sovereignties and political jurisdictions are carefully guarded by authorities that feel little direct responsibility for the condition or fates of the lakes. Governmental bodies do not normally seek to act beyond their legally defined jursdictions, and there is today no single governmental entity in North America specifically authorized to implement a basinwide ecological approach to management for the Great Lakes. Only the two federal governments are presently competent to form such an entity.

These obstructive realities being conceded, the Great Lakes governments are nonetheless committed to a policy which confronts them with a dilemma. To seriously undertake basinwide ecological implementation of Great Lakes management is to act against the interests and preferences of large numbers of public officials, to intrude upon the jurisdictions and territorialities of both Canadian and American governmental institutions. A basinwide ecological approach to the problems of the lakes might require that governments act against the present interests of important constituents, action not likely to elicit enthusiasm from responsible public officials. On the other hand, if the governments and their officials decline to act responsibly to address the problems of the lakes, they may be held accountable for dereliction. Even in government and international relations, established institutional arrangements are not immutable. For the responsible public authorities it would seem a better choice to rise above policies of caution and delay than to risk the consequences of an aroused public, rejecting binational diplomacy in favor of state-provincial and private initiatives to safeguard the future of the Great Lakes.

The response options of governments are limited. The ecological systems approach appears to be the only choice with a realistic prospect for saving the lakes. In theory there may be other choices, but in fact none of them appear to be sustainable. One unrealistic option appears to be rejection of the evidence of deterioration; another is reliance upon nature to set matters to right. Equally unrealistic and politically unacceptable is to regard the Great Lakes as sacrifice areas, to continue to use them as sinks for the industrial and municipal wastes of the surrounding hinterland. Neither Canadians nor Americans in any significant numbers are today willing to regard the loss of quality in the Great Lakes as a price of progress, or to accept sacrifice arguments of economistic rationalization. Deliberate inaction being unacceptable, the closest approximation would be to declare in favor of a basinwide ecological approach and to then do as little as possible under the excuse (too often justified) of jurisdictional or budgetary restraints.

A more acceptable but ultimately unsustainable option would be a compensatory transposition of values—from ecological to exclusively economic benefits. The strategy here would be to focus on economic development—on reindustrialization, shipping, tourism, and recreational uses of the lakes. But these goals cannot be sustained in an ecologically deteriorating environment. All the economically sustainable goals of development in the Great Lakes region require a high level of quality in the lakes and their hinterlands.

Another unsustainable option to a basinwide ecological approach would be an incremental strategy of taking one issue at a time and trying to resolve it before moving on to another; and in fact, that was the approach taken to management for the lakes when threats to their quality were first perceived. Efforts to approach each issue incrementally revealed that the threats to the lakes were interlinked and that little was gained in efforts to remove one hazard only to have that achievement negated by a counteractive consequence or a parallel hazard. For example, protection and restoration of Great Lakes fisheries could not be accomplished by removing the threat of the lamprey eel if poisoning of the water made fish unavailable for human consumption. Water-dependent recreation and tourist development in the lakes region could hardly flourish where beaches were lined with decaying masses of dead alewives or rendered unattractive and odiferous by accumulating masses of algae. The siting of power plants, steel mills, and other industrial structures on the shores of the lakes without regard to ecologic or aesthetic considerations has conferred an unneccssary competitive disadvantage on the recreational potential of the region. An ecosystem approach would imply that more than strictly economic and technical convenience should govern siting.

Failure to implement an ecological basinwide approach to the lakes should not, however, be attributed solely to economistic thinking, jurisdictional jealousy, and institutional conservatism. Under salutary and sustainable conditions institutional conservatism may be desirable. It becomes harmful when it handicaps the ability of governments to respond adaptively to dangers to the public welfare. To respond effectively, public officials must know, and equally importantly their constituents should know, what response will be required. They not only need some estimate of the political and economic cost of an effective response, but they must be able to compare this cost with the price of failure to respond. No one with any real knowledge of the Great Lakes today would argue that their problems are neither real nor serious. But the failure to address effectively the problems of the lakes can be explained in large measure by the absence of a sound and persuasive analysis of the true costs and benefits of a basinwide ecological approach to management for the lakes as contrasted with the costs and benefits of reliance upon incremental action.

Commitment to a basinwide ecosystem approach to management for the Great Lakes is now realistic because we have sufficient understanding of the ecology of the lakes and the threat to their future to know what must be done to protect them, and we have the technical means and the research capabilities to take the indicated action. More needs to be learned, but the major problem now is how to mobilize the political will to move ahead with the task.

THE GROWTH OF POLICY COMMITMENT

With the foregoing discussion as background, the basis of an ecosystems approach to basinwide management for the Great Lakes can now be summarized. A mixture of three elements form this basis: (1) practical experience, (2) scientific findings, and (3) environmental awareness.

The prospects for implementing a policy commitment depend upon the strength of conviction behind it. The idea of a basinwide ecosystem approach did not originate with the framers of the 1978 agreement. We have noted its earlier development by the ad hoc committee of the Great Lakes Research Advisory Board and the report of that board to the IJC, which may be regarded as a definitive statement of the ecosystem approach to environmental policy generally. Most importantly, this approach puts humans into the biospheric system of the earth rather than separated from it, as was implied in previous law and policy affecting natural resources, nature, and the environment. Commitment to an ecosystem approach is no longer a unique or exceptional policy position. It has, in principle, a broad base of acceptance amongst persons and organizations concerned with the future of the lakes.

The IJC is not the only governmental entity to have directly or by implication endorsed the basinwide ecosystem approach. For example, the *Five Year Program Strategy for Great Lakes National Program Office 1986-1990* published by the U.S. Environmental Protection Agency listed the following as the first of five goals: "To apply an ecosystem approach to management by considering effects of use of the lakes on the health of biota and human health." And the Great Lakes Charter adopted in 1984 by the governors and premiers of the Great Lakes states and provinces declares the following:

> The planning and management of the water resources of the Great Lakes Basin should recognize and be founded upon the integrity of the natural resources and ecosystem of the Great Lakes Basin. The water resources of the Basin transcend political boundaries within the Basin, and should be recognized and treated as a single hydrologic system. In managing the Great Lakes Basin waters, the natural resources and ecosystem of the Basin should be considered as a unified whole.

If this statement is taken as a declaration of intent, it clearly implies an effort to reconcile and harmonize economic resources and ecologic values in Great Lakes policy.

We have noted that almost every problem arising in relation to the uses of the lakes is connected to other problems or issues. The explanation is that each specific Great Lakes problem arises within the context of ecological systems which, large or small, are characterized by the interconnectedness of their components. When governments and the IJC have been confronted with particular complaints or problems concerning the lakes (such as shoreline erosion, winter navigation, water levels, wildlife protection, especially in relation to wetlands, and atmospheric deposition), it has proved impossible to deal effectively with the problem by isolating it from all other issues. Informed and practical-minded administrators and engineers have been convinced by experience that nothing short of a basinwide ecosystems concept will enable the governments of the Great Lakes region to provide the integrative management for the lakes that their preservation requires.

The influence of science on the idea of an ecosystem approach to policy for the Great Lakes has been both general and specific. It has been general in two respects: first, through advances in ecology, systems science, computer technology, and analytic methods; second, through specific studies of the effects of dispersion of contaminants and alien organisms throughout the lakes. Scientific studies of particular problems, notably in relation to fisheries and containment of the lamprey eel, have made clear the systemic nature of the problems and the necessity for using a systems approach to their solution.

Science-based information picked up by the popular news media creates a public opinion that, even when sometimes mistaken, forces itself onto the agenda of political decisionmakers. The premature notice of the death of Lake Erie is a case in point. The ability of scientists to detect the presence of substances in parts per million has in no way changed the condition of the lakes, but it has affected the perception of people concerning the air they breathe, the water they drink, and the food they eat. Scientific findings of measurable toxicants in fish and water triggered the application of public health standards and advisories. When fishermen are told not to eat the fish they catch, sudden conversions to environmental concern may be expected.

Scientific information has thus induced and reinforced the rise of organized citizen action for protection of the lakes. We have noted that different groups with different interests in the lakes initially saw the issues of concern to them, but not the relationship of their concerns to other issues. Throughout the Great Lakes region there has gradually grown an awareness of depletion of the native fishes, the intrusion of alien species, the pollution of waters and beaches, and the variability of lake levels. This concern has led to the mobilization of nongovernmental organizations for the study and conservation of the lakes within a basinwide ecological context.

Almost every user interest in the Great Lakes is represented by one or more nongovernmental organizations, some of which are binational in membership. Organizations and conferences have focused attention on individual lakes, as, for example, in conferences on Lake Erie organized in the 1960s by the League of Women Voters or in the state-sponsored Illinois Governor's Conference on Lake Michigan in 1985. The basinwide ecosystem perspective is evident in privately funded organizations such as Great Lakes Tomorrow, Center for the Great Lakes, and a coalition of environmentally concerned organizations called Great Lakes United. Even a cursory survey of organized public interest shows that collectively there is widespread concern for the lakes even amongst specialized interests and that in many of the more recent organized efforts the ecosystem approach is explicit.[3]

In the universities and independent institutes, research on the Great Lakes had for many years focused on specific biological and hydrological problems. A very large number of institutions was listed in the *Dictionary of Universities, Research Institutes, Libraries, and Agencies Concerned with Water and Land Resources in the Great Lakes Basin* published in 1976 by the U.S. Federal Council for Science and Technology. Canadian and American scientists have collaborated for many years on problems of mutual scientific concern, but the formal structure of academic science has not been conducive to looking at the lakes as a total ecosystem. To do so has required an interdisciplinary commitment which seldom leads to high recognition from peer groups in the specific sciences. Moreover, when an ecological (man-in-system) approach to restoration and preservation of the lakes became an objective, involvement of the disciplines of economics, political science, and law also became necessary—subject areas in which few physical scientists and biologists feel comfortable. Conversely, social scientists largely lack the understanding of natural systems and ecological concepts needed in any ecosystemic approach to laws and policies pertaining to the Great Lakes.

In 1971, however, an interdisciplinary, interuniversity, binational seminar on the Great Lakes was organized (see chapter 2). Over the following decade, with changing membership, this binational research group developed concepts and papers pertaining to policy and management for the lakes from the perspective of a basinwide approach. This effort, assisted by private foundation funding, demonstrated not only the feasibility of dealing with problems of the lakes in basinwide systemic terms, but also the ability of scholars from a broad range of natural and social sciences, law, and engineering to collaborate on the basis of a shared perception of the field of investigation. This book is in large part a consequence of that effort.

POLICY IMPLICATIONS OF ECOLOGICAL GOALS

We now have both a policy and a research commitment to an ecological approach to the Great Lakes because no other way of dealing with their problems offers as much promise for success. A growing body of opinion in Canada and the United States accepts this belief, including some who nonetheless feel that it cannot be implemented (or at least implemented soon) because of political realities. There are also those persons who believe that the alleged problems are exaggerated, that they will cure themselves if let alone, or that they can be lived with. The governments have attempted to encompass these perspectives by boldly declaring an ecological approach, by calling for research (seldom matched by funding), and by acting cautiously. Even so, rhetorical commitments are forms of action and generate expectations that become forces for implementation of declared principles.

For the present, the greater concern of governors and premiers in the Great Lakes region has been for economic redevelopment and growth. They have endorsed the ecosystem approach in principle, but its practical implementation is almost certain to restrain or conflict with someone's economic objectives. The business community in the Great Lakes region has not shown much interest in the lakes as a basinwide ecosystem. Instead the lakes and their environs have been approached largely as natural resources—storehouses of materials capable of being used as commodities or services. *A Background Report: Critical Decisions for the Region,* prepared by the Northeast-Midwest Institute for the 1983 Congress on the Economic Future of the Great Lakes States, noted the following:

> Policy makers from the Great Lakes states agree that natural resources occupy a critical place in the region's economic future. However, they are less in agreement about the proper means of using these resources for economic growth, and at the same time, conserving them for future generations.

There are many ways, however, to advance economic development and to use natural resources—and not all of them need be ecologically harmful. Ill-conceived economic growth has caused much of the harm evident in the lakes today. Ecologically uninformed and unsound economic development has thus offset or destroyed many of its intended benefits. Under an ecosystem approach to policy, economic development and growth would be planned to be consistent with ecological realities. The greater elasticity, however, must be sought through options in economic planning, because the "laws" of nature tend to be unvarying.

It is not difficult to deduce the political implications of an ecological approach to management for the Great Lakes. There is a programmatic and organizational logic that follows from viewing the lakes and their environment as a single complex interactive system, allowing for local variation within the whole. It would seem that the implications should be clear to adequately informed and thoughtful people. In fact, it appears that many otherwise well-informed persons are unaware of contradictions in their purposes and values. They do not appear to see the numerous opportunities for conflict between their commitments to economic growth and environmental protection. What is also not clear is how and when these areas of conflict, present or potential, could be addressed in actuality. To some extent a human generational succession accompanied by changing assumptions and values may be required.

Official studies have concluded that if a basinwide ecological approach is taken to management for the Great Lakes, basinwide coordinative institutional arrangements must be strengthened. But before coordinative management can occur, there must be coordinative operational policy. The structure and mission of any new institution cannot be completed until some policy for its operation is officially established. This policy should put into effect the policy in principle enunciated in the 1978 Great Lakes Water Quality Agreement. There are a number of different ways of achieving a basinwide integrative policy in action, but the number is not indefinite and not all are equally promising of success. It seems safe to assume that neither Canadians nor Americans will create a new institutional entity solely for the purpose of achieving a theoretically desirable objective. The historic tendency of democracies is to back into more comprehensive institutional arrangements when temporizing, make-do measures fail. The risk to ecological systems in this tendency is that when failure of policy becomes obvious, it may be very late for remedial measures.

It is erroneous to believe that an ecological approach to management for the Great Lakes can be accomplished solely through technological or scientific means. Management for the lakes occurs by and through people and is thus inherenntly social and political. Governments cannot realistically be expected to execute policies for which they feel no real commitment. Elected and appointed officials are often reluctant to carry out policies which they feel are disregarded, opposed, or not understood by influential constituents. Candidates for elective office try to ascertain the state of public opinion on issues believed by them to be relevant to elections. There is, however, evidence that they often misread public attitudes, especially on matters of fundamental, long-range concern that are not believed to be of immediate urgency.

Under present circumstances of politics and public opinions, an ecological approach to management for the lakes is an innovation that requires a phased undertaking to achieve effective implementation. The first phase, already begun, is scientific assessment of the condition of the lakes and of the trends that threaten their future. Phase 2 involves the discovery or development of the scientific or technical measures most likely to deal effectively with the problems revealed in phase 1. Phase 3 requires consideration of the problems of law, politics, and economics to be overcome in putting these measures into effect. Phase 4 requires identifying or building a constituency supportive of a basinwide ecological approach to management for the lakes. These phases need not necessarily occur sequentially; they may in part occur simultaneously, and phase 4, popular support, should logically precede and accompany all of the others.

Implicit in the foregoing discussion and observed over several decades has been a movement toward more inclusive adoption of binational environmental policies. However, this course of action has been largely issue-specific and incremental. Establishment of the Great Lakes Fisheries Commission (1955) is a case in point. The functions specified for the Great Lakes Water Quality Board and the Great Lakes Science Advisory Board in the 1978 Water Quality Agreement, taken literally, were narrower than the scope of the agreement, but subject to expansion by interpretation. In contrast, the U.S. Great Lakes Basin Commission was charged by its enabling legislation (1967) to approach its mission with a comprehensive basinwide perspective. The framework studies sponsored by the commission assumed a basinwide system as their field of inquiry, although their specific concern was with natural resources, not ecosystems. But visions of a comprehensive grand design for governance of the Great Lakes have not been seriously entertained at policy levels on either side of the international border. Work of the commission was stopped by the Reagan administration through Executive Order No. 12319, September 9, 1981 [F.R.45591].

The patchwork appearance of the institutional structure of management for the Great Lakes fairly reflects the ad hoc way in which that structure was evolved. There is, however, more coordination within the structure than its disjunctive appearance would suggest. Intergovernmental cooperation may be insufficient to the need, but it does occur. Even so, the absence of a comprehensive basinwide arrangement for policy development and implementation presents a formidable barrier to an ecosystem approach to policy or management. The institutional structure has been built pragmatically in response to particular issues as perceived by the two federal governments, the state and provincial authorities, and concerned organized groups of citizens. However, once the lakes are viewed holistically—as an articulated drainage system including not only the water bodies but also the surrounding land within the Great Lakes basin—a different perception of organizational needs and structural implementation emerges. But it is a perception of organizational needs that first appears—not necessarily a vision of any particular organizational model. There may be various models that could provide a structure capable of implementing an ecosystem approach to management. What is required of any feasible organizational plan is that it facilitate a holistic way of dealing with those problems of management that affect the entire basinwide system.

If we assume a basinwide, holistic, ecological systems perception of the management task for the Great Lakes, at least five implications follow, all of which pertain to institutional arrangements:

1. We need coordinated scientific work, including research, monitoring, interpretation, and those aspects of evaluation amenable to scientific inquiry. (This need appears to be widely accepted in principle but is often set aside in practice when interdisciplinary investigation and funding are proposed.)

2. Conventional institutional assumptions and arrangements will be stressed by demands for action beyond the competence of existing agencies to respond. (This fact appears to be recognized by persons familiar with ecosystem analysis but is troubling to those who foresee possibilities for binational political embarrassment.)

3. We need a purposeful and articulate transnational constitutency able to pressure governments on both sides of the international border toward a common course of action. (This has yet to be created; it now exists in embryo, and is being encouraged by coalitions such as Great Lakes United.)

4. Institutional innovations must be appropriate and responsive to the environmental problems of the lakes and to their qualitative enhancement. (Opinions now differ over how much and what kind of institutions and powers are needed; a relatively politically neutral arrangement such as a monitoring and surveillance system may be the place to begin.)

5. An authoritative institution for Great Lakes management is more likely to evolve piece by piece in response to demonstrated needs than to be created as a fully developed entity. (A stronger transnational consensus is a prerequisite.

There is wisdom, however, in avoiding the tyranny of small incremental decisions that foreclose or delay advantageous innovation.)

When conditions are favorable, conceptual change moves rapidly and policy implementing institutional change follows. It is evident that the decade of the 1970s was a period in which concepts germinating in the 1960s, and before, achieved political acceptance and institutional expression. A comparison of the Water Quality Agreements of 1972 and 1978 reveals the extent and direction of conceptual change, but it also reveals the well-known institutional lag between new ideas and their practical expression. As noted, the rhetorical commitments of the 1978 agreements are innovative and by implication far-reaching, whereas the specifics are conventional and limited. There are apparent inconsistencies within the 1978 agreement, as, for example, between the goal of zero discharge of pollutants and limited-use zones. These inconsistencies should not be surprising, however; when concepts and policies are in transition, compromise makes good sense politically even though sometimes that is the only sense it makes.

Had the water quality agreements signed in 1978 been negotiated three years later, it is questionable whether they would have contained the expansive language of declaration and purpose. Although opinion polls in the early 1980s showed no significant decline in a basic public concern for environmental quality, other issues took center stage in the theater of politics. Nevertheless, a New York Times/CBS poll taken in January 1986 found that 66 percent of the respondents agreed that "protecting the environment is so important that requirements and standards cannot be too high, and continuing environmental improvements must be made regardless of cost."[4] To political parties and leaders, the salience of issues and the immediacy of their constituents' concerns are more significant than underlying predispositions that for the time being are unaroused.

In the 1980s relatively conservative governments came into power in both Canada and the United States. Environmental concerns generally had not been contested political issues in either country. Although environmental conservation would seem a logical issue for conservative support, economic development (seldom defined) has usually held a higher place on the conservative agenda. In Canada, however, all political parties favored action to abate acid raid, whereas in the United States no party wanted to become identified with the issue. To other environmental issues the governments of both countries appeared to give little more than routine attention. Especially in the United States, new initiatives were not considered, and a reexamination of legislation enacted during the 1970s was undertaken. Nevertheless, one may infer from cumulating opinion analyses that the public is far more concerned over environmental issues than are their political representatives, especially in the executive branch.[5] Opinion trends indicate the likelihood that future elections might significantly upgrade environmental values on the scale of national priorities.

Meanwhile, throughout the Great Lakes region and the Midwest, decline in the steel and automotive industries has become a major focus of political and economic concern. Regional redevelopment has been a major political theme of conferences, seminars, and the action programs of American state governments. These efforts largely emphasize attracting new industries, increasing the competitiveness of old ones, developing new industrial products and processes, and using more persuasive public information and advertising. Recreational opportunities in the Great Lakes region have not been overlooked, but the emphasis more often has been on attracting industries and tourists than on protecting or enhancing the environment as an incentive for investment in the region.

There is, however, a countercurrent to this largely economic concern; it is a rising public awareness of the menace of toxic wastes and of the contamination of the Great Lakes by toxic substances. The concern is not confined to the lakes; the groundwater supplies of growing numbers of communities are being lost to contamination. There is also suspicion that contaminated groundwater has been slowly making its way into the Great Lakes, thus adding to the burden of pollutants from point sources and from atmospheric deposition. Communities surrounding Lake Ontario have demonstrable reason for concern over toxic wastes leaking (some visibly) into the Niagara River from dump sites in the state of New York.

Promoters of economic development and tourism have thus been confronted by a dilemma. Publicity regarding pollution and of course the pollution itself is bad for business and damaging to the prospects for attracting new enterprise. The greatest asset of the region—an abundance of fresh water—is being threatened, but remedial measures are costly and complicated by numerous legal and jurisdictional considerations. Cleanup and prevention of toxic contamination would impose new economic burdens on the region in production and treatment costs that would be reflected in prices and taxes; but failure to deal effectively with toxics would almost certainly accelerate economic decline and add new burdens to human health. Some local officials and business interests have been reported to favor suppressing discussion of the issue, yet the basinwide dispersion of toxics makes this alternative no more than a short-run expedient. At federal, state and provincial levels of government there has been no basic disagreement in principle over the necessity for dealing with the toxics problem. The practical questions have been where and how action should be taken, how rapidly, and at whose expense.

A very different problem, record-high water levels in the Great Lakes in 1985–86, has further demonstrated the interconnected systemic character of Great Lakes phenomena. It has reinforced the point that human decisions regarding land use, unguided by ecological and hydrological realities, have been major contributors to environmental (and thereafter to economic) distress in the region. In the conventional view, high water levels were the problem; from an ecological viewpoint, the problems experienced by people building on the lakeshore and lakeside cities resulted from failure to take account of the variation in lake levels over time. An ecosystems approach to policy would require a reconcilitation of land use policy and the behavior of nature.

EXTENDING THE WATER QUALITY AGREEMENT

To assist the IJC in the exercise of the enlarged powers and responsibilities assigned under the 1978 agreement, two joint advisory bodies and a regional office were reconstituted from the 1972 agreement. The former consisted of two boards of equal numbers of members from Canada and the United States. Under the terms of the agreement, a Great Lakes Water Quality Board was designated as principal advisor to the Commission. A Great Lakes Science Advisory Board (formerly Research Board) was to provide advice on research to the commission and to the Water Quality Board. In addition, the agreement reauthorized the Great Lakes Regional Office of the IJC, now situated at Windsor, Ontario. The duties of these bodies were detailed in the "Terms of Reference" attached to the agreement. This structure for assistance in implementing the 1978 Water Quality Agreement is essentially fact finding and advisory, supplementary to the similar role of the IJC itself. But the 1978 agreement also, in effect, conferred certain powers of initiation on the IJC.

Of particular significance are the provisions for surveillance and monitoring under Annex 11 of the agreement. Whereas the development and implementation of a joint monitoring and surveillance program are declared to be a responsibility of the federal, state, and provincial governments, the IJC is the agent, common to the parties, with competence to develop such a system. In October 1984, the IJC sponsored in Philadelphia the Transboundary Monitoring Netowrk (TbMN) Workshop on the development of a transboundary system encompassing not only the Great Lakes but the entire five-thousand-mile international boundary region.[6] This extended geographic scope of surveillance and monitoring has become more pertinent to the Great Lakes Water Quality Agreement because of growing indications that some significant portion of contaminants in the lakes is the result of airborne deposition originating from without the Great Lakes basin. And, pursuant to the 1978 agreement, the Great Lakes Water Quality Board has developed the *Great Lakes International Surveillance Plan* (1981) to monitor individual lakes as well as the whole system.

Following its Third Biennial Report on the Agreement of 1978, the International Joint Commission proposed amplifications and clarifications of the 1978 provisions. These changes were embodied in The Protocol of 1987 to the Water Quality Agreement of 1978 and were adopted at a meeting of the I. J. C. in Toledo, Ohio 18 November 1987. The Protocol proposed no new international arrangements or conferences concerning the future of the Lakes. It did, however, give increased recognition to the role of state and provincial governments and reaffirmed commitment to the ecosystem approach to policy and management. For example, Annex 2, Remedial Action Plans and Lakewide Management Plans stated as General Principle (a) "Remedial Action Plans and Lakewide Management Plans shall employ a systematic and comprehensive ecosystem approach to restoring and protecting beneficial uses in Areas of Concern or in open lake waters." The Research and Development agenda proposed in the Protocol, followed the almost exclusively scientific and technical emphasis characterizing the document. Neither the Commission nor the Parties (the two federal governments) seemed persuaded that the objectives of its 1978 Agreement and 1987 Protocol could not be achieved through present institutional arrangements.

REVIEWING IMPLEMENTATION OF ECOSYSTEM MANAGEMENT

Under Article VII of the agreement, the IJC is required to report to the respective governments "no less frequently than biennially concerning progress toward the achievement of the General and Specific Objectives including, as appropriate, matters relating to Annexes to [the] Agreement." The Canadian and United States governments declared their intention to review the agreement following the third biennial report of the IJC on its implementation. This review was reflected in the Protocol of 1987. In anticipation of that report and review, the Water Science and Technology Board of the United States National Research Council held a conference in April 1984 in Buffalo, New York, "to identify scientific, technical, and institutional issues on which a review of the Agreement might focus." Canadian experts also attended this meeting, which led to a binational review of the agreement sponsored by the Royal Society of Canada (RSC) and the National Research Council (NRC) of the United States.

The joint report of this review, *The Great Lakes Water Quality Agreement: An Evolving Instrument for Ecosystem Management,* was published by the U.S. National Academy Press in 1985 and included amongst its findings and recommendations:

> The 1978 Agreement has not served as a stimulus for further rapid progress with respect to the ecosystem approach. The years since the Agreement was signed may ultimately be seen as a maturation period, leading in future years to strong advances in ecosystem management for large systems, and the emphasis of recent IJC, WQB, and SAB reports of 1984 and 1985 show promise of such an advance.

Referring specifically to the ecosystem approach, the RSC-NRC review recommended

> that the overall objective of the Agreement should, therefore, continue to emphasize the systemic characteristics of the basin including the human activities taking place in it. Four kinds of information are needed: time series of monitored data, maps of key features of

the ecosystem and of its use and abuse by humans, models of causal relationship integrating human uses and ecosystem responses, and case studies of management actions to demonstrate what has worked and what has not.

Therefore, the committee recommends that the interests of future generations be considered more explicitly in the Agreement. We should be guided in our actions by two principles of intergenerational equity: the first is conservation of quality, defined as leaving the Great Lakes basic ecosystem in no worse condition than it was received from previous generations; the second is to conserve the diversity of the natural resource base so as not to eliminate future options for use of the resource.

Therefore, the committee recommends that the Great Lakes basin ecosystem be managed not only reactively for unintended impairments but with foresight so as to anticipate and prevent any further diminishment of the resource.

In addition, the committee recommends that the parties to the Agreement carry out a focused binational study addressing questions as to what has happened as a consequence of a number of major interventions, as disclosed by subsequent surveys and monitoring. The aim would be to "mine" the existing data base so as to advance ecosystem understanding most effectively, an activity for which past support has been minimal in comparison with the costs of the interventions.

Therefore, the committee recommends that the parties to the Agreement hold a binational conference on the Great Lakes and that they establish a Preparatory Committee to develop a draft statement of principles and a draft action plan to be acted on formally at a conference to be held before the end of the present decade.

Of the foregoing recommendations, the proposal for a major conference and action plan could prove to be the most significant. Much would depend upon the climate of opinion preceding the conference. The 1972 United Nations Conference on the Human Environment at Stockholm occurred at the apex of the environmental movement of the 1960s and 1970s. The official positions of Canada and the United States were clearly more favorable to domestic and international environmental protection measures than they have been during the 1980s. And even before Stockholm, observers noted that while science advisors were urging bold international action upon their national delegations, sovereignty-conscious foreign office representatives were advising caution and reserve. The selection of delegates and terms of reference for such a conference would be of critical importance.

In concluding its summary of findings and recommendations, the RSC-NRC committee declared that "substantial further reforms are needed in the Great Lakes basin, far beyond the programs specified in the 1972 and 1978 Great Lakes Water Quality Agreements. Now is an appropriate time to face that challenge."

This conclusion leads to two questions which the review did not address. First, is there a binational constituency effectively supportive of the recommendations made by the review committee and of "further reforms" unspecified? Second, what kinds of institutional (political and jurisdictional) changes would be necessary to carry out the broad objectives of the 1978 agreements as interpreted and explicated by the RSC-NRC committee? As of the end of 1987 it seems probably that no one really knows the answers.

To discover what people in the Great Lakes Basin know and believe about the lakes and their tolerance for institutional change would be a logical first step to dealing with the constituency question. This kind of information can be obtained through techniques of survey research that are among the more reliable achievements of the social and behavioral sciences. There is demonstrated competence in opinion polling in both Canada and the United States. Although the IJC is responsible to governments rather than directly to people, the fate of its recommendations may depend upon the informed and uninformed preferences of people. If the objectives of the 1978 agreement and the recommendations of the RSC-NRC review, amongst others, are to be realized, increases in personnel and funding will be required and changes in law and jurisdiction are probable. For these requirements to be met, governments will need clear and positive signals from the governed.

A binational conference on the Great Lakes could be a powerful catalyst for action, raising public awareness and understanding. Surely a task for a preparatory committee recommended by the RSC-NRC review would be to discover the public awareness informational base upon which a binational conference could build. The opinions of scientists and public officials are not sufficient for this purpose. The public political constituency must also be considered if for no other reason than to learn where and how it needs to be informed and persuaded regarding the present and future of the Great Lakes and their environs.

Future organizational and institutional structures for the Great Lakes Basin will logically (but not inevitably) be based on the tasks to be performed. To propose new institutional arrangements apart from programmatic considerations appears at present to be premature. Nevertheless, the comprehensive view of the task of restoration, preservation, and enhancement of the Great Lakes set forth by the 1978 Water Quality Agreement and reiterated in the 1987 Protocol and in related studies raises reasonable doubts regarding the ability of the present highly fractionated, decentralized structure of governance to meet the challenge.

SOME ALTERNATIVE ARRANGEMENTS FOR ACTION

Implementation of an ecological approach requires an appropriate structure through which action may be taken. A structure of governance now exists, but in both theory and practice it contradicts assumptions regarding a basinwide ecosystem approach to the lakes. The existing structure of governance for the region was based on utterly different premises. How far it could be adapted to the objects of an extended water quality agreement is uncertain. Yet the action plan undertaking proposed by the RSC-NRC committee could hardly accomplish its task without considering the institutional issue with its political and jurisdictional considerations. Any realistic plan for action must consider how that action is to be accomplished. Consideration of institutional changes for the Great Lakes is not a utopian development.

The individual chapters that follow, each in its own way, address the needs and strategies for attaining basinside ecosystem management for the Great Lakes. Nine differing perspectives provide alternative ways of understanding a common problem: the application of scientific concepts and findings to the sociopolitical milieu of the Great Lakes Basin. The common focus of these chapters is the ecosystem concept, with the partial exception of chapter 7, "The Great Lakes as a Water Resource." This chapter affords a perspective on a contrasting way of seeing the water of the Great Lakes—as a commodity rather than as an essential element of the Great Lakes ecosystem. With this exception, specific uses of the lakes are only considered incidentally to the larger theme, which is treated throughout in historical depth. Public and international policy regarding the Great Lakes appears to be in transition from fractionated reactive management in the past to more coherent, comprehensive, and anticipatory action in the future. The chapters in this reader record and reflect this transitional process.

PRINCIPAL DOCUMENTS RELATING TO AN ECOSYSTEM APPROACH

The Ecosystem Approach: Scope and Implications of an Ecosystem Approach to Transboundary Problems in the Great Lakes Basin. Special Report to the International Joint Commission by the Research Advisory Board, Windsor, Ontario: IJC Great Lakes Regional Office, July 1978, reprinted 1980.

Environmental Management Strategy for the Great Lakes System: Final Report to the International Joint Commission from the International Reference Group on Great Lakes Pollution from Land Use Activities—PLUARG. Windsor, Ontario: IJC Great Lakes Regional Office, July 1978.

Anticipatory Planning for the Great Lakes—Workshop Report, vols. I–II. Workshop held March 5–7, 1979, sponsored by the International Joint Commission's Science Advisory Board through its Societal Aspects Expert Committee. Windsor, Ontario: IJC Great Lakes Regional Office, 1979.

The Great Lakes Water Quality Agreement: An Evolving Instrument for Ecosystem Management. Report of a joint project of the Royal Society of Canada and the National Research Council of the United States. Washington, D.C.: National Academy Press, 1985.

NOTES

1. For interpretations of the ecosystem concept that are applicable to geographic areas such as the Great Lakes basin, see the following references:

Brock, Thomas. "The Ecosystem and the Steady State." *BioScience* 17, no. 3 (1967): 166–169.

Caldwell, Lynton K. "Problems of Applied Ecology: Perceptions, Institutions, Methods, and Operational Tools." *BioScience* 16 (1966): 524–27.

———. "An Ecosystems Approach to Public Land Policy." In *Public Land Policy: Proceedings of the Western Resources Conference,* 1968, edited by Philip O. Foss, 43–56. Boulder, Colorado: Colorado Associated University Press, 1970. Revised and extended as "The Ecosystem as a Criterion for Public Land Policy," *Natural Resources Journal* 10 (April 1970): 203–21.

Kesteven, G. L. "The Ecosystem as a Biotic Entity." *Intecol Bulletin* 2 (1970): 8–23.

Likens, Gene E., ed. *An Ecosystem Approach to Aquatic Ecology: Mirror Lake and Its Environment.* New York: Springer Verlag, 1985. (A microcosmic study outside the Great Lakes basin but which illustrates many of the factors to be considered in an ecosystem approach with primary focus on biogeochemical factors.)

Maelzer, D. A. "Environment, Semantics, and System Theory in Ecology." *Journal of Theoretical Biology* 8 (May 1965): 395–402.

Stoddert, D. R. "The Ecosystem as a Geographic Principle and Method." *Geography* 50 (July 1965): 242–51.

United States Environmental Protection Agency and Environment Canada. *The Great Lakes: An Environmental Atlas and Resource Book*, jointly produced by Environment Canada, United States Environmental Protection Agency, Brock University and Northwestern University, Chicago: Great Lakes National Program Office, E.P.A. and Toronto: Great Lakes Environment Program. Environment Canada, 1987.

Van Dyne, George M., ed. *The Ecosystem Concept in Natural Resource Management*. New York: Academic Press, 1969.

2. The workshop was jointly sponsored by the International Joint Commission; the Great Lakes Fisheries Commission; the International Association for Great Lakes Research; and Great Lakes Tomorrow. For a summary report of findings and conclusions, see Christie, W. J., et al., "Managing the Great Lakes Basin as a Home," *Journal of Great Lakes Research* 12, no. 1 (1986): 3–17. (Provides references to numerous unpublished papers prepared for the workshop relative to the Great Lakes as an ecosystem.)

3. See "New Groups Signal Growing Great Lakes Region Identity," *The Great Lakes Reporter* 2 (March–April 1985): pages unnumbered.

4. See *CBS/The New York Times Poll* news release 1/27/86, and R. W. Apple, Jr., "President Highly Popular in Poll: No Ideological Shift Is Discerned," *New York Times* (1/28/86): A1, A14. See also John M. Gillroy and Robert Shapiro, "The Polls: Environmental Protection," *Public Opinion Quarterly* 500 (1986): 270–79.

5. A 1983 report by L. J. D'Amore and Associates, Ltd., to the Department of the Environment (Canada) found that "general concern for the environment peaked in 1970 and declined shortly thereafter, but has recovered to the point where most recent polls show it near the top of the noneconomic agenda." Opinion studies by Lester W. Milbrath likewise indicate continuing strong popular support for environmental protection. Nevertheless there appeared to be a distinct difference between the evaluation of environmental priorities by the political and economic leaders in Canada and the United States and the preferences of a majority of the general public. The priority commitment of business and government to economic growth and development over ecological and environmental values has been documented by Samuel P. Hays in *Beauty, Health, and Permanence: Environmental Politics in the United States, 1955–1985*, Cambridge and New York: Cambridge University Press, 1987.

6. Haug, Peter T., Bruce L. Bandurski, and Andrew L. Hamilton, eds. *Toward a Transboundary Monitoring Network: A Continuing Binational*

Exploration, vols. 1-2. Ottawa, Canada, and Washington, D.C.: International Joint Commission, 1986.

7. *The Protocol of 1987 to the Great Lakes Water Quality Agreement of 1978.* Signed at Toledo, Ohio, 18 November 1987.

CHAPTER 1. THE ECOSYSTEMS APPROACH: A STRATEGY FOR THE MANAGEMENT OF RENEWABLE RESOURCES IN THE GREAT LAKES

In this chapter, substitution of the plural "ecosystems" for "ecosystem," as in the Great Lakes Water Quality Agreement of 1978, is not an editorial inconsistency. The authors intention is to emphasize the complexity and diversity of the various systems that comprise the Great Lakes ecosystem in its entirety.

The concept of an ecosystemic approach to management implies a plan of action or at least a plan toward action. Achieving the complex, comprehensive, long-range goals implied in the expression *ecosystems approach* requires a strategy to match the challenge of the task. The authors are four scientists with governmental responsibilities for implementing the 1978 Water Quality Agreement outlines a strategy and indicates its interrelating phases. They develop this strategy against a background of issues that drive public and international action toward remedial action for the threatened lakes. The logic and rationale for the strategy are thus made explicit and clear.

R. L. THOMAS, J. R. VALLENTYNE,
K. OGILVIE, and J. D. KINGHAM

1

THE ECOSYSTEMS APPROACH: A STRATEGY FOR THE MANAGEMENT OF RENEWABLE RESOURCES IN THE GREAT LAKES BASIN

In Windsor, Ontario, on July 17, 1978, the cochairmen of the International Joint Commission, Maxwell Cohen (Canada) and Robert Sugarman (United States), convened the annual meeting of the Great Lakes Water Quality Agreement organizations. This meeting was a high point in the affairs of the commission. The final report of the Pollution from Land Use Activities Reference Group (PLUARG) was presented to the commission on July 19. This report was followed on July 20 by a report of the Research Advisory Board: *The Ecosystem Approach.* These two reports paved the way for incorporation of the ecosystem concept into the 1978 Great Lakes Water Quality Agreement and the formal adoption of the concept by the governments of Canada and the United States.

From this auspicious beginning and the expression of high hopes and expectations of the governments, implementation of the ecosystem approach to management of the Great Lakes has not progressed. Efforts have been made but have not been sustained, in part because of changing priorities induced by the economic recession of the late 1970s and early 1980s, during which the concern of governments and of the public shifted away from environmental considerations to focus on highly personalized economic concerns.

The following chapter defines Great Lakes issues and strategies which, if applied collectively, may help to return the program to the full intent of the Great Lakes Water Quality Agreement of 1978. This chapter is based on a strategic plan developed for Canadian federal organizations involved in the conduct of the Canadian Great Lakes water quality program.

The Great Lakes are a unique global feature containing 18 percent of all fresh water on the earth's surface. They provide a navigation route 3,200 kilometers long from the Atlantic to the Great Plains. They modify climate and have provided essential ingredients (such as coal, water, and steel) in the evolution of North American society and its accrual of wealth. The basin is home to some 37 million people, accounting for one-seventh of the U.S. population and one-third of the Canadian population. The true value of the lakes is incalculable. Their uniqueness makes it essential that they continue to survive without degradation for the benefit of future generations. The citizens of the basin must regard themselves as custodians or tenants with a responsibility to ensure that the lakes are maintained and passed on in a condition satisfactory to future generations.

THE ECOSYSTEMS APPROACH

In their paper on the Great Lakes, Christie et al. (1986) state that "ecosystems are natural or artificial subdivisions of the biosphere with boundaries arbitrarily defined to suit particular purposes." Odum (1969) defines an ecological system as any unit of nature in which living organisms and nonliving substances interact with an exchange of materials between the living and nonliving parts. The report to the International Joint Commission (IJC) on the ecosystem approach states, "This ecosystem approach is based on a man-in-a-system concept rather than on the system-external-to-man concept inherent in the 1972 Great Lakes Water Quality Agreement" (IJC, 1978). It has become apparent that living matter, the hydrosphere, atmosphere, and lithosphere are interactive, and that the biosphere is both influenced by and influences human activities. The use and abuse of the system will determine both future environmental quality and the quality of human existence.

The interactiveness of the ecosystem has been eloquently summarized by Khan (1986).

> It is . . . this lack of conceptual framework for understanding the environment and its interaction with man which has resulted in part from our fragmented, piecemeal approach of the problem. Because every element of the environment is adjusted to every other (although often distantly), a change induced by man usually sets off a chain of repercussions, or indirect and extended effects. In general, however, the variety, intensity, and geographical spread of environmental change by man is accelerating. And as problems of air contamination or water pollution worsen they demand our attention. But reaction to crisis is not enough, for technology may not be able to save us from the repercussions of our own actions. The critical questions is: can we overcome our ignorance and apathy concerning our environmental action soon enough?

These prophetic words lay down a challenge to both developed and developing societies to interact with and manage human activities in a way that will sustain in perpetuity those renewable resources upon which we are dependent. The ecosystem approach to the management of the Great Lakes must therefore be defined as the management of human uses of the natural resources of the Great Lakes basin on a sustainable basis. It must also be recognized that the management of one use must be accomplished within a multiple-use system. All uses must be optimized within the social fabric of the society most affected.

OVERALL OBJECTIVE OF THE STRATEGIC PLAN

Any form of management requires a purpose, a goal or objective. Obstacles standing in the way of achieving the objective are identified and strategies are developed to overcome them. These strategies, balanced against current or changing patterns of use or the social fabric, represent the essential management skills needed to achieve the purpose. In complex, multiuse systems, such as the Great Lakes Basin ecosystem, management is widely divested among agencies and political jurisdictions. Clearly the adoption of a common objective (more clearly defined the "ecosystem approach") is essential if the current management of the Great Lakes is to be focused on resolving the great issues that face the Great Lakes today.

An objective for the Great Lakes Program may be stated as follows:

To restore and secure the chemical, physical, and biological integrity of the Great Lakes Basin ecosystem as a multiuse resource with full commitment to renewable resource management principles, to provide for the requirements of society for

- food and drinking water,
- human health,
- shelter and energy,
- industrial and commercial opportunity, and
- culture and recreation.

This objective is more detailed than that given in the Great Lakes Water Quality Agreement of 1978. It provides a purpose and some indication of management principles whereby the objective might be attained.

To provide for a common understanding of this objective, some definitions are necessary. The use of the word *restore* implies that the basin ecosystems are degraded. *Restore thus means that action must be taken in different parts of the basin to obtain an improvement that may include one or more of the chemical, physical, and biological components of the degraded area.* To *secure* implies conservation. Either the present condition is maintained or the restored condition is maintained. *Integrity* implies that the three elements of the ecosystem as defined are collectively balanced and function in a manner that is self-sustaining by virtue of natural processes. The *Great Lakes Basin ecosystem* is defined as the interacting components of air, water, land, living organisms, and associated processes (chemical, physical, and biological) that produce the self-sustaining whole. People and their activities are included as an integral component of the ecosystem. The phrase *requirements of society* recognizes that human benefits must be balanced with minimal environmental degradation and with a minimum of conflict among uses.

The phrase *integrity of the Great Lakes Basin ecosystem* encompasses the concept that management of human activities in the basin and manipulation of the basin's resources must be such that the basin ecosystem will not be degraded. The quality of the aquatic environment becomes the measure of the effectiveness of the management. Implicit in *culture and recreation* is the concept of conservation of habitat and protection of the health and well-being of the fish and wildlife that it sustains.

This objective is a general statement of purpose or use. To place it in a proper perspective, further specification of the major uses of the basin and its waters is necessary. Six major uses are defined, each with a subobjective, as follows:

USER OBJECTIVES

1. Drinking Water

To ensure and preserve an adequate water quality for drinking.

This objective requires a water quality at source that will not impair human health, both in the Great Lakes and in the rivers and groundwaters of the basin that are used for the production of potable water.

2. Recreation and Aesthetics

To restore and secure the chemical, physical, and biological integrity of the waters of the Great Lakes Basin in order to provide healthful and pleasant recreational, cultural, and aesthetic benefits to society.

3. Habitat

To restore and secure the integrity of the Great Lakes Basin ecosystem in order to conserve the health and diversity of wildlife, fish, and other organisms, and to ensure the preservation of heritage features reflecting human history and interaction within the basin.

4. Industry

To continue to ensure adequate quantity and quality of water for industrial use.

This objective refers solely to the supply of water for industry as opposed to waste disposal, which is discussed in objective 6 below.

5. Navigation

To preserve and continue to develop environmental conditions required for a safe navigation system for the Great Lakes, their connecting channels, harbors, and ports.

Since this subobjective requires control of lake levels and maintenance of minimum channel depths by dredging, there is obviously potential conflict with other users. Dredging may be required because of translocation of sediments and soil loss elsewhere in the basin. Disposal is also complicated by contaminants. Strategies for reducing soil loss and contaminants will help meet the requirements of this subobjective.

Since the maintenance of normal lake levels and variations is a necessary part of conserving habitat for wildlife and fisheries, this concern is also directed to other uses. Serious conflicts arise in near-shore or restricted waters, where wake effects from passing vessels perturb wildlife, fish, and their habitats. Conflicts may be exacerbated by extensions of the navigation season or by large-scale diversions of Great Lake waters.

6. *Waste Disposal*

> To ensure the provision of current and innovative programs and facilities for waste treatment and recycling in order to establish and meet the guidelines and criteria for waste management in the Great Lakes Basin ecosystem for municipal, industrial, urban, and agricultural wastes.

This objective is specific to wastes discharged directly to aquatic systems. However, it is now recognized that the atmosphere is serving as a transitional sink for many contaminants, resulting in increased dispersion of contaminants throughout the basin.

This issue is particularly important with respect to persistent contaminants that build up proportionally to the manufacture and use of those substances. Further, resolution of local or regional problems can lead to global buildup through atmospheric transport. Therefore, the following waste disposal objective pertinent to the atmosphere is proposed:

> To develop and implement programs for the identification of airborne pollutant sources and relative source contributions, and to develop innovative technologies for the elimination of these sources.

This objective relates to a much broader area than the Great Lakes Basin proper and must therefore be viewed in the context of other air quality agreements and activities that exist or may be developed.

ASSUMPTIONS ABOUT THE FUTURE

Managing the uses of the Great Lakes requires that some projection of societal, economic, and physical conditions into the future must be made. The following trends are anticipated in several key areas of importance to the management of the Great Lakes over the next decade.

Public Attitudes and Expectations

Despite the fact that a basinwide public opinion survey has never been undertaken, smaller surveys have revealed a number of trends in public attitudes and expectations that are likely to influence government programs over the medium to long term. In particular, the general feeling that government is too big and costly, combined with the volatile economic outlook, places downward pressure on budgets and new initiatives. However, a majority of people still see protection of the environment as a governmental responsibility that must be maintained.

Economic and social problems are increasingly viewed by the public as linked, and people are showing greater interest in the decision-making processes of government as conflicts between economic, social, and environmental goals arise. Greater use of the courts is being made, especially by issue-oriented citizen groups. Most people do not believe that economic growth requires acceptance of higher pollution levels, and tougher environmental standards are frequently advocated. Long-term prevention policies are favored over remedial actions. Toxic chemicals are a particular concern, with human health as the focus for public anxiety.

The coming decade will probably see increasing public debate over both the quality and quantity of water in the Great Lakes. The predominant issues of concern will be the threat posed by toxic substances in the lakes, the possibility of diversions of Great Lakes waters, and the necessity for an ecosystem approach—that is, designing with nature. Winter navigation proposals have evoked widespread opposition in the United States and Canada and will continue to be of concern to the public as further initiatives are taken.

The result of a 1982 Gallup poll showed that 98 percent of Ontario residents felt it was important to clean the Great Lakes of pollution that 75 percent felt it to be critical. Public interest groups and private citizens are likely to demand government initiatives to protect the Great Lakes. They also expect greater involvement in decision making and greater access to information on the Great Lakes.

Fiscal Restraint

If fiscal restraint on the part of governments continues through this decade, Great Lakes managers will have to initiate innovative efforts to improve the efficiency and effectiveness of the Great Lakes Water Quality Program.

Scientific Uncertainty

A total and comprehensive understanding of the ecological sciences will never be achieved because of uncertainties caused by chance and the complexity of interactions. In view of this fact, the decision-making process must assess the point at which sufficient scientific evidence exists for a rational decision to be made. Uncertainty will always remain but must not be allowed to delay environmental decisions on the basis of a perceived need for more study, greater resolution of process and understanding, or supposed reduction of the level of uncertainty. Such requirements merely delay controls and allow problems to worsen. If this desire to reduce uncertainty had been manifest in the phosphorus management program in the Great Lakes, the lakes would have been irretrievably lost to the ravages of eutrophication while studies of the process were continued. A similar situation is projected to arise with respect to more hazardous issues such as toxic chemicals. The paradox is that although scientific certainty is unattainable, scientific credibility is an essential ingredient for gaining public confidence and establishing the will to implement solutions.

The Economy

Slow economic growth and relatively high unemployment levels are expected over the next several years. Structural adjustment linked with economic recovery has the potential to make industry more competitive and less wasteful than at present. Service-oriented industries appear to be more environmentally benign, and modernization of resource-based industries will probably yield environmental benefits as pollution controls, resource recovery, and recycling are encouraged through tax measures and modernization incentives. Emerging industries based on genetic engineering and biotechnology are likely to bring an increased public emphasis on moral and ethical issues, thus calling for even greater political attention to economic, social, and environmental concerns.

The increasing interaction between governments and economic activities in weakened industrial sectors has important implications for the way in which the economy will develop over the next decade. For example, in the agriculture sector, individual farmers often lack the capital to take advantage of new knowledge and farming techniques that are clearly of long-term benefit both to the agricultural sector and to environmental objectives. To the extent that governments want to affect decisions made at this level, they will have to develop policies (such as loans and other investment incentives) that encourage the desired actions to be taken. It is assumed that governments will continue to intervene in the economy to effect these changes, and that this intervention will have a major influence on industrial developments in certain sectors.

The demand for recreational uses of Great Lakes waters and shorelines is likely to increase as a result of continuing high unemployment levels and the growing number of people in part-time and seasonal work. This demand will conflict with demands for urban, industrial, and population growth, thus further stressing the management capabilities of governments.

Intergovernmental Relations

Resolution of transjurisdictional questions is likely to have a bearing on the future development of management programs relating to the Great Lakes. The overall climate for federal-provincial, federal-state relations may change as a result of elections and continuing economic and social problems. However, current indications of a desire for greater cooperation among governments suggest that tensions may decrease over the longer term. Moreover, improved knowledge of the effects of toxic chemicals in food, air, and water will undoubtedly focus public and political interest on the need for greater cooperation.

Current U.S. policies, including deregulation and the transfer of federal regulatory authority and administration to the state level, have the potential to adversely affect that country's environmental protection capability and its stance on transboundary resource and environmental issues related to the Great Lakes. However, there is evidence that the American public does not accept environmental deterioration as a necessary companion of economic growth.

We assume that, philosophically and strategically, levels of government throughout the Great Lakes Basin will come closer together as a result of the cost effectiveness of shared approaches to the economy and the environment. Pressures outside the basin for water diversions and winter navigation will provide incentives to develop a common front. The concept of the need to manage on an ecosystems basis is recognized, at least on the surface. However, the present institutional framework still supports narrow attitudes that have characterized Great Lakes management over the last few decades. The single-discipline (rather than transdisciplinary) and single-mandate focus within the present educational framework continues to hinder the attainment of a management process that accommodates the joint interest of affected groups.

Water Levels and Diversions

With the continuing and accelerating overexploitation of water in the western and southwestern United States, there will be increasing pressure for large-scale diversions from the Great lakes to the Mississippi and Ohio watersheds. The major social and economic investment in the U.S. Southwest will result in political efforts to transfer the water benefit of the lakes to the large infrastructure that has developed there, and to distribute the costs among all.

This interplay of forces will hinge on the relative costs of energy and water, and the extent to which users will assume capital costs. The outcome may be uncertain in the short term, but the issue of water supply can be expected to become paramount in the twenty-first century. The need for conservation of the Great Lakes will become increasingly important, and the information base required to demonstrate this need must be developed. The impact of water diversions on water quality is of lesser importance than their impact on water levels.

Climate Change

Recent projections of trends in the level of carbon dioxide in the atmosphere due to the burning of fossil fuels indicate that the level could double in the next eighty to one hundred years. Such an increase would alter the climatic patterns of North America and contribute to increases in temperature and changes in precipitation patterns over the medium to long term. The strong possibility of drier conditions in the U.S. Sun Belt and western regions lends support to the concern over demands for diversion of Great Lakes waters. The Great Lakes Basin itself is very vulnerable to the effects of climate change and, because of the small size of the basin relative to the surface area of the lakes, a small decrease or increase in precipitation could have major effects on Great Lakes water levels. The scenario of a warming trend in the Great Lakes Basin would increase evapotranspiration and could also stimulate further agriculture development with a possible increase in demand for irrigation. An increase in precipitation associated with increased humidity and associated increases in water levels would have a profound impact on the social and economic fabric of the Great Lakes.

PRINCIPLES FOR RENEWABLE RESOURCE MANAGEMENT

The objective given above explicitly states "with full commitment to renewable resource management principles." Resources may be renewable (forests, fish) or nonrenewable (coal, oil, gas). The common denominator is time, geological time for nonrenewable resources, and years to decades for renewable resources. The supply of either can be altered as a result of human exploitation, both in quality and quantity. Renewable resources are subject to greater perturbation as a result of human activity than are nonrenewable resources: if exploited beyond their natural ability to restore themselves, they become nonrenewable. Endangered species are an example of this phenomenon.

Human interventions must be harmonized with nature so that the natural cycles and energy flow are disturbed to the least extent possible. Implicit is the necessity that humans see themselves as part of the natural ecosystem—subject to its laws and limitations. Management philosophies, or principles, must reflect this basic reality.

Sixteen management principles are summarized below. It is recognized that managers may not be ecologists, yet these principles are so fundamental that a rudimentary knowledge must become an essential ingredient in the makeup of the individuals who have the designated authorities to manage the resources of the Great Lakes. The principles are not listed in priority; they should be regarded as having equal weight in providing the fundamental concepts of rational resource use management.

    1. The ecosystem concept is holistic. It opposes the classical idea that the world can be analyzed as separate, independent parts. The parts are seen to be intimately connected, their

dynamic relationships depending, in an irreducible way, on the state of the whole system. The Great Lakes Basin ecosystem is defined in the 1978 Great Lakes Water Quality Agreement as "the *interacting* components of air, land, water and living organisms including man." The ecosystem concept implies that it is not the separate components themselves, but the interactions between the components, that are essential to understanding the nature and dynamics of things. It also embodies recycling as a major ecological concept.

Therefore, the separation of each component for analytical purposes and special study is artificial. A full understanding of the components and changes in these components requires a consideration of the interactions of the whole.

2. The maintenance of economic value, and the sustainability of the economic process, are ultimately and irrevocably dependent on the nature of the interactions described in 1, above. Accordingly, it is useful to consider two kinds of interactions on a human time scale that influence or transform the various ecosystem compartments, and ultimately the whole system: human-environment interactions that create *irreversible* changes (mining the soil and forests, soil erosion, and toxic contamination, for example); and interactions that involve exploitation and *active* conservation, with inherent resource maintenance feedbacks (fisheries and agriculture, for example). The first kind is purely exploitive, and is not sustainable but self-destructive. The second kind is integrative and forms the basis of sustainability. Prospects for development, growth, and progress depend on the second kind of interaction.

3. It is inherent in the notion of an ecosystem (living organisms and their environments as interactive systems) that there exists knowledge of ecosystem interrelationships and humans' role in nature. Ian McHarg, in his book *Design with Nature,* demonstrates the need to further our knowledge of nature.

As a society we neither know nor value the chemical elements and compounds that constitute life, and their cycles, the importance of the photosynthetic plant, the essential decomposers, the ecosystems, their constituent organisms, their roles and cooperative mechanisms, the prodigality of life forms, or even the greatest values, the genetic pool with which we confront the future. (McHarg, 1969, p. 25)

Developing this knowledge requires first identifying the components and relationships within the ecosystem, both natural and imposed by human (for example, socioeconomic and institutional); and second, understanding these relationships. As knowledge is acquired, the wisdom to apply it in an ecosystem context must be developed. Quoting from Schumacher, "We can say to-day that man is far too clever to be able to survive without wisdom. One may be clever enough to manipulate nature through powerful modern technologies, yet not wise enough to consider the full range of consequences that could follow from that action" (Schumacher, 1973, p. 30). Only after accomplishing this can the ecosystem be measured in terms of its own intrinsic value as well as its level of tolerance to stress—that is, development. This knowledge provides the fundamental basis for managing ecosystem resources in a manner that causes the fewest perturbations to the natural system. In this way prospective uses can be fitted to specific ecosystems. The closer that management strategies fit the natural system, the less the stress and the less the investment in mitigative actions. In this way humans maximize their benefits while minimizing costs in social, economic, and ecosystem terms. As stresses to the environment increase, so do the intensity and cost of ecosystem management.

4. The principles of ecological succession bear importantly on the resolution of the environmental crisis (Odum, 1969). Basically, the human desire to maximize production is at odds with successional processes that result in increased biomass and the shunting of energy from production into maintenance in order to improve control over external perturbations. The wounding of an ecosystem is followed by a natural healing process.

Overharvesting of fish, clear-cutting of forests, depletion of topsoil, monoculture, urbanization, and toxic chemical discharges are well-known instances of stresses imposed on the Great Lakes Basin ecosystem. The costs in terms of environmental harm and vastly increased needs for planning, research, and management have risen sharply in recent decades and show few signs of abating. The shift from piecemeal management to ecosystem management is not accidental; it is necessary if costs are to be limited and harmful perturbations avoided.

5. In order to appropriately assign prospective uses to specific ecosystems, consideration must be given to adjacent uses to minimize the transfer of impacts from one use to another. This principle leads to recognition of the need for "reconstruction of the Biospheric in the interests of freely-thinking humanity as a single totality" (Vernadsky, 1945).

6. Natural ecosystems must be preserved to maintain renewal of resources and stability.

7. The natural components around us (the "natural capital" must not be used or stressed to the point where remediation is no longer possible. If this happened, then life itself would be threatened. The natural resources of the Great Lakes Basin are a good example of natural capital that if lost to pollution would have dramatic effects on the populations which they now support. In this regard, the functioning of the Great Lakes Basin ecosystem is "dependent upon the presence of a suitable combination of species each of which performs a specialized task within the total system" (Dasmann, Milton, and Freeman, 1973, p. 29).

8. Genetic diversity, when lost, cannot be regained.

9. Readily exploitable nonhuman components of the Great Lakes Basin ecosystem need protection to survive. This statement applies to native stocks that are protected through licensing regulations (hunting, fishing); endangered species and habitats (bald eagles, forests, wetlands); and diversity of cultures, species, and habitats. This principle underlies the necessity for ecological impact assessments of new development projects.

10. Since human societies are capable of inadvertently destroying their environmental support base through pollution, overexploitation, or accident, there is a need for the extension of a human-centered ethic to an ecosystem-centered (nature-centered) ethic.

11. Any condition that approaches or exceeds the limits of tolerance of any organism or group of organisms constitutes a limiting factor to growth (Odum, 1971). The principle of limiting factors has found application in the phosphorus control strategy used to control eutrophication in the Great Lakes Basin. The logic is that phosphorus, by its removal

from detergents and sewage treatment plants, can be made to limit plant growth through reduced supply.

12. Renewable resources should be managed so as to maintain their capability to supply in perpetuity as high a level of output as is indefinitely sustainable. The yield of natural resources from the Great Lakes Basin ecosystem provides a matrix of multiple uses. In this context, the sustainability of these uses over time depends on management of factors such as fish harvest quotas, waste loading limits, marshland conservation, and even population control. Demand management applied to all uses is a major requirement. The need is to limit the catch, rather than catch the limit.

13. Renewable resources should be allocated to those single or multiple uses that are most likely to produce the greatest economic and social benefits. In the context of the Great Lakes Basin, this principle must be interpreted so as to encompass the needs and values of the noncultural components. Wise use requires an optimizing process that recognizes the interdependence between cultural and noncultural components in the long term.

14. The quality and quantity of renewable resource systems should be safeguarded to permit flexibility in the production, development, and use of renewable resources for current and future generations. The responsibility to future generations embodied in this stewardship principle requires active protection and intervention. The ecosystem must be seen to have intrinsic and not just aesthetic or human value.

15. Cooperation among managers of shared renewable resources must be encouraged while minimizing infringement on the rights and responsibilities of public and private renewable resource owners. The principle of cooperation applies especially to the Great Lakes Basin ecosystem because it is a prime example of a resource shared by two nations, with two senior levels of government. Eleven state, provincial, or federal jurisdictionns cooperate in the management of this ecosystem. Waste is the integrator which forces cooperation.

16. Owners and managers of renewable resources should be encouraged to capture a just return for the use of those

resources and to reinvest in maintaining and enhancing resource productivity. In the case of the Great Lakes Basin ecosystem, this principle requires significant interpretation and focus. Owners and users must be carefully defined. Ownership resides with the government in trust. Each user exerts some kind of polluting influence on the resource that reduces its value to other users. A more appropriate statement of the principle would be that pollutors must pay the cost of treatment to ameliorate the disbenefit to other users.

ISSUES

Issues are defined as obstacles that hinder the achievement of objectives. The identification of substantive issues is essential to the development of strategies that can be used to guide resource allocation decisions and management practices.

Agencies involved in Great Lakes programs and activities must grasp these issues in their entirety without regard to the limitations imposed by mandates and resources. They must strive to make substantive, positive contributions to the resolution of these issues and must encourage other agencies and interests to address those aspects of the issues requiring their input. Achievement of the long-term goal hinges on coordinated actions.

Chemical Disruption

Chemical loadings to the waters of the Great Lakes Basin have resulted in major disruptions of valued ecosystem components and have directly affected human activities and uses of Great Lakes waters. These chemicals originate from various sources, including liquid and solid waste disposal and atmospheric deposition from both within and outside the Great Lakes Basin.

Ecosystem impacts from chemical loadings include eutrophication, which results in degradation of fish and wildlife habitat; loss of recreational and aesthetic uses of Great Lakes Basin waters and shorelines; and taste and odor problems in drinking water. Chemical disruption further results in contamination of wildlife and fish with toxic chemicals and contamination of sediments and benthic organisms. Potential adverse effects on human and ecosystem health from exposure to toxic contaminants in the Great Lakes Basin are increasing public concerns.

The situation is further complicated by atmospheric deposition of toxic contaminants. It is now established that many environmental contaminants are recycled through the atmosphere and subject to increasing global distribution. The persistent nature of many of these contaminants indicates the probability of a global buildup with resultant ecological consequencies. The Great Lakes are both a source and a recipient of these contaminants, and impacts upon the more sensitive ecosystems of the upper Great Lakes have been identified from atmospheric sources (for example, PCBs).

The problem of eutrophication of the Great Lakes, particularly the lower lakes, is a persisting issue despite the increasing concern over toxic chemicals. Increasing population pressure, urban and industrial development, and agricultural expansion in the Great Lakes Basin will result in even greater stress on the ecosystem from herbicides, pesticides, and nutrients. Human abuses of water resources in the basin arise in large measure from burgeoning urbanization and industrialization.

The ecosystem impacts impose economic burdens on society. This problem is evident in cases such as the loss of the eel fishery in the St. Lawrence River from contamination by Mirex, the temporary Japanese ban of Canadian fish products in 1983 because of a misperception that Lake Erie fish contained high levels of toxic contaminants, changes in the fishery in Lake Erie from oxygen depletion in the central basin, losses of revenue from fish consumption guidelines and fishing bans, and increased costs of dredging from sediment contamination and related disposal guidelines.

Other adverse economic consequences, including effects on human health, can be identified but are not easily quantified. However, the essential point is that substantive losses of beneficial uses of the Great Lakes have occurred. More severe losses may occur in the future if society does not adequately respond to the issue of chemical disruption.

The problem of chemical loadings is pervasive, severe, and costly to society, and will be with us for many (perhaps hundreds of) years to come even if agressive controls are imposed now. The problem is complicated by our lack of knowledge in many areas and by the absence of cost-efficient technology to measure, and ultimately to prevent, these chemicals from entering the Great Lakes Basin ecosystem.

Biological and Physical Disruption

Human activities have in the past, both inadvertently and deliberately, resulted in extensive biological and physical disruptions to the Great Lakes Basin ecosystem. Many of the more severe abuses have been controlled as a result of improved knowledge and management practices. However, the growth of human population and technology in the Great Lakes Basin imposes a need for constant vigilance and for continued evolution of processes that allow for a balance between human needs and the requirements of a healthy ecosystem. Over the long run, human needs and ecosystem needs are complementary, but decision-making processes often ignore this linkage.

Human activities that have greatly contributed to biological and physical disruption include the overexploitation of the Great Lakes fishery; the destruction of the Atlantic salmon (indigenous to Lake Ontario) because of loss of river spawning areas; reduced populations of top fish predators, leading to changes in fish species composition; the general destruction of fish habitat and stream and near-shore spawning areas; the introduction of exotic fish and other species (thirty-three species in all, including the sea lamprey, alewife, and pink salmon); the loss of recreational and aesthetic uses of the Great Lakes because of bacterial contamination and physical alterations; and the substantial destruction of wildlife habitat (especially wetlands) because of a variety of human activities, in particular agriculture and urbanization. Changes in phosphorus loadings and the introduction of exotic fish species, such as Pacific salmon, are having a direct effect on the primary and secondary producers of the lakes with wide-ranging implications to the food web dynamics of the lakes and their ability to sustain a viable and desirable fish community. Management of the Great Lakes to produce protein with a full recognition of food web dynamics (trophodynamics) is essential.

Many of the human activities that have disrupted the biological and physical components of the Great Lakes Basin ecosystem continue to occur today. The emergence of a more affluent society has intensified the competition among uses of the ecosystem and has given rise to a greater number of individuals and interest groups dedicated to the preservation of valued ecosystem components. Thus, conflicts over use have become a major issue in such areas as recreation, aesthetics, industrial development, and fish and wildlife habitat preservation. The economic importance to society of these uses has increased over time and is projected to increase more rapidly than traditional industrial uses. In addition, the emergence of significant interest in major physical alterations of the Great Lakes Basin ecosystem for economic reasons, such as water diversions and winter navigation, has raised the possibility of future large-scale biological and physical disruptions. Biological and physical disruption is a key issue to be tackled in the management of the Great Lakes Basin ecosystem and its beneficial use by society.

Response to Public Concern

Public concern and the response by governments and others to this concern is a key issue and is an important consideration in all government programs and activities. Since the public, in a broad sense, is both the client for government agencies and the ultimate source of authority for these agencies, it is crucial that governmental processes and decisions allow for two-way consultation and participation with the public.

There is little question that the rapid development of technological capabilities in areas such as analytical techniques and instruments has resulted in the generation of new knowledge on the existence and extent of chemical contamination of the Great Lakes Basin ecosystem. The significance of this knowledge is not always clear in terms of the potential effects of these chemicals on human and ecosystem health. However, instances in which certain chemicals have had clearly defined impacts, combined with the pervasive nature of chemical contamination, have caused widespread and growing public concern to which governmental agencies have had great difficulty in responding. Substantive scientific and technical answers to this public concern are not likely to be available in the foreseeable future, thus increasing the importance of establishing processes for adequately informing the public of governmental knowledge or lack thereof and for making the government accurately aware of public concern.

In summary, public concern is a key issue for which a coordinated governmental response is required. This response should encompass education, information, consultation, and participation to the extent required to ensure adequate two-way communication in the development of programs and activities and in the general interaction between agencies and the public.

Conflicting Uses and Institutional Arrangements

The issue of conflicting uses and institutional arrangements is important for management agencies since the legislative and other decision-making authority and capability to attain the objective often fall outside the mandate of any single government or level of government. Thus, the development of a coordinated societal response to the resolution of the problems confronting the Great Lakes Basin ecosystem is of vital importance. The need is to ensure connections among loose ends. Also vital is the development of decision-making processes and institutional arrangements that allow for a balanced perspective on competing uses and the full participation of those individuals and interests likely to be affected by proposed modifications to the ecosystem, including the ecosystem itself.

Competing uses can be identified in such areas as recreation versus industrial development, recreation versus wildlife habitat, and fisheries versus chemical waste disposal. Many other conflicting uses could be cited. Where such conflicts arise, their resolution is frequently complicated by the existence of several different jurisdictions with different decision-making processes and different objectives for management of the same resource. The decision-making processes do not always allow proper access to all competing interests or adequate time for meaningful identification and resolution of conflicts. The cost of intervention in these processes may be quite high, and the criteria by which decisions are made are not always clear.

The resolution of this issue in whole or in part is an essential contribution to the effort to maintain the integrity of the Great Lakes Basin ecosystem and its use and enjoyment by society.

MANAGEMENT STRATEGIES

Strategies are defined as comprehensive long-range plans to deal with issues; thus strategies lead to the attainment of objectives. They must be directly relevant to the issues and objectives that have been defined. They form the basis upon which policy and resource allocation decisions are made. Four general strategies have been identified which outline actions that all Great Lakes jurisdictions and interests should consider within their respective authorities.

Chemical Management Strategy

There already exist many policy documents and action plans related to the management of toxic chemicals. Some examples include the following:

- Toxic Chemical Management Program Strategic Plan (Environment Canada)
- Fish Toxics Action Plan (Fisheries and Oceans Canada)
- National Program on Drinking Water (Health and Welfare Canada)
- Toxic Substances Control Act (TOSCA—United States Environmental Protection Agency)

These strategies and action plans and their complementary programs provide valuable perspectives. In addition, toxic chemical problems in the Great Lakes Basin have had a major influence on the setting of objectives and the development of programs at national levels. It is desirable that reciprocal influences among federal, provincial, and state programs be strengthened wherever linkages exist.

The chemical management strategy is reduced to three essential management and control ingredients or substrategies, as follows:

SUBSTRATEGY 1: ELIMINATION AT SOURCE

There is a continuing need to identify sources (production, use, and disposal) of chemical loadings to the Great Lakes Basin and to conduct research into environmental pathways and the fate and effects of toxic chemicals. Research in the area of human toxicity and bioindicators for toxic chemicals should be conducted and linked, where necessary, to the development of standards and regulations that can be used to limit and ultimately eliminate the discharge of toxic chemicals at source. There is a strong sentiment within the agencies involved in Great Lakes programs toward eliminating sources of toxic chemicals because of the pervasive and unpredictable nature of this problem and the certainty of large-scale ecological disruption if discharges continue at present rates. The "virtual elimination of discharges of persistent toxic chemicals," as stated in the Canada–United States Great Lakes Water Quality Agreement of 1978, is a valid long-term objective to which many concerned agencies subscribe. To achieve this goal, additional consideration must be given to the deposition of contaminants from the atmosphere and to the cleanup of poorly designed hazardous waste disposal sites. In addition, the development of further phosphorus reduction programs is required to maintain the present trend in the control of eutrophication. The problem of eutrophication remains an important program area requiring a specific focus within the Great Lakes Water Quality Program.

SUBSTRATEGY 2: TECHNOLOGY

There is also a need to develop cost-effective analytical technologies and methodologies for toxic chemicals of concern. Hundreds of chemicals found in the Great Lakes Basin cannot be properly identified and quantified, and those that can are often extremly expensive to measure. If precise data on the existence and quantity of toxic chemicals discharged at source and subsequently found in the ecosystem are required as a prerequisite for control actions by governments, then it could be decades before existing legislative mechanisms can be applied. Methods must be found to accelerate the acquisittion of information for those chemicals that pose a risk to human and ecosystem health.

Of even greater urgency is the development and implementation of source control technology in support of substrategies 1 and 2. Elimination of persistent toxic chemicals at source is required since there is no viable long-run alternative.

SUBSTRATEGY 3: INTERIM CONTROL

The economic base of our industrial society is heavily dependent upon the production and use of chemicals. Major reductions in production and use of industrial, new-to-the-biosphere chemicals, in the short term, could result in negative economic repercussions. In the long term, control of the discharge of industrial, new-to-the-biosphere chemicals to the Great Lakes Basin through reuse, recycling, substitution, or destruction is essential. A major concerted effort by industry and government to accelerate these efforts should be instituted. Governments should promote this work and should consider using a full range of policy instruments to assist industry. These instruments should range from standards and regulations to tax incentives, loans, effluent charges and technology research, and development and demonstration programs. All levels of government should coordinate their efforts to minimize overlap and to reduce the uncertainty generated by inconsistent programs and objectives. A more concerted effort by industry and governments to assess the direct and indirect economic impacts of control measures should be pursued to ensure that a balanced perspective on social, economic, and ecological considerations is used as a guide to decision making.

Conservation and Restoration Strategy

This strategy is directed toward the biological and physical disruption issue. Major disruptions of biological regimes and physical habitat and other components of the Great Lakes Basin ecosystem have proceeded to such an extent that we must go beyond merely conserving what is left. An effort to reverse past damage and to protect and sustain high-quality areas is needed even though it is recognized that we may not be able to restore certain systems to what they once were (for example, Lake Erie, Atlantic salmon in Lake Ontario, marshlands of Essex County). Particularly severe degradation and destruction is evident in relation to the Great Lakes fishery and shoreline (wetland) habitat for wildlife. Potentially severe effects on shoreline habitat could occur in the future from fluctuations in lake levels, consumptive use and diversions of Great Lakes waters, or the effects of climate change from the buildup of carbon dioxide in the atmosphere.

Restoration includes the identification of degraded resources and areas and the options available for rehabilitation, the establishment of priorities for remedial action, and the securing of public support and jurisdictional cooperation. Conservation efforts should include the strategies identified under the Chemical Management Strategy, complemented by the identification of sensitive organisms and areas on which conservation efforts should be focused. The sources of external stresses on or within the ecosystem should be identified and research conducted on the response of the ecosystem to those stresses. A holistic approach to conservation of valued ecosystem components should be pursued, founded upon the development of an ethic or sense of environmental responsibility by government, industry, and the public. Implicit in this strategy is the need to preserve the health and well-being of the communities of organisms in the Great Lakes so that they are self-sustaining and fulfill their roles in the ecological food web of the basin. An understanding of biological communities and their interactions with each other and their habitats is an essential ingredient of this strategy.

Two substrategies are identified, as follows:

SUBSTRATEGY 1: PUBLIC EDUCATION

The quality of public education programs should be improved on many subjects, such as the presence and significance to human health of contaminants in drinking water and food. These programs should explain the roles and responsibilities of each level of government and should demonstrate that multiagency programs are in place to assure the pubic that the issues are being addressed in a comprehensive manner. The level and extent of the knowledge, assumptions, and uncertainties should be made clear, and the methods by which public and ecosystem health and security are safeguarded must be described.

The best way to protect the uses of the resources of the Great Lakes Basin ecosystem is to instill and enhance an ecosystem ethic with an accent on environmental responsibility in the public, industry, and government agencies. The concept of protecting the ecosystem as an end in itself is fundamental to the maintenance of valued uses.

SUBSTRATEGY 2: PUBLIC PARTICIPATION IN DECISION MAKING

The public places a high value on the quality of the environment and looks to government to provide leadership. However, when governmental programs have inconsistencies and internal conflicts or when decision-making processes exclude legitimate public intervention, the demand for consultation and direct public participation in decision making increases. This demand is particularly strong in relation to local issues, and it is gaining strength in relation to broader concerns, such as overall governmental programs and policies.

There is a need for governments to develop policies, programs, legislation, and regulations that are more comprehensive, equitable, consistent, and effective, and that are adequately monitored and reported to the public. The public itself should be encouraged to assume more responsibility for its own actions where such actions contribute to Great Lakes Basin issues. Governments should assist the public by increasing their awareness of sources of environmental problems (such as product labeling for chemical content) and institutional mechanisms for resolving conflicts.

There is a pressing need for multiagency agreements and other coordinating mechanisms. These agreements should be structured to include public involvement, since public concern is often the result of exclusions. Governments must be particularly sensitive to this issue and should provide opportunity for meaningful public contribution.

Jurisdictional Cooperation Strategy

The resolution of the issues outlined in this strategic plan depends heavily upon interjurisdictional and intrajurisdictional cooperation. The following activities form the basis of the jurisdictional cooperation strategy.

SUBSTRATEGY 1: INTERNATIONAL COOPERATION

International Joint Commission
- *Support* the IJC in its role and responsibilities under the 1978 Great Lakes Water Quality Agreement.
- *Respond* in a timely manner to IJC recommendations regarding the continued implementation of the agreement.

SUBSTRATEGY 2: INTERAGENCY COOPERATION

- *Strengthen* coordination of activities under the agreement. More work is required to ensure the compatibility of initiatives taken by the national governments, the provinces, and states in requirements of the agreement.
- *Demonstrate* leadership in scientific research. This leadership can be shown in a number of ways, such as through the International Association of Great Lakes Research and the International Joint Commission Great Lakes Science Advisory Board, and through ensuring coordinated planning of research undertaken on the Great Lakes.
- *Improve* interagency awareness and understanding of the scientific basis of regulatory and operational activities as well as the institutional variables that affect the implementation of the agreement. This can be accomplished by holding more interagency joint scientific and planning forums.
- *Establish* formal interagency mechanisms to enhance communication, information exchange, and joint management procedures.

IMPLEMENTING THE ECOSYSTEM APPROACH

It appears that virtually every significant stakeholder group in the basin—including governments at all levels, industries, citizen groups, and review agencies—supports the need for an ecosystem approach to restoration and enhancement of water quality in the basin. The question, then, is, why has implementation been so slow?

A major part of the problem is that until recently *localized initiatives* for the practical development of an ecosystem approach have been lacking. With the new focus of the International Joint Commission Great Lakes Water Quality Board on "areas of concern" in its 1985 report to the commission, the situation has changed. The board created six categories to describe the extent of resolution of water quality problems in forty-two "areas of concern" in the Great Lakes Basin. These categories ranged from areas in which causes were unknown and no program was under way (category 1) to removal of the status as an area of concern (category 6). Written remedial action plans with time schedules have been requested for all of the forty-two current areas of concern.

Persons and organizations interested in accelerating implementation of the ecosystem approach in the basin would do well to focus on the extent to which these remedial action plans identify causative factors beyond the simplistic approach of controlling chemical discharges from point or diffuse sources. To what extent do the remedial action plans attempt to grapple with outdated attitudes, perceptions, and behaviors antecedent to the immediate causes of water pollution? How complete is the identification of stakeholders (such as school boards) and remedial measure (educational programs)? To what extent will the Water Quality Board fulfill the criteria for an ecosystem approach in categorizing the fifteen areas of concern initially identified for remedial action plans? To what extent will the jurisdictions come together to fully coordinate the development and implementation of the plans?

The areas of concern are normally the areas where people interact with the waters of the Great Lakes. This is where citizen involvement will be optimized and where the direct results and socioeconomic benefits are likely to be most easily recognized and quantified. This is where the ecosystem approach will be first truly applied. Success in these areas will reduce and eliminate the transfer of materials to the open lakes. The cleanup of these areas will restore and conserve the lakes themselves. It is then that the significance of atmospheric deposition will be realized and efforts made to resolve this, the most pervasive source of contaminants to the Great Lakes.

ACKNOWLEDGEMENTS

The authors would like to thank the many people who participated in a workshop that was held at Geneva Park to discuss Great Lakes users' requirements. Particular thanks are expressed to Don

Williams, Tom Muir, and Ron Shimizu for their enthusiastic participation in the discussions, which led up to the finalization of the concepts expressed in this paper.

REFERENCES

Christie, W. J., Becker, M., Cowden, J. W., and Vallentyne, J. R. 1986. "Managing the Great Lakes as a Home." *J. Great Lakes Res.* 12:2-17.

Dasmann, R. F., Milton, J. P., and Freeman, P. H. 1973. "General Ecological Considerations." In: *Ecological Principles for Economic Development.* John Wiley and Sons, New York. 252 pp. pp. 27-50.

International Joint Commission. 1978. *The Ecosystem Approach.* Research Advisory Board Report to the International Joint Commission. Windsor, Ontario.

Kahn, A. 1986. *Concept paper on Water Quality Management.* Pakistan Council of Research in Water Resources. A. No. 4, St. No. 41, F-6/1, Islamabad.

McHarg, I. L. 1969. *Design with Nature.* Natural History Press, Garden City, New Jersey. 198 pp.

Odum, E. P. 1969. "The Strategy of Ecosystem Development." *Science* 164:262-270.

―――1971. *Fundamentals of Ecology.* W. B. Saunders Co., Philadelphia, London, Toronto. 3rd Edition. 574 pp.

Schumacher, E. F. 1973. *Small is Beautiful. Economics as if people mattered.* Harper Torch Books, Harper and Row, New York. 290 pp.

Vernadsky, V. I. 1945. "The Biosphere and the Noösphere." *American Scientist* 33(1):1-12.

CHAPTER 2. THE GREAT LAKES: 1955-1985

This chapter makes two important contributions to this reader. First, it provides a historical perspective on policy for the Great Lakes, and second, it summarizes economic and geographic data helpful to an understanding of the context in which management for the lakes occurs. It includes chronological tables of major events affecting the Great Lakes, and a tabular comparison of the water quality agreements of 1972 and 1978. The author concludes with an account of the Canada-United States interuniversity seminar, out of which this book evolved. The article summarizes substantive issues, for example,—acid rain, energy, land use, and water levels—not specifically dealt with in other chapters.

LEONARD B. DWORSKY

2

THE GREAT LAKES: 1955–1985

The Great Lakes are the most important natural resource shared by Canada and the United States. The joint responsibility for this shared resource has produced large-scale cooperative arrangements such as the St. Lawrence Seaway, the Niagara Falls Treaty, the Great Lakes Water Quality Agreement, the Great Lakes Fishery Commission, and three Lake Levels Boards of Control (International Section of the St. Lawrence River, Lake Superior, and Niagara River).[1]

Because the United States and Canada contain two highly dynamic societies in which social, economic, and technologic change are accepted norms, solutions to problems occurring at one time may not remain pertinent at some future date. In addition, new problems must be confronted as the two societies evolve in relation to one another and to the world environment.

A reaffirmation of this statement is contained in a January 1985 advisory by the International Joint Commission (IJC) of Canada and the United States to the two governments.[2] The main themes on which the commission's advice is centered are contained in three excerpts from that advisory:

> . . . [t]he need to consider the interrelationship of Great Lakes water quantity and water quality in the context of an ecosystem, including the other than economic importance of this vast body of water to the millions of people who live and will live in the basin.
>
> [T]he Commission considers that, based on the experiences of the United States and Canada with regard to the 1972 and 1978 *Great Lakes Water Quality Agreements,* the two governments would be

well advised at this state to engage in broad but systematic discussion of their use of Great Lakes water before they are faced with any sense of crisis, actual or imminent, and before any relationships deteriorate or become jeopardized.

[T]he shared waters of the Great Lakes have a regional, national and international significance that requires that they be treated as a joint responsibility of the governments and peoples of both nations. They are a priceless resource in their own right. The multiplicity of uses to which they are put makes it imperative that closest attention be paid not only to the present needs of diverse users but also to the needs of future generations. The waters must be protected, conserved and managed with insight, determination and prudence if they are to continue to play the role they have played in the past. The Commission therefore urges the governments of the two nations and the people whom they represent to examine carefully the conclusions, recommendations, observations and counsel to be found in this Report. The Commission stands ready to provide whatever assistance the Governments may request in this regard.[3]

This article attempts a comprehensive overview of the management of a shared binational resource, management that is an outstanding example of international comity. It also traces many of the forces that evolved over the thirty-year period that led to the IJC advisory and that, over time, will provide the basis for marked changes in management of the Great Lakes. Presented first is a tabulation of major events, followed by a description of the current setting. Tabular information on the uses of water and related land resources of the Great Lakes and examples of environmental effects are next, followed by a detailed discussion of issues and the status of efforts to manage them. The concluding section addresses current institutional (primarily governmental) arrangements for management, describes some proposals that have been suggested for change, and recommends specific measures for change as a result of the author's experience.

TABULATION OF MAJOR EVENTS UP TO 1959[4]

1570   Hiawatha legend dates the founding of the five-, later six-nation Iroquois Confederation on the Great Lakes by Haion-Hwe-Tha about this time.[5]

1535   Jacques Cartier reaches Montreal.

1615	Samuel de Champlain sights the Great Lakes.
1701	Detroit founded.
1749	Toronto (York) founded.
1797	Northwest Fur Company built small lock for canoes and bateaux on St. Mary's River, Sault Ste. Marie.
1804	Ft. Dearborn (Chicago) founded.
1825	First diversion of Niagara River to Erie Canal.
1826	Erie Canal opened.
1829	Welland Canal diversion between Lakes Ontario and Erie.
1829	St. Lawrence Canals opened.
1848	Lake Michigan to Illinois River diversion through Illinois and Michigan Canal.
1855	State of Michigan lock opened at Sault Ste. Marie.
1856	St. Clair–Detroit River system opened by dredging.
1880	Alewife Fishery entered Lake Ontario.
1881	First U.S. electric generating station at Niagara Falls.
1893	First Canadian hydroelectric plant at Niagara Falls.
1900	Beginning at this time, studies for lakes regulation were done in 1911, 1920, 1926, and 1952.
1909	Chicago Sanitary and Ship Canal completed; Lake Michigan to Illinois River Basin.
1912	First reference to IJC by Canada and the United States to survey pollution in the Great Lakes.
1921	Sea lamprey recorded in Lake Erie.[6]
1932	Welland Canal (Canada) completed.
1933	Sea lamprey taken in Lake Huron.[7]
1939	Long Lake diversion from Hudson Bay drainage to Lake Superior.
1943	Ogoki River diversion from Hudson Bay drainage to Lake Superior.
1946	Second reference to IJC by Canada and the United States to survey pollution in the Great Lakes.
1950s	Last large expansion of power plants: Sir Adam Beck (Canada) and Robert Moses (United States).
1950	Niagara River Treaty for power and Niagara Falls preservation.
1955	Great Lakes Fishery Commission.
1959	St. Lawrence Seaway opened.

THE CURRENT SETTING

The Great Lakes and their connecting channels and the St. Lawrence River System provide a continuous 2,400-mile deep-draft waterway that extends from the Atlantic Ocean into the heart of the North American continent.[8] The system serves the eight Great Lakes states, eleven contiguous states, and the Canadian provinces of Ontario, Manitoba, and Saskatchewan. For the purpose of this inquiry, the Great Lakes Basin extends from the downstream end of the International Rapids section of the St. Lawrence River to fifty miles west of Duluth on Lake Superior.[9] A map of the Great Lakes Basin is shown in figure 1. Physical,[10] hydrologic, and rainfall and runoff data on the Great Lakes are presented in table 1.

About 83 percent of the population within the Great Lakes Basin reside in the United States, and 17 percent in Canada.[11] The United States portion of the basin produces one-sixth of the national income and accounts for over one-fifth of manufacturing employment and capital expenditure. In Canada the figures are more dramatic, for the basin produces nearly one-third of the national income and accounts for over one-half of the manufacturing employment and capital expenditure.[12] Basin agricultural production accounts for 7 percent of all United States output and 25 percent of total Canadian output. There are fifty-nine thousand square miles of commercial forest in the U.S. portion of the basin, and over seventy thousand square miles in the Canadian portion. Iron ore, coal, limestone, and grain account for 85 percent of the 220 million tons of waterborne freight carried each year on the waterway. The remaining 15 percent includes overseas general cargo, petroleum products, cement, and chemicals.

The hydroelectric installations in the Great Lakes Basin produce more energy than thermal plants using fossil or nuclear fuels. They produce far more than most other hydroelectric plants of the same installed capacity because the Great Lakes have the unique feature of an extremely high degree of natural regulation. The existing hydroelectric plants affected by regulation of the Great Lakes have a total installed capacity of nearly eight million kilowatts, of which over three million are in the United States and almost five million in Canada. The principal hydroelectric power producers are the publicly owned utilities.

The institutional setting[13] is defined primarily by the two federal systems of the United States and Canada, and responsibility for governance is shared by the federal, state (provincial), and local governments within each system. Basin governance is diffused among two federal governments, eight states, and the Province of Ontario,[14] as well as among numerous regional, local, and special-purpose districts of government. In addition, international institutions have been developed to aid in cooperative approaches to Great Lakes Basin resource protection and management. The following framework exists for Canada–United States cooperation on the Great Lakes:[15]

> 1. Treaty between the United States and Great Britain relating to boundary waters and questions arising between the United

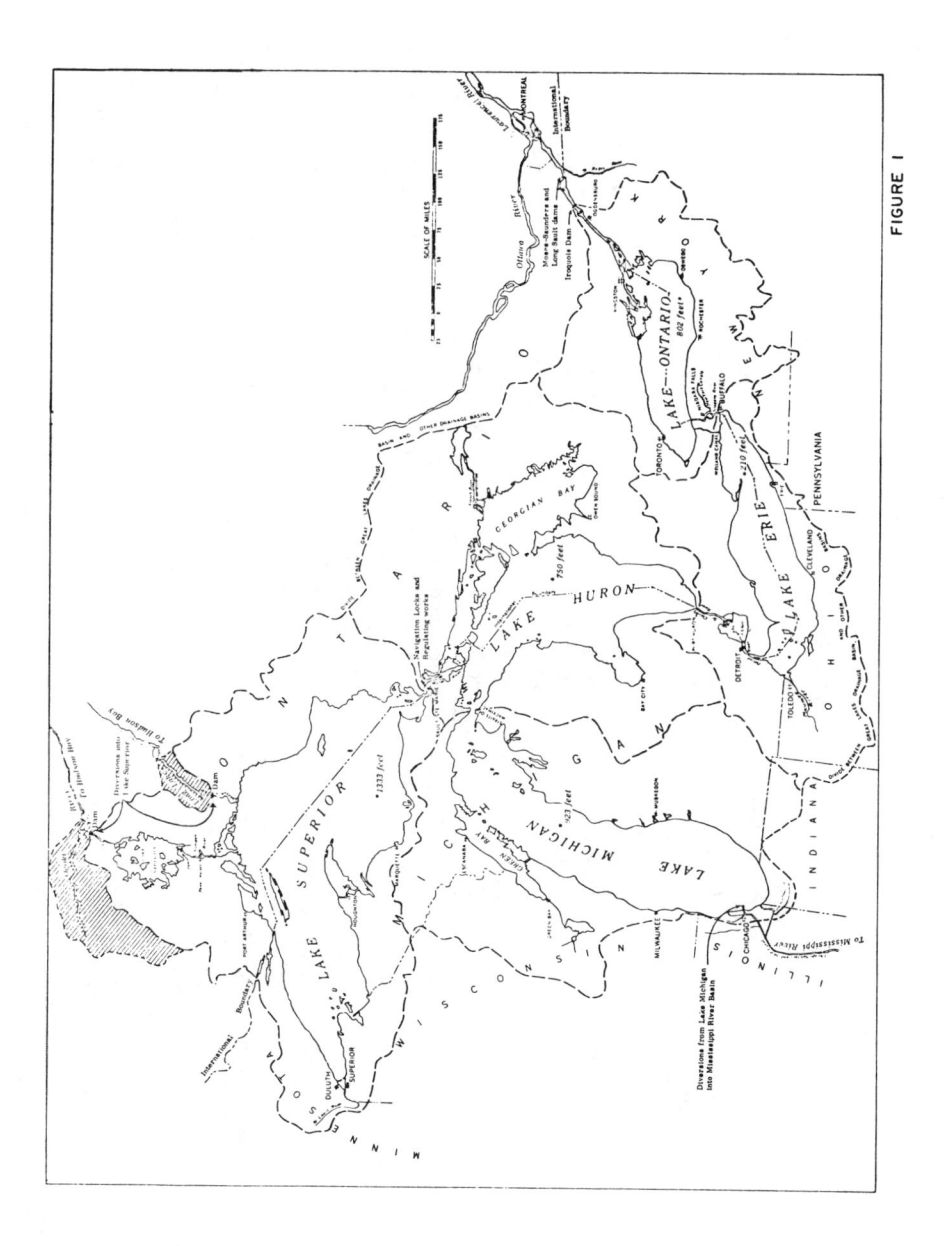

FIGURE 1

Table 1. Great Lakes Data

PHYSICAL

Lake	Water surface	Drainage area (square miles) Land area	Total	Storage capacity CFS months per foot	Outlet river	Length of shoreline including islands (miles) U.S.A.	Canada
Superior	31,700	49,300	81,000	317,000		1,245	1,481
Michigan	22,300	45,600	67,900			1,638	0
Huron	23,000	51,800	74,800	481,000		955	3,119
St. Clair	400	6,100	6,500	5,000		171	149
Erie	9,900	23,600	33,500	105,000		541	460
Ontario	7,600	23,200	34,800	80,000		713	758
TOTALS	94,900	203,600	298,500	1,008,000		5,265	5,967

NOTE: Water areas do not include the connecting channels. Land areas and shoreline lengths include the area up to the outlet of the upstream lake. For Lake Ontario the land area and shoreline length also include the St. Lawrence River downstream to the Saunders Munes Dam

HYDROLOGIC

Lake	Monthly mean elevations IGLD (1955) Maximum	Mean	Minimum	Range	Annual fluctuation (feet) Maximum	Mean	Minimum	Outlet river	Monthly outflows CFS Maximum	Mean	Minimum
Superior	602.1	600.4	598.2	3.9	1.9	1.1	0.4	St. Mary	127,000	75,000	41,000
Michigan-Huron	581.9	578.7	575.4	6.5	2.2	1.1	0.1	St. Clair	245,000	188,000	99,000
St. Clair	576.2	573.1	569.9	6.3	3.3	1.8	0.9	Detroit	246,000	189,000	100,000
Erie	573.5	570.4	567.5	6.0	2.7	1.5	0.5	Niagara	265,000	202,000	116,000
Ontario	248.1	244.8	241.4	6.7	3.5	1.9	0.7	St. Lawrence	350,000	240,000	154,000

NOTE: Mean outflow from Lake Michigan through Mackinac Strait is estimated to be 52,000 CFS

Table 1. Great Lakes Data (cont'd.)

RAINFALL AND RUNOFF

Lake	Annual Precipitation (inches) Maximum	Annual Precipitation (inches) Minimum	Mean	Runoff (annual mean in inches)
Superior	18.0	24.0	29.7	12.4
Michigan	17.8	22.2	31.2	11.1
Huron	39.0	25.8	31.3	11.1
Erie	42.6	24.5	33.8	10.2
Ontario	43.7	27.6	34.3	10.5

States and Canada
   (Boundary Waters Treaty), 1909
   International Joint Commission, 1912
   Great Lakes Water Quality Agreement, 1972
   Great Lakes Water Quality Agreement, 1978
   Protocol to 1978 Agreement, 1987

2. Treaty of Niagara Falls, 1950

3. Convention on Great Lakes Fisheries, 1955
   Great Lakes Fishery Commission, 1956
   Joint Strategic Plan for the Management of Great Lakes Fisheries, 1981

USES OF THE WATERS AND RELATED LAND RESOURCES

Reacting to the high water levels in the Great Lakes in 1976, the two nations in 1977 authorized a study by the IJC of diversions and consumptive uses of Great Lakes Waters. Table 2 provides information on the amount of water withdrawn for various uses and the amount of water lost to the atmosphere through the process of consumption and thus not returned to the lakes.

Table 3 provides information on a wider array of water and related land uses for the year 1970, and focuses on the effects of change that may take place by the year 2020 for each of the various resource categories.

Recirculation practices could reduce the amount of municipal and industrial wastewater needing treatment, while at the same time implementing the goals of the Federal Water Pollution Control Act Amendments of 1972.[16] It is hoped that by the year 2020 implementation of progressive federal and state legislation, coupled with pollution control management systems, will be effective so that the Great Lakes Basin environment will be minimally affected by discharges from municipal and industrial wastewater treatment facilities. The Great Lakes are presumed to be able to provide all of the water required for cooling condensers for the production of energy, and the withdrawals are judged not to have a significant effect upon the quantity or quality of the lakes' waters. However, the location of power plants along or near the shore lands implies a significant increase in the amount of shore land allocated to power plant construction, along with elimination of valuable waterfowl and fish

Table 2. Water Withdrawals and Water Consumed for the Entire Great Lakes: United States and Canada

Water uses	Withdrawals,[a] 1978 (cfs)	Consumed,[b] 1975 (cfs)
Manufacturing	26,030	2,490
Municipal	7,060	830
Power	40,070	480
Irrigation	480	360
Rural-Domestic	560	330
Mining	1,210	250
Livestock	210	210
United States	66,600	4,300
Canada	9,400	600
Rounded totals	76,000	4,950

a. Withdrawals are waters taken from the Great Lakes for use.
b. Consumed waters are that portion of withdrawals not returned to the Great Lakes.
International Joint Commission, Great Lakes Diversions and Consumptive Uses (report to the two governments made under the reference of February 21, 1977), (Jan. 1985), p. 28.

habitat.[17] The large increase in electrical power demands expected in the Great Lakes Basin will require adequate land for power plant sites and transmission line rights-of-way.[18] Problems of aesthetics and land loss and disruption result from distribution and transmission lines. However, many manufacturers and utilities have developed new designs and materials that can improve the appearance of these power facilities.

With the exception of petroleum, natural gas, and a few other resources, mineral reserves within the Great Lakes Basin are adequate to meet projected demands. Mineral-bearing land requirements are expected to grow about 900 percent by the year 2020. In addition, certain mineral producers need large acreages for processing plant sites, ore storage areas, overburden and waste rock dumps, and tailings ponds. State policy for each individual state controls drilling for oil or gas in the beds of the Great Lakes. Offshore drilling presents a possibility for environmental damage; an appaisal of the value, location, and extent of mineral deposits in beds of the Great Lakes is needed and then decisions can be made on the feasibility of lake bed mining.

Projected flood damages in the Great Lakes Basin, excluding flooding on the lakes, can be alleviated through a two-pronged

Table 3. Significant Environmental Changes in the Great Lakes Basin due to Growth and Proposed Framework Programs

Resource use categories	Units	Base year condition (1970)	Projected condition (2020)	Future change (Ratio of 2020—1970 condition)
Water supply [a]	MGD	15,427.9	31,351.7	2.0
Irrigation	MGD-consumption	682.1	2,763.5	4.1
Mining	1,000 acres disturbed	65.4	571.8	8.7
Thermal power cooling	MGD-cooling consumption	165.0	2,220.0	13.4
	1,000 acres of plants [b]	4.6	68.9	15.0
Municipal waste-water discharge	MGD-effluent requiring treatment	3,063.7	9,787.0	3.2
Sport fishing	1,000 angler days	80,700.0	153,500.0	1.9
Recreational boating	1,000 boat days	29,010.0	39,850.0	1.4
Commercial navigation	Million tons/year accommodated	343.0	754.3	2.2
Agricultural land, treatment	1,000 acres	20,453.0 [c]	15,500.0	0.76
Agricultural land, cropland drainage	1,000 acres	6,213.0 [c]	2,610.0	0.42

Table 3. Significant Environmental Changes in the Great Lakes Basin due to Growth and Proposed Framework Programs (Cont'd.)

Resource use categories	Units	Base year condition (1970)	Projected condition (2020)	Future change (Ratio of 2020– 1970 condition)
Forest land, treatment	1,000 acres	27,930.0 [c]	21,800.0	0.78
Shoreland erosion	Miles protected by structures	317.7	5621.8	1.6
Streambank erosion	Miles protected	346.5	3,277.0	9.5
Flood damage prevention	Thousand $ AAD (avg. annual damages)	60,609.0	222,548.0	3.7
Wildlife management	1,000 acres	74,818.0 [d]	79,739.0	1.1
Outdoor recreation	1,000 recreational days	637,167.0	1,863,787.0	2.9

Source: *Great Lakes Basin Commission, Environmental Impact Statement of the Great Lakes Basin Framework Study Program* (1976), p. 26.
a. For municipal, self-supplied industrial, and rural domestic water supplies.
b. Assume maximum land required for plants at 0.17 acres per megawatt of installed capacity.
c. Land requiring treatment ratio of 2020 to 1970 indicates portion of these needs met.
d. 1960 data.

approach to floodplain management that includes nonstructural and structural measures. By 2020, approximately 54 percent of the urban flood damage that could occur and 39 percent of the rural flood damage that could occur in the basin will have been alleviated through structural measures.[19] Nonstructural measures such as floodplain management and zoning regulations are also projected.

The environmental effects of channel maintenance and selected segmented deepening would be felt in (1) the extent of polluted or unpolluted dredged material removed; (2) the negative short-term effect of dredging on water quality and benthic population; (3) the land required for disposal of dredged material (often including valuable fish and wildlife habitat); and (4) the land required for harbor area development stimulated by channel and harbor deepening.

The effects of dredging on aquatic flora and fauna are variable, and a site-by-site analysis of impacts would be required to judge their severity. Waterfowl and waterfowl habitat need to be protected from on-land disposal practices. Adverse effects could lead to disturbance of valuable fish-spawning areas, increased temperatures in side channels and wetland areas, extended periods of turbulence, and increased gouging of shore land. Although recreational diversity and opportunity is a desirable goal for the Great Lakes Basin, more intensive use of existing lakes and streams will burden some already overused resources. The problem now and in the future for basin wildlife is the influx of people. An accelerated rate of attrition of habitat is occurring, with wetlands, the habitat of highest value, the most affected. Destruction of shore wetlands is proceeding at an alarming rate. In nearly all of the Great Lakes land areas, the demands for consumptive and nonconsumptive wildlife uses are projected at least to double. Considering the fact that total basin wildlife area demand exceeds supply, and that the supply in terms of acres of wildlife habitat may be steadily diminished in the future, accommodation of any major increases in the current demand is not at all likely.

ISSUES, CURRENT STATUS, AND FUTURE OUTLOOK

Water Quality[20]

Following the 1909 treaty, from 1912 until the present day, Canada and the United States have authorized investigations and have struggled with the development of procedures to control the pollution of the boundary waters of the Great Lakes, excluding Lake Michigan. A synopsis of these activities follows.

1912   The two governments refer the matter of pollution of the Great Lakes to the IJC.

1918   The IJC reports to the governments that the "situation along the frontier is generally chaotic, everywhere perilous and in some cases disgraceful."[21]

1920   Canada proposes a treaty to control pollution to the United States; agreement was not reached.

1946   Reference sent to IJC similar to 1912 reference pertaining to the St. Clair River, Lake St. Clair, and the Detroit River.[22]

1946   Reference extended to include St. Mary's River.[23]

1948   Reference extended to include Niagara River.[24]

1954   In its report on reference, the IJC found injury being caused to health and property from municipal and industrial wastes and shipping sources, and recommended the governments adopt specific water quality objectives and extend authority of the IJC to maintain surveillance of water quality to ensure achievement of quality objectives. The governments approved both recommendations and further authorized establishment of advisory boards on each of the connecting channels to report semiannually to the IJC.[25]

1964   Reference resulting from deteriorating conditions in Lakes Erie and Ontario was given to the IJC by the two governments.[26]

1970   Final report submitted by the IJC to the two governments relative to the 1964 reference.[27] Between 1964 and 1970, the IJC's International Advisory Boards submitted ten semiannual reports, three major interim reports, and a special report on oil drilling.[28] In addition, six public hearings were held by the boards, and further public hearings were held by the IJC.

1969–1972   Various activities, including the formation of the Canadian Department of the Environment and the U.S. Environmental Protection Agency.[29]

1972   On April 15, 1972, the Great Lakes Water Quality Agreement was signed in Ottawa by President Richard Nixon and Secretary of State William Rogers for the United States, and by Prime Minister Trudeau and Secretary of State for External Affairs Mitchell Sharp for Canada.[30]

1972   The Water Quality Agreement of 1972 attached two additional references as tasks to be undertaken by the IJC.[31]

1978   Following the first five-year review, the Great Lakes Water Quality Agreement of 1978 was signed at Ottawa on November 22, 1978.

1979   The IJC in May provided the two governments with a report on the water quality of the upper Great Lakes.[33]

1980   The IJC in March provided the two governments with a report on pollution in the Great Lakes Basin from land use activities.[34]

1981   The IJC in January provided the two governments with a special report on pollution in the Niagara River.[35]

The Water Quality Agreements: 1972 and 1978

The texts of the agreements in English and in French run over seventy pages (1972) and fifty pages (1978). A side-by-side comparison of the tables of contents of the two agreements, excluding annexes, is provided here, together with brief notes to indicate the topics and changes in the substance of the agreements as stated in the IJC's Second Biennial Report.[36]

1972 Agreements	1978 Agreements
Article I—Definitions[37]	Article I—Definitions[38]
(No comparable article)	Article II—Purpose
Article II—General Water Quality Objectives	Article III—General Objectives
Article III—Specific Water Objectives	Article IV—Specific Objectives (This includes a nondegradation clause; a policy that flow augmentation is not a substitute for adequate treatment; exclusion of in-shore areas where natural phenomena prevent achievement of objectives; and designation of limited-use zones.)
Article IV—Standards and Other Regulatory Requirements	Article V (Reiterates prohibition against flow augmentation as a substitute for adequate treatment.)
Article V—Programs and Other Measures	Article VI—Programs and Other Measures (Changes compliance date from 12/31/75 to 12/31/82. Requires pretreatment for industrial waste; establishment of effective enforcement programs; and adds new sections on industrial sources, inventories, eutrophication, pollution from land uses, persistent toxics, and airborne pollutants.)
Article VI—Powers, Responsibilities and Functions IJC	Article VII—Powers, Responsibilities and Functions of the IJC. (Changes "Great Lakes Water Quality" to "Great Lakes Basin Ecosystem" with regard to research and investigation authority. Changes reporting schedules.)

Article VII—Joint Institutions	Article VIII—Joint Institutions and Regional Office. (Changes the function of the Regional Office from "to assist it [the IJC] in the discharge of its functions" to "provide . . . support and . . . assistance to the two Boards.")
Article IX—Consultation and Review	Article X—Consultation and Review (In lieu of prior five-year review, review following third biennial report.)
Article X—Implementation	Article XI—Implementation
Article XI—Existing Rights and Obligations	Article XII—Existing Rights and Obligations
Article XII—Amendment	Article XIII—Amendment
Article XIII—Entry into Force and Termination	Article XIV—Entry into Force and Termination
	Article XV (Supersession changes reference to "Great Lakes Water Quality Agreement of 1978."

The short phrases selected for the topics discussed in this section inadequately reflect the commission's voice, tone, and balanced concerns. It is important to recognize its concern for the integrity and validity of the agreement; a presentation that tells of gains and unattained objectives; a proper reading of the responsibilities of the two governments, their federal partners of state, provincial, and local levels; and the responsibilities of the two societies, the citizens of the two democracies who have the ultimate responsibility. Finally, the commission speaks to its own role with a sense of historic perspective. It relates explicitly to its traditional place in Canada–United States relations; it does not want to be saddled with performance tasks, and budgets and administration, that are the proper work of others; and it definitely wants to be free to carry out its essential role of advising governments.[39]

The commission opens its Second Biennial Report by noting the following:

> In the twelve years since Canada and the United States signed the 1972 Great Lakes Water Quality Agreement, the Commission's advisory boards have reported annually on progress in meeting the Agreement goals. In 1972, the Great Lakes Basin community faced serious problems that threatened the ecology of the Lakes and the uses of this large natural resource. The substantial efforts and funds directed by governments have not eliminated the problems, but important milestones have been reached.[40]

The commission closes this opening note by saying the following:

> There are limits to what technical and scientific programs can accomplish when fundamental elements are not only technological but also societal and attitudinal. As technological and scientific limitations on progress become more apparent, the challenge becomes increasingly one of engaging public support for the new approaches and programs that are needed.[41]

The commission's report addresses four major areas: (1) progress under the agreement; (2) problems of the management of science under the agreement; (3) ecosystem approaches and their implications; and (4) roles under the agreement.

Under the first area, the report states that controlling eutrophication through the management of phosphorus was a main focus of the 1972 agreement. The goal was to reduce phosphorus concentrations to 1.0 milligram per litre in municipal wastewater treatment plants that were discharging more than one million gallons per day, and to limit phosphorus in household detergents. Regarding these point sources of pollution, the report states that Canada and the United States had spent more than $7.6 billion to construct and upgrade municipal plants in the basin.[42] The report also explains that unless nonpoint sources of phosphorus pollution from land use, agriculture, forestry, mining, and similar activities are controlled, the full extent of the phosphorus problem will not be addressed.[43]

Continuing under the progress area, the report notes the following:

> Unlike the efforts to control phosphorus, there had been limited success in coming to grips with the overall problem of toxics in the Great Lakes basin . . . [I]t is becoming increasingly apparent that their individual, combined, and long-term effects do present serious environmental problems . . . The Commission has previously recommended that a comprehensive toxic substances control strategy be implemented by governments.[44]

Although, as the IJC notes, the agreement does not explicitly address groundwater problems, it recommends that the parties give serious attention to developing toxic monitoring strategies for groundwater resources in the Great Lakes region.[45] The commission reports its support for the application of an "ecosystem approach" to research and monitor the transport and behavior of toxic materials concerning water and air bases throughout the Great Lakes Basin.[46] The commission also raises its concern about the adequacy of present risk assessment methods and the confidence placed in them.

Areas of concern that do not conform to the requirements of the agreement occur throughout the system and, despite considerable attention from governments and the public, eighteen "class A" areas of concern remain the same as in 1981.[47] The ecosystem of the Niagara River and Lake Ontario is pointed out as one environment that "will continue to be degraded by pollutants for the foreseeable future."[48] Twenty-one "class B" areas also remain of concern, but, because of low priority, they may be "neglected until their problems escalate."[49]

Water quality goals include reference to thirty-eight specific objectives for chemical substances. The IJC has recommended new or revised objectives for eleven of these substances. Although the limitations of using single water quality parameters for assessing progress are recognized, they are a basic part of the current agreement.

The concept of limited-use zones is included in Article IV of the agreement but, after formal adoption by the United States, the U.S. Environmental Protection Agency informed the Commission that these zones are inconsistent with U.S. domestic law. The commission "believes that the Parties should consult at the earliest opportunity to resolve this issue and provide clarification to the Commission."[50]

Finally, in addressing the subject of progress under the agreement, the IJC states that it "is not satisfied that the information it now receives enables it to assess adequately programs and progress required under the Agreement." The Water Quality Board has formed a committee to review the commission's information needs and to recommend appropriate data requirements.[51]

Under the second major area, problems of management, the commission combines a number of previous concerns into an entirely new and vital dimension of its supervisory responsibilities. The problem is the design of a science policy for the Great Lakes Basin. The background summary statement is an excellent description of current problems in planning, funding, administration, and management of science under the agreement. The commission expresses concern for scheduling and allocation of funds, availability of expertise, uncertain levels of support, timing of awards and receipt of funds, and effects on personnel and coordination. Similar concerns are expressed regarding planning of scientific research, priorities, and laboratory operations. The commission encourages the parties to take steps to address these concerns.[52]

The third major area, ecosystem approaches, reflects a restatement of the IJC's commitment to an ecological approach to resource management in which land, water, air, and biota interact and are mutually influenced. "A seemingly unrecognized dimension [is] the extent to which institutional arrangements limit the ability of scientists and scientific institutions to focus on relevant research leading to the technical resolution of environmental problems."[53] The first recommendation of the commission's first biennial report states the following: "[T]he Commission recommends therefore that: 1. Parties, Jurisdictions and others foster and encourage policies, programs and institutions that (a) help develop and maintain a long-term ecosystem perspective with respect to their other legitimate goals and to be more anticipatory in their actions."[54]

In the final major area, roles under the agreement, the commission, after indicating that the agreement is between the two governments, makes it clear that the role of the IJC is one of assisting the two governments. In clarifying its specific role, the commission says that "it must ensure that its own integrity as an independent commentator on governmental programs be maintained."[55] It gives the following unambiguous statement:

> [I]t is the task of federal, state and provincial governments to integrate and coordinate governmental activities, supply scientific personnel and provide technical and financial resources. They can foster public consideration of Agreement principles and issues and provide the public with a credible base of information.[56]

ADDITIONAL ISSUES

Lake Levels and Flows[57]

The very large size of the Great Lakes creates, to a high degree, a self-regulatory mechanism. Variations of two to three feet from the long-term average affect shore property, navigation, and power interests. Shore property owners seek a stable water level regime; navigation is best served by high water levels; and hydropower generation prefers maintenance of minimum flows as large as feasible. The issue of lake levels and flows has been the search for a balancing of benefits and detriments among these interests.[58] In 1985 the consensus was that further regulation of the Great Lakes, except for modest adjustments in outflow rates for Lakes Superior and Ontario using available regulatory devices, is not justified. Instead, heavy reliance must be placed on man's adjustment to and respect for the natural self-regulation of the lakes.

Waterway Transportation

A 1980 Workshop on Anticipatory Planning listed sixteen major problems of concern in the planning, developing, and monitoring of a Great Lakes regional transportation system.[59] Although there is a Great Lakes Waterway System, it should not be inferred that there is unified system management. In fact, there is a Canadian system, and an American system; the workings, however, are primarily cooperative. Changes in the Welland Canal are the responsibility of that ownership. Winter navigation studies have been primarily a responsibility of the Corps of Engineers. The study of the potential for an All-American Canal some years ago was a unilateral study on the American side. Perhaps the future is more clouded than ever before by the new policies on deregulation. It will bear watching to see if a free marketplace and more open competition will operate to rationalize who will be carriers of what at what prices, and what the Great Lakes Water Transportation System will look like when the situation clears.

Fisheries

The Great Lakes Fishery Commission (GLFC), established in 1955, initiated the long-needed task of changing the direction of exploitation of Great Lakes fisheries towards one of protection, if not yet one of restoration or rehabilitation. Professor Henry Regier has noted that by 1960

> [a]ll the major traditional commercial fisheries on the Great Lakes were in a shambles of collapse . . . The most important proximate causes in the twenty year period prior to 1960 were: eruptions of exotic sea lamprey, alewife and smelt; improper fishing, especially by some commerical interests; eutrophication and its ramifications; and nearshore pollution by obnoxious and toxic materials.[60]

The GLFC had limited responsibilities. The Great Lakes Water Quality Agreement had a strong agenda to restore and control water quality, which is of vital concern to fisheries. For roughly five years, between 1972 and 1977, little if any communication occurred between the IJC and the GLFC, but beginning in 1977 joint meetings were initiated.[61] In 1980, the Great Lakes Basin Commission hosted a conference to consider a strategic plan to guide the GLFC in the management and rehabilitation of the fishery resources of the entire Great Lakes.[62]

There is renewed, but guarded, optimism about the rehabilitation of the Great Lakes fishery from a biological, species, point of view. Yet, there is much concern about the problem of toxic substances and the processes of bioaccumulation of toxics in fish life. Public health agencies maintain their warnings against human consumption. Carcinogenic effects in fish and the transferability of disease to man are under continued scrutiny. The remainder of the rehabilitation task is proving to be much more difficult than were the catchup efforts of the initial phases to meet long-standing, known needs for municipal sewage and industrial works.[63]

Energy

The electrical generating capacity in those portions of the eight Great Lakes states in the basin is calculated to be 52,151.2 megawatts. This capacity represents a mix that relies on coal (48 percent), oil (24 percent), uranium (18 percent), and hydropower (10 percent). Ontario has a capacity of 24,489 megawatts generated by coal (38 percent), oil (9 percent), uranium (21 percent), and hydropower (26 percent).[64]

The Science Advisory Board of the IJC published two reports, both dealing with broad-ranging energy questions. The first brought forward eight so-called factors of importance that led to matters termed "IJC active or monitoring roles."[65] The second report[66] had a more detailed technologic base, but concentrated its recommendations in four IJC "shoulds," suggesting that the IJC should (1) request integrated information from the parties regarding their programs for making more effective use of energy; (2) encourage the parties to undertake studies to identify energy alternatives best suited to achievement of overall environmental quality and to promote the use and development of those alternatives; (3) encourage the parties to coordinate in planning and using energy alternatives; and (4) encourage research into hazardous substances associated with alternative energy use and production, monitoring those substances that may produce significant environmental or health hazards.[67]

Acid Rain

The energy work group of the 1980 Anticipatory Planning Workshop began its report on sulfur emissions and acidic precipitation by noting that "acidic precipitation is perhaps the most serious environmental problem faced in the Great Lakes Basin."[68] United States contributions of sulfur dioxide (SO_2) emissions from states in the basin amounted to 10,586,000 tons per year; Ontario accounted for 1,500,000 tons.[69] Although the Great Lakes are not highly susceptible to acidification because of their buffering capacity and volume, the report said that "a large number of highly susceptible streams and small lakes . . . will undergo acidification within ten to twenty years."[70] The Library of Congress Congressional Research Service has prepared an information pack on acid rain that provides summaries of the major elements of the problem.[71] In the political arena, President Reagan and Prime Minister Mulroney, in 1985, appointed country representatives to a panel that was to recommend courses of action during that year.[72] The panel's report, made early in 1986, indicated that the problem resulted from sulphur emissions of power plants and other industrial sources; specific solutions remained to be determined.[73]

Land Use

The development of institutions and procedures to correlate land and water management in the Great Lakes Basin has proceeded slowly, in spite of the concept that land use is the driving force that determines water use and water quality. During the past thirty years, major studies and reports by the IJC and others have laid an adequate basis for needed action.[74] However, the IJC's 1985 biennial report to the two governments made clear its concern for lack of appropriate action in the land management area.[75]

Perhaps the strongest voice providing specific direction to institution building for land resources management was that of Professor Zigurd L. Zile:[76]

> Those who have contemplated and urged "alternative institutional arrangements" for resource management . . . appear to assume that the International Joint Commission lacks the requisite powers to work toward their envisioned goals, including land resource management. I believe that this assumption is unwarranted and that certainly none of the Commission's constituent jurisdictional documents needs revision as a condition to pragmatic progress toward improved binational land management practices.
>
> The reference mechanism first conceived in Article IX of the Boundary Waters Treaty and expanded in Article VI of the Agreement on Great Lakes Water Quality seems adequate for both surveillance and mediation functions with respect to planning or programming, designation, enforcement, and dispute settlement. The dormant article, Article X of the Boundary Waters Treaty, possibly provides a mechanism for the making of binding decisions in a

pinch. The perceived inadequacies of the Commission are traceable to the unwillingness of the parties to utilize what they already have rather than to a lack of linguistic embellishment on the sparsely-worded treaty framework.

I am convinced that the parties can draft a reference to authorize the International Joint Commission to engage in as much binational land resource management as could be realistically accommodated at this time even with substantially augmented resources of the Commission. The reference might direct the Commission to look into the condition of the land resources, to talk to the national, state (provincial) and local authorities about the practices and needs of land resource management in the area, and to prepare a responsive management plan or program for an indicated future. In addition, if the affected interests were ready for it, the reference might propose specific land use designations subject to approval under the applicable domestic law of the two countries. The mandate would simultaneously give the Commission an initiatory role regarding any action within the scope of the reference. Adequate staffing and an operating budget could be given to enable the Commission to perform the assigned tasks.

The parties should take procedural care in formulating the reference. In particular, they should secure the cooperation of all relevant government units through their principal resource management agencies.[77]

INSTITUTIONS

Joint institutions established under the premier agent of the two governments, the IJC, include three control boards and two technical boards pertaining to management or investigation of Great Lakes levels and flows, one study board on diversions and consumptive uses, and several special committees and groups.[78] The Niagara Falls Treaty of 1950 provided an assured flow of water over Niagara Falls in competition with hydropower interests.[79] The Great Lakes Fisheries Treaty of 1955 brought to a conclusion matters that had been discussed by no fewer than twenty-seven commissions and conferences since 1875.[80] Agreements, lacking the force of treaties but binding nonetheless, were used in 1954 and 1972 for the arrangements then thought necessary to control pollution in the Great Lakes.[81]

The activities of the two countries in the arena of Great Lakes Basin water, land, and environmental resources during the past three-quarters of a century, but primarily during the last thirty years, include boundary agreements; institution building; agreements on levels and flows, diversions, and fisheries; agreements on scenic resources; allocation for hydropower; air quality in the Windsor-Detroit area; and water pollution control. In light of comparable arrangements in similar international arenas, their record is impressive. Of equal importance in the longer term is the inevitable direction of the two countries toward the bilateral multipurpose management of the basin. It is this direction toward comprehensive, integrated, multipurpose water, land, and environmental management to which both countries have subscribed, not only in concept but by action, that allows an optimistic outlook for the future management of the basin.

An impressive start toward the development of a modern and effective management plan was outlined by J. W. MacLaren, one of Canada's foremost consulting engineers, and R. F. Clevinger, a former chairman of the Great Lakes Basin Commission, nearly twenty years ago.[82] Their plan laid out the basic reasoning to justify a comprehensive, integrated approach by showing the relationship among seven water use categories.[83] The organizational framework was to be, like the IJC, a coordinating agency. Each country would provide its own planning agents, envisioned as the Great Lakes Basin Commission, then in existence, and a counterpart agency, a Great Lakes Resources Commission, on the Canadian side, to be built upon an agreement of the governments of Canada and the Province of Ontario.

Planning Philosophies

The approach taken by MacLaren and Clevinger towards an integrated arrangement for the Great Lakes was in keeping with the evolution of complex resource management systems in both countries as well as with philosphical realities in the relations between Canada and the United States. Comprehensive, integrated, multipurpose water resource planning and development by river basins is an idea that has been extant for about a hundred years. Professor Norman Wengert of Colorado State University has traced the concept through three eras.[84]

> The first is the preparatory period from the 19th century to the New Deal, during which a set of related ideas were being expressed and tested in the market place of public discussion. Toward the end of this period a variety of ideas were being woven together as a basis for public action, data being accumulated on rivers as

systems, and multipurpose projects rather than single purpose projects were being proposed. The second period extends from 1933–1965 when, to ideas about multipurpose integrated planning were added goals for socioeconomic development within regions traversed by major rivers. Finally, the present period from 1965 is that when river basin planning, and programs rationalized in river basin terms, began to be crowded from their previous dominant position with respect to water policy, as new concerns, new goals and objectives, and new concepts with respect to water, to the environment, to development, and to the government role, were articulated and received political support.[85]

Institution building to make real the sought-after concept of river basin development evolved in periods approximating the three identified by Wengert.[86]

The first period was one in which separate agencies were or had been assigned separate tasks: the Army Corps of Engineers was responsible initially for navigation and flood control, and towards the end of the period for selected multipurpose development planning; the Bureau of Reclamation was responsible for western irrigated agriculture, as well as for water power and related matters. These assignments continued into the second period, when new tasks for water pollution control were given to the Public Health Service; small watershed protection, to the Department of Agriculture; and fish and wildlife protection, to the Department of the Interior. The second period, ending in 1965, saw two reasonably successful efforts at joining together the federal and state agencies. The first, during the 1930s and early 1940s, was the establishment of the National Resources Planning Board (NRPB). The board's reports on the several regions of the country were landmarks in intergovernmental cooperation. The second effort, following the demise of the NRPB, was the voluntary formation in 1943 of the Federal Interagency River Basin Committee.[87] Over the next decade, field committees, including state participation, were established in the Columbia, Missouri, and Arkansas-White-Red basins, the Pacific Southwest region, and New England, including New York.[88]

During both of these periods, beginning with President Theodore Roosevelt just after the turn of the century, the concept of comprehensive, integrated, multipurpose development of the river basins of the nation was supported by several attempts to institutionalize the concept. Finally, as an outgrowth of a 1960 Senate report on the nation's waters,[89] the U.S. Congress enacted the Water Resources Planning Act of 1965.[90] This act established the United States Water Resources Council and authorized the establishment of river basin commissions with federal and state members having equal voting power. From 1965 until 1981, the commissions were established in the Columbia, Missouri, Upper Mississippi, Ohio, Great Lakes, and New England drainage basins.

The principal task of the commissions was to develop comprehensive, coordinated, joint plans for basin development. Planning authority was limited, as was authority for plan implementation; nevertheless, the commissions were of value. Their major benefit was to bring together state and federal water authorities on a regular basis to consider the development and management of water quality and quantity and related matters. In 1981, the Reagan administration chose not to continue the commissions and other arrangements made by the Water Resources Planning Act of 1965. Whether, over the long term, this action signals a retreat from the seventy-year effort to evolve a federal-state cooperative arrangement to manage the nation's waters is not clear.

A SAMPLING OF MANAGEMENT PROPOSALS

At a conference held to celebrate the seventieth anniversary of the IJC, Professor Don Munton said the following:

> At the ripe old age of three score years and ten, when many institutions have passed the point of redundancy, the need for the International Joint Commission is increasing. Indeed, the IJC is still being recognized internationally as one of the most ambitious examples of a joint boundary water authority. But its future does remain something of an enigma. Almost no one, it seems, wants just to leave it alone. Over the years a host of observers have found it in need of restructuring, reforming, expanding, strengthening, even narrowing and weakening. What accounts for all this attention? Its success is one factor . . . Paradoxically perhaps, its limitations also attract attention.[91]

The most complete and authoritative study of the entire range of Canada–United States relations that has appeared in recent years was a 1965 report entitled "Canada and the United States—Principles for Partnership," by former Ambassadors Livingston T. Merchant of the United States and A. D. P. Heeney of Canada.[92] Although the emphasis of the report is on the economic issues between the two countries, Ambassadors Merchant and Heeney address themselves to nearly every significant aspect of the bilateral relationship. In a section entitled "Machinery for Consultation," the authors describe the IJC as "one which has been of continuing importance to both countries since its establishment . . . a unique institution" with a "solid foundation of law and precedent." Its "long and successful record in the disposition of problems along the boundary," which "justify consideration of some extension of the Commissions's functions," suggests that the two governments "examine jointly the wisdom and feasibility of such a development."[93]

Views from the U.S. Congress, 1965

Ten Republican members of the House of Representatives, meanwhile, detailed their own reaction to the Merchant-Heeney study in a statement inserted in the Congressional Record.[94] Their overall view was laudatory, although they expressed some differences in their own and the author's perspectives. They then listed suggestions for a broader IJC function: (1) include Lake Michigan in the definition of boundary waters; (2) empower the IJC to make recommendations relating to continental development of water and energy resources; (3) establish a permanent institutional location at the IJC offices for international discussion of technical foreign policy questions; (4) grant priority emphasis in both countries to IJC studies on water levls and pollution of the Great Lakes; and (5) give the commission a leading role in fulfilling the "obvious need for comprehensive advance planning in the development of water resources."[95]

International Pollution Control, 1969

Professor Frederick Jordan of McGill University noted shortcomings of the IJC,[96] pointing out that it has no specific jurisdiction over boundary pollution matters and consequently no control over the timing, extent, or nature of the investigations that it undertakes. Jordon suggested that the most fundamental difficulty is the lack of power to put into effect the standards and measures of control recommended by the IJC following completion of its study and in the exercise of its surveillance function. Even though both governments may adopt the recommendations of the IJC, in the absence of legislative enactments to carry out the recommendations, their implementation and enforcement remain academic. Within the context of a perception that neither Canada nor the United States would be prepared to vest broad powers over international pollution control in an international agency, he suggested changes he felt would strengthen the commission. They included (1) amending the Boundary Waters Treaty to place the air pollution concern on the same level as that of water; (2) doing away with the reference procedure in cases involving transboundary air and water pollution; and (3) giving the IJC certain supervisory powers over implementation of its recommendations.

Thirteenth Conference on Great Lakes Research, 1970

Existing institutional arrangements define the essential terms and conditions for establishing the political feasibility of any program of action relating to the water resources of the Great Lakes Basin. Therefore, the characteristics of the different political regimes bearing upon the basin need to be well understood before an effective analysis of its water resource problems can take place. Conferees noted that most studies of institutional arrangements focus on one or, at best, a limited number of governmental instrumentalities in relation to a complex system and that little is known about the patterns of interaction between and among public and private enterprises in the Great Lakes Basin system.[97] The Great Lakes represent a classic example of a common-pool resource in which a user draws from the resource until the marginal costs equal the marginal benefits without taking into account the external costs imposed on other users. This pattern will continue unchecked unless institutional arrangements require all users to take external factors into account.

Institutional Analysis, A Report from the Great Lakes Basin Commission, 1972

Dr. Lyle E. Craine, consultant to the Great Lakes Basin Commission, prepared this report.[98] Because the commission was a U.S. entity, the report was limited to the consideration of alternative institutional arrangements for the Great Lakes within the United States. Dr. Craine's purpose was to lend structure to the complex problem of institutional arrangements and to offer some general guidelines on how to proceed with any reform. His main point was that more geographic integration is needed. This means more formal links between, and coordinated management among, the various governments and agencies and departments of those governments operating within a particular geographic region that is ecologically related, such as the Great Lakes.

In this context, Dr. Craine assessed four institutional alternatives: interstate compacts, Title II river basin commissions, federal-interstate compacts, and basin interagency committees. He concluded that no single one of the four forms appeared to completely fill the need for geographic integration. According to Craine, a systems approach to geographic integration would be concerned

> [f]irst about the degree of policy, planning, and management powers which should be delegated to a geographic agency as compared to those exercised by agencies of general purpose government; second, about the constitution of the governing body of the geographic agency, with due attention to the requirements for representation and to the decision rules; and third, about the operational links among geographic agencies and functional agencies in general purpose governments.[99]

Binational Environmental Cooperation, 1972

Only a few months before the Stockholm meeting of the United Nations Conference on the Human Environment, *Controlling Great Lakes Pollution: A Study in United States–Canadian Environmental Cooperation* by Richard Bilder was published.[100] Recognizing that the cooperative arrangements resulting from the U.N. conference would have little in the way of precedent and law to guide them, Bilder attempted to fill some void with a detailed case study of United States–Canada cooperation on boundary matters. He began by reviewing major factors relevant to the pollution problems of the international Great Lakes. He pointed out the limitations in the ability of the federal governments to intrude, particularly in Canada, and the "complex hodgepodge of proliferating and occasionally inconsistent laws, regulations, and ordinances" governing Great Lakes pollution.[101]

Bilder commended the IJC for having dealt successfully with a wide range of problems over the years. But he injected a word of caution about making predictions for the future on the basis of that experience, suggesting that the IJC had been left relatively free from political pressures by the two governments. With the growing political importance of the problems with which the IJC deals, "the two governments may in the future prove less inclined to respect its [IJC's] traditional independence. There may be at least some pressures toward its politicization."[102] He suggested, however, that a more politicized IJC might actually be more useful. A politically responsive commission, he reasoned, might even be trusted with regulatory or enforcement powers.

Bilder also reviewed the 1972 coordinating agencies in both countries with responsibilities for resource management in the Great Lakes and proposed alternatives for coordination: (1) an advisory board operating under the IJC that would include responsible officials from all concerned planning, research, and operating agencies, and (2) some type of "internationalized" Great Lakes Basin Commission combined with the establishment of a new high-level joint U.S.–Canadian interagency committee on Great Lakes pollution.[103] In addition, he discussed potential alternatives that would go beyond the scope of the present Great Lakes Water Quality Agreement. One would be to expand the IJC's authority under the existing treaty framework. Another alternative, a supranational Great Lakes Authority, would, in his view, permit "problem-shed" management; eliminate the recurrent problems of jurisdictional conflict, duplication, and lack of coordination; and encourage effective decision making in a sufficiently broad context to permit a more complete analysis and balancing of policy alternatives.[104]

Improving Management, 1973

During the period from December 1971 to June 1972, the first session of a Canada–United States university seminar explored ways in which the institutional structures for management of water and land resources in the Great Lakes Basin might be strengthened to the mutual advantage of both countries.[105] The undertaking of this seminar in a sense reaffirmed the growing cooperation between Canada and the United States on Great Lakes problems. Participants recognized the progress and positive contributions being made in biophysical research on the lakes as exemplified by the International Field Year on the Great Lakes, which began in the spring of 1972. They also were aware of the negotiations then taking place between the two nations to strengthen the hand of the IJC in controlling transboundary water pollution. Although it acknowledged these accomplishments, the seminar also felt it was necessary to ask what else had to be done. The scope of attention would have to go beyond cooperation on controlling transboundary water pollution and joint efforts on water research, but how far, and in what way?

Two major substantive proposals came from the seminar. There was general agreement on the necessity for additional institutional change and the need to develop some framework as a prerequisite for more detailed plans, studies, and consultations required in the institutional remodeling process. In addition, two distinct alternative options were identified. The first would seek organizational improvements within the framework of a significantly strengthened IJC. Its key feature was that the IJC would be freed from the present treaty constraint of acting only when a matter is referred to it by both countries, so that it could assume an active role in the public decision-making processes. This process is already under way, in part as a result of the Great Lakes Water Quality Agreement of 1972. That agreement provides significantly more freedom for IJC action than any other previous arrangement by the two countries. The first alternative seeks to have this type of greater IJC freedom extended to other water and land problems in the Great Lakes.

The second alternative would call for a specifically created international body to supplant the IJC in the Great Lakes Basin. The IJC would be relieved of its treaty responsibilities within the basin and the function of the existing permanent and temporary Great Lakes Boards absorbed by the new treaty-established body. The responsibility of the IJC for that portion of the international border lying outside the Great Lakes Basin would remain unaffected. This alternative would require the negotiation of a new treaty by Canada and the United States as well as modifications to the 1909 treaty. The Columbia River Treaty would provide some precedent for this arrangement.

Either alternative requires developing relationships among existing federal, provincial, state, and regional agencies. The arrangements considered in these two alternatives would not constitute a management body in the sense of a control and operating organization such as state, provincial, or federal agencies with legislative mandates. Neither would they change the equality status between the two countries nor create a supranational bureaucracy with authority over the existing three levels of government. Instead, they would give rise to a joint Canadian–American body intended to serve as the locus of recommendatory policy guidance and coordination for those public programs and private activities that affect the water and related land and air environments of the Great Lakes Basin.

The organization would be assigned two basic management functions, those of surveillance and mediation. Surveillance, defined in this instance as information gathering, data interpretation, and dissemination, is a function concerned with problem identification and definition. Mediation is viewed as a management function that goes beyond surveillance in requiring broader authority and responsibility, an active role in which joint activities are agreed upon and conflicts resolved through discussion and consultation. The joint Canadian–U.S. body would be actively involved in a coordinative and mediative capacity with the operating agencies in developing joint programs to attack common problems within the basin. This role could include, among other things, promulgation, after appropriate coordination among the agencies concerned, of regulations, standards, and compliance schedules. Although the joint body under the definition and recommendations of this report would have no enforcement authority, these promulgations would provide clear evidence of acceptance of common goals and agreement on joint programs. The public notice of these actions would be a large step forward in securing public credibility, improving government accountability, and providing public reports for public assessment of progress. The report makes the following recomendations:

1. The governments of the United States and Canada should initiate, on a joint basis, a comprehensive examination of the problems associated with multiple-purpose management of the Great Lakes in order to conserve, develop, and use that unique resource for the mutual benefit of the people of both countries.

2. The alternative proposals formulated by the Canada–United States university seminar should be used by the two governments as a basis for initiating discussion and debate on the management of the Great Lakes.

3. In the United States, a study bill should be introduced early in the 93rd Congress for the purpose of opening the doors to serious public debate on the question of the joint management of the Great Lakes Basin by local, state, regional, and federal officials, and by private persons and nongovernmental organizations concerned with the public interest.

4. In Canada, the findings of the seminar should be discussed with officials in the federal government, the Ontario provincial government, and selected regional and local governments in Ontario. The purpose would be to encourage informal consultations on the new steps and responsibilities needed for the Great Lakes Basin, with the view to developing more detailed proposals for consideration at the Cabinet level of the two senior governments and to providing material for bilateral consultations.

A Canadian Parliament Report, 1975

This report by the Standing Senate Committee on Foreign Affairs of the Canadian Parliament is Volume I of a continuing study of Canada–United States relations.[106] While praising the IJC, the committee also listed suggestions for its improvement. Present environmental concerns that could not have been foreseen by the treaty makers of 1909, they noted, may force certain modifications in the

IJC procedures. The committee urged the Canadian government to examine two recommendations with a view to their joint implementation with the United States.

The committee recommended that the IJC should be given the authority to make, on its own initiative, preliminary examinations or assessments of potential pollution problems along the boundary, to point out potential sources of trouble and dispute, and to suggest to the two governments that a reference should be made. At present, the IJC must await a reference from the governments before inquiring into or investigating these problems.[107] The committee also recommended that the IJC should have extended power to publicize all its recommendations. Although it now has power to publicize its views under the Great Lakes Water Agreement, this authority is not automatically given in respect to other areas of IJC competence under the Boundary Waters Act.

Improving Management—Second Session, 1978[108]

Recomended long-term objectives of a critique and draft proposals, approved in general terms by the second session of the Canada–United States university seminar, are the rehabilitation and restoration of the Great Lakes. To achieve this goal, participants suggested an integrated problem analysis of the lakes so that proposed solutions could better fit existing and future conditions. Integrated problem analysis is sought through strengthening the role of the IJC within the context of the Boundary Waters Treaty. Rehabilitation and restoration of the Great Lakes, implicit in the 1972 and 1978 water quality agreements, requires the two countries to make a strong, irreversible, and concerted commitment to this goal in the new agreement.

Recommendations

The seminar participants made the following specific recommendations:
1. The IJC should be authorized to establish a board to interface with the planning activities in both countries, and this board should report not less than annually to the IJC on current and potential problems that may require action.
2. The two countries should explicitly recognize the authority of the IJC to recommend references to them, and should encourage the IJC to proceed on its own initiative to rec-

ommend references on current or potential management problems of the Great Lakes.

3. The governments of Canada and the United States should submit a reference to the IJC asking it to create a group, or board, on Great Lakes rehabilitation and restoration.

4. The IJC professional and support staff should be increased.

5. The term of office of IJC commissioners, board members appointed by them, the Great Lakes Fishery Commission, and other boards whose decisions bear substantially on Great Lakes management should be defined for specific periods of time.

6. The Canadian Parliament and the Congress of the United States should hold annual legislative oversight hearings on the management of the Great Lakes.

7. The two governments should formulate a science policy for the Great Lakes as an indication of their commitment to restore, rehabilitate, and improve the management of the lakes and to support the development of new knowledge needed to achieve those ends.

Anticipatory Planning, 1979[109]

The IJC's Science Advisory Board brought together nearly one hundred persons to define major actions that might be taken to improve the management of the Great Lakes. Main themes were identified by the group, and key questions posed: How are we to develop a "Great Lakes Perspective"—a view of the international Great Lakes as a whole? What is the role of information and analysis in creating a "Great Lakes Perspective"? What is the role of the IJC in arranging for the development of a "Great Lakes Perspective," and how should it use the results of such a process?

To move toward a strengthened collaborative arrangement allowing the two governments, acting through the IJC, better access to an improved information and analysis procedure, the following proposals were made:

1. The IJC should establish a standing board on information acquisition and analysis, including a core staff qualified to integrate, synthesize, and interpret such information, to improve the capability of the IJC to advise governments on needed programs and policies for the Great Lakes Basin.

2. The Canadian federal government and the Province of Ontario should develop an agreement that the preparation of reports for the Canadian portion of the Great Lakes will allow necessary coordination with reports by U.S. institutions for the U.S. portion of the Great Lakes.

3. Under its mandate in the Great Lakes Water Quality Agreement of 1978, the IJC should monitor the evolution of human settlements in the Great Lakes region from a comprehensive, holistic stance, reorienting its operations to include a view toward the future as well as considering the past.

Integrated Ecosystem Management

What new tasks are imposed on the governments of Canada and the United States and the IJC as greater recognition emerges of the interrelationships of water, land, the atmosphere, plant and animal life, and the effect of human behavior? The IJC and the two nations need new ways to speed their responses so that problems that influence each other can be dealt with sooner and more holistically. Because integrated management of the Great Lakes Basin is a very large task, priorities will have to be established. Development of an effective management process would extend over several years. To begin this process, Canada and the United States, with the assistance of the IJC, should undertake studies to consider program linkages and priorities, to expand the roles and capabilities of the standing boards, and to strengthen the role and staff capabilities of the regional office.

Regional and Economic Perspectives

The Great Lakes represent a geographic region shared by Canada and the United States. What is the significance of regional and economic factors in developing a management strategy for the lakes? What impact does the Great Lakes region have on other North American regions, and what is the impact of the other regions on the Great Lakes? How can the nature of these complex issues be more clearly identified so that effective regulatory programs can be implemented and monitored?

How should the Boundary Waters Treaty and the Water Quality Agreement be modified, if necessary, in order to allow the two nations to solve regulatory problems arising as a result of energy development, human settlements, water transportation, regulation of lake levels, increasing pressures for diversions into and out of the Great Lakes Basin, increasing consumptive use of water in the basin, and atmospheric pollution of land, lakes, rivers, and human settlements? How can the IJC address the emerging problem of scarce economic resources for support of water quality regulatory and control programs?

Institutional Arrangements and Capabilities

What changes may be needed in the institutional arrangements that have been established within and between the United States and Canada for dealing with Great Lakes issues in an anticipatory and forward-looking manner? What changes do these in turn imply for the IJC as the major binational bridging agency for the Great Lakes? The development and strengthening of an anticipatory capability for the Great Lakes Basin ecosystem can be done within the basic policy framework for governance as outlined above. The IJC has a crucial role to play as major facilitator for consultations on goals, issues, and problems requring the attention of both countries. Existing intergovernmental arrangements within each nation should be modified and strengthened where necessary to provide the intelligence function in support of binational cooperation. Steps need to be taken to strengthen the involvement of municipal governments in working out implementable programs for resolving problems pertaining to the Great Lakes ecosystem, and elected officials at all levels of government should be brought much more into the consultation process. Public awareness and involvement also must be widened. It is desirable that the two countries issue a strong statement confirming their expectations that the IJC will take the initiative to advise them on current or emerging problems in order that they may respond in a timely manner, and on what specifically has to be done to create a strengthened anticipatory capability to respond to emerging problems in the Great Lakes Basin ecosystem. The IJC should create a special panel or advisory board to develop the strategies needed to implement such a directive, in part by reviewing the nature and extent of ongoing planning and development activities that bear significantly on Great Lakes issues and in part by consulting with other Great Lakes commissions on the programs they are facilitating or coordinating. Such a panel or board could then initiate consultations with various individuals or groups of professionals and impacted publics along the lines proposed for creating the communication networks necessary to develop a futures orientation toward planning and management of the Great Lakes ecosystem.

Communication for Implementation

Strategies to improve the ecosystem quality of the Great Lakes Basin cannot succeed without widespread public understanding and acceptance of whatever goals the strategies are meant to achieve. They also require mobilization of strong political support. How can effective communication networks be brought together with one another to facilitate information sharing and a great degree of public involvement in matters affecting ecosystem quality in a large region such as the Great Lakes Basin? What is the crucial role of the IJC in helping to bring this about? How can the IJC develop effective two-way information sharing and communication processes with local groups, elected officials, and citizens in both countries, even though it must also formally work through official channels of communication to governments?

What approaches are being taken to anticipate and assess technical innovations, changing cultural values, and social futures? In what ways can the IJC maintain communication with these activities so that it can be better prepared to deal with the future? Following are some proposals, developed at greater length by Professors Munton and Francis in chapters 8 and 9 of this volume.

Dealing with the Future

Professor Munton provides a deeper and more critical analysis of management proposals.[110] He notes: "In 1973 a bilateral group of professors, mainly of resource planning and engineering, under the banner of the Canada–United States University Seminar produced the most thoroughly developed set of proposals to date."[111]

In the final report of that seminar to the secretary of the Department of the Interior,[112] the principal investigator summarized the value of the 1971–72 and 1976–77 seminars, saying that both had contributed substantially to the establishment of concepts and the formation of attitudes and implementation processes, all of which were in part used by various publics, the governments, and the IJC during the past decade. He noted there was no record of any similar binational disucssion group that concentrated its efforts on the Great Lakes and their management for the long future.

Although the Boundary Waters Treaty of 1909 and the formation of the IJC were first and major steps toward managing through a unitary body many of the issues arising out of new developments (but not treating the issues themselves in a unitary manner), the largest step toward the evolution of a management process that substantially recognized interrelationships, integration, ecology, or, stated another way, "the totality of the whole," occurred with the approval of the binational Water Quality Agreement of 1972, extended in 1978. It was the felt need to look into management processes concerned with the totality of the whole that led to the initiation of the Canada–United States university seminar.

The findings of the two seminars heightened the debate in Canada and the United States on management matters, and several significant occurrences took place. In 1973 the U.S. Congress held, for the first time, a hearing on Great Lakes institutional arrangements;[113] the IJC undertook, for the first time, a self-review in 1974;[114] and the Standing Senate Committee on Foreign Affairs of the Canadian Parliament did the same in 1975.[115] Additional growth of the idea of "managing the whole" took place during the first five-year program of the Great Lakes Water Quality Agreement. As a result of impressive special presentations, the IJC agreed to initiate a management process guided by the idea of ecosystem management[116] that was further enlarged in an IJC-funded workshop in 1979 under the sponsorship of its Science Advisory Board–Societal Aspects Committee. The workshop report, *Anticipatory Planning for the Great Lakes,* had as one of its main themes the idea of "integrated (ecosystem) water resources management."[117]

In furtherance of the integrated management idea, the Great Lakes governors and provincial ministers in 1982 resolved that the time had come to examine institutional arrangements as a means of looking forward to the improved management of the Great Lakes. And in June 1982, the IJC made it clear that institutional roles and opportunities represented a major concern in preparing for future developments.[118]

Institutional Summary

The impressive record of the two countries when compared with that of other nations facing similar international boundary water problems has been noted. Of equal importance in the longer term is the inevitable direction of the two countries toward the bilateral multipurpose management of the Great Lakes Basin. It is the direction taken by Canada and the United States toward comprehen-

Table 4. Interdependence Matrix for the Great Lakes Basin

Affects	Water quality	Land use	Lake level control	Recreation	Flood control	Municipal/industrial Water supply	Fish and wildlife protection	Agricultural water supply	Solid waste	Air quality	Navigation	Hydropower
Water quality	—	2	5	3	3	0	0	0	1	3	3	5
Land use	2	—	1	2	1	2	1	2	5	1	4	2
Lake level control	0	4	—	0	1	1	0	3	2	0	0	1
Recreation	1	1	3	—	3	0	2	0	4	1	5	5
Flood control	0	3	1	0	—	2	0	0	3	0	0	5
Municipal/industrial water supply	1	0	3	4	5	—	0	4	3	4	5	0
Fish and wildlife protection	1	1	2	2	2	0	—	0	2	4	3	2
Agricultural water supply	1	5	3	5	5	3	0	—	3	5	5	0
Solid waste	1	1	3	0	3	0	0	0	—	0	1	5
Air quality	4	1	0	0	0	0	0	0	4	—	5	0
Navigation	0	2	1	5	4	0	0	0	1	0	—	0
Hydropower	0	0	1	0	4	0	0	0	4	0	0	—

Ranking of priority on a scale 1-5; 1 = highest; 0 if no significant interdependence is thought to exist.
Canada-U.S. University Seminars. A Proposal for Improving the Management of the Great Lakes of the United States and Canada 17 (1971).

sive, integrated, multipurpose water and related land and environmental management that allows an optimistic outlook for the future management of the Great Lakes Basin.

One of the reasons that ecological planning has not moved forward as well as it might has been the lack of activity to identify the elements and their specific interdependencies that would better define the ecosystem to be managed.[119] A first order of concern in attempting to design institutional characteristics is the need to determine the objectives sought and the problems to be confronted. An interdependence matrix for the Great Lakes Basin is presented in table 4.

A report on Lake Erie water levels,[120] authorized by a reference in 1977 and published in 1981, considered geographic location;

physiography; climate; hydrology and hydraulics; population; environmental conditions, water quality, wildlife-wetlands, and fish; coastal zone, economic areas, areas of concern, and land use–shorelines; power development, St. Lawrence, Niagara, and St. Mary's; Great Lakes–St. Lawrence navigation system; public beaches; and recreational boating.

A report authorized by a reference in 1977 and published in 1981 on Great Lakes diversions and consumptive uses[121] considered hydraulic methodology—forty-three possible scenarios of diversion flow changes; economic evaluation—navigation, power generation, beaches and boating, and coastal zone–shore property; environmental evaluation—fisheries, near-shore habitat, wetlands, and water temperature; wildlife; water quality—oxygen, phytoplankton, embayment water quality, phosphorus, and turbidity; consumptive uses—municpal, rural-domestic, manufacturing, mining, rural-stock, and irrigation; thermal power; consumption quantities by basins, nations, sectors of the economy, and lake and nonlake categories; and general assumptions and parameters such as population growth, migration trends, employment, GNP, per capita consumption, energy use, economic growth, and government policies.

In a 1984 report on great lakes hydrometeorologic and hydraulic data needs,[122] the findings and conclusions of which were transmitted with substantial approval by the IJC to the two governments on January 1985, the need for improved coordinating mechanisms for Great Lakes technical information was outlined. The report concluded that institutional arrangements among the boards of the IJC, data-gathering agencies, and other users lack cohesion and the authority needed to make optimum use of technological advances.

The report recommended continuing review and coordination of the ever-changing needs of the IJC boards; formal coordination with data collection agencies to ensure meeting present and future technical information needs of the Great Lakes boards and agencies in both countries using internationally coordinated data; promotion of the development of climate forecasts; and promotion of the development of predictive large basin water supply models. To accomplish these goals, the board proposed that the IJC establish a permanent International Great Lakes Technical Information Network Board to provide a mechanism for institutional coordination in making studies and gathering and providing data on the Great Lakes system. This board should also function as a coordinating committee on hydraulic and hydrologic data.

Without citing additional reports, it is apparent from those detailed above that the data requirements of the IJC boards, study committees, and the like are broad and growing. Integrated ecosystem planning data require technical information of a specific kind, but also needed are socioeconomic data, statistics on water use and consumptive use, resource and environmental evaluations, and land, atmospheric, climate, and quality data.

At the end of 1985 the two countries appeared close to acting to achieve integrated ecosystem planning and management for the Great Lakes and to articulating, through carefully defined policy and institutional capacity, means to implement such a program. Alerted to changing legal policies affecting diversions of water[123] and concerned about such diversions affecting the Great Lakes, the riparian states and the Provinces of Ontario and Quebec joined forces in February 1985 to sign a Great Lakes Charter. The charter calls for each signatory state to use similar formats to collect and maintain data on major water uses, diversions and consumptive uses, uses for navigation, recreation, hydroelectric power, and water allocation.

The workshop on anticipatory planning[124] laid out the basic lines of action that, if implemented by the two countries, can bring about an effective start to the long-term and unending task of binational management of the Great Lakes.

An Ending, Perhaps a New Beginning

The Great Lakes Basin Commission, organized under the Water Resources Planning act of 1965, provided an important (but incomplete by itself) institution to forward the idea of Great Lakes Basin integrated ecosystem management. Representing the eight basin states and the relevant federal agencies, the commission moved forward the idea of comprehensive, coordinated, joint planning for the basin through publication of its twenty-seven-volume *Great Lakes Basin Framework Study.*[125]

In September 1981, all basin commissions under the Planning Act of 1965 were terminated by the federal government,[126] leaving a vacuum in federal-state-local relations and institutions in basinwide water and related land resources planning. Alerted to the changing legal policies affecting diversions of water and concerned about such diversions affecting the Great Lakes, the lake states, joined by the Provinces of Ontario and Quebec, joined forces in February 1985 to sign a Great Lakes Charter.[127] The charter calls for each state and province to use similar formats to collect and maintain data on major water uses and diversions and addresses uses for navigation, recreation, hydroelectric power, and water allocation. Governor Blanchard of Michigan emphasized, in signing the charter, that it was "a first step not only in preventing diversions but also in addressing many of the other common issues this region faces."[128] The signatories to the charter agreed that "without careful and prudent management, the future development of diversions and consumptive uses of the water resources of the Great Lakes Basin may have significant adverse impacts on the environment, economy, and welfare of the Great Lakes region."[129]

Institutionally the charter working committee, entitled the Water Resources Management Committee, "will be charged with responsibility to identify specific common water data needs: to develop and design a system for the collection and exchange of comparable water resources managemennt data."[130] The charter action by the signatory parties should be watched with a great deal of interest by the two national governments and by the IJC. There are a number of cautionary signals that need to be considered in determining the role of the charter in the management of the Great Lakes, which the Great Lakes framework report[131] had earlier commented upon: (1) any mechanism fashioned to deal with basinwide resource issues must be capable of dealing with the problems of multiple-use resources; (2) failure to coordinate information generation and planning constitutes a grave handicap of the ability to identify problems and to formulate policy goals; and (3) an institution created to deal with the total Great Lakes picture must have authority to establish priorities. Otherwise, there is a probability that any agreement on policy goals and objectives would be a hollow gesture.[132]

Professor George Francis, in "Institutional Arrangements and Capabilities,"[133] responded to two questions: what changes may be needed in the institutional arrangements that have been established within and between the United States and Canada for dealing with Great Lakes issues in an anticipatory and forward-looking manner, and what changes do these in turn imply for the IJC as the major binational "bridging agency" for the Great Lakes? He expounded as follows:

> The basic policy framework for governance over the Great Lakes Basin is set primarily by the international boundary between Canada and the United States, the constitutional division of powers among levels of government within both countries, and the major statutes bearing on planning, management, and use of the Great Lakes Basin ecosystem within each of the major jurisdictions. The secondary, but nonetheless crucial, components of this framework are the various intergovernmental coordinating devices which have been created to help to facilitate the handling of specific kinds of problems arising from the many uncoordinated uses of Great Lakes resources.

> The binational commissions, the IJC and the Great Lakes Fishery Commission, are the only bodies whose mandates permit them to view the lakes' ecosystem as a totality. Within the United States there is an additional complementary role for water and land use planning provided by the Great Lakes Basin Commission, and some coordination of user group interests by the Great Lakes Commission. In Canada, several federal-provincial agreements, especially the Canada-Ontario Environmental Accord, also serve to facilitate joint inter-jurisdictional cooperation on matters concerning the Great Lakes.[134]

In order to strengthen these capabilities, Professor Francis suggests the creation of a Great Lakes Basinwide "intelligence" operation to monitor ecosystem quality changes and to exercise surveillance over ongoing activities and new initiatives that appear to have impacted most heavily on the basin ecosystem. In addition, he sees a need for a wider measure of informal binational and interorganizational consultation on policy issues and common goals to be sought for the Great Lakes by each country working through its own system.

It is important to recognize the significance of the action of the leaders of the Great Lakes Basin states and the two Canadian provinces in furthering the idea of comprehensive, multipurpose, integrated water and related land and environmental planning and management, and ecosystem planning and management. They have moved the idea to a new plateau, and it is to be hoped that by their action they will have created a new atmosphere within which the two governments can once again more comfortably undertake those consultations and studies that will lead in time to an improved and effective management arrangement for the Great Lakes.

The advisory provided for the two governments by the IJC in part 2 of its January 1985 report on diversions and consumptive uses,[135] excerpts from which were included in the introduction to this article, stands as a strong complement to the Great Lakes governors' and provincial ministers' charter. In concluding its advisory, the IJC asks, and answers, a provocative question: are we prepared for a nonlinear future? A portion of that response follows:

> Major changes in the economic and social conditions of our two nations have occurred in the past, and substantial policy shifts have taken place in reaction to them. One has only to think first of the Great Lakes in the early 1800s, not greatly different from what they were before the arrival of the Europeans, and then of the Great Lakes a century later, at the center of a rapidly industrializing and

urbanizing North America. The Great Lakes made this change possible with their seemingly unlimited supply of water for domestic and industrial use, for navigation, for power generation, for recreation; but they also paid the price in terms of pollution and eutrophication. In little more than a century, an apparently inexhaustible supply of pure water had become fully committed—if not over-committed—to supporting a variety of beneficial uses, leading inevitably to a variety of control measures to balance the needs of competing forces.

If this rapid change could occur in little more than a century, discontinuities must also be expected in the future. Though some trends leading to major change may be discernible now, their nature and scope are to a large extent unpredictable, for the Great Lakes and elsewhere. For example, a change in attitudes or in economic imperatives could make water a widely accepted article of commerce. While the commission does not believe that there is now a critical situation, at least one that would be felt in the Great Lakes region with respect to the quantity of water, it questions whether the institutions of government are in a position to make thoughtful and forward-looking decisions about the use of water, should the need arise. We know with little precision the present and future uses and values of Great Lakes water. Policies should therefore provide adaptive mechanisms for dealing with change and the unexpected.[136]

If the two governments find it within their agendas, under this new climate, to initiate conversations looking toward the strengthening of institutional arrangements for the shared international Great Lakes, action will be needed to bring together representatives of urban and rural constituencies and federal, provincial, and state government representatives, in a setting that will provide for communication among the several parties.

Several proposals have suggested an international committee format.[137] In keeping with these views, and based upon the author's own research and experience, an initial step to support the IJC's advice to governments that they would "be well advised at this stage to engage in broad but systematic discussion of their use of Great Lakes waters before they are faced with any sense of crises, actual or imminent"[138] would be the creation of an ecosystem study board under usual reference procedures to the IJC and under IJC oversight. Such an arrangement would involve minimal formality and could be established for a specified period of time, for specific tasks, or for any number of directed actions. It could be discharged at the will of the governments. It would be experimental, enlightening, and would provide a guide, positive or negative, to the future.

The primary purpose of such a reference would be to provide an authorization by the governments of the United States and Canada to allow the IJC to initiate a comprehensive examination of the problems associated with the ecosystem management of the Great Lakes in order to conserve, develop, and use that unique resource for the mutual benefit of the people of both nations. Such a report would be of great value in providing the basis for the broad but systematic discussions recommended by the IJC.

Professor Munton[139] implied the difficulty the two governments may have in assessing the need for, the value of, and the usefulness of the IJC. Particularly, their concern is rooted in ensuring that they do not overkill a good thing and that they maintain control over their responsibilities. But Munton's conclusion appears to be that the times, the problems, and the experience to date do require some change. In responding to the suggestion for an ecosystem study board, the two governments could initiate a process that would lead to a variety of opportunities to allow responsible actors at all levels to evolve, ultimately, a procedure which will be practicable and workable in the real world.

NOTES

*Professor Emeritus of Civil Engineering, Department of Environmental Engineering, Cornell University.

1. For descriptions of these arrangements see *Great Lakes Water Level Problems, Hearings before the Senate Comm. on Foreign Relations,* 94th Cong., 2d Sess., 3–34 (1976).

2. International Joint Commission, *Great Lakes Diversions and Consumptive Uses* (January 1985).

3. Ibid., Pt. 2, at 41.

4. Engineering Institute of Canada & American Society of Civil Engineers, *Proceedings of Great Lakes Water Resources Conf.* (June 24–26) (hereinafter cited as *EIC&ASCE Proceedings*).

5. R. Erdoes & A. Ortiz, *American Indian Myths and Legends* (1984).

6. J. Legault & T. Kuchenberg, *Reflections in a Tarnished Mirror: The Use and Abuse of the Great Lakes* (1978).

7. Ibid.

8. The Great Lakes, with the exception of Lake Michigan, are divided approximately midway between the United States and Canada. Seldom do

reports from either country provide a total perspective. For such a perspective, see International Joint Commission, *Further Regulation of the Great Lakes,* Ch. 3 (1976). For an additional Great Lakes perspective see Misner and Daniels, eds. *Decisions for the Great Lakes,* A Project of Great Lakes Tomorrow, (1982), Natural Setting for the Ecosystem pp. 23–84.

9. The maximum dimensions of the Great Lakes Basin are approximately 740 miles from north to south and 940 miles from east to west. The total area of the basin, both land and water, is 298,500 square miles. The basin is unique in that water covers approximately one-third of its total area, that the land areas which drain into the lakes are only from ten to one hundred miles from the shoreline, and that it has no dominant tributary system.

10. Most of the Great Lakes Basin is within two major physiographic regions. The areas north and west of Lake Superior and north of Lake Huron are in the Laurentian Uplands dominated by hills, a few low mountains, many lakes, and numerous swamps. The central lowlands cover most of the remainder of the basin. The eastern limit of the basin is in the foothills of the Adirondacks; the basin's outlet is in the wide St. Lawrence Valley, a relatively flat marine plain.

11. One-seventh of the U.S. population resides in the Great Lakes Basin, which includes four of the twelve largest cities in the United States: Chicago, Cleveland, Detroit, and Milwaukee. The relative importance in Canada is even greater because one-third of that country's population lives in the Ontario portion of the basin and, if the wholly Canadian portion of the St. Lawrence River Basin is added, the proportion of the total population rises to 60 percent.

12. The region accounts for 40 percent of U.S. and 80 percent of Canadian iron and steel production.

13. For an excellent discussion of the institutional setting, see *Decisions for the Great Lakes,* supra note 8, "Governing the Basin Ecosystem," pp. 101–177.

14. The states of New York, Pennsylvania, Ohio, Indiana, Illinois, Michigan, Wisconsin, and Minnesota. Although the Great Lakes are bounded in Canada by the Province of Ontario only, the St. Lawrence drainage and the results of Great Lakes management have substantial effects in the province of Quebec.

15. Taken from Francis, "How Governments Behave," *Decisions for the Great Lakes,* pp. 101–112.

16. Federal Water Pollution Control Act Amendments of 1972, Pub. L. No. 92-500, 86 Stat. 816.

17. The dissipation of heated water discharge from thermal power plants could have serious localized effects upon wildlife and fishery habitat

by increasing the water temperature to unacceptable limits. By 2020, a major portion of the total energy produced in the Great Lakes Basin may be from nuclear power plants. The potential threat of nuclear accident and radiological contamination requires stringent public health and environmental safeguards.

18. The land requirement for thermal plants varies from about 0.09 acre/MW to 0.17 acre/MW, depending on the size and type of plant. For the steam-generating capacity projected to be installed in the basin by 2020, and using the 0.17-acre/MW figure, the amount of land required for thermal plants would be about 69,000 acres. Assuming that 150 to 200 plant sites would be required, all situated on the lakeshore, a maximum of about 200 miles of shoreline would be needed.

19. These measures include reservoir storage, channel modification, levees, and flood walls, which will significantly disrupt fish and wildlife habitat, both in the areas of construction and in other areas that depend on periodic flooding to maintain their productivity.

20. Prior to the establishment of the IJC in 1909, under the Boundary Waters Treaty, January 11, 1909, United States–United Kingdom, 36 Stat, 2448, 2451, T.S. No. 548, the United States had established two commissions, in 1906 and 1908, to investigate water pollution in Lake Erie and Lake Michigan. In both of these early commissions and the subsequent studies under the IJC, the part played by the sanitary engineers of the United States Public Health Service was significant.

21. International Joint Commission, *Final Report on the Pollution of Boundary Waters Reference* (1918).

22. 1946 IJC Docket No. 54.

23. Ibid.

24. 1948 IJC Docket No. 55.

25. International Joint Commission, *Pollution of Boundary Waters* (1951); International Joint Commission, *Safeguarding Boundary Water Quality* (1961) (a cooperative effort between the United States and Canada under International Treaty).

26. 1964 IJC Docket No. 83.

27. International Joint Commission, *Pollution of Lake Erie, Lake Ontario, and the International Section of the St. Lawrence River* (1970).

28. International Lake Erie Water Pollution Board, *Potential Oil Pollution Incidents from Oil and Gas Well Activities in Lake Erie—Their Prevention and Control* (September 1969).

29. These activities included the Canada–United States consultation in anticipation of the IJC's final report (1969); a ministerial meeting in Ottawa to set phosphorus limits on detergents (1970); the U.S. Environmental

Protection Agency formed (1970); the first Great Lakes environmental conference of governors (1970); the Canada Department of the Environment formed (1971); the second ministerial meeting (1971); the Canada Federal Government and Province of Ontario Agreement on Lower Great Lakes (1971); and draft texts of agreements (1971-1972).

30. Canadian Department of the Environment, *A History and Analysis of the Agreement Between Canada and the United States on Great Lakes Water Quality* (September 18-22, 1972) (prepared for the NATO/CCMS workshop symposium at Presque Isle).

31. Great Lakes Water Quality Agreement, April 15, 1972, United States-Canada, 23 U.S.T. 301, 24 U.S.T. 2268, T.I.A.S. Nos. 7312, 7747 (with Appendix I dated November 21, 1973). The first reference was to study pollution in the Great Lakes system from agricultural, forestry, and other land use activities. The second was to study pollution problems of Lake Huron and Lake Superior.

32. Great Lakes Water Quality Agreement, November 22, 1978, United States-Canada, 30 U.S.T. 1384, T.I.A.S. No. 9257.

33. International Joint Commission, *Water Quality in the Upper Great Lakes* (May 1979).

34. International Joint Commission, *Pollution in the Great Lakes Basin from Land Use Activities* (March 1980).

35. International Joint Commission, *Special Report on Pollution in the Niagara River* (January 1981). Annual or biennial reports of the IJC, the Water Quality Board, the Science Advisory Board, or of special committees established by those entities have not been included in the summary. Copies of most publications of the Great Lakes Water Quality Agreement agencies can be received by writing the International Joint Commission, Great Lakes Regional Office, 100 Ouellette Avenue, Windsor, Ontario N9A 6T3, or the Canada or United States Sections IJC in Ottawa, Ontario, or Washington, D.C., respectively.

36. International Joint Commission, *Second Biennial Report under the Great Lakes Water Quality Agreement of 1978 to the Governments of the United States and Canada and the States and Provinces of the Great Lakes Basin* (December 1984) [hereinafter cited as *Second Biennial Report*].

37. These pertain, in part, to boundary waters, the boundary waters treaty, the Great Lakes system, harmful quantity, hazardous polluting substance, phosphorus, and specific water quality objectives.

38. The same as note 37. The 1978 definitions also include the Great Lakes Basin ecosystem, monitoring, research, surveillance, and toxic substances.

39. On a personal note, as an observer of the IJC for four decades and as a friend or working colleague of many of the commissioners and

staffs on both sides, the author's admiration must be expressed for the fairness, objectivity, and willingness to serve in the best public service tradition that pervades this agency.

40. *Second Biennial Report,* supra note 36, at 1.

41. Ibid.

42. "Though significant progress has been made . . . 39 of the 390 major (municipal treatment) facilities in the basin missed the December 31, 1982 construction deadline and difficulties have been encountered in operating some plants to their design capabilities. In November, 1983 . . . nine major municipal . . . plants in the lower lakes were still discharging effluents with phosphorus concentrations exceeding the 1 mg/litre limit. These . . . control programs have improved water quality. Nutrient goals for Lake Superior have been met; Lakes Erie and Ontario continue to show declines in phosphorus concentrations; Saginaw Bay on Lake Huron . . . is also improving. The Commission reminds the Parties, however, of their commitment in the 1978 Agreement to achieve the effluent discharge requirement of 1 mg/litre at all major municipal waste treatment facilities and where necessary to reduce the effluent discharge to 0.5 mg/litre in order to meet target goals" (ibid., at 3).

43. "The Commission again recommends a comprehensive strategy be developed for dealing with non-point pollution, including phosphorus . . . While there have been some successful demonstration programs . . . a widespread, coordinated, and systematic approach has not been implemented" (ibid., at 4). The commission then reminds the governments that in signing Annex 3 of the agreement they confirmed their commitment to specific phosphorus reductions, and concludes by noting: "The Commission reiterates its support for the kind of broadly-based efforts such as those outlined by the Commission's Task Forces on Non-Point Source Control (1983) and Phosphorus Management Strategies (1980) as well as the Commission's 1981 Supplemental Report on Phosphorus Management Strategies" (ibid.).

44. Ibid., at 4. The commission also called for more research in the area of toxics, specifically for new and broader technologies to treat toxic chemicals, for pretreatment technologies for certain industrial wastes, and for the disposal on land or through incinerator of toxic materials.

45. Ibid., at 5.

46. See International Joint Commission, *Report of Workshop on a Transboundary Monitoring and Surveillance Network* (Oct. 1984) (Philadelphia Academy of Natural Sciences).

47. *Second Biennial Report,* supra note 36, at 7.

48. Ibid.

49. Ibid.

50. Ibid., at 8. In connection with this concept, reference should be made to Agreement Article IV, which states that the "flow augmentation is not a substitute for adequate treatment." Where limited-use zones are intended to provide an area of a lake for dilution purposes, such action would appear inconsistent with Article IV as well as with U.S. domestic law.

51. *Second Biennial Report,* supra note 36, at 9.

52. Ibid., at 11–12. A series of Canada–United States university seminars addressed, from 1971 to 1977, the problem of improving the management of the international Great Lakes. The second seminar recommended that the two governments formulate a science policy for the Great Lakes as an indication of their commitment to restore, rehabilitate, and improve the management of the lakes and to support the development of new knowledge needed by decisionmakers. Subsequently, the two cochairmen of the seminars, Professor George Francis of the University of Waterloo in Ontario, and Professor Leonard Dworsky of Cornell University in Ithaca, New York, were appointed members of the Societal Aspects Expert Committee (SAEC) of the IJC's Research (later Science) Advisory Board. The draft minutes of the twenty-sixth Research Advisory Board meeting, May 23, 1978, note that Dworsky as chairman of the SAEC proposed an SAEC agenda of six items, one of which was "A Science Policy for the Great Lakes." The draft minutes of the twenty-seventh meeting note that Professor Francis led further discussion to clarify the idea. Although the idea was accepted as a vital question that should be given further attention, implementation of further action was not accomplished because of lack of resources.

53. *Second Biennial Report,* supra note 36, at 13.

54. International Joint Commission, *First Biennial Report Under the Great Lakes Water Quality Agreement of 1978 to the Governments of the United States and Canada and the States and Provinces of the Great Lakes Basin* (June 24, 1982) [hereinafter cited as *First Biennial Report*].

55. *Second Biennial Report,* supra note 36, at 15.

56. The commission writes the following:
Specifically it is the prerogative and responsibility of governments to undertake, among other things, the following:
(a) adoption of new water quality objectives;
(b) provision of reliable information for adequate program assessment;
(c) development of demonstrative programs for non-point source reduction of phosphorus and other pollutants;
(d) consideration of a comprehensive toxic substance strategy; and
(e) implementation of clean-up programs in areas of concern.
(Ibid., at 15)
This summary of the main areas considered by the IJC in its second biennial report provides some idea of the tasks involved in carrying out the Great Lakes Water Quality Agreements of 1972 and 1978.

57. International Joint Commission, *Further Regulation of the Great Lakes* (1976). See also EIC&ASCE, *Proceedings,* supra note 4; International Joint Commission, *Great Lakes Diversions and Consumptive Uses* (Sept. 1981); International Joint Commission, *Lake Erie Water Level Study* (July 1981); Great Lakes Basin Commission, *Great Lakes Basin Framework Study,* Appendix 11 (1975); *Great Lakes Water Level Problems, Hearings before the Senate Comm. on Foreign Relations,* 94th Cong., 2d Sess., 33–34 (1976); *The Great Lakes: Hearings before the Subcomm. on InterAmerican Affairs of the House Comm. on Foreign Affairs,* 93rd Cong., 1st Sess., 634–713 (1973) [hereinafter cited as *The Great Lakes Hearings*]; and Dworsky, *Setting Great Lakes Water Levels: Institutional Aspects of the IJC* (1974) (Great Lakes Mgmt. Ser. Working Doc. No. 3).

58. In 1964, the two governments requested the IJC to determine whether further regulation of Great Lakes levels would be in the public interest. Existing regulation was provided at the St. Mary's River for Lake Superior and at the St. Lawrence power facilities for Lake Ontario; the other lakes were unregulated directly, but may be affected by Lake Superior controls. When, nine years later, these studies had not been concluded by the agencies responsible for reporting to the IJC, the U.S. Congress authorized a study to see what effect diversions up to 10,000 cfs at Chicago would have on lake levels. See *The Great Lakes Hearings,* supra note 57. In addition, a study of the general problem of diversions and consumptive uses of Great Lakes water was authorized in February 1977. See International Joint Commission, *Great Lakes Diversions and Consumptive Uses,* (1981), a report to the governments of Canada and the United States made under the Reference of February 21, 1977.

59. Four of these problems involved the management of available economic aid and environmental data to facilitate planning; three were environmental in nature and concerned dredging, transportation-related environmental problems, and recreation; five concerned either technical or economic equations including length of navigation season, intermodality and intersystem considerations, locks and channels, port planning, and the relation of the Great Lakes system to the nation's water needs; and the other four involved energy transport and consumption, future outlook, Corps of Engineers studies in relation to IJC activities, and a general catchall of other factors.

60. Regier, "The Rehabilitation of Great Lakes Fishes and Fisheries," *J. Great Lakes Research* (forthcoming 1987).

61. Great Lakes Fisheries Commission, Report of Meeting (October 20, 1977) (Ann Arbor, MI).

62. *The Effects of Environmental Issues and Programs on Great Lakes Fisheries: Directions for the Future* (Ann Arbor, Michigan, January 10–11, 1980).

63. See J. Legault & T. Kuchenberg, supra note 6.

64. U.S. Dept. of Energy, study on Great Lakes Basin States electric

power capacity (1980). See also Royal Commission on Electric Power Planning, (Ontario) *Report on Electric Power Planning* vol. 4 (1980).

65. International Joint Commission Science Advisory Board, *Anticipatory Planning for the Great Lakes* vol. 2, 59–113 (Feb. 1980). The eight "factors" were the long lead time to bring new energy facilities into service in sufficient quantities to have Great Lakes Basinwide effects; an adequate total energy and electrical energy supply in the near term, based on lower expected growth rates in energy demand; a shortage of oil and natural gas predicted for the Great Lakes Basin beginning in the late 1980s–1990s; the Great Lakes region's extreme dependence on imported energy, with about 80 percent of its gas and oil coming from outside the basin; a growing U.S. interest in the natural gas potential in Lake Erie; the apparent need for increased reliance on coal and uranium in order to meet the Great Lakes' future energy requirements; more work on the extent of environmental difficulties associated with coal; and accelerated exploration of alternative energy supply technologies.

66. International Joint Commission Science Advisory Board, Environmental Implications of Alternative Energy Futures for the Great Lakes Basin (March 1982).

67. Ibid.

68. International Joint Commission, *Anticipatory Planning for the Great Lakes* vol. 2 (Feb. 1980) [hereinafter cited as *Anticipatory Planning*].

69. Ibid., at 130.

70. Ibid., at 132.

71. Congressional Reference Service, U.S. Library of Congress, *Background Material on Acid Rain* (1984) (Washington, D.C.).

72. "Reagan, in Quebec, Agrees to a Study of Acid Rain Issue," *N.Y. Times,* March 18, 1985, § A, at 1, col. 6.

73. "Joint U.S.–Canada Report on Acid Rain is Delivered," *N.Y. Times,* January 9, 1986, § B, at 6, col. 1.

74. See International Joint Commission, *Pollution in the Great Lakes Basin from Land Use Activities* (March 1980); Great Lakes Basin Commission, *Great Lakes Basin Region Summary Report for the National Assessment of Water and Related Land Resources* (April 1977) (prepared for the U.S. Water Resources Council); International Joint Commission, *Further Regulation of the Great Lakes,* supra note 57, at chs. 1,2,4; Ontario Dept. of Treasury & Econ. & Ontario Dept. of Municipal Affairs, *A Strategy for Southwestern Ontario Development* (March 1970); Province of Ontario, *Design for Development Reports* (1970–1977); *A Reader on Management Improvement Strategies: The Great Lakes of the United States and Canada* (L. B. Dworsky & C. F. Swezey, eds. 1974).

75. *Second Biennial Report,* supra note 36.

76. Zile, *Binational Land Resource Management for the Great Lakes Area: Powers of the International Joint Commission* (Study Doc. No. 1, Canada-U.S. University Seminar, Great Lakes 1974).

77. Ibid., at 61-62.

78. The boards are the International Lake Superior Board of Control, the International Niagara Board of Control, the International St. Lawrence River Board of Control, the International Great Lakes Levels Board, the American Falls International Board, the International Niagara Committee, the Coordinating Committee on Great Lakes Basin Hydraulic and Hydrolic Data, and the Winter Navigation Board. Great Lakes Basin Commission, *Great Lakes Basin Framework Study* 173-179 app. II (1976). See also International Great Lakes Commission, *Executive Summary* (1981), supra notes 57, 58.

79 International Joint Commission, *Further Regulation of the Great Lakes* 90 (1950).

80. Convention on Great Lakes Fisheries, September 10, 1954, United States-Canada, 6 U.S.T. 2836, T.I.A.S. No. 3326 (entered into force October 11, 1955).

81. The first (1954) resulted from studies under 1946-1948 IJC Docket Nos. 54 & 55 of the Connecting Channels of Lakes Superior, Huron, and Erie, and of Lakes Erie and Ontario. The second (1972) resulted from 1964 IJC Docket No. 83 and is the Great Lakes Water Quality Agreement of 1972, later extended with amendments to 1978. Within this agreement fall the Water Quality Board and the Science Advisory Board.

82. MacLaren & Clevinger, "New Requirements in Water Resources Planning on the Great Lakes," in *Proceedings of Great Lakes Water Resources Conference* 361-389 (1968) (conference held June 24-26, 1968, at Toronto, Canada, Paper No. 7).

83. Ibid. The seven water use categories discussed are domestic water supply, wastewater disposal, navigation, power development, agricultural irrigation, fisheries, and recreation. The paper notes that unless a comprehensive plan for the staged development of Great Lakes water and related land uses is effectuated, all problems will become increasingly complex and difficult and it presents an outline of an early work plan.

84. Wengert, "A Critical Review of the River Basin as a Focus for Resource Planning, Development, and Management," in *Unified River Basin Management Symposuim Proceedings* 9-28 (1980).

85. Ibid., at 10-11.

86. Ibid. See also Dworsky & Allee, "Unified/Integrated River Basin Management: Evolution of Organizational Arrangements," in *Unified River Basin Management Symposium Proceedings* 28-45 (1980).

87. The Federal Power Commission, along with the Departments of the Army, Agriculture, and Interior, jointly formed the Federal Interagency

River Basin Committee in 1943. The Federal Interagency River Basin Committee and the subsequent field committees in various basins of the United States are described in Schad, "Water Resources Planning—Historical Development," 105 *J. Water Res. Plan. & Mgmt. Div. Am. Soc. Civ. Eng.* 9 (1979).

88. This practical approach was used by the U.S. federal government and the states in the interstate basins of the United States from 1943 until 1965, when the Water Resources Planning Act of 1965 was enacted. See case studies of the Missouri and Columbia Basin Interagency Committees in Dworsky, *A Study of Potential Institutional Arrangements for Water Quality and Water Resources Planning and Management* 79–148 (Mar. 1974) (Cornell Univ. Water Resources & Marine Sciences Center, Tech. Rep. No. 83); see also Schuefle, *History of the Columbia Basin Interagency Committee* (1967) (report prepared for U.S. Army Corps of Engineers North Pacific Division, Portland, Oregon).

89. Staff of Senate Select Comm. on National Water Resources, *Report on U.S. Water Resources* 86th Cong., 2d Sess. (1960).

90. Water Resources Planning Act of 1965, 79 Stat. 244–254 (1965).

91. Munton, "Paradoxes and Prospects," in *The International Joint Commission Seventy Years on* 60 (R. Spencer, J. Kirton, & K. R. Nossal, eds. 1981).

92. Merchant & Heeney, "Canada and the United States—Principles for Partnership," *Dept. State Bull.* 193–207. (Aug. 2, 1965).

93. Ibid., at 199.

94. 111 Cong. Rec. 25,394 (1965).

95. Ibid.

96. Jordan, "Recent Developments in International Environmental Pollution Control," 15 *McGill L. Rev.* 277 (1969).

97. Ostrom, Ostrom, & Whitman, "Problems for Institutional Analysis of the Great Lakes Basin, in *13th Conference on Great Lakes Research Proceedings* 156–67 (1970).

98. Craine, *Final Report on Institutional Arrangements for the Great Lakes* (1972) (unpublished report prepared for the Great Lakes Basin Commission).

99. Ibid., at 2–3.

100. Bilder, "Controlling Great Lakes Pollution: A Study in United States-Canadian Environmental Cooperation," 70 *Mich. L. Rev.* 469 (1972).

101. Ibid., at 478.

102. Ibid., at 521.

103. Ibid., at 537.

104. Ibid., at 547-48.

105. Faculty members from some twenty universities and colleges in both countries, with Professors George Francis and Leonard Dworsky acting as cochairmen, joined in dialogue and published a report entitled *A Proposal for Improving the Management of the Great Lakes of the United States and Canada,* which was reported in *The Great Lakes Hearings,* supra note 57. The seminar continued with changing participation until January 1984 and was the stimulus for the publication of this reader.

106. Standing Senate Comm. on Foreign Affairs, Canada-United States Relations, *The Institutional Framework for the Relationship* (1975).

107. Ibid. As an example, the committee is of the opinion that the current Garrison Diversion problem might have been headed off had the IJC had this watchdog capacity. The committee hoped that an extension of authority could be granted without opening up the treaty, because the two governments had already given the IJC a similar watching brief in regard to air pollution, and presumably the same technique could not be used to provide an extension into other pollution problems. If not, perhaps a standing reference could be given.

108. Dworsky, "The International Joint Commission—A Critique," in *Proceedings of the Canada-United States Natural Resources and Environmental Symposium* (J. Carroll & D. Carroll, eds. 1978) (the Report of the Canada-United States University Seminar, Second Session).

109. *Anticipatory Planning,* supra note 68.

110. Munton, supra note 91.

111. Ibid., at 70.

112. Dworsky, *Report on Office of Water Research & Technology Proect No. C-5305,* Funding Agreement No. 14-31-0001-4238 (1974).

113. *The Great Lakes Hearings,* supra note 57.

114. International Joint Commission, *Self Review* (1974) (unpublished mimeo prepared at two-day conference held at Montreal, Quebec).

115. Standing Senate Comm. on Foreign Affairs, supra note 106.

116. Great Lakes Water Quality Agreement of 1978, supra note 32.

117. *Anticipatory Planning,* supra note, 68.

118. International Joint Commission, *Institutional Roles & Opportunities* (June 1982) (annual report, under Great Lakes Water Quality Agreement of 1978, supra note 32).

119. Jack Vallentyne, *The Ecosystem Approach* (1978) (report prepared for Great Lakes Advisory board, IJC). Vallentyne states explicitly that integration is the essential feature of the ecosystem approach. Although his

comment was addressed to management, it applies equally to integration among the tasks to be managed.

120. International Lake Erie Regulation Study Board, International Joint Commission, *Lake Erie Water Level Study: Main Report* (July 1981).

121. International Joint Commission, *Great Lakes Diversions and Consumptive Uses: Executive Summary* (1981); International Joint Commission, *Great Lakes Diversions and Consumptive Uses: Final Report (1985).*

122. International Great Lakes Technical Information Network Board, *Great Lakes Hydrometeorologic and Hydraulic Data Needs* (1984) (report to the IJC).

123. Sporhase v. Nebraska, 458 U.S. 941 (1982), Colorado v. New Mexico, 459 U.S. 176, 183 (1982).

124. *Anticipatory Planning,* supra note 68.

125. Great Lakes Basin Commission, supra note 57.

126. Exec. Order No. 12319, 3 C.F.R. 175-76 (1981).

127. On February 11, 1985, in Milwaukee, Wisconsin, the governors of Michigan, New York, Ohio, Illinois, Wisconsin, and Minnesota signed the antidiversion Great Lakes Charter at a ceremony attended also by representatives of the governors of Indiana and Pennsylvania and of the premiers of Ontario and Quebec who were to sign the charter at a later date.

128. Hon. James J. Blanchard, Governor of Michigan, Statement on the Signing of the Great Lakes Charter 3 (Feb. 11, 1985).

129. Great Lakes Charter, supra note 127, at 1, Findings.

130. Ibid., at 42.

131. Great Lakes Basin Commission, *Great Lakes Basin Framework Study: Final Environmental Impact Statement* 22, 25-28 (1976) (Leonard Crook, Staff Director).

132. Ibid., at 106.

133. Francis, "Institutional Arrangements and Capabilities," in *Anticipatory Planning,* supra note 68, at 37, 39, 40.

134. Ibid., at 39.

135. International Joint Commission, supra note 2.

136. Ibid., at 44.

137. I.e., Bilder supra note 100; Craine, supra note 98.

138. Dworsky, *The Great Lakes of the United States and Canada: An Ecosystem Perspective* (Dec. 1985) (report prepared by a Cornell Univ. seminar, Leonard B. Dworsky, leader).

139. Munton, supra note 91.

CHAPTER 3. INSTITUTIONAL ARRANGEMENTS FOR GREAT LAKES MANAGEMENT

In considering the adequacy of present institutional arrangements for Great Lakes management and the possible need for new institutions, it is sensible to examine what presently exists and how it functions or fails to advance water quality agreement objectives. This chapter is an audit of the existing institutional framework for Great Lakes management. It analyzes the factors that explain the apparent inability of the several binational institutions for Great Lakes governance to implement an effective basinwide ecosystem approach to protection of the lakes. If future governance for the lakes is to build on past experience, it is necessary to know what has worked well and what has proved ineffective. This chapter provides a critique of what we presently have to work with in institutional arrangements for Great Lakes management.

MICHAEL J. DONAHUE

3

INSTITUTIONAL ARRANGEMENTS FOR GREAT LAKES MANAGEMENT

Recent years have witnessed a revitalization of a regional consciousness among the public officials and citizenry of Great Lakes political jurisdictions. Born of multijurisdictional environmental crises and the desire to tap the economic potential of the expansive resource, an ecosystem philosophy had gained credence, and with it the initial indications of an emerging regional identity for the Great Lakes. Accompanying this revitalization is a renewed interest in the institutional arrangements that have evolved to translate this regional consciousness and ecosystem philosophy into implementable programs for management of the water and related land resources of the Great Lakes Basin.

This renewed interest has been fueled, in part, by the collective thoughts of participants in the interuniversity seminar on the Great Lakes. A 1984 conference theme, "sustainable redevelopment for the future in the Great Lakes region," afforded a welcome opportunity to explore the means by which these positive trends can contribute to the enhanced managemnet of this international resource.[1] This, and subsequent initiatives of a similar nature provide a refreshing and challenging opportunity to set aside, at least for the moment, our current preoccupation with what is, and to focus instead on what could be. The generation and subsequent application of principles for sustainable redevelopment is indeed a most timely, and perhaps long overdue exercise. It is also a logical precursor to subsequent efforts to generate recommendations for future redevelopment. As Lyle Craine has observed, too often we concern ourselves with how to manage the Great Lakes resource without first determining why it should be managed at all.[2] Initiatives such as the interuniversity seminar on the Great Lakes, through goal-setting exercises, assist in discouraging any tendency toward logic that puts the cart before the horse.

Recommendations developed by the interuniversity seminar and related initiatives contribute substantively to the future direction of Great Lakes management. It is essential, however, that the formulation of alternative futures includes a blueprint for achieving them. The blueprint must reflect an understanding of the existing Great Lakes management framework and its potential value as a foundation for change rather than an obstacle to such change. The *Great Lakes Basin Framework Study* (1975) correctly observes that "the current array of government units must not be viewed as immutable constraints on the formulation of alternative courses of action."[3]

The intent of this paper is to address, at least modestly, the following four objectives:

1. To demonstrate the importance of institutional analysis as a means of enhancing Great Lakes management efforts

2. To provide an overview of the present institutional framework for Great Lakes management

3. To present selected research findings relating to desired characteristics for the institutional framework

4. To suggest guidelines for institutional analysis

These objectives have been carefully selected to provide a starting point for futher analysis; it is not the intent, at this time, to present a polished set of findings. The latter is the collective responsibility of participants of the interuniversity seminar on the Great Lakes and others dedicated to the wise use and protection of the Great Lakes resource.

The preponderance of this material is derived from Sea Grant–sponsored research at the University of Michigan. The research is designed to assist decisionmakers in ongoing efforts to enhance the efficiency and effectiveness of Great Lakes management through the development of research-based alternatives for the revision of existing Great Lakes institutional arrangements and the design of new ones.[4] By its very nature this research effort raises many more questions that answers. In fact, it is hoped that the reader will find in these remarks a point or two to challenge and debate. This questioning will ensure that the investigation has touched upon many of the sensitive and unsettled elements associated with the Great Lakes management effort.

THE ROLE OF THE INSTITUTION IN THE GREAT LAKES MANAGEMENT PROCESS

An inextricable link exists between the prescribed mission of a given organization and the institutional arrangements and processes created to fulfill that mission. The institutional arrangement as a determinant of goal attainment is capably articulated by the National Academy of Sciences' Commission on Natural Resources:[5]

> The characteristics of anticipated problems are shaped by existing institutions, and any attempt to improve matters that ignores this fact will probably come to very little. No amount of monitoring, or science advising, or project modelling is going to improve our record if the relevant problem recognition system, the approaches to mitigate the problems, and the incentive systems to provide alternatives remain unchanged.

Although these remarks were addressed primarily to research and development initiatives at the federal level, their consideration is equally appropriate in a broader policy context. If policy is to be viewed as an output of organizations, the institutional arrangements that shape, interpret, and administer policy become a critical determinant of the policy's impact upon society.[6] The institution—at any level of government—is not merely a vehicle for operationalizing policies formulated by legislatures of officials of a given administration. The institution itself provides an environment in which policies can be devised, altered, interpreted, advocated, ignored, or otherwise transformed. The institution can determine not only the success or failure of a given policy, but the very essence of that policy.

The argument that institutional arrangements are a dominant factor in the policy process is convincingly substantiated in the arena of resource management in the international Great Lakes Basin. Ostrom et al. observe that existing institutional arrangements are instrumental in determining the political feasibility of Great Lakes management efforts.[7] For this reason, they argue, a thorough understanding of those institutional arrangements, as well as the political influences associated with them, is a requisite, and perhaps dominant, component of any analysis of Great Lakes water resource problems. Similarly, Hennigan has pointed out that an understanding and subsequent reform of the Great Lakes institutional ecosystem is the critical factor in establishing a "workable system incorporating the action elements of persuasion and education, legal action and economic incentives which can make effective water management attainable."[8] Following an exhaustive analysis of resource-based problems and opportunities in the basin, the *Great Lakes Basin Framework Study* concluded, "In sum, the critical deficiency in the Great Lakes Basin is that institutional arrangements for arriving at a political consensus do not exist."[9] Clearly, any effort to affect policy change in the absence of institutional analysis will come to very little.

The requisite, yet elusive, harmony between institutional form and management function has been the focus of unrelenting debate within the Great Lakes Basin throughout this century.[10] Historically, five principal causal factors might be identified:

1. *The diversity of regional resource management goals among political jurisdictions.* Regional management institutions in the Great Lakes Basin have historically been membership organizations vested with limited autonomy and a mandate to represent the collective will of the membership. The inevitable diversity of resource management goals and strategies advocated by the individual jurisdictions within that membership ensures that institutional adequacy will be questioned by some membership sector at any given time. Such is the outcome of what Fesler has termed a "competitive, special interest milieu."[11]

2. *The experimental nature of regional resource management.* Regional management institutions, in the Great Lakes Basin and elsewhere, fall victim to the perpetually experimental and chronically undefined role of regional government in the federal system. Martin describes regional organizations as "excrescences on the constitutional system."[12] Derthick suggests that they share a common handicap "in being unusual cases, deviant new growth in a government landscape."[13] Some years ago, the federal Bureau of the Budget, ever cognizant of new institutional forms that might make claims on the federal treasury, once described one regional resource management institution—the Delaware River Basin Commission—as a "constitutional anomaly to be treated with caution."[14] Although the existence of regional resource

management institutions has come to be accepted, and in many cases welcomed, the question of "what we do with them" remains a relevant one.

3. *The complexity of the Great Lakes management framework.* The perceived complexity of what one might call the Great Lakes "institutional ecosystem" has contributed to this century-old debate on institutional adequacy as well. In its final report on U.S. National Water Policy, the National Water Commission observed that the "plethora" or organizations in the Great Lakes region impeded decisionmaking.[15] Bilder has derided the "complex hodgepodge of proliferating and occasionally inconsistent laws, regulations and ordinances" issued by an equally complex series of governmental authorities.[16] As a major obstacle to coordinated and effective management, such jurisdictional complexity has been accused of fostering uncoordinated and overlapping missions;[17] a lack of responsiveness to perceived management needs;[18] and general public confusion.[19] Senator Gaylord Nelson once characterized the Great Lakes institutional system as a "bureaucratic mess."[20] More recently Senator Kasten referred to the "bureaucratic maze" in Great Lakes management.[21] Although one might argue that the latter observations are somewhat overstated, they are indicative of attitudes that have generated debate over the adequacy of institutional arrangements for Great Lakes management.

4. *The tendency toward institutional inertia.* Schon's principle of "dynamic conservatism" is reflected in the Great Lakes management framework.[22] This framework is characterized, in Hennigan's words, by "unresponsive institutions created to grapple with the problems of much simpler times."[23] Increasingly, the Great Lakes states and provinces are being confronted by economic and environmental problems and challenges of a regional nature. The ever-widening gap between scientific and technological capability and the institutional forms to fully employ that capability has been a long-standing focus for debate.

5. *The continuing maturation of the "ecosystem management" concept.* Resource managers and policymakers have become increasingly aware of the interrelatedness of the basin's resources and the concomitant need for an integrated, systems-oriented management approach.[24] This awareness has

prompted a rethinking of traditional approaches that rely upon issue-specific authority and political jurisdiction. The ability and willingness of existing regional institutions to embrace the ecosystem management philosophy has been questioned.

Collectively, all these factors have fueled the ongoing debate over the adequacy of institutional arrangements for Great Lakes management. One need only review the historic status of regionalism in the federal system to realize that this debate is unlikely to be silenced by even the most innovative and successful institutional form.

THE PERCEPTION OF A NEED FOR REGIONALISM

An examination of regional approaches to resource management in North America is an exercise in contradiction.[25] These entities generally tend to be ill-defined, experimental, and of limited authority and resources, unknown effectiveness, reluctant acceptance, and perpetual involvement in redefinition of goals and problems. They tend to be something of a "Band-Aid" solution to the failings of traditional resource management approaches on a political jurisdictional basis. Generally speaking, when present, they draw more criticism than accolades. When absent, however, their resurrection or successor is earnestly sought. Their presence, in some form, has become a necessity. The challenge is to advance beyond their use as a Band-Aid solution, and to develop their full potential as a vehicle for ecosystem-based resource management.

Despite their failings and frustrations in practice, the argument for regional management institutions is a strong one. These entitites serve to transcend the parochialism of more established levels of government, and hence respond to solvable regional problems and needs. "At its most daring," explains Munro, "the case for regional organization argues that the state governments are artificial creations, obsolete and too numerous, which should be replaced by larger governments rationally adapted to the natural or sociocultural features of American society."[26] A more modest perspective views these institutions as coordinative, service-oriented bodies designed to assist political jurisdictions in joint problem solving. Clearly, beyond their intergovernmental and resource-based characteristics, these institutions vary significantly in purpose, structure, and function.

The seeds of regionalism have long been sown in the Great Lakes Basin. The Rush-Bagot convention of 1817—limiting naval armaments on the Great Lakes—was perhaps the first recognition of the Great Lakes system as a regional (international) resource demanding multijurisdictional management. A series of U.S.–Canadian agreements addressing mutual navigation rights followed, as did the establishment of various binational waterways commissions in the 1880s and 1890s leading up to the international Boundary Waters Treaty of 1909.[27]

The concept of resource management on a regional basis gained credence on both sides of the border in the early decades of the century.[28] On the U.S. side, President Roosevelt submitted, in 1937, a proposal for regional planning bodies covering the entire country. Subsequent decades saw the formation of predecessor agencies to the now defunct Water Resources Council; the formation of the Tennessee Valley Authority; Basin-Interagency Committees; various interstate compact commissions; Title V regional development commissions; Title II River Basin Commissions; Federal Regulatory Councils; and other regional entities.

Despite the progression of regional resource management approaches in North America over the last century, there is widespread agreement in the literature with the following statement by Derthick: "None of the different approaches . . . embodied in regional organizations is sufficiently superior to the rest to make it preferable, nor is any approach so clearly successful as to contribute substantially to justification of the regional form."[29] This statement capsulizes both the frustration and the challenge associated with institutional design for Great Lakes management. Despite the historical absence of a systematic analysis of the Great Lakes institutional system and its components, there appears to be a compelling, yet inadequately articulated, sense of dissatisfaction with present arrangements.[30] In the absence of criteria for evaluation, "success" is a matter of personal perception. Furthermore, there appears to exist an unalterable faith that a "preferred approach," albeit yet undiscovered or even understood, holds the promise of resolving the myriad issues present today. Discovering this approach, or simply realizing that we must settle for something less, is the challenge before us.

THE EXISTING INSTITUTIONAL FRAMEWORK FOR GREAT LAKES MANAGEMENT

The magnitude and complexity of the physical and socioeconomic attributes of the basin are exhibited in terms of governance as well.[31] The Great Lakes system is a shared, multipurpose resource intensively used and managed at every level from the local to international arena. Eight states and two Canadian provinces share the basin. Well over a dozen federal agencies—on both sides of the border—have a mandated interest in some aspect of the resource. Literally hundreds of governmental entities are charged with some resource management responsibility, including municipalities, county health boards, state departments of natural resources, a variety of regional bodies, and several international bodies. Most are limited in management authority to a defined political jurisdiction or a specific management function, such as water supply, flood control, or water quality, to name a few. A constellation of research institutions, citizen groups, policy centers, foundations, and special interest coalitions have flourished as well, using the various access points to the institutional framework to influence the direction of Great Lakes management.

Full documentation of the management functions of these various entities is clearly beyond the scope of this paper. For example, Haynes and Madau identified 91 Canadian governmental units (exluding municipalities) involved in Great Lakes management.[32] Bulkley and Mathews identified 650 governmental units—from the municipal to the international level—with some Great Lakes management responsibility.[33] Indeed, the resource management structure in the region is a complex one. Yet, one need only be reminded of the immensity, diversity, and geographic expansiveness of the resource to realize that such a management structure is not only inevitable, but in some ways desirable.

This overview of Great Lakes institutional arrangements will focus on a small yet significant subset of the overall management structure—regional management institutions. Specifically, reference is made to those institutions that are public, resource-based entities, that possess a basinwide orientation, that are multijurisdictional in nature, and that at least attempt to examine issues from what has come to be known as an "ecosystem perspective." The term *management* is employed rather loosely to describe an institution with one or more of the following charges: planning, research, coordination, regulation, enforcement, monitoring and surveillance, policy making, advocacy, and the like. The existing Great Lakes institutions within this classification include the International Joint Commission, the Great Lakes Commission, the Great Lakes Fishery Commission, and the Council of Great Lakes Governors. The balance of the discussion will focus primarily upon them, keeping in mind their links with, and function within, the overall management framework.

This discussion serves as a starting point for attaining our ultimate goal: the design of institutional forms capable of managing the resource to ensure sustainable development in a manner responsive to the collective needs of society.

In focusing upon the means by which existing or future institutions can realize this goal, the following thesis is presented as a guide for analysis:

> The evolution of effective institutional arrangements for Great Lakes management has been hampered by an inadequate review of past institutions as well as "parallel" institutions responsible for water resource management in other geographic areas. As a consequence, we find a resultant failure to incorporate their positive attributes into the establishment of new management institutions or the revision of existing ones. A systematic review of selected past and present institutional arrangements will facilitate the identification and analysis of proven management strategies and organizational characteristics. These can be integrated into new or existing institutional arrangements to enhance Great Lakes management capabilities.[34]

With this thesis in mind, a very brief overview of the aforementioned institutions will follow, as well as a comparative analysis of their functions, and, finally, selected ideas that might be considered as guidelines for further institutional analysis.

International Joint Commission

The International Joint Commission (IJC) is a permanent bilateral body created under the auspices of the Boundary Waters Treaty of 1909 to prevent disputes relating to boundary water usage and to settle questions arising along the common frontier.[35] The commission has provided the framework for cooperation on questions relating to water and air pollution and the regulation of water levels and flows.

Three principal functions are undertaken by the commission:

1. *Quasi-judicial.* The commission approves or disapproves applications from governments, companies, or individuals for obstructions, uses, or diversions of water that affect the natural level or flow of water on the other side of the international boundary.

2. *Investigative.* The commission investigates questions on matters of difference along the common frontier, under-

taking references that are presented to the commission by the two governments. In such cases, the commission reports to the governments the facts and circumstances of the issue, as well as recommendations for action. These recommendations are not binding; the governments decide whether or not the commission's recommendations will be acted upon.

3. *Surveillance/Coordination.* The commission monitors and coordinates the implementation of recommendations accepted by the governments. It also monitors compliance with orders of approval for structures in boundary waters.

The IJC has specific Great Lakes responsibilities under the Great Lakes Water Quality Agreement of 1972 (amended in 1978).[36] The 1978 agreement directs the two parties to the commission to "restore and maintain the chemical, physical, and biological integrity of the waters of the Great Lakes Basin Ecosystem" This effort is undertaken through efforts to "make a maximum effort to develop programs, practices and technology necessary for a better understanding of the Great Lakes Basin Ecosystem and to eliminate or reduce to the maximum extent practicable the discharge of pollutants into the Great Lakes System."

The technical studies and fieldwork required to carry out the commission's functions are performed by twenty-eight binational advisory boards, the members of which are appointed by the commission and are generally drawn from government agencies. The U.S. commissioners are appointed by the president of the United States with the advice and consent of the U.S. Senate. The Canadian members are appointed by the governor in council in Canada. The commission includes U.S. and Canadian cochairmen who serve in their positions on a full-time basis. The commission maintains professional staffs in Washington, D.C., Ottawa, Ontario, and Windsor, Ontario. The latter was established in 1973 to assist in fulfilling the provsions of the Great Lakes Water Quality Agreement.

Great Lakes Commission

The Great Lakes Commission (GLC) is an interstate compact commission composed of gubernatorially appointed and legislatively mandated representatives of the eight Great Lakes states. Established by joint action of the Great Lakes governors in 1955 and granted congressional consent in 1968, the GLC seeks "to promote the orderly, integrated, and comprehensive development, use, and conservation of the water resources of the Great Lakes Basin" (Article I, Great Lakes Basin Compact).[37] The objectives associated with these overall goals, as stated in the compact, include the following:

> 1. To plan for the welfare and development of the water resources of the Basin as a whole as well as for those portions of the Basin which may have problems of special concern.
>
> 2. To make it possible for the states of the Basin and their people to derive the maximum benefit from utilization of public works, in the form of navigational aids or otherwise, which may exist or which may be constructed from time to time.
>
> 3. To advise in securing and maintaining a proper balance among industrial, commercial, agricultural, water supply, residential, recreational, and other legitimate uses of the water resources of the Basin.
>
> 4. To establish and maintain an intergovernmental agency to the end that the purposes of this compact may be accomplished more effectively.

The commission pursues this broad mandate through three principal functions: (1) informative sharing among the Great Lakes states; (2) coordination of state positions on issues of regional concern; and (3) advocacy of those positions on which the states agree. Advocacy activities take various forms, including the passage and dissemination of resolutions, the presentation of testimony to Congress, frequent contact with the Great Lakes congressional delegation, and contact with federal officials.

The commission addresses a range of issues involving environmental protection, resource management, transportation, and economic development. A task force structure, in which commissioners and advisors from all states participate, is the vehicle for identifying and developing issues, and subsequently recommending the adoption of positions by the full membership. Federal and provinical observers participate, but do not vote, in all Commission activities.

The GLC is the only Great Lakes organization with a statutory mandate to represent the collective views of the Great Lakes states. As such, it provides a variety of services and works with a range of public and private sector organizations in the interest of best serving the needs of its member states. The staff is based in Ann Arbor, Michigan.

Great Lakes Fishery Commission

The Great Lakes Fishery Commission (GLFC) was established pursuant to the binational Convention on Great Lakes Fisheries, ratified in October 1955.[38] The convention stipulates five areas of responsibility:

1. The formulation of programs to determine the means by which fish stocks of common concern to the United States and Canada can be managed for maximum sustained productivity.

2. The coordination or undertaking of this research to support those programs.

3. The development of recommendations to the two parties on the basis of research findings.

4. The eradication or reduction of sea lamprey populations in the Great Lakes.

5. The publication of scientific reports and other information prepared in the performance of duties.

The convention specifies that the commission should work through official agencies of the contracting parties (and the Great Lakes states and the Province of Ontario) in the performance of its duties. The commission contracts with Fisheries and Oceans Canada for sea lamprey control and research, and maintains a contractual arrangement with the U.S. Fish and Wildlife Service as well. The balance of its program is pursued through a committee structure that involves the academic community and representatives of the agencies with fishery management and other natural resources mandates. The three principal committees include the Sea Lamprey Committee, the Board of Technical Experts, and the Fish Habitat Advisory Board. A number of technical committees have also been appointed to address issue- and lake-specific concerns within the mandate of the commission.

A major initiative for the commission in recent years has been the development and implementation of a joint strategic plan for management of the Great Lakes fisheries.[39] Under the plan, the commision works along with its committees, principal cooperators, and other Great Lakes agencies.

The commission is composed of Canadian and United States sections, each served by four commissioners appointed by their respective governments. A secretariat, appointed by the commission, assists the commission in carrying out its duties. The staff is based in Ann Arbor, Michigan.

Council of Great Lakes Governors

The Council of Great Lakes Governors is an organization composed of the governors of the six westernmost Great Lakes states. Formed in 1982, it provides a forum for identifying, discussing, researching, and formulating policy on various regional economic and environmental issues of common interest. As stated in its Articles of Incorporation, the council is mandated

1. To develop, plan, execute and coordinate programs and projects which will stimulate economic, community and environmental development within the states of Minnesota, Wisconsin, Michigan, Illinois, Indiana and Ohio;

2. To facilitate coordination of multi-state capabilities to identify and effectively respond to problems and issues common to the states represented by the membership;

3. To promote effective communication and cooperation among the states represented by the membership and governmental units in Canada with regard to issues and problems of mutual concern and responsibility;

4. To provide a forum at which communication and discussion regarding such problems and issues can take place;

5. To assist in the development, coordination and execution of plans and programs under multi-national, national, state and local authority which shall promote the general welfare of the citizens within the area represented by the membership;

6. To stimulate economic, community and environmental improvement by promotion of domestic and international trade, tourism, business development, and other methods which shall be determined to have a common beneficial effect; and

7. To assist in the orderly conclusion of unfinished work of the Upper Great Lakes Regional Commission, including the provision of technical assistance for project completions and general phase-out responsibilities of said Commission.[40]

Early initiatives included the establishment of a Machine Tools Task Force to examine opportunities for revitalizing the industry in the region. Studies were also conducted to examine the region's economy and its relationship to the Great Lakes, as well as to assess the feasibility of joint international business development programs and joint tourism promotion initiatives among member states. A Great Lakes Economic Development Commission was established in 1987, with seven task forces drawn from member states, to develop an action strategy on a range of issues including higher education, rural development, and capital investment, among others.

Two recent initiatives are directed at promoting uniformity among Great Lakes states and provinces in management of shared water resources. The Great Lakes Charter, signed by Great Lakes governors and premiers in 1985, is a historic good faith agreement establishing principles for water quantity management and setting in place a joint consultative mechanism on major water withdrawals. The Great Lakes Toxic Substances Control Agreement, signed by the governors a year later, establishes water quality management principles and outlines a uniform regional strategy to address a msot insidious threat—toxic contamination of the Great Lakes.

The council is a greatly modified "successor" to the Upper Great Lakes Regional Commission which was established pursuant to Title V of the 1965 Federal Economic Development Act. Following the Presidentially mandated demise of that organization in 1981, the governors of the party states (Michigan, Minnesota, Wisconsin) created the Council of Upper Great Lakes Governors. New bylaws were adopted in 1982 permitting membership by Illinois and Indiana.[41] Ohio was granted membership soon thereafter, upon its own request. New York and Pennsylvania have not been offered full voting membership, but participate on an issue-specific basis. The staff is based in Chicago, Illinois.

A comparative analysis, in general terms, of selected structural and programmatic characteristics of these institutional arrangements is helpful in illustrating the range of approaches taken. From the standpoint of institutional structure, we can focus on membership, geographic jurisdiction, organizational resources, and authority. From a programmatic standpoint, we can conduct a comparative review of institutional goals, program scope, and management functions.

Selected Structural Characteristics—A Comparison

MEMBERSHIP

Membership on both the International Joint Commission and the Great Lakes Fishery Commission is international in nature, appointive, and generally reflective of a federal orientation toward binational resource management. A variety of advisory boards and committees involving state, provincial, and academic representation have been established to provide various planning, research, monitoring, surveillance, and coordinative services.

Conversely, membership on the Great Lakes Commission and the Council of Great Lakes Governors is limited to the United States, is either elective or appointive, and generally reflective of an interstate orientation toward binational resource management. The Great Lakes Commission appointment process varies from state to state and involves three to five members, at least one of whom is appointed by the governor. The Great Lakes Commission has historically provided for the designation of federal and provincial observers, having created in 1982, for example, a Technical Advisory Committee on Research and Development composed of nonvoting state, federal, provinical, and academic representatives.

The governors of the six westernmost Great Lakes states constitute the membership of the Council of the Great Lakes Governors, with New York and Pennsylvania holding "associate" membership on water resource issues. The council works primarily through governors' offices and state agencies, although provincial representation has been solicited on an issue-specific basis, such as in deliberations relating to the Great Lakes Charter and Toxic Substances Control Agreement.

GEOGRAPHIC JURISDICTION

All four institutions maintain a special focus upon the Great Lakes Basin, although in some cases actual geographic jursidiction is much broader. The Great Lakes Fishery Commission, by virtue of its mandate, is most clearly oriented toward basin management. Both the Great Lakes Commission and the Council of the Great Lakes Governors, as policy-oriented institutions, address interstate issues of interest that primarily (but not exclusively) include basin-specific issues. The International Joint Commission has jursidiction over all United States–Canadian border disputes; the Great Lakes Water Quality Agreement of 1978 provides basin-specific jurisdiction as a subset of this overall authority.

ORGANIZATIONAL RESOURCES

Organizational resources include items such as funding arrangements, staffing, and membership support. A common thread runs through all four entities: funding is modest with respect to mandated responsibilities, staffs are largely skeletal, and institutional viability is generally dependent upon staff support from member entities.

Present fiscal year funding for the Great Lakes Regional Office of the International Joint Commission is set in the area of $2.4 million, and is shared equally by the United States and Canada. These funds support a staff of thirty, fifteen of whom are professionals. The Water Quality Board, Science Advisory Board, and associated committees are actively involved in commission activities; membership is drawn from federal, state, and provincial agencies as well as from academia.

The Great Lakes Fishery Commission is also funded binationally. Funds for sea lamprey control are provided as follows: 69 percent through the U.S. Department of State, and 31 percent through Fisheries and Oceans Canada. This ratio reflects the historical commercial lake trout harvest between the two countries before the sea lamprey impact. Administration and general research funding is split evenly between the two countries. The total annual budget is approximately $7 million. The majority is allocated toward contract agents (primarily the U.S. Fish and Wildlife Service) and sea lamprey control programs. A small general research budget is maintained, as is a professional staff of five. The commission's three principal committees (identified earlier) are composed of federal, state, and provincial agency representatives, and take an active role in carrying out the commission's mandate.

The Great Lakes Commission is funded solely by the eight Great Lakes states, with current annual dues set at $35,000. The current annual budget of approximately $360,000 is drawn in part from funds made available when the Great Lakes Basin Commission ceased operation. The preponderance of the commission's research, planning, and coordination activities is conducted by an in-house staff of four to seven professionals and three support personnel. The commission accepts and lets contractual work on an issue-specific basis. As previously noted, commission membership is composed of gubernatorially appointed and legislatively mandated representatives from the eight Great Lakes states. Through the commission's task force structure, these individuals provide staff direction, and, as appropriate, assist in the development of work products.

The six state members of the Council of Great Lakes Governors are assessed annual dues of $20,000, and additional funding assistance is derived from project-specific grants from foundations and U.S. federal agencies. The council's research and planning activities are largely contracted out, since the small staff (presently four full-time professionals) is largely involved in coordination and advocacy activities.

AUTHORITY

All of the institutions of concern were created as instruments of formal international or intergovernmental agreement. The Great Lakes Water Quality Agreement of 1972 (amended in 1978) provided the basis for establishing the Great Lakes Regional Office of the Internatinal Joint Commission. The commission itself was established in 1911 under the authority of the Boundary Waters Treaty of 1909. The Great Lakes Fishery Commission was created to carry out the mandate embodied in the International Convention on Great Lakes Fisheries, which entered into force in 1955. The Great Lakes Basin Compact, passed by the eight Great Lakes states during the period 1955–63 and ratified by Congress in 1968, set out the mandate for the Great Lakes Commission. The Council of Great Lakes Governors, a greatly modified successor to the Upper Great Lakes Regional Commission, was formed in 1982 and operates under a set of bylaws approved by its membership.

Selected Program Characteristics—A Comparison

From a programmatic standpoint, a comparative analysis of institutional goals, program orientation, and management functions provides useful insight into the Great Lakes management structure.

INSTITUTIONAL GOALS

The stated goals and objectives of the institutions of concern are largely compatible and focused in a single direction—the protection and enhancement of the resource through multijurisdictional cooperation. Their goal statements are quite broad. A case in point is the goal of the Great Lakes Commission: "to promote the orderly, integrated, and comprehensive development, use and conservation of the water resources of the Great Lakes Basin" (Article I, Great Lakes Basin Compact). Goal statements for the other three institutions of concern are somewhat more focused but are consistent with this all-encompassing statement.

PROGRAM ORIENTATION

Program orientation varies considerably among the institutions of concern. International Joint Commission programs are oriented primarily (but not exclusively) toward water quality and quantity issues (levels, flows, diversion) in the international Great Lakes. The Great Lakes Fishery Commission focuses its programs toward maximizing the sustained productivity of the Great Lakes fishery. The Great Lakes Commission's program orientation is a function of the collective resource management priorities of the Great Lakes states; numerous policy-oriented issues are under examination at any given time. The Council of Great Lakes Governors operates in a similar mode, although the issues examined are generally fewer in number and are typically reviewed in substantial depth.

Although a number of issues are under active consideration by one or more of the institutions at any given time, program orientation is, in general, sufficiently different to preclude duplicative efforts. However, a strengthening of coordinative practices may be in order.

MANAGEMENT FUNCTIONS

The four institutions of concern pursue several of the same management functions: data collection and analysis, research, coordination, and policy development. The nature and extent of these activities, however, vary significantly with regard to the resource characteristics, uses, and development impacts of interest. In addition to these fundamental management functions, the International Joint Commission does possess regulatory powers relating to lake levels and flows, is involved in monitoring and surveillance activities, and maintains a public information program.

The Great Lakes Fishery Commission is primarily involved in fishery-related data collection and analysis, research, and coordination. It has distinguished itself in terms of basin planning with the preparation of its joint strategic plan for management of the Great Lakes fisheries.

Management functions emphasized by the Great Lakes Commission include advocacy, policy development, and coordination. Other functions, such as research, data collection, and analysis, are undertaken on an issue-specific basis. This statement is generally reflective of the Council of Great Lakes Governors as well.

A review of these institutions also provides an indication of the management and resource functions (1) that are not consistent with a specific institution's existing mandate; and (2) that are consistent with the existing mandate but are not presently undertaken. Examining the institutions collectively, examples of the former include (for most institutions) regulation, enforcement, and arbitration and conflict resolution. Examples of the latter (for most institutions) include advisory services, basin planning, public participation and education, and impact assessment. This second category is particularly important. It demonstrates the fact that not one Great Lakes regional institution is presently exercising full authority under its existing mandate. Consequently, one can convincingly argue that any institutional design exercise must be preceded by a careful review of existing institutions and their present mandates. This activity is, in fact, fundamental to the previously articulated thesis regarding the evolution of Great Lakes management institutions. Simply put, we must overcome the tendency to start anew until we have determined whether the foundation for an enhanced management structure is already in place.

THE DESIRED INSTITUTIONAL FRAMEWORK FOR GREAT LAKES MANAGEMENT

The perception of institutional adequacy—in the Great Lakes or any other region—is characterized by polarized opinions and laden with subjectivity. Regional resource management institutions, particularly those involved in coordination, research, monitoring, and other nonregulatory functions, are notoriously lacking in objective techniques for measuring performance. Perceptions of institutional adequacy therefore tend to be a reflection of a given individual's experience with the institution rather than an objective evaluation of the institution's ability to address its mandate.

The contrasts relating to institution-specific performance are pronounced as well. Zile has hailed the International Joint Commission's techniques of continuous consultation as a "model for the world."[42] Other investigators have questioned that agency's ability, under its treaty limitations, to react promptly to emerging problems. Similarly, Rexford G. Tugwell, an early supporter of the Tennessee Valley Authority, boasted that TVA would "furnish a new pattern for civilization."[43] Most other reviews yielded an understandably more modest statement of success.

In this author's research, over two dozen personal interviews were conducted with a variety of individuals actively involved in one or more of the four Great Lakes institutions of concern.[44] Perceptions of institutional performance and structural adequacy varied significantly among these individuals as well. This finding lends credence to Derthick's claim that there is no undisputed "preferred" approach to regional resource management in a federal system.[45]

The absence of measures of success constrains, but does not prohibit, meaningful institutional analysis. One might argue that the adequacy of existing institutions can be examined by comparing their characteristics with a descriptive listing of desired institutional characteristics drawn from the literature, case studies, and the creative thoughts of those committed to ecosystem management in the Great Lakes Basin. It is, in fact, an approach this author has undertaken in some detail. Examples of desired characteristics for a regional resource management entity were retrieved from the literature, and their conceptual bases identified and subsequently generalized to reflect consensus findings. The result is a series of abstract statements, or application concepts, that can be subsequently developed, tested, and diffused for broad utilization.

The forty-nine application concepts elicited during this effort were placed in eight broad categories: management philosophy; participatory management; management functions; role of the management entity in the institutional ecosystem; physical jurisdiction; breadth of activity; membership and constituent relations; and compatibility of form and function. The list goes beyond, but is found to be compatible with many basic elements of a Great Lakes governance structure posited by Milbrath.[46] The list provides a useful benchmark for examining institutional arrangements and for determining the means by which they might be strengthened. Although further detail is not possible here, this approach to strengthening the institutional framework for Great Lakes management does appear to have merit and warrants further consideration.

REALITIES FOR INSTITUTIONAL REVIEW

Earlier discussion has (1) demonstrated the importance of institutional analysis as a means of enhancing the Great Lakes management effort; (2) provided an overview of existing regional institutions; and (3) alluded to a series of desired characteristics that might be used as a benchmark for examining institutional adequacy. To conclude this discussion, eight realities that must be kept in mind during any review of institutional arrangements in the Great Lakes region are presented. They consist of findings, observations, and impressions generated from literature reviews, interviews, case studies, and related investigations. Many are rather obvious yet tend to be ignored or overlooked during investigations of this nature. They are presented as guidelines for use in traversing the gap between the identification of institutional needs and the design or alteration of institutions to address those needs.

1. Not one of the four Great Lakes institutions of concern has exercised all powers available under its existing mandate. These opportunitites should be thoroughly investigated before attempts are made to add another layer to the current management framework or to dispose of the framework entirely. In fact, using existing institutions as a foundation for change is perhaps the only means of reconciling the ideal and the politically feasible.

2. Problems of intergovernmental cooperation and coordination in the Great Lakes cannot be legislated away solely through the creation or revision of a regional institution. A *commitment* to the cooperative management of a shared resource is the key element—a commitment that must be fostered within each individual involved. Hence, fostering an ecosystem consciousness in the region is perhaps more important than investigating an institutional design for the same purpose.

3. One must not assume that all political jurisdictions in the Great Lakes Basin are ready and willing to involve themselves in regional management efforts; a states rights attitude is very strong, and in many cases well founded. Great Lakes institutions exist only because the various political jurisdictions allow them to. Any institutional design effort that fails to recognize this fact will probably come to very little.

4. Given the historical aversion to large-scale reform of governmental institutions, it is politically more feasible to fine-tune present arrangements. Institutional analysis and design efforts should reflect this fact.

5. There is common agreement in the literature and among practitioners that no ideal prototype of a regional management institution is in existence today. Furthermore, the uniqueness of the basin's hydrology, geography, and political jurisdictional status tends to discourage the application of institutional forms in place in other regions. We must therefore accept the fact that regional management efforts remain experiments, and hence must remain open to change.

6. The perceived absence of an ecosystem approach to Great Lakes management is not necessarily a failure of existing institutions; they simply were not designed with that purpose in mind. Given their generally broad mandates, however, integrating such an approach into their present functions is an opportunity that warrants thorough investigation.

7. Performance evaluations of existing institutions should be conducted cautiously and their findings carefully qualified. The absence of measures of success as a benchmark for evaluation inhibits objectivity. Developing such measures should be a priority concern, since they provide institutions with a learning capability.

8. Political will is the overriding determinant of the success of a regional resource management institution. When present, it can transcend even the most restrictive institutional form. When absent, even the most innovative form can become impotent. Hence, institutional responsiveness to the political jurisdictions served is a necessity.

In closing, it might be argued that Great Lakes management is not a perfect puzzle in which all the pieces fit. It is an unending process, with many players, by which the pieces of that puzzle are continuously reshaped and reworked. The goal—a complete picture acceptable to all—is an elusive one, but certainly worth striving for. Participants in the interuniversity seminar on the Great Lakes, and other interested individuals and organizations, can serve an impotant role in ensuring that the picture we develop is one we all want to see—an ecosystem managed for sustainable resource development.

NOTES

This chapter is one of a series of contributions prepared in partial fulfillment of the requirements for the degree of doctor of philosophy in urban, technological, and environmental planning at the University of Michigan. The research in support of the chapter has been made possible by a grant from the Michigan Sea Grant College Program.

1. Interuniversity Seminar on the Great Lakes. Conference on Sustainable Redevelopment for the Future in the Great Lakes Region. Wingspread Conference Center, Racine, Wisconsin, July 23–24, 1984.

2. Craine, Lyle E. (1972). *Final Report on Institutional Arrangements for the Great Lakes,* prepared for the Great Lakes Basin Commission, Ann Arbor, Michigan.

3. Great Lakes Basin Commission (1975). *Great Lakes Basin Framework Study: Report* Ann Arbor, Michigan.

4. Donahue, Michael J. (1986). *Institutional Arrangements for Great Lakes Management: Past Practices & Future Alternatives.* Submitted in partial fulfillment of requirements for the Ph.D. in Urban, Technological and Environmental Planning, University of Michigan. Funded by the Michigan Sea Grant College Program, NOAA-DOC Sponsored research, Grant Contract #NA80-AA-D-00072.

5. Panel on Sources and Control Techniques, Environmental Research Assessment Committee, National Research Council (1977). *Sources of Residuals and Techniques for their Control, Research and Development Needs: A Report.* National Academy of Sciences, Washington, D.C. p. 185.

6. Zile, Zigurd L. (1974). *Binational Land Resource Management for the Great Lakes Area: Powers of the International Joint Commission.* Madison, University of Wisconsin Law School, Grant No. C-5305, Office of Water Resource and Technology, U.S. Dept. of the Interior.

7. Ostrom, Vincent A.; Ostrom, E.; and Whitman, I. L. (1970). "Problems for Institutional Analysis of the Great Lakes Basin," Proceedings of the Thirteenth Conference on Great Lakes Research, 1970: International Association for Great Lakes Research, Ann Arbor, Michigan.

8. Hennigan, Robert D. (1970). "Effective Water Quality Management: Impossible Dream or Attainable Goal," Proceedings of the Thirteenth Conference on Great Lakes Research, 1970: International Association for Great Lakes Research, Ann Arbor, Michigan.

9. Supra note 3.

10. Derthick, Martha (1974). *Between State and Nation: Regional Organizations of the United States.* The Brookings Institution, Washington, D.C.

11. Fesler, James W. (1964). "National Water Resources Administration," in *Economics and Public Policy in Water Resources Development* (Smith and Castle eds.) Iowa State University Press, Iowa City, Iowa.

12. Martin, Roscoe, et al. (1960). *River Basin Administration and the Delaware.* Syracuse University Press, Syracuse, New York.

13. Supra note 10.

14. Supra note 10.

15. National Water Commission (1973). *New Directions in U.S. Water Policy: Final Report to the National Water Commission.* U.S. Government Printing Office, Washington, D.C.

16. Bilder, Richard B. (1972). "Controlling Great Lakes Pollution: A Study in United States–Canadian Environmental Cooperation," *Michigan Law Review,* Vol 70, No. 3 (January, 1972), pp. 469–556.

17. Supra note 3.

18. Dworsky, Leonard B.; and Swezey, Charles F. (eds.) (1974). *The Great Lakes of the United States and Canada—A Reader on Management Improvement Strategies.* Based on the Report of the Canada–United States Interuniversity Seminar, "A Proposal for Improving the Management of the Great Lakes of the United States and Canada." Cornell University, Ithaca, New York.

19. Kelnhofer, Guy J., Jr. (1972). *Preserving the Great Lakes.* Prepared for the National Water Commission. Contract No. NWC 72-010. National Water Commission, Arlington, Virginia.

20. Nelson, Senator Gaylord (1977). "America's Great Lakes Program: The Bureaucratic Mess in the United States" (speech of February 21, 1977).

21. Kasten, Senator Robert (1984). "Bureaucratic Maze of the Great Lakes Management." *Congressional Record,* June 15, 1984 (Vol. 130, No. 82).

22. Schon, Donald A. (1971). *Beyond the Stable State: Public and Private Learning in a Changing Society.* Random House, New York, N.Y.

23. Hennigan, Robert D. (1970). "Effective Water Quality Management: Impossible Dream or Attainable Goal," Proceedings of the Thirteenth Conference on Great Lakes Research, 1970: International Association for Great Lakes Research, Ann Arbor, Michigan.

24. International Joint Commission (1980). *Workshop Report: Anticipatory Planning for the Great Lakes.* A report by the Science Advisory Board through its Societal Aspects Expert Committee. Great Lakes Regional Office, Windsor, Ontario.

25. The discussion contained herein reflects, in part, findings by Derthick, supra note 10.

26. Munro, William B. (1928). *The Invisible Government.* Macmillan, New York, N.Y.

27. International Joint Commission (1909). *International Boundary Waters Treaty of 1909.* International Joint Commission, Washington, D.C.

28. For further elaboration, see Derthick, supra note 10.

29. Supra note 10.

30. This finding is based on a review of the literature, as well as on a series of personal interviews with appropriate Great Lakes management officials and academicians. See Donahue, supra note 4.

31. Donahue, Michael J. (1984). "Great Lakes Related Organizations" (unpublished).

32. Haynes, David; and Madau, Mario (1978). "Current Status of Canadian Organizational Arrangements for Planning and Management in the Great Lakes Basin," in *Toward the Future in the Great Lakes Basin—An Agenda for Negotiation: Canada-U.S.* (December, 1978). Cornell University, Ithaca, New York, and Waterloo University, Waterloo, Ontario.

33. Bulkley, J. W.; and A. R. Mathews (1973). "Water Quality Relationships in the Great Lakes" *Proceedings,* International Association for Great Lakes Research, pp. 872-879.

34. Supra note 4.

35. Supra note 27.

36. International Joint Commission (1972). *Great Lakes Water Quality Agreement.* International Joint Commission, Great Lakes Regional Office, Windsor, Ontario.

37. Great Lakes Commission (1955). *Great Lakes Basin Compact.* Great Lakes Commission, Ann Arbor, Michigan.

38. Great Lakes Fishery Commission (1955). *Convention on Great Lakes Fisheries Between the United States of America and Canada.* Great Lakes Fishery Commission, Ann Arbor, Michigan.

39. Great Lakes Fishery Commission (1980). *Joint Strategic Plan for Management of the Great Lakes Fisheries.* Ann Arbor, Michigan.

40. Council of Great Lakes Governors (1982). Articles of Incorporation. Madison, Wisconsin.

41. Council of Great Lakes Governors (1982). *Bylaws of the Council of Great Lakes Governors.* Madison, Wisconsin.

42. Zile, Zigurd L. (1974). *Binational Land Resource Management for the Great Lakes Area: Powers of the International Joint Commission.* Madison, University of Wisconsin Law School, Grant No. C-5305, Office of Water Resource and Technology, U.S. Dept. of the Interior.

43. Tugwell, Rexford G. (1935). *The Battle for Democracy.* Columbia University Press, New York, N.Y.

44. Interviews have included representatives from state, provincial, federal (U.S. and Canada), regional, and international agencies, as well as academia. See Donahue, supra note 4.

45. Supra note 10.

46. Milbrath, Lester W. (1984). "A Governance Structure Designed to Learn Would Better Protect the Great Lakes," paper prepared for the Interuniversity Seminar on the Great Lakes. State University of New York at Buffalo. Chapter 4 of this Reader.

CHAPTER 4. A GOVERNANCE STRUCTURE DESIGNED TO LEARN WOULD BETTER PROTECT THE GREAT LAKES ECOSYSTEM

There appears to be growing opinion that implementing basinwide ecosystem policies for the lakes requires institutional innovation. There are differences of opinion, however, regarding what kinds of institutional arrangements would be acceptable and effective. If we knew for certain what husbandry of the lakes required, new forms of governance could be negotiated. In fact, the size, complexity, and novelty of the management task implied by an ecosystem approach further implies the need for flexible and expansible institutional arrangements that will enable experience and scientific advances to point the way toward effective governance. This chapter proposes a structure to assist this process of social learning; the structure is based upon a charter of commitment to transboundary, regional action toward protection of the Great Lakes.

LESTER W. MILBRATH

4

A GOVERNANCE STRUCTURE DESIGNED TO LEARN WOULD BETTER PROTECT THE GREAT LAKES ECOSYSTEM

WHY DO THE GREAT LAKES NEED PROTECTION?

Over the past twenty years the public's awareness that the Great Lakes are in peril has undeniably been growing. The Great Lakes and the St. Lawrence River constitute the largest body of fresh water on the planet. We have learned to use this treasure in a multitude of ways. Not only do we drink from it, swim in it, and use it to cleanse ourselves, our homes, and our factories, but we also use it for fishing, boating, the transport of goods, irrigation, hydropower, cooling water, and as a sewer to dispose of our wastes. The plentiful availability of water and ease of navigation attracted many people to shoreline settlements that have developed into major cities. About 70 percent of Canadians live within one hundred miles of the Great Lakes. On the U.S. side, the following major cities front on the Great Lakes: Rochester, Buffalo, Erie, Cleveland, Toledo, Detroit, Gary and Hammond, Chicago, Milwaukee, and Duluth and Superior. About forty million people now live in the Great Lakes watershed, but fifty to sixty million live close enough to use the

Great Lakes in one way or another. It is becoming increasingly clear to the people in the Great Lakes community that protecting the natural integrity of the Lakes is crucial to their long-range well-being.

As the people in the basin built an industrial civilization, they were slow to become aware of the long-range consequences of the way they used the Great Lakes. Overfishing eliminated certain desirable fish species altogether. Slashing down forests and converting them to farmland led to silted and polluted rivers. As the farms increasingly used fertilizers and pesticides, the pollution load on the lakes increased. Millions of homes used lake water to flush their household wastes back into the lakes. Factories hungrily drew upon the water for cleansing and cooling processes, adding their load of pollution to the returning water. Chemical factories, attracted to the lakes because of plentiful water and cheap hydropower, buried toxic wastes in landfills not far from the water. Now we are discovering these wastes seep into the groundwater and eventually enter the lakes. This pollution injures aquatic life, contaminates fish so that they cannot be consumed, and threatens drinking water. Ironically, the people in the basin are discovering that, even though the Great Lakes are crucial to their well-being, human mismanagement threatens to make this great natural treasure a danger rather than a value. We no longer can treat it as a free resource that any person or firm can draw from or dump things into without careful consideration of the long-range consequences of such actions.

But how can we require careful and considered action when two countries, eight states, and two provinces have official responsibility for actions that affect the adequate functioning of the Great Lakes ecosystem? Our ancestors perceived rivers and lakes as clearly identifiable breaks of land that made handy political boundaries; water boundaries were easier to draw and more defendable than land boundaries. They did not perceive that lakes and rivers are central elements of ecosystems requiring the people on each side of the boundary to eventually find ways to collaborate to protect the integrity of their common ecosystem.

The people in the basin are recognizing their common stake in protecting the Great Lakes. They are experimenting with a variety of institutions that are making valiant efforts, but are only partially successful, in protecting the resource. Most thoughtful observers recognize that we must go further to overcome the unfortunate historical legacy of political boundaries that divide us. The people in the Great Lakes Basin are becoming a community that crosses national, state, and provincial boundaries. The time has come, or will soon arrive, to give institutional expression to the community's strong desire to preserve its natural treasure.

One of the clearest expressions of this sense of community is found in the second Great Lakes Water Quality Agreement signed by Canada and the United States in 1978. This agreement is an extension of the Boundary Waters Treaty of 1909 and pledges that both countries will take an ecosystem approach to the protection of the Great Lakes. Implementing that goal has turned out to be considerably more difficult than agreeing to it. A great deal of thought needs to be devoted to what this goal means in actual practice and to how the governance of the Great Lakes should be structured so as to effectively implement the goal.

EVALUATION OF THE EFFECTIVENESS OF OUR PRESENT INSTITUTIONS FOR PRESERVING THE INTEGRITY OF THE GREAT LAKES

The original human settlers in the basin, native Americans, intervened very little in natural ecosystems; the European civilization that supplanted them intervened dramatically. More than one hundred years passed before Canada and the United States began to recognize the damage inflicted by their way of life and took any significant steps to regulate and protect the Great Lakes. The Boundary Waters Treaty of 1909 was the first and still is the major treaty that governs the relationships between Canada and the United States with respect to their care of the Great Lakes. At first the treaty was used mainly to control navigation, withdrawals of water, and water levels. It also contained a provision forbidding pollution of boundary waters that was used later (during the 1960s and 1970s) to control pollution. The treaty set up an International Joint Commission (IJC), composed of three Americans and three Canadians, to oversee these activities. As the functions performed under the treaty have expanded, so have the power and influence of the commission. It now has its own office in Windsor as well as sizeable secretariats in each national capital. The water quality agreements between the two countries in 1972 and in 1978 have added a Water Quality Board and a Science Advisory Board to the IJC's institutional structure.

Although the IJC is the most prominent public body shaping policy with respect to the Great Lakes, there are many additional binational bodies that play meaningful roles, such as the Great Lakes

Fishery Commission, the Great Lakes Commission, and the Conference of Great Lakes Governors. In addition, provincial, state, and local governments not only make policies in their jurisdictions but also collaborate in a variety of ways in policies and practices that affect the lakes. For example, New York State, the Province of Ontario, and the national governments of Canada and the United States recently cooperated in a three-year study of toxic contamination of the Niagara River; in February 1987 these same four governments signed an agreement for toxic abatement in the river. There also are many nongovernmental organizations, several of them with binational memberships, that strive to protect the Great Lakes by trying to influence public policy. The development of this institutional structure for the protection of the Great Lakes is, itself, a long, complicated, and fascinating story that is thoroughly discussed elsewhere.[1]

Many observers believe that the institutional structure that has evolved is working reasonably well and probably represents the furthest development that the people and their two national governments are willing to accept.[2] The Boundary Waters Treaty grants certain powers that have never been carried into practice; presumably those powers would have been activated if the two governments were in agreement that they should be. The structure surely has shown considerable adaptability in other respects. If the present structure is somewhat effective, and the governments seem not at all eager to change it, what is the point of discussing a new governance structure for the Great Lakes?

But is the structure really effective? The IJC has only a small budget and has no power to make authoritative decisions. It can recommend to governments, but there are dozens of instances in which recommendations have been ignored; sometimes letters go unanswered for several years.[3] Recently, wholesale budget cuts have crippled Great Lakes research programs and demoralized staff. Some progress has been made in cleaning up pollution, particularly that arising from excessive phosphate discharges into the water, but this change has come agonizingly slowly and only after public opinion overwhelmingly demanded remedial action. Indeed, the IJC has learned that its best weapon for protecting the lakes is to stimulate citizens to demand protection of the lakes from their governments.

The most eloquent evidence for the limitations of the present structure is the continuation of physical injuries and threats to the well-being of the Great Lakes ecosystem. Some sectors of the lakes, such as Green Bay and Saginaw Bay, continue to be so polluted that their waters are a threat to all forms of life; the main body of the lakes, although useable, can hardly be said to be clean and safe. Little progress has been made in eliminating the toxics entering the Niagara River from old chemical dumps along its banks. The Canadians cry vainly against the U.S. government's inaction that results in toxic pollution of their drinking water. Are economic development projects in the basin taken with foresight as to their impact on the ecosystem? Do we have a knowledge base that enables us to forecast the ecosystem consequences of new human initiatives?

Another way to evaluate the adequacy of the present institutional structure for protection of the Great Lakes is to compare it against an ideal structure. We could imagine the capabilities that such a structure would need to possess if it were completely effective in protecting the ecosystem of the Great Lakes while simultaneously reconciling the many uses humans make of the lakes. We could then imagine how these new capabilities could be added to the present structure to make it more effective. Since it is difficult to foresee all of the needs this structure will be required to fulfill, we should strive to make it flexible. As a matter of fact, *we should design the structure to learn.*

THE BASIC ELEMENTS OF A GREAT LAKES GOVERNANCE STRUCTURE DESIGNED TO LEARN

All systems learn by trial and error. Some learn faster than others, but typically the learning is very slow. This is very expensive learning. Wouldn't it be better to design a governance system to maximize learning? It should not only be flexible to enable it to change as new understandings develop among the actors in the system, but it should also help citizens learn how their environmental-social-economic-political system works. As we proceed to try and do this, we should keep in mind that all of the natural elements of an ecosystem—the water, the soil, the mineral resources, the animals (including humans), the plants, the air, and the energy from the sun that drives the system—are systemically interrelated. The human add-ons (such as cities) also constitute systems that are inextricably intertwined with the ecosystem. Whatever humans do in their man-made systems affects the ecosystems in which they are embedded. The ecosystem, in turn, feeds back upon and affects the functioning of the human social systems. Although it is easy to recognize that these systems exist and that they are interconnected, we cannot say that we understand them well.

In the following section I will try to avoid becoming structural too soon. Instead, I will speak of capabilities that identify a need and a function but that leave open how that function would be fulfilled by a concrete structure (institution). To be sure, a given function implies something about structure, but there would be some leeway to design different structures to fulfill a needed capacity.

A Great Lakes Information System to Facilitate Learning

A Great Lakes governance structure that emphasizes learning needs a well-functioing information system. Natural and social scientists have developed considerable understanding of ecosystems and social systems. This important research, much of which is multidisciplinary, not only must continue but should be accelerated. Frequently the data supporting research reports are lost, and sometimes the reports themselves are lost. Surely, many people who could use the information never learn about its availability. Modern computer technology makes it possible to store data, reports, and bibliographies in retrievable data bases. This technology further eases problems of search, retrieval, and data manipulation.

Some institution should be identified (or created) and assigned the responsibility to set up and maintain a comprehensive information management system for the Great Lakes. This system would constitute a general-purpose resource to serve many needs, some of which cannot be anticipated. Data should be stored in retrievable bases that could be used for a variety of purposes. Research that develops new information relevant to the Great Lakes could be initiated by governments, universities, and private individuals or groups. However, the other institutions to be proposed for this learning governance structure would have a special responsibility to initiate and support relevant research.

Information achieves its full value only when it is used. Therefore, an information dissemination capability for the Great Lakes should be established and maintained. Utilization is much greater if the meaning in technical reports can be translated into everyday language and carried into public discourse. The meaning from research also should be converted to recommended practices for people to use as they go about their daily work. The Extension Service of the U.S. Department of Agriculture, working with the land grant universities in each of the fifty U.S. states, has had considerable experience in translating technical research into ordinary language and in carrying recommended practices to persons needing advice and assistance. That experience should be used in designing the information dissemination capability proposed here. A Great Lakes extension service should reach into all sectors of the basin and would need to be supported by both countries. It is possible that such an extension service could one day be the major vehicle for changing the daily practices of the humans in the basin and thus helping them to preserve their great natural treasure.

The media, particularly television, should be used extensively to disseminate information about the Great Lakes. Public service television could be used creatively and effectively not only to inform people how the Great Lakes ecosystem works but also to lead people to reflect on how their life-style affects the ecosystem and the other people in their community. This education could lead them to a deeper understanding of their basic values. Information resources are always scarce; there is a scarcity of money and talent to produce messages that communicate effectively, and there also is a scarcity of attention time among intended audiences. The information dissemination system of this proposed governance structure will need to make thoughtful and farsighted choices about the deployment of its informational resources.

A Systemic and Futures Thinking Capability

Most of the activities in modern industrial societies, particularly in the West, are governed by market interactions. Although markets are reasonably effective in allocating goods and services to various activities, they are weak decisional structures for integrating a variety of elements that are related systemically; they also provide little opportunity and capability for thinking about the future. Our societal capability for integrative systemic thinking is further weakened by the extreme division of labor and the narrowness of expertise that has developed in modern industrial societies.

Past human actions around the Great Lakes, guided primarily or solely by individuals seeking to maximize their personal advantage in a market system, have resulted in the resource depletion and environmental degradation mentioned in the introduction. Each individual may take only a little water, or dump only a little waste, but the cumulative effects of these individual actions have begun to overwhelm the natural balance in the lakes. We are being forced to conclude that human activities that impact on the Great Lakes must be guided by knowledge of the systemic relationships that bind elements into an ecosystem and by skilled interpretation of that knowledge to arrive at reasonably accurate estimates of the future consequences of contemplated actions. An effective governance system for the Great Lakes, then, must self-consciously develop and maintain a capability for systemic and futures thinking; let us call it the "Great Lakes Futures Review Board" (GLFRB).

How might such a capability work? First, the people working in it would need to know how ecosystems and social systems function; particularly, they would have to understand the intricate interrelationships between ecosystems and social systems. If the information capability discussed above is well designed, it should be able to provide the detailed information about systems needed by the board; if not, the board should have the authority and resources to commission the research needed to fill the identified gaps. It might choose to convene special panels or committees to evaluate the adequacy of present knowledge and to estimate the need for new research and data gathering. It should publish special reports stating these findings.

The GLFRB would need thinkers with special talents. These persons would not only need capacious minds but also should be comfortable in receiving, processing, and integrating information from a wide variety of disciplines. The persons making up such a "think group" would need depth as well as breadth. This depth could be achieved by including specialists from many knowledge areas who would know when and how to access further expert information from their area of specialization but who could also work as part of a multidisciplinary team to arrive at integrated composite judgments about the wisdom of proposed actions.

Although it would be the primary mission of this group to learn to think systemically and to anticipate the future as best it can, the group must also reach out to affect actions in the real world. *I propose that all major human initiatives that could significantly impact the Great Lakes ecosystem should be brought to this group for review of their consequences for the ecosystem* **as well as their consequences for the social system.** This process would commence by requiring that each initiative be preceded by the preparation of an impact assessment that would be reviewed by this think group. I will discuss more fully below the components that should be included in an impact assessment.

Boards with decision-making functions are fairly common in both Canada and the United States. Typically people are chosen for these boards because of their expertise or because they are representative of certain blocs of citizens. The GLFRB would be different in that persons would be chosen to serve on it because of their broad integrative knowledge and their ability to use that knowledge to estimate the future consequences of proposed actions. *The GLFRB would not make authoritative decisons;* it would only make recommendations. It would acquire proper information, evaluate it for its adequacy (reliability and validity), use it to forecast future consequences of proposed initiatives, and make recommendations to public authorities (and the public) who have the legal responsibility for making decisions.

The GLFRB should not be thought of as trying to be representative; its task, rather, would be to think integratively for the whole basin. On the one hand, it should be insulated from politics so that it would be free to fully use its knowledge and judgment to make the wisest recommendations it could conceive of; on the other hand, its members must be selected and would need to be supported with funds; surely elected officials ultimately should play some role in those matters. The officials appointing the board would need some guidance in choosing board members, and the practice known as "peer review" would probably be best suited to recommending prospective members. Persons who have worked closely with someone on projects or committees are usually best equipped to judge how a person would be likely to function on this very special kind of board. The GLFRB should be small in size (I propose approximately ten members), and it should be supported by a professional staff. Members should be appointed for staggered fixed terms (let us say seven years) with possibility of renewal for one additional term. When the IJC (or similar body) makes the appointments, they should seek the advice of professional associations concerned with the Great Lakes.

Surely it is possible for ten people, even wise ones, to make mistakes. (Remember that the board will not make authoritative decisions.) What institutional corrective might be found for that problem? One useful corrective is to rquire that all findings, reports, and decisions be made public. The GLFRB would not be the creature of, or subservient to, any given government; hence, no government would have the power to suppress a report or dictate its contents. A second useful corrective would be to invite, even finance, other review teams to offer a second opinion. These proposed correctives reflect the premise that the role of the board should be primarily educative. It must persuade people to act so as to protect the ecosystemic integrity of the Great Lakes by the power of its information, its analyses, and its recommendations. It would be tidier, but unrealistic, to propose to give the board the power to make legally binding decisions.

Some critics have suggested that the people will never accept the establishment of a board to rule over the Great Lakes. Once more, I point out that the board would not rule; it would only have the power to recommend. Its main function would be to facilitate learning. To do that, it must be composed of poeple who are broadly informed and more experienced that the average citizen; it is especially important for the members of this board to have learned to think integratively, systemically, and with an eye to the future. Ordinary common sense, as it is spoken of colloquially, would not suffice. Instead, the board should make its findings and recommendations known, and then people could react to the new information using their common sense.

The board's reports and recommendations should go to governments, organizations, and people with the hope of having an impact on governmental decisions. One might ask, "Why not simply let the governmental bodies decide as they do now?" Experience has shown that governmental officials, by and large, are so caught up in immediate problems and crises that they seldom can think deeply about the future consequences of their actions; therefore, they take a short-range perspective and find it difficult to anticipate even a moderate distance into the future. This proposal is a step toward programming government to learn by designating a special group to give full time to acquiring the best information, thinking about it integratively and systemically, and projecting the future consequences of proposed actions.

An Intervention Capability

There will be a natural tendency for some people to ignore or deny problems that others will recognize as having a potential for seriously damaging the Great Lakes ecosystem. For example, it may be in the interest of a local community to allow pollution discharges knowing that the moving waters will sweep away part of the problem, loading it, instead, on communities downstream. An intervention capability is needed to identify such problems, to get them on the public agenda for review, and to press for satisfactory resolution. Although an existing governmental agency might occasionally press another governmental entity, or a private entity, to deal with a problem, the people of the basin could hardly count on governmental agencies alone to intervene.

A new governance structure for the Great Lakes community should explicitly grant the right to nongovernmental organizations (NGOs), to intervene anywhere in the basin (no matter which country) to obtain review action for a problem they have identified. For example, NGOs could identify failures of responsible officials to act and could seek an official review by the GLFRB of the long-range consequences of that inaction. They could request or demand that a proper impact statement be filed before a project is undertaken. They could bring new knowledge to the attention of the GLFRB and request a new review of an impact statement.

Sometimes governmental agencies are officially assigned a responsibility but given so little money that they cannot carry out the responsibility effectively. NGOs might be given the right to noisily intrude on the governmental budgetary process, perhaps by being given the right to testify at budgetary hearings, and to thus be able to alert the public so that it will not be fooled by the common tactic of starting a remedial program but not providing sufficient funding to make it viable. (The rights of intervention to be exercised by NGOs also should be available to governmental units; it often happens that a given unit of government needs some procedure to get another unit of government to carry out a responsibility.)

NGOs might form themselves into a consortium (Great Lakes United is a consortium of NGOs already in place) to take on this watchdog, intervention role. It might even be wise to provide some modest public funding to a binational NGO consortium so that it could more effectively play this watchdog role. When NGOs are effective watchdogs, they typically generate conflict; but NGOs might also contribute to conflict management and resolution. They could be dynamically effective in both directions. The main task for the intervention capability would be to facilitate learning. Providing this intervention capability, and locating it primarily with NGOs, would help avoid the present pattern of governments waiting for each other to act, blaming each other for inaction, passing the buck, and doing as little as possible while hoping that other governments will meet the problem.

A Capability for Conflict Resolution

Any attempt to manage a major natural resource like the Great Lakes is likely to engender conflict. Fresh water has a multitude of uses, and some uses are incompatible; accentuation of one use may require diminution of another use. Some conflicts can be averted if impact assessments thoroughly explore the ramifications of a potential project. Sometimes seeing an arena of conflict in the context of its total ecosystemic relationships will facilitate conflict resolution. GLFRB reviews of impact assessments, pointing out the systemic consequences of proposed actions, should help to reduce conflict. Interventions by NGOs also could have the effect of resolving conflict.

Environmental mediation is another useful institutional device for conflict resolution. There are a variety of forms of environmental mediation; in nearly all of them skilled practitioners try to find common ground between protagonists that can serve as a basis for conflict resolution. A number of environmental mediation consulting firms have been set up in the United States and Canada. The methods that they have worked out probably could effectively be applied to the kinds of conflicts that can be anticipated for the overall management of the Great Lakes.

Even if the two forms for mitigating conflict just discussed are moderately successful, there will be conflicts requring authoritative resolution. The International Joint Commission as currently constituted could suitably be assigned the power to make final decisions in cases brought before it. The 1909 Boundary Waters Treaty would seem to grant this power to the IJC, but the two national governments have seldom allowed it to use it. Alternatively, a special Great Lakes Court might be established to receive disputes and to render final disposition on them. This court could be given jurisdiction over all disputes within the basin that affect the Great Lakes ecosystem. State or national courts could not claim exclusive jurisdiction. The Great Lakes Court itself would decide if it has jurisdiction; in this respect it would be like the U.S. Supreme Court, which also decides whether or not it has jurisdiction in specific cases. Since this court would be part of a transnational governance structure, there would be no appeal from its decisions to national courts. The signatory governments to the agreements establishing the court would be obliged to enforce its decisions in the same way that they enforce judicial decisions in their own territories.

The Necessity of Impact Assessments

Two hundred years ago the natural resources available on the North American continent were so plentiful, and the human population so small, that society could afford the luxury of allowing people to avail themselves of natural resources with only a few controls about ownership accompanied by comparatively little concern for damage to nature or neighbors. Now the population is so large, and the human capability for technological intervention is so huge, that our societies have begun to require environmental impact statements before major projects can be undertaken. The U.S. National Environmental Policy Act of 1969 was the first major piece of national legislation requiring impact assessments. Now more than one hundred national governments require environmental impact statements.

At first, impact statements were confined to concern for the natural environment, but, but the mid 1970s, the idea had been expanded to *social impact assessment*. By now, considerable literature has developed addressing both kinds of assessments.[4] I recommend that the idea of impact assessment be expanded still more to incorporate *"value impact assessment."* In deciding how to allocate a resource, or in deciding what strategy to pursue to protect a resource, it is very useful to identify as comprehensively as possible all the values at stake for a given initiative or project. Very often, project proponents and project reviewers consider only the first order consequences of an action and ignore second-, third-, and fourth-order consequences. If people knew what impact the second-, third-, and fourth-order consequences would have on their values, they might well have a different perspective on the wisdom of the proposed project. Value impact analysis would attempt to identify the value impacts of second-, third-, and fourth-order consequences. (It goes without saying that second-, third-, and fourth-order environmental and social impacts also should be considered.)

Since value impact assessments are only now beginning to be discussed, it might be helpful to suggest briefly how a value assessment could be conducted. It is typical for values to be assumed when a project is contemplated; therefore the value analyst needs to search for the hidden values that are *implicit* in the statements made in the environmental and social impact assessments. Many projects call for benefit-cost analysis; each benefit and cost that is identified has value attached, and these might be called the "obvious" values. It is also important to try to identify the values that would be enhanced or diminished as the second-, third-, and fourth-order consequences of a project are realized; these can be called the "consequential" values.

The explicit identification of the implicit, obvious, and consequential values at stake in a project, in and of itself, constitutes the first step toward weighting these values. How else might weights be assigned to values? Economists typically try to weigh values in monetary terms. If all values could be monetized, money would provide a useful and familiar metric for making comparative judgments. Unfortunately, many values cannot be monetized without gross distortions of their essence; the efforts of some economists to monetize all values should be viewed with extreme skepticism. The practice of excluding from consideration those values that cannot be monetized also is unacceptable. Values exist only in our minds and are necessarily subjective; these subjective judgments seem imprecise; we thus feel it is difficult to compare across individuals and groups.

Objectively measuring subjective value judgments is actually not as difficult as popularly supposed. Those who deny that values can be measured, but who still must make decisions that have value components, inevitably assign some weight to those values. They are crudely measuring values despite their denial of the possibility of measuring them. It is better to employ the simple seven- or ten-point rating scales commonly used in sample surveys, which are reasonably effective for weighing values and for comparing across individuals or groups. The use of these value scales means that all values can be measured and compared using approximately the same metric. They are not precise, but they are serviceable and can be quantified. They certainly are less misleading than using money to weigh values. They also are less misleading than using hidden value judgments, or assuming values without making them explicit. *In sum, we have no choice but to value; we have no choice but to weigh values; we serve our societal values by making our values explicit and by measuring them as openly and as effectively as possible in a value impact assessment.*

Environmental impact assessment, social impact assessment, and value impact assessment should eventually come to be thought of as a total package. It is this total impact assessment that I propose be required for every major project or initiative taken in the Great Lakes Basin. As with present environmental impact assessments, the proposer of a project would have responsibility for preparing the assessment. Impact assessments would be required for such projects as new power plants (nuclear, fossil fuel, or hydro), new factories on or near (using) waterbodies; water diversion for irrigation, power production, or coal slurry (or any other major quantitative demand); commercial fishing; new locks or channel deepening; extension of the winter navigation season; new resort complexes or other major shoreline real estate developments; drilling for gas and oil in the lakes; building (or failing to build) sewage treatment plants; undertaking (or failing to undertake) toxic dump cleanups; introduction of new fish species; and all proposals for disposal of wastes in waterways of the Great Lakes Basin.

Actual experience with impact assessments over a period of time, accompanied by cases brought for conflict resolution to the Great Lakes Court (possibly as a result of NGO intervention), would gradually define a boundary between projects requiring the full impact assessment (and review by the GLFRB) and projects that society can afford to exempt from this basinwide oversight. Requests for exemption would be directed to and reviewed by the GLFRB. The GLFRB also should have the capability to order an impact assessment if, in its judgment, one is required for a proposed project (it might obtain this information from an intervention by an NGO). The Great Lakes Court also would have the power to grant an exemption or to require a review. States and other governmental units would have the same right to request impact assessments as would NGOs.

An impact assessment methodology and lore will develop over time; actually, a great deal already is known from the experience with environmental impact assessments. The United States has more experience than Canada with impact assessments, but this lore can easily be shared across boundaries. Reviews of the impact assessments by the GLFRB are likely to feed back upon and sharpen impact assessment preparation and to contribute to development of the lore.

Finally, the structure proposed here would need administrative support, a secretariat, to hire the staff, to pay them, and to provide and maintain offices, labs, libraries, and so forth. These necessities are so obvious and the methods required for their provision so well known that no further discussion is required.

THE SYSTEMIC INTERCONNECTIONS IN THE PROPOSED GREAT LAKES GOVERNANCE STRUCTURE

Figure 1 displays the components of the proposed governance structure and illustrates, with arrows, the systemic interrelations of the components. The motor that would keep the system going would be the requirement for impact assessments for all major human interventions that could impact the ecosystem of the Great Lakes. The governmental signatories to the governance agreement would pledge by their assent to it that they would require such impact assessments. All such impact assessments would be forwarded to the GLFRB for review. These assessments would be made public so that NGOs, with their intervention capability, could focus public attention on impact assessments that they believe are inadequate; they also could request impact assessments for projects that they believe would threaten the integrity of the Great Lakes ecosystem.

The information system would acquire new knowledge from disciplinary and multidisciplinary research; new knowledge also would be generated from the data base management system. This new

FIGURE 1
A GOVERNANCE STRUCTURE FOR THE GREAT LAKES COMMUNITY

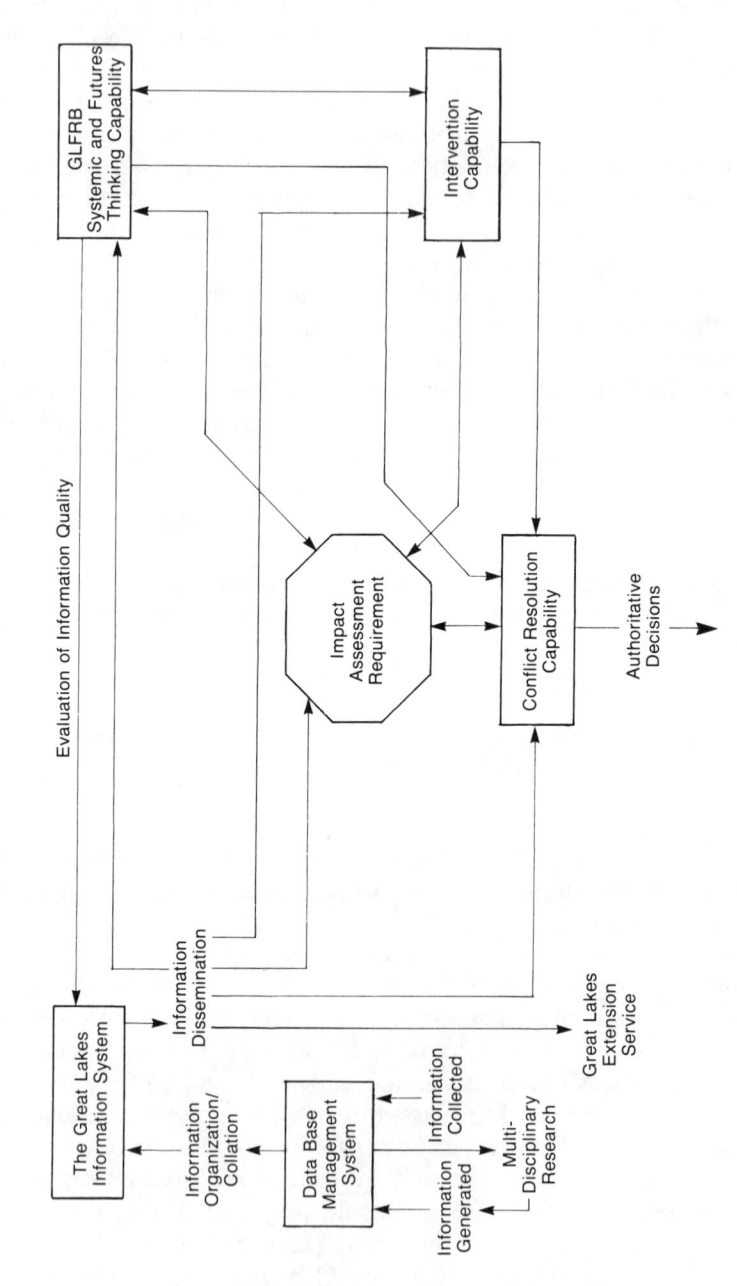

information would regularly be disseminated to the other elements of the governance structure: the systemic and futures thinking capability, the intervention capability, and the conflict resolution capability. The information also would be publicly available and would be especially relevant for impact assessments. As mentioned above, the new knowledge and practices also should be disseminated as widely and swiftly as possible through the media (especially television) and an extension service that would reach into all sectors of the basin, and to all the walks of life for which the information would be relevant.

The systemic and futures thinking capability (the GLFRB) would be a major consumer of new information from the information system. It should evaluate that information and should help to direct the future information-gathering activities of the information system. Many of the inputs to the GLFRB would come in the form of impact assessments, but the board should be given the power to initiate impact assessments if they have not been generated by initiatives taken elsewhere in the system.

Over the years governments have undertaken rehabilitative actions to improve the quality of the Great Lakes; the GLFRB should have the power to review those actions and to pay particular attention to their synergistic effects on the multitudes of elements that make up the Great Lakes ecosystem. As mentioned above, the findings and recommendations of the GLFRB must be made public and would constitute inputs to other sectors of the system; this input would be particularly relevant for the intervention capability.

The persons and groups active in the intervention sector would receive information from the GLFRB, from the impact assessments, and from the information system. The nongovernmental organizations in their watchdog role would be alert to possible problems and could make inputs to the impact assessment process and the GLFRB review process, and could also take cases to the conflict resolution sector of the governance system.

The conflict resolution capability would receive information and other messages from all the other sectors of the system. Presumably it would receive specific concrete cases on which it would bestow authoritative decisions.

In its totality, this proposed governance structure constitutes an institutional capability for implementing the ecosystem approach to management of the Great Lakes. Most large natural resources are used freely at first, but, as the withdrawals increase in size and number, we run the danger of experiencing the "tragedy of the commons." The governance structure proposed here would provide basinwise oversight and would help to avoid the tragedy of the commons. This structure also is designed to facilitate learning and presumably would evolve into an increasingly effective institution as social learning with respect to it would progress.

FUNDING

Although it might be desirable for this governance structure to have its own power to generate funding (the ability to levy and collect taxes), that power is not very likely to be granted at this time. Experience has shown that when international agencies are dependent on contributions from member governments, those agencies must constantly be concerned about the withdrawal of contributions should the agency do something to displease a member government. It would help alleviate that problem somewhat if the intergovernmental agreement carried a pledge that each government would provide to the Great Lakes agency a certain percentage of its annual budget (let us say one-tenth of 1 percent). With eight states, two provinces, and two countries contributing to its funding each year, the agency would have a sufficiently stable funding base to launch and sustain the many-faceted governance programs outlined above. The drain on any member government would be tolerable, and the benefits in the form of protection of a major natural treasure would be substantial.

Another possibility would be to establish a special lottery dedicated to support of the Great Lakes agency for the preservation of the Great Lakes ecosystem. The lottery would be administered by the secretariat for the agency and would be offered throughout the basin. Persons from anywhere in the world could buy lottery tickets, but presumably most sales would be in the basin itself. Even though lottery sales are not as secure a source of funding as the power to tax, they would probably be more secure than depending on contributions from member governments.

HOW WOULD THIS STRUCTURE INTEGRATE WITH EXISTING INSTITUTIONS?

Some of those who think carefully about how to manage the Great Lakes believe that we should supplant existing institutions with an entirely new governance structure. Others believe that the present institutions are working reasonably well and represent what is possible to achieve in the present political climate. These people believe that any efforts at improvement should be focused on modest amendments to the powers and functions of present institutions.

Either approach could be used to implement the ideas suggested in this document. Even though this author believes that it would be preferable for a brand new charter to be written and adopted, the option of adapting existing institutions is a viable one and may well be the most effective route for obtaiing meaningful progress. Let us see how the structural changes proposed here could be added on to existing instututions.

The International Joint Commission undoubtedly is the centerpiece of existing institutions for binational management of the Great Lakes. It does not have much formal power but has accrued considerable political power from the quality of its work and the strong public support in the basin for its efforts to protect the Great Lakes ecosystem. It has shown itself to be adaptive and to be able to develop new understandings and new programs as it has faced new challenges. Most observers of public institutions would rate it as being successful, especially considering the weak formal political powers granted to it by the two national governments. The strong support the IJC now enjoys makes it unlikely that the agency will be discarded in favor of the structure proposed here. How could the IJC be changed to take on the functions proposed here?

The IJC could continue to be the centerpiece of the revised institutional structure. It could be the main office and provide a secretariat for the various structures and functions proposed here. It could appoint, or advise in the appointing of, the members of the GLFRB and the Great Lakes Court. Conceivably, it could even be given the conflict resolution functions of the proposed Great Lakes Court.

The IJC already has considered information generation and dissemination capability; the functions proposed here, such as the extension service, could readily be added to the existing structure. The IJC's information system has been hampered to date by lack of funds; if sufficient funding were granted, the IJC would be the most natural agency to house and nurture the Great Lakes Information System.

The requirement for impact assessments, and for their review by the GLFRB, also could be added to the present binational institutional structure. This should be done basinwide; therefore, the requirement to file impact assessments would probably have to be added by a new agreement under the general umbrella of the 1909 Boundary Waters Treaty (as the water quality agreements of 1972, '78 and '87 were added), or by a new treaty. The requirement for impact assessments would have to have the force of law; establishment by treaty would achieve that status. As suggested earlier, the members of the GLFRB could be appointed by the IJC. Proposed members should be screened and nominated by professionals who have given many years of research and thinking to Great Lakes issues. (Several reviewers of this chapter strongly emphasized that they did not wish the members of the GLFRB to be appointed by governments, presumably because they do not have faith that they would be wise appointments.)

The NGOs that would constitute most of the intervention capability already exist and are active. The new treaty, or agreement, that would establish the capabilities discussed above also could explicitly grant NGOs the right to intervene in the process and to demand the preparation of impact statements. This right also should be extended to governments. For example, a government in Ontario should have the right to demand (through legal suit in the Great Lakes Court, if necessary) that a government in Ohio file an impact assessment for a new resort development it is promoting on the south shore of Lake Erie. As mentioned earlier, the IJC could be assigned conflict resolution functions. Alternatively, a new treaty or agreement could set up a Great Lakes court with an administrative and budgetary tie to the IJC. The agreement establishing the court also would specify the kinds of cases the court would hear and who would have standing to sue (bring cases). It also would be important to specify the link between the court and the GLFRB. For example, the GLFRB could use the powers of the court to enforce its demand for the preparation of satisfactory impact statements.

The rationale for using this gradualist approach to getting these new governance capabilities in place has been eloquently stated by George Francis, professor at the University of Waterloo, former member of the Great Lakes Fishery Commission's Board of Technical Experts, and long-time careful observer of Great Lakes issues.

> The conclusion I draw is that our challenge is not so much to come up with a "Grand Design" and a ringing statement of what ought to be, but rather to give life and substance to the basic institutional arrangements we already have, recogniziing they reflect important historical and political realities. While one might be tempted as a matter of strategy to argue that they have failed us to the point the whole business needs to be scrapped and re-designed

along the lines you suggest (this could certainly draw media attention) in my view it is not a strategy with much appeal. Most (of the few) people in Canada who know about the Boundary Waters Treaty for example, don't want to see it tampered with, and rightly or wrongly, not many Canadians would believe we would get a "square deal" from the U.S. on any major rearrangement of binational relationships. (Personal letter to the author; see also his chapter in this volume)

HOW COULD A NEW CHARTER BE ADOPTED?

Now let us examine the prospects and pitfalls of trying to bring about the adoption of a new governance structure for the Great Lakes—a new charter. Some of the pitfalls already have been mentioned: the disbelief among Canadians that they can get a square deal from the United States; the tremendous effort required to get two nations, eight states, and two provinces to move ahead with this initiative; and the general disillusionment with government in North America (in fact, worldwide) that makes many people reluctant to hand any new powers to government. To this list must be added the strong emotional attachment to nation (and to national sovereignty) that characterizes the whole world today; the governance structure proposed here would require the two nations to relinquish some sovereignty. In addition, we should expect that most public officials in the twelve governments would be reluctant to hand over some of their powers to another entity.

These are formidable obstacles indeed. It seems clear that a new charter could only be adopted if there were overwhelming public sentiment in favor of it in both countries. Is there such a sentiment? Beware of simplistic yes or no answers. Skeptics can point out that there are many potentials for further development of binational governance of the Great Lakes in the 1909 Boundary Waters Treaty. If the people really wanted further elaboration of that structure, it already would have happened; the fact that it hasn't happened is good evidence that it can't happen. (This argument assumes that the people are paying attention and have chosen not to press for action, or that they are not paying attention because they don't perceive the problem as serious.) Skeptics also point out that national security and economic concerns outweigh environmental concerns in both countries; in this public mood the preservation of the Great Lakes simply has no chance of getting a prominent place on the public agenda in the two countries.

There is some valid evidence on the other side suggesting that there is strong public sentiment for new initiatives with respect to the Great Lakes. Sample survey studies from a variety of reputable survey research firms over the past fifteen years show a continuing high level of concern for environmental issues, despite the preoccupation with economic woes in our two nations. The attempt by the Reagan administration to deemphasize environmental protection has met with vigorous public reaction that eventually forced James Watt and Anne Gorsuch Burford from office. Survey studies in the Great Lakes Basin show that an extraordinary high level of importance is assigned to the Great Lakes as a treasured resource in the region and an equally high willingness to pay higher prices and taxes to protect the integrity of the lakes. Furthermore, these studies show great displeasure with the inaction of governments in letting the lakes become so severely threatened.

There is quite a lot of other evidence suggesting the emergence of a sense of Great Lakes community. Numerous public conferences have been held throughout the basin in recent years with strong public attendance by people from many walks of life. Television, radio, newstories, and editorial attention to the Great Lakes have significantly increased. A substantial and demanding credit-free course sponsored by Great Lakes Tomorrow and entitled "Decisions for the Great Lakes" has received large and enthusiastic enrollments. One critic challenged me to show that a sense of Great Lakes community is emerging; the survey evidence just mentioned was acknowledged to be interesting and suggestive but not conclusive. For most skeptics the evidence would not be conclusive until a new charter had been adopted. But, is it necessary to wait for conclusive evidence of community before trying to obtain the adoption of a new charter?

The process of gathering support for a new charter would significantly contribute to developing this sense of community. Many people may be ready to accept a stronger structure for their community but simply have not thought about the prospect of a new governance structure for their basin. We cannot really know how much community is there until a proposal such as that described in this document is put forth and thoroughly debated. In 1972, for example, a proposal to join the European Economic Community was debated extensively in both Norway and Denmark; eventually Denmark joined and Norway refused; neither outcome was clear before the public referenda.

It probably would be worthwhile to put forth a proposal such as this and to encourage thorough debate on it, even if it should eventually fail. It would encourage media attention, raise the level of awareness of the people, and build community. It might engender the public support needed to amend the present institutional structure (as discussed in the previous section) even if it did not result in the adoption of a completely new charter. The evidence is overwhelming that our present institutional structure is not providing adequate protection for the Great Lakes ecosystem. The presupposition of unfettered national sovereignty that underlies the 1909 Boundary Waters Treaty (and the IJC) is a significant barrier to wise amendment of that structure. Putting forth a proposal that challenges the wisdom and presumed necessity of defending unfettered national sovereignty may be the most effective way of breaking the mental logjam that interferes with clear thought and planning on these matters.

I have often heard that we must make the Great Lakes number 1 on the national agenda if we hope to get a substantial change of institutional structure. Not only is that unlikely, but it also is not essential. If there is substantial support for a change in governance structure, it can get on the national agenda of the two countries, even if it is not at the top of the list. It would be essential, however, to demonstrate that a new charter has strong support in the Great Lakes Basin.

A possible scenario for the adoption of a new charter for the Great Lakes could go something like this. The idea must first be tightly and clearly articulated. Supporting reasons that consider both pro and con arguments must be clearly stated. Both should be published in a single attractive document and widely circulated. The first and crucial debate would probably occur within the NGOs; unless the great proportion of them would concur and would be willing to push for the new charter, there would be little point in pursuing the matter.

Assuming that most of them would concur, a basinwide conference on the Great Lakes should be called. This conference could be pattered after the Stockholm conference on the world environment that was held under the United Nations auspices in 1972. The proposed new charter should be a major topic for consideration at the conference. If the conference endorses the charter's basic ideas, the next step would be to bring the proposal to the attention of the two national governments. At about the same time the idea should be brought to the state and provincial governments to seek resolutions of endorsement. Assuming that at all of these steps there would be a substantial amount of support for the idea, the final official establishment of the new charter could be achieved through a new binational treaty; another possibility would be a new agreement under the 1909 Boundary Waters Treaty; a third possibility would be to have the governments call a constitutional convention to which delegates from all sectors of the basin would be elected. The proposed constitution resulting from their deliberations could be submitted to the voters of the basin in a referendum.

WHAT MIGHT WE EXPECT FROM THE GOVERNANCE STRUCTURE PROPOSED HERE?

Since the governance structure proposed here is somewhat unusual, it may be difficult to imagine how it would work. It is based on a recognition that there is little likelihood of displacement of present governments, as well as on the recognition that the slight powers proposed to be relinquished here will be given up slowly. Hence, the emphasis here is on a governance structure that learns and that achieves its purposes by education and persuasion. A total system for protection of the integrity of the Great Lakes ecosystem will only be successful to the extent that the people in the basin are persuaded that this protection is a valuable social goal and that they must thoughtfully act in concert to protect their natural treasure. If the people are persuaded of its desirability, the system will work; if they are not persuaded, even a coercive system probably would fail.

The strong points for this governance system are that it is designed to take a systemic view, to take a long-range perspective on the future, and to operate in a learning mode. Provision is made for the generation, dissemination, and assimilation of new information. Protecting the right of intervention helps to ensure that the available information is used and that appropriate practices are instituted. Decisions can be made and work can progress, but there also are manifold opportunities for new information and relearning.

The requirement for impact assessments is the central energizing aspect of the system. Critics will point out that preparing these comprehensive assessments, and waiting for their review, will be likely to slow down work on new projects. We must learn to plan for such delays. We can no longer afford the degradation that results from letting each individual, each firm, or each community do whatever it wishes with our common resource. Projects that are well designed to minimize their impact on the ecosystem and the social system, and that are truly needed, will proceed to fruition. Projects that will not have substantial social benefit and projects that are likely to inflict unacceptable damage to the ecosystem are likely to fail. That is how we would like things to turn out, is it not? The people on the North American continent have sufficient wealth to afford the luxury of taking a long and careful look at new initiatives. We should be designing our governance structure to encourage that, and to encourage all of us to learn.

POSTSCRIPT

It would be premature at this time to draft a proposed new charter in detail. That should follow after the extensive discussion that this chapter, and other writings, hopefully will spark. An important step toward such a charter was taken in February 1985 when the governors of the eight states and premiers of the two Canadian provinces signed the Great Lakes Charter.

Compared to the proposal made in this chapter, the 1985 charter is a very modest document. It deals primarily with possible major diversions of water out of the basin. Each signatory government pledges to give prior notice to all of the other governments and the IJC if it plans to divert out of the basin, or consume, more than five million gallons of water during the average day in any thirty-day period. The consultation processes are agreed to in the charter, and other governments have a right to object. The charter does not have the force of law sufficient to forbid any government to allow a major diversion; but the moral force of strong protests from other governments would be a significant deterrent.

In order to arrive at coordinated management policies, the governments also pledge in the charter to establish a basinwide water resources management program and a research program. The first step would be to set up a Great Lakes data base. The 1985 charter is intended to have a legal impact nationally in forestalling possible action by the U.S. Congress to establish and fund a gigantic engineering project that would divert water from the Great Lakes Basin to recharge the swiftly depleting Ogallala Aquifer that underlies the high plains region of the United States.

The draft preamble that follows is intended for the charter discussed in this paper. It is my attempt to capture in words our sense of community here in the Great Lakes Basin, and it proclaims the values we would wish to preserve by adopting a new charter.

A CHARTER FOR THE GREAT LAKES COMMUNITY

Preamble

We the people living in the drainage basin making up the five Great Lakes and the St. Lawrence River acknowledge our intimate and inseparable connection to the ecosystem of the basin from which we draw our sustenance. From this natural treasure we draw our water, on its bordering lands we grow our food, and in its waters we fish for food and recreation. It provides plentiful sites for recreation, it situates our homes and places of work, it allows us to transport ourselves and our goods, it nourishes other species of plants and animals, it furnishes us with energy, and it receives our wastes.

Since this ecosystem serves so many of our needs, we are resolved to protect its integrity. We pledge to strive in all the ways we use it to leave it as close to the way that nature made it (before human intervention) as possible. In those respects in which human activity has already degraded it away from nature's cleanliness, balance, and beauty, we pledge sustained cooperative effort to restore it to its natural integrity. Since the people living in this basin, and sharing this natural treasure, are scattered across eight states and two provinces in both the United States and Canada, we must make special provision for its governance and nurturance. This charter pledges our adherence to the goal of maintaining a clean, beautiful, and delicately balanced Great Lakes ecosystem and establishes governmental procedures to help us achieve that objective. The transcendent importance of that goal leads us to transcend traditional allegiances to province, state, and nation and to work cooperatively as one people to protect our great natural treasure.

NOTES

1. See the article by Michael J. Donahue, "Institutional Arrangements for Great Lakes Management," in this volume.

2. Don Munton is one of the more prominent scholars of Canadian–American binational institutions holding this view; see his "Paradoxes and Prospects," ch. 4, in Robert Spencer, John Kirton, and Richard Nossal, eds., *The International Joint Commission Seventy Years On,* Toronto, Best Printing Co. 1981, 60–97. See also his "Great Lakes Water Quality: A Study in Environmental Politics and Diplomacy," in O. P. Dwivedi, ed., *Resources and the Environment,* Toronto, McClelland and Stewart, 1980, 153–178.

3. U.S. General Accounting Office (GAO) report to the Secretary of State, *International Joint Commission Water Quality Activities Need Greater U.S. Government Support and Involvement,* June, 1982; also GAO report to Congress, *A More Comprehensive Approach is Needed to Clean up the Great Lakes,* May, 1982.

4. EIA literature is voluminous; social impact literature is rarer; see Kurt Finsterbusch and C. P. Wolf, eds. *Methodology of Social Impact Assessment,* Stroudsburg, PA, Dowden, Hutchinson & Ross, 1977, also Kurt Finsterbusch, "State of the Art in Social Impact Assessment in the United States," paper delivered at the 10th World Congress of Sociology, Mexico City, 1982.

CHAPTER 5. REMEDIATION AND REHABILITATION OF THE GREAT LAKES

To assess effectively the prospects of applying ecosystem science to management for the lakes, it is useful to know what has been accomplished toward this objective and what is now being undertaken. This chapter is, in effect, a status report on implementation of the ecosystem approach and an indication of where remedial action is needed to achieve a rehabilitation of the lakes. Neither Canada nor the United States receives high marks on this report card. The chapter indicates where specific action must occur to bring the ecosystem concept from a generalized idea to an itemized list of things that must be done in order to achieve the goals of the 1978 water quality agreement. It references major scientific studies that provide an information base for public policy and administration.

HENRY A. REGIER
WITH THE ASSISTANCE OF LEE BOTTS
AND JOHN E. GANNON

5

REMEDIATION AND REHABILITATION OF THE GREAT LAKES

In the 1978 Great Lakes Water Quality Agreement, Canada and the United States committed themselves to an ecosystem approach with respect to Great Lakes water quality issues. Whether or not this commitment was implicitly related to general system theory, the latter does provide a context in which the concept of an ecosystem approach may be addressed. Rapoport's (1986) two-dimensional perspective on general system theory may be helpful here. One dimension is the analytic-holistic contrast (related to the nature of knowledge), and the other is the descriptive-normative contrast (related to values).

Analysis provides understanding of a phenomenon by examining the structures and processes of its internal constituent parts. Holistic understanding is achieved by comprehending the whole phenomenon. For analysis, proper methodology is usually specified carefully, as in conventional science. For holistic understanding, the approach to an understanding of the whole phenomenon may be specified carefully. The descriptive-normative contrast relates to whether the purpose of study is to achieve a value-free understanding of what exists or to achieve some practical valued purpose. The two dimensions may be seen as a sophisticated version of internal-versus-external examination and basic-versus-applied study.

Rapoport (1986) has shown how different schools within each area of economics, sociology, psychology, and biology are biased toward different edges of this two-dimensional matrix of general system-theory (see References). Regier (1980) has provided a compatible classification for different schools within ecology. For Rapoport the challenge for this theory is to integrate the analytic (using rigorous methods) and the holistic (using intuitive approaches), together with the descriptive (objectively disinterested) and the normative (practical and value oriented).

How does all of this relate to the 1978 water quality agreement? Clearly the predominant emphasis within the text of the agreement is toward the analytical and the practical. Since 1978, most of the efforts undertaken ostensibly to satisfy the commitment to an ecosystem approach have involved more comprehensive analysis of the internal workings of Great Lakes ecosystems and more comprehensive and detailed specifications of the practical purposes to be achieved by the agreement. These have been focused in the analytical-normative cell of Rapoport's 2 x 2 matrix of emphases. Two other cells have received some attention: the analytical-descriptive (as in conventional, basic scientific research) and the intuitive-normative (as in discussions of rights of different ecosystem entitites as affecting practical actions). The fourth cell, the intuitive-descriptive, has received comparatively little attention within the networks of experts involved with the 1978 agreement.

Sibley (1986) has proposed a project to achieve the following quote from Ronald Reagan: "We seek to restore the family, the neighborhood, the community, and the workplace as vital alternatives in our national life to ever-expanding federal power." Sibley expects the disciplines of art and the humanities to be the best tools to achieve this restoration, and not the conventional sciences, which are now largely programmed to serve centralized federal power. Sibley's proposal, and somewhat similar initiatives by the bioregionalists (Berg 1986), may help to stimulate broader interest in Rapoport's fourth cell, the intuitive-descriptive focus. This may be seen as a necessary precondition to the mature development of the ecosystem approach with respect to the Great Lakes. Efforts to interest children in Great Lakes issues through art, as in the IJC's 1983 biennial meeting in Indianapolis, may be a step in this direction.

In this paper I consider further the implications of an ecosystem approach to the Great Lakes from a perspective that I take to be generally consistent with that of general system theory as elaborated by Rapoport (1986). In a sense this paper is a sequel to an earlier paper by Caldwell (1969).

CONVENTIONAL EXPLOITIVE DEVELOPMENT

For the past two centuries a dominant process within our human culture, of the Great Lakes Basin and elsewhere, has been conventional exploitive development, which involves progressive commercialization, industrialization, urbanization, and "technization" (Ellul 1985). Here some of this development's general adverse consequences to the natural features of the basin ecosystem will be emphasized. That exploitive development has had desirable consequences for many humans needs no emphasis.

Exploitive development has always operated from a hierarchy of centers of organization created by the leading *developers* to suit their purposes. It was arranged that resources should flow toward these centers, in what may be termed *"contributary streams."* The wastes that resulted from the processing and consumption of these resources emanated from the centers in *"distributary streams."* There were also distributary streams with respect to commerical goods, but these streams were less massive and less disruptive ecologically than the waste distributaries. The commerical goods distribuaries will be ignored here to keep the sketch simple.

To participate as an entrepreneur with respect to a resource contributary stream has generally been more rewarding than to do so with respect to a waste distributary stream. Organized crime has entered the latter field, in part because our culture has not developed adequate institutional arrangements to deal with the necessity to offload wastes. It is as though we have sought to deny the reality of waste. The ecosystem approach implies the need to recognize that waste is real and not necessarily all bad.

The contributary streams were fed resources through a process of *progressive high-grading* (Regier and Baskerville 1986). The highest-quality resources nearest a development center were harvested in a first wave. The next wave involved prime-quality resources at an intermediate distance as well as second-quality resources from nearby. The succeeding wave involved prime-quality resources from far away, second-quality resources from an intermediate distance, and third-quality resources from nearby. For the term *resources* we may insert forest trees, fish, furbearers, waterfowl, water, minerals, and soil. Soil was seldom transported physically to the development centers, but the crops that entered the contributary streams were often grown in such a way as to degrade or mine the soil.

There were few legal or cultural impediments to this progressive high-grading. The worst types of abuses with this harvesting were eventually forbidden, but relatively little was done to develop husbandry practices for sustainable production of high-quality resources. The overall effect of this progressive hygrading was the progressive *degrading* of the natural processes that generated the quality resources. Incidentally, the natural processes that generated the high-value resources in the first place involve *natural upgrading* in the sense of Odum (1983).

The distributary streams that fanned out from the development centers carried wastes from commerce, industry, and urban human consumers. The organization of the distributary streams has always been more primitive that that of the contributary streams. Initially the wastes were simply off-loaded within meters of where they were produced. Some wastes were burnt, and some of the transformed wastes were then vented into the atmosphere to be transported off the site. Some wastes were piped to the nearest stream or lakeshore, to be hidden there or carried away. Some were carted to a convenient ravine or wetland, incidentally to create new developable flatland.

As the nearby environment became excessively fouled, the wastes were diluted with water or air, and some were distributed to locales at an intermediate distance. Eventually the distributary streams extended outward to the outer sources of the contributary streams, with the help of long-range transport by natural hydrological and atmospheric currents. The wastes came to pollute the resources in a variety of ways so as to exacerbate the degrading effects of progressive high-grading by crippling the processes of natural upgrading.

Technology was mobilized to mitigate both types of adverse effects, those due to harvesting and those due to pollution, through *technological upgrading* of the abundant low-quality resources that remained after high-grading. Inevitably technological upgrading contributed its own wastes.

Ways were also found to compensate for some of the more polluted features of resources, such as by adding biocides to drinking water or by innoculating humans against diseases transmitted by pollution. Technological compensation became so extreme that at the very focus of development centers very little life other than human beings could be found. Amidst the skyscrapers, everything outdoors consisted of concrete, glass, and steel. The further this process progressed in the metropolis, the greater the degrading effects on the hinterland through the disruptive influences of the contributary and distributary streams. The effects of the two streams interacted synergistically in many locales of the hinterland.

ECOSYSTEM DEGRADATION

With respect to local degradation, consider a small ecosystem—comprising a stream, a wetland, a bay, and the near-shore part of a lake—situated within an urbanized region in the Great Lakes Basin. This ecosystem will have been influenced progressively by all the following *stresses* (modified from Francis et al. 1985):

> *Natural background processes:* battering storms; rains and floods; water level cycles; spells of hot or cold weather; forest and marsh fires; disease outbreaks; local bluff erosion
>
> *Harvesting of renewable resources:* fishing, whether commercial, angler, or by party boat; hunting for ungulates, upland birds, or waterfowl; trapping for fur bearers; withdrawal of water for consumption
>
> *Loading by substances and heat energy:* inert solids and suspensions of sand and clay; organics that putrify and remove oxygen; nutrient materials that fertilize plants and plankton; poisons that kill organisms; contaminants that cripple the young and cause tumors in older organisms; heat that raises the temperature of the water
>
> *Restructuring the morphometric form of water bodies:* filling in deeper parts with sediments; damming streams; modifying the shoreline by bulkheading, infilling, etc.; dredging to deepen parts of the basin; stirring up bottom by boating and shipping; erosion that makes streams wider and shallower
>
> *Introduction of nonnative organisms:* intentional stocking of preferred organisms, which may nevertheless become pests; accidental invasion through canals; accidental introduction through bilge water, private aquaria, anglers' bait buckets

Cultural *stress* means some activity, influence, or force caused by humans that intereferes with the normal, natural functioning of an ecosystem. Some of these stresses relate to resource extraction, some to waste loading, some to urban construction initiatives that physically modify some ecosystemic structures, and some to direct human contact.

The ecological consequences of the action of these development stresses may be summarized as follows (modified from Francis et al. 1985):

- The major stresses, or effects of human uses, often act synergistically to exacerbate each other's adverse effects. They seldom act antagonistically to cancel out adverse effects.

- The stresses alter the fish association from one that is dominated by large fish usually associated with larger streams, the lake bottom, and the lake edge to one characterized by small, midwater species. A similar change happens with respect to vegetation: firmly rooted aquatic plants near the shore originally are replaced by dense suspensions of open-water planktonic algae or filamentous algae in shallow areas. In addition, the association of relatively large invertebrates such as mussels and crayfish living directly on bottom substrates is supplanted by an association characterized by small burrowing insects and worms such as midge larvae and sludge worms.

- With the above changes comes an increased variability from year to year in the abundance of particular species, and in particular in landings of different fish species by anglers and commercial fishermen.

- The shift from large organisms associated with the bottom to small organisms in the bottom and in midwater is not accompanied by a great increase in the total biomass of living material, at least not of the valued species.

- Market and sport value per unit of biomass is generally much lower with small midwater fish species than with large bottom species, and processing costs are higher. Similarly, the aesthetic value of the rooted plants near shore with the associated animals is higher than a pea-soup-like mixture of suspended algae or swaths of decaying filamentous algae.

- The effect on fisheries is that labor-intensive specialized fisheries (sport and commerical) tend to disappear, but highly mechanized, capital-intensive enterprises may persist if the combined stresses do not become excessive and if the fish are not so contaminated as to become a health threat for those who would eat them. Beyond that, people generally find such degraded systems offensive and quite literally turn their backs to them.

The *general degradation syndrome* sketched above is likely to be most severe where a variety of cultural stresses act and interact within an ecosystem. The interactions among effects of different stresses are usually not such as to cancel each others effects—as when both acids and bases are loaded into a locale in just the right proportions to neutralize each other. Usually the interactions are such as to exacerbate each others' adverse effects—they are synergistic. But this is not always the case; for example, simple acidification may lead to ecosystemic effects different from those depicted in the characterization of the general degradation syndrome given above.

The occurrence of a general degradation syndrome within a degraded ecosystem complicates the task of identifying the main cause of the degradation. Different combinations of various stresses can cause such a syndrome; even individual stresses may do so if sufficiently intense (Rapport, Regier and Hutchinson 1985). As with the diagnosis of the causes of human maladies, identification of the causes of ecosystem degradation from an examination of only the effects or symptoms can be difficult (Regier et al. 1988). Usually some of the causative stresses are themselves readily apparent from direct observation, but some may not be obvious.

The normal systemic maturation of natural ecosystems unstressed by humans and the rejuvenating role of natural perturbations are coming to be well understood. Some of the features of systemic degradation due to massive interventions by careless humans are increasingly being described in general terms, as in a context analogous to that of the organism as system according to Bertalanffy (Davidson 1983). Superficially some general features of most forms of ecosystemic degradation due to humans resemble some features of ecosystemic rejuvenation due to natural perturbations. But a deeper examination of degradation shows that system crippling or incapacitation is usually involved, with effects that are not at all characteristic of natural rejuvenation (Rapport and Regier 1988).

It is important not to draw false analogies, as between cultural degradation and natural rejuvenation. The premature aging or death of Lake Erie may or may not involve a false analogy between the character of a degraded lake ecosystem and that of a senescent or moribund human. In both cases the system is about to be transformed to a state that exhibits relatively more of the small decomposer organisms than it did in its natural or healthy state. If the great abundance of these organisms is taken as a sufficient indicator of system aging or death, then the existence of a rough analogy may be accepted. But if death implies a complete and irreversible transformation of the "essence" of the system, then the analogy has never been appropriate for Lake Erie, through which waters flow from the Upper Lakes to Lake Ontario. In particular, the organismic analogy of ecosystemic enrichment or eutrophication may better be obesity (due to overfeeding) rather than aging or death due to sensescence. It is only under special circumstances that the physical obliteration of a lake (its death) is accompanied by enrichment of the type associated with conventional eutrophication.

People generally find degraded ecosystems repulsive. They have low economic value in that they do not produce highly valued resources. The values of properties near degraded locales are also depressed because of aesthetic and safety considerations. With intense degradation, people who live nearby may condone the obliteration, or "death," of an ecosystem for the purpose of some form of conventional exploitive development that is less objectionable. So it may be to the short-term interest of development that ecosystems become degraded in locales where new conventional development is being planned. Certainly such degradation is commonplace in locales slated for development.

SLUMIFICATION AND REMEDIATION

In the Great Lakes Basin, commercialization, industrialization, and urbanization operated largely without cultural restraints until midway through the twentieth century. The regional effects of conventional exploitive development became apparent to informed observers, though perhaps not to the developers. The following sketch is modified from Regier (1986).

In the 1950s, the southerly third of the basin was degrading rapidly into a vast ecological slum. Human sewage received little or no treatment before being dumped into rivers and lakes, and poliomyelitis, spread through contact with the polluted waters, was epidemic. Industries were loading increasing amounts of wastes that were increasingly more hazardous into the air, water, and land with relatively little meddling from government.

Farmers had come to use inexpensive persistent pesticides such as DDT with little awareness of consequences except to the pests being sprayed. Fisheries scientists were noting reduced reproductive success of lake trout in nearby waters, which they attributed to DDT. Fish-eating eagles and ospreys were becoming less abundant because pesticides interfered with reproduction.

These were the years of atmospheric testing of nuclear weapons. Milk contaminated with Strontium 90 was perceived as a risk to infants in particular. This risk presaged other threats, especially to infants, of chemicals that pose some threats similar to those of radioactivity, such as persistent pesticides and chemical contaminants.

Nonbiodegradable synthetic detergents were providing copious long-lasting suds in the washing machines, in sewage treatment plants (where such existed), and where the sewers emptied into the river. Sometimes waves of suds frothed out of sewer manholes to blanket residential streets.

Debased wetlands were being filled with waste soil and rubble that was often polluted. Transportation interests encountered little opposition to placement of major roads next to the shore, thus blocking access to the lakes—a process that had begun decades earlier with the location of railroads and heavy industry along the waterfront. Urban developers, road builders, and farmers cared little about soil, and much eroded away into the streams and bays. Urban streams became ugly and obnoxious to the point that their burial underground was accepted as desirable progress.

The lower reaches of the rivers, the harbors, the near-shore waters of the lakes, and the beaches had all become offensive, and people had turned their backs to these waters. Lake Erie, in particular, was undergoing a comprehensive transformation due to synergism among a number of stresses. A multitude of unpleasant organisms thrived in its depths; the most desirable fish species disappeared from the lake.

The sea lamprey, to which lake trout were particularly vulnerable, had used ship canals and perhaps anglers' bait buckets to reach the farthest end of Lake Superior. Synthetic fibres greatly increased the effectiveness of fishing gear, leading to severe overfishing. Fisherman anger was aroused that was vented destructively, mostly on other fishermen.

Also in about 1950 it became apparent that the older parts, the cores, of the basin's cities were rotting. Their towers of business and commerce were ringed by urban slums. The large concentrations of industry in the suburbs were surrounded by the terrestrial version of ecological slums. Farms in areas only marginally suited to farming were being abandoned and were reverting to scrubby wilderness, of a sort. Farms near cities were being bought by speculators and left to grow weeds. Useless holes in the ground, from which gravel and sand had been removed, were being filled with garbage and with chemical wastes of unknown composition. Macro developers were dreaming of a megalopolis extending from Madison and Milwaukee to Montreal and Albany.

A long period of decline ran its course, especially in the American Great Lakes states. It had ecological, social, and economic dimensions. The *Pollution Belt,* the *Slum Belt,* the *Rust Belt*—these terms came to have some relevance to ecological, urban, and industrial aspects of the southern third of the basin. People and investors began to look elsewhere, for instance, to the Sun Belt, for a good life and for opportunities.

In the middle third of the basin the degradation was less intense and less pervasive, and was limited mostly to smaller locales. In the northerly third, it was even less apparent except with respect to fish and fisheries and near mines and pulp mills. All but a few of the dozens of distinct stocks of lake trout of the upper lakes were extinguished during the 1950s under the impact of the parasitic sea lamprey and a technologically innovative commercial fishery that raced the sea lamprey for the remaining lake trout.

There is a growing consensus among expert observers that the Great Lakes Basin is now recovering ecologically, and perhaps socially and commercially as well. If so, when did it reach its lowest point of degradation? An answer may depend on one's more specific concerns. With respect to sea lamprey predation and overfishing, the low point may have occurred about 1960. The highest contamination with persistent pesticides such as DDT probably came in the latter 1960s. Phosphate enrichment peaked in the 1970s. Deposition from the atmosphere of acids and contaminants from combustion may peak in the latter 1980s. Currently anglers who fish salmon that are somewhat contaminated are pleased with the recovery of the lakes; meanwhile, people who are concerned about the effects of contaminants on the health of infants and of future generations are far from happy.

The following is a kind of report card on efforts to remediate some of the worst features of conventional exploitive development in the basin. As of 1987 the degree of success has been quite limited. Different issues are of very different degrees of importance to different interests in society.

Good Progress in the Past

- Reduced dumping of trash and of materials with high biological oxygen demand into streams, bays, and lakes
- Reduction of transmission of diseases such as cholera and typhoid fever through human wastes by sewage treatment and water purification
- Reduction of waters diverted to flush Chicago's wastes out of the basin
- Controls on flows through hydroelectric power plants

- Outlawing the most destructive fishing practices, whether by anglers or commercial fishermen
- Controls on overkill of migratory birds and waterfowl
- Reduced use and bans of certain persistent pesticides, such as DDT, aldrin, and dieldrin.
- Controls on loadings of mine tailings
- Restricting discharge of wastewater from ships and controls on dumping of other refuse from vessels
- Controls on the disposal of contaminated dredge material from harbors and navigation channels
- Controls on direct discharge of industrial waste into water bodies
- Controls on emissions of acutely toxic substances such as arsenic and mercury
- Less destructive practices in mining and dredging of sand and gravel
- Some correction of destructive channelization practices
- Reduction of phosphorus loadings through detergent bans and more efficient sewage treatment plants
- Use of low-till agricultural practices in areas subject to erosion
- Reduction of loadings into sewers of industrial chemicals even of only moderate toxicity
- Controls on the commerce and use of some contaminants, such as PCBs
- Coping with small to moderate catastrophes by coordinated emergency response organizations
- Controls on excessive fishing even by acceptable methods
- Integrated management of sea lamprey with less reliance on solely chemical controls
- Restrictions on the willful introduction of exotic species
- Programs to reduce transmission of fish diseases through fish hatcheries

- Stocking of large piscivorous salmonines to control small exotic fish that foul beaches and exacerbate eutrophication
- Controls on the intense use of natural parks by recreationists
- Siting of nuclear power plants

Relatively Poor Progress in Recent Years

- Identification of sources of atmospheric inputs, and quantification of leaching and runoff of contaminants such as dioxin from landfill and diffuse sources
- Coping with atmospheric pollutants, such as acid rain and polynuclear aromatic hydrocarbons, at the sources
- Putting waste heat loading by electric utilities to good ecological use
- Reducing entrainment and impingement of organisms by water intakes
- Controls on erosion at urban developments and construction sites
- Controls of storm water runoff and combined sewer overflows in urban areas
- Prevention of inappropriate shoreline development
- Controls on eutrophication through nutrients from diffuse sources such as feedlots
- Reduction in air pollution in the Sarnia—Port Huron area
- Prevention of destruction of wetlands and restoration of degraded wetlands
- Reestablishment of naturally reproducing stocks of native salmonines other than in Lake Superior
- Prevention of synergistic interactions of adverse ecological impacts of the many human uses and abuses, especially in "areas of concern"
- Controls on local water diversions at Sault Ste. Marie Rapids

to preserve key fish habitats, though a small remnant may be preserved
- Reduction of gross inputs of industrial and municipal wastes into the St. Lawrence River in Quebec
- Inadequacy in distinguishing between historical, in-place pollutants and active sources in rivers and harbors
- Mitigation of in-place pollutant problems in river and harbor sediments

Continuing and New Fears: Potential Future Problems

- Accidents in nuclear-powered electric generating facilities
- Major accidents with ships, trains, and trucks transporting hazardous substances in the basin
- Winter navigation in narrow and shallow connecting waters
- Massive diversions of water into and out of the basin
- Increased consumptive use of water by cooling towers and irrigation
- Increased mineral and oil extraction from under the lakes
- Persistance and unknown effects of dioxins and other contaminants on aquatic life
- Cumulative health effects through inhalation and ingestion of contaminants over an extended period of time on mammals, including man
- Long-range atmospheric transport of toxic contaminants, including DDT and toxaphene, into the Great Lakes Basin
- Long-term effects from runoff of deicing salts into the Great Lakes on the chemical balance of ions
- Long-term contamination of groundwater aquifers most everywhere now and subsequent seepage into the Great Lakes
- Increasing accumulation in sediment and biota of polynuclear aromatic hydrocarbons
- Intense synergistic interactions of persistent and toxic contaminants in polluted sediments

- Continued invasions by nonnative species by way of ship canals, bilge water, and ill-advised introductions
- Warming of the climate through the "greenhouse effect" and its terrestrial and aquatic consequences
- Rising water levels in the lakes to record highs, for unknown reasons

A SET OF GOALS FOR AN ECOSYSTEM APPROACH

Vallentyne (1986) has long been admonishing us to develop "homelike" relationships to the Great Lakes Basin rather than to merely treat it as a "house." Table 1 is an attempt to explain the ecosystem approach as Vallentyne might view it (see also Christie et al. 1986).

The first three objectives have been enunciated for decades with respect to water quality, broadly defined in various political platforms, legislative acts, and so forth. They have not yet been realized in many waters, such as in the forty-two areas of concern (GLWQA 1985). The last three have, implicitly and imperfectly, guided binational efforts in the Great Lakes Fishery Commission. Nevertheless, it is now time to take the second set of three objectives more seriously, in the context of an ecosystem approach. Implementation of the 1978 Agreement, as revised in 1987, should deal more explicitly with all six, as an interactive set.

Sustainable as a policy objective has been developed in the World Conservation Strategy (IUCN 1980). In a practical sense, it means more than *maximum sustainable yield,* as in conventional, Alpha-type fisheries science. For example, it means husbandry of a desirable natural resource system as well as husbandry of the most preferred species on a species-by-species basis. The latter approach, dominant in recent decades, has not worked in practice in any case. Berg (1986) argues: "Restore natural systems, satisfy basic human needs and develop support for individuals: those are the most fundamental requirements for sustainability and should be the goals of watershed-scaled bioregional politics."

Enjoyable here refers to aesthetic and naturalistic values in an ecosystem: it means the enjoyment of the aquatic ecosystem by lcoal humans, the attraction of tourists and anglers, and the enhancement of the value of compatible economic developments near the shores

Table 1: A schema to illustrate how our perspectives on the Great Lakes Basin must be "deepened" to implement an "ecosystem approach".

Political objectives	Systemic focus	Vallentyne's analogy	Remediation/ Rehabilitation
Swimmable	Human health in an epidemiological context	▲ Environment as House	▲ Alpha, E
Drinkable			
Fishable	Biota and resource health in an economic context	▲ Ecosystem as Home	▲ Beta
Sustainable			
Enjoyable	Cultural health in a man-nature ecosystemic sense	▲ Species as Resources	▲ Alpha, R
Equitable			

of those waters. For all three purposes, the aesthetic features are very important.

Equitable relates to interpersonal, intergenerational, interjurisdictional, and interspecies relationships. The tacit assumption that externalizing the undesirable consequences of some enterprise is broadly acceptable is now fully obsolete. The myriads of social, economic, and ecological connections in our man-nature ecosystem ensure that the bad consequences of abuses often fall on the innocent. The benefits and disbenefits of ecosystemic abuses fall very inequitably on some persons, some generations, some jurisdictions, and some species. It is impossible to achieve "homelike" relationships where such inequities prevail. It has long been realized that there is no such thing as a free lunch; we now know that there is no such thing as a free off-loading of the wastes from that lunch.

As a set, the six objectives of table 1 may be seen as one version of a purpose enunciated for the U.S. National Environmental Policy Act of 1969, that is, "to assure for all Americans safe, healthful, productive and aesthetically and culturally pleasing surroundings." One need only recognize that current multifarius inequities are not "culturally pleasing" to complete the parallelism. And, of course, the set of objectives must be seen to be applicable to more than only Americans.

ECOSYSTEM STRATEGIES

The term *remediate* has come to be widely used within the agencies, such as the International Joint Commission, with responsibilities for the 1978 Great Lakes Water Quality Agreement. Presumably it derives from *remedy,* with *remediate* meaning to rectify or make good. Alternatively it could be interpreted as deriving from *mediate,* in which case *remediate* might mean to reconnect two parties for the purpose of reconciling them; here the parties might be humans and the rest of nature.

The term *rehabilitate* has been used within fisheries circles in the Great Lakes, as in the Great Lakes Fishery Commission. It might be taken to derive from *habilitate* to connote refurnishing with working capital in the sense of the stocks of fish as renewable resources. Generally, *rehabilitate* is interpreted more broadly to encompass concepts such as restoring, preserving, mitigating, and remediating (Regier et al. 1988).

Table 2. A Table of Contrasts Showing a Possible Transition in the Consensus View of What Remediation/Rehabilitation Means

	Alpha	*Beta*
Policy goals	Six goals (Table 1) stated narrowly and separately	Six goals (Table 1) related to systemic interactions of different uses/abuses
Policy objectives	Multiple use, large quantities of natural "services"	Sensitive use, high qualities of ecosystem features
Overall strategy	Simple optimization, down-play risks	Satisficing, minimize risks
Focus of formal studies	Physical effects downstream and downwind of original causes, exploitation processes of separate stocks	Original causes in the context of regional man-nature system, synergisms and antagonisms among effects
Bias of mix of disciplines*	Technocentric, with conventional experts	Ecocentric, together with affected public
Locus of practical intervention	Proximal to site of ecological degradation or bad fishing practices	At the origin of the degrading influences and harvesting activities
Type of intervention	Reduce worst abuses, partially	Reduce all abuses, more fully
Re ecosystem recovery	May occur spontaneously, gradually	Rapid recovery is fostered, directly
Means of environmental management	Structures of concrete, steel and glass	Husbandry of water, soil and biota
J.R. Vallentyne's perspective	Environment as house, species as resources	Ecosystem as home

* See Pepper (1984) for further discussion.

Different people use these terms in somewhat different ways, and there is an overlap in the spectrum of connotations now current. A shift in the centers of gravity of these ranges of connotation appears to be underway: for remediation and rehabilitation as a combined spectrum, the shift appears to be from an alpha toward a beta gestalt; see table 2.

An ecosystem approach may be structured hierarchically into nested ecosystems of increasing scale: the local, as in the case of the *areas of concern* (IJC/WQB 1985) with nearby terrestrial areas; the individual lake or connecting channel; the Great Lakes Basin (GLB); and the Great Lakes and St. Lawrence Valley, (GL/SLV), including the marine Gulf of St. Lawrence.

Alpha-type remediation and rehabilitation have been most thoroughly developed at the level of a lake but there is progress currently underway with connecting channels and local areas of concern. Not much conceptual, scientific, or practical progress is apparent with the ecosystems of larger scale, that is, with GLB and GL/SLV. Acid rain and toxic fallout due to long-range atmospheric transport of pollutants from the combustion of fossil fuels may be comprehended at the larger scale. Hydrological and biotic transport of contaminants downstream from their sources, as from the shores of the Niagara River to the Gulf of St. Lawrence, are phenomena of larger scale. This is also the case with the intermedia cycling of contaminants such as volatile PCBs—from land to water to air and back again.

The transition from an alpha to a beta gestalt on man-nature interactions may be furthest along with respect to local ecosystems (Lerner 1986). Informal networks of knowledgeable and committed people now exist to make notable progress with the various lakes and connecting channels (Francis 1986). At the GLB and GL/SLV scales, the beta gestalt is, as yet, only a hope.

The man-nature ecosystem of the Great Lakes and St. Lawrence Value is now well along in the transition from a century of conventional exploitive development to something else. But what that something else will be is not clear. The first major step in the transition has involved expenses of many billions of dollars for the purposes of alpha-type remediation and rehabilitation. Gradually alpha-type programs are being complemented by those of a beta type. Will the latter type of ecosystem approach eventually become dominant?

We are still some generations away from resolving the disastrous practices and legacies of exploitive development. Two or three decades may elapse before the contaminants now already in the ecosystem become inactivated or buried so that attendant risks fall to low levels. Perhaps more time will be required to bring the airbone acids and contaminants from combustion to low levels. That still leaves the radiatively active or greenhouse gases to be reduced, which may require a massive shift to energy sources other than the carbon-based fossil fuels.

We note progress in the realization of an ecosystem approach at the local level as well as with individual lakes and connecting channels. This is occurring at a time when basin-level, regional, and biospheric effects of conventional exploitive development are still continuing to expand and intensify. Will the more local progress of recent decades be overridden by the more global degrading influences? The answer is unknown—the question itself has hardly been considered.

ACKNOWLEDGEMENTS

Lee Botts and John Gannon collaborated in developing the report card on page 178. Financial support from the Donner Canadian Foundation is acknowledged with appreciation.

REFERENCES

Berg, P. 1986. "Growing a Life-Place Politics" *Raise the Stakes: The Planet Drum Review* (San Francisco) No. 11: 9-12.

Caldwell, L. K. 1969. "Health and homeostasis as Social Concepts: An Exploratory Essay," pp. 206-223. In G. M. Woodwell and H. H. Smith (eds), *Diversity and Stability in Ecological Systems*. Brookhaven Symposia in Biology No. 22, Brookhaven National Laboratory, Brookhaven, N.Y.

Christie, W. J., M. Becker, J. W. Cowden, and J. R. Vallentyne. 1986. "Managing the Great Lakes as a Home." *Journal of Great Lakes Research* 12: 2-17.

Davidson, M. 1983. *Uncommon Sense: The Life and Thought of Ludwig von Bertalanffy (1901-1972), Father of General Systems Theory.* J. P. Tarcher, Los Angeles. 247 pp.

Ellul, J. 1985. Foreword, pp. ix-xix. In W. H. Vanderburg, *The Growth of Minds and Cultures: A Unified Theory of the Structure of Human Experience.* University of Toronto Press, Toronto, 334 pp.

Francis, G. R. 1986. "Great Lakes Governance and the Ecosystem Approach: Where Next?" *Alternatives* 13(3):61-70, Chapter 9, this volume.

Francis, G. R., A. P. Grima, H. A. Regier, and T. H. Whillans. 1985. *A Prospectus for the Management of the Long Point Ecosystem.* Great

Lakes Fishery Commission, Ann Arbor, Mich., Technical Report 43. 109 pp.

Holling, C. S. 1986. "The Resilience of Terrestrial Ecosystems: Local Surprise and Global Change," pp. 292-317 in W. C. Clark and R. E. Munn Eds., *Sustainable Development of the Biosphere* Cambridge University Press, Cambridge, 491 pp.

IJC/WQB. 1985. *1985 Report on Great Lakes Water Quality.* Water Quality Board of the International Joint Commission, Windsor, Ont. 212 pp.

IUCN. 1980. *World Conservation Strategy.* Internat. Union Conservation of Nature and Nat. Resources, Morges, Switzerland.

Lerner, S. C. 1986. "Environmental Constituency-Building: Local Initiatives and Volunteer Stewardship." *Alternatives* 13(3): 55-60.

NRC/RCS. 1985. *The Great Lakes Water Quality Agreement: An Evolving Instrument for Ecosystem Management.* U.S. National Research Council and the Royal Society of Canada. National Academy Press, Washington. 224 pp.

Odum, H. T. 1983. *Systems Ecology: An Introduction.* John Wiley and Sons, New York. 644 pp.

Pepper, D. 1984. *The Roots of Modern Environmentalism.* Croom Helm, London. 246 pp.

Rapoport, A. 1986. *General System Theory: Essential Concepts and Applications.* Abacus Press, Tunbridge Wells, U.K. 270 pp. See Table 1-1 and 1-2, pp. 5-7 for referenced illustration.

Rapport, D. J., and H. A. Regier. 1988. "Disturbance and Stress Effects on Ecological Systems." In B. C. Patten (Ed.), *Progress in Systems Ecology,* Vol. 2 (in press).

Rapport, D. J., H. A. Regier, and T. C. Hutchinson. 1985. "Ecosystem Behavior under Stress." *American Naturalist* 125: 617-640.

Regier, H. A. 1980. "The Culture of Ecology." *INTECOL Bull.,* 1980 (7/8). pp. 25-29.

―――. 1986. "Progress with Remediation, Rehabilitation and the Ecosystem Approach." *Alternatives* 13(3): 45-54.

Regier, H. A., and G. L. Baskerville. 1986. "Sustainable Redevelopment of Regional Ecosystems Degraded by Exploitive Development," pp. 75-101. In W. C. Clark and R. E. Munn (eds.), *Sustainable Development of the Biosphere.* Cambridge Univ. Press, Cambridge. 491 pp.

Regier, H. A., R. L. Welcomme, R. J. Steedman, and H. F. Francis. 1988. "Rehabilitaton of Degraded River Ecosystems." *Canadian Journal of Fisheries and Aquatic Sciences* (in press).

Sibley, G. 1986. "Rediscovering the Lost Vision." *MANAS*. (San Francisco) 39(30): 1,2,4,8.

Vallentyne, J. R. 1986. "The Necessity of a Behavioral Code of Practice for Living in the Biosphere, with a Special Reference to an Ecosystem Ethic," pp. 406–414. In N. Polunin (ed), *Ecosystem Theory and Application*. John Wiley and Sons, New York. 445 pp.

CHAPTER 6. BIODANCING: THE 1 - 2 - 3 OF GREAT LAKES MONITORING

In this set of individual perspectives there is room for at least one with a distinctly different way of expressing the common theme. The author of this chapter examines the ecosystem perspective on the Great Lakes from an historical, literary, folkloric point of view. This view entails a degree of complexity and allegory in a narrative in which some readers may find insight, but which others may at first find perplexity. The theme of the chapter is the monitoring of the Great Lakes region as an ecosystem. But the author views his topic in a large and evolutionary dimension. His observations are not confined to formal technoscientific monitoring, which he nonetheless views as very important. But perhaps of greater importance is the change in popular attitude, understanding, and behavior, as the "dance of life" on the three stages that he describes moves from exploration and exploitation to an era of conservation and remediation. As Aesop and his emulators over the centuries have demonstrated, allegory often provides a quicker avenue to insight than that reached by linguistically more straightforward routes.

BRUCE L. BANDURSKI

6

BIODANCING: THE 1-2-3 OF GREAT LAKES MONITORING

Transboundary monitoring is as easy as 1-2-3. Also, when you really get into it, it is as difficult as 1-2-3—in a foreign language with different linguistic rules and different symbols. For two days in October 1984, about a hundred of us really got into it in Philadelphia. Now we coudn't get out of it even if we wanted to. Transboundary monitoring—even in the Great Lakes Basin—is not some unusual activity. It isn't something you can take or leave or get out of. It goes on all the time, at every level of every living system, from cell to ecosphere. Again and again, we participants in the Transboundary Monitoring Network (TbMN) Workshop were reminded of this fact during that two-day meeting convened by the International Joint Commission of the United States of America and Canada. In that conclave the Great Lakes provided much of the nutriment for our discussions, but not the only nutriment: examples and perspectives from all over the world were used. It became obvious to us that, for the health of the Great Lakes, we need to look well beyond their watery attention-getting margins. For their health and for the health of humans depending on them, we need to look farther than we now can see.

Net human benefit was the cause bringing together Americans and Canadians at the TbMN Workshop in Philadelphia to discuss a shared transboundary monitoring network—a TbMN for mutual benefit. But U.S. and Canadian national perspectives proved too narrow. As the workshop participants got a grip on their human ecology, it became evident that "net human benefit" requires the consideration of living systems at a variety of scales. In looking beyond national and binational concerns, participants seemed to increasingly recognize the need to consider both supranational and subsystem dynamics, and to take into account relationships between and among various large-, medium-, and small-scale living systems in the United States of America and Canada. Even with the most careful and systematic monitoring measures, the *net* human benefit is not obtainable by North Americans—even including Mexico—working alone.

In fact, monitoring, if done by itself, is seldom worth the effort and expense, whether it's done on a small scale or on the scale of the Great Lakes Basin Ecosystem. For effectiveness, monitoring needs integration into alert systems capable of response. In sensitively moving in synchrony to design a decision support system (DSS), Canada and the United States are as likely to arrive at comparable transboundary region data as when they rely on the International Joint Commission for a disinterested study; but they are less likely (considering the differences in the government seats to which they then repair) to arrive at the same DSS configuration following that exercise. Their extant cooperative international network of gauging stations for monitoring stream flow and water levels in the transboundary region is indicative of these likelihoods.

The U.S. Council on Environmental Quality found in a recent study that

> monitoring . . . ought to be designed to serve as an essential complement to research, and must be closely linked to it, yet it raises such additional and difficult questions of long-term priorities as the following: No monitoring system can be designed to serve all purposes equally well, and most monitoring systems were designed to facilitate enforcement of existing pollution control regulations rather than to track basic ecological variables or to anticipate new problems. Good environmental research, monitoring, and management are iterative and interdependent. Research yields hypotheses about how environmental systems work; the outputs of monitoring are data about the status of those systems that permit both testing of those hypotheses and management responses. Few substances are monitored at all in the environment or in humans, and even fewer biological variables are systematically observed.[1]

There is room for improvement.

TRACKING TRANSCENDENT VALUES

Monitoring for the Great Lakes Basin or other ecosystems requires a broader framework.[2] With a framework only enfranchising humankind, Gertrude Stein's dictum proves correct: "When you get there, there's no *there* there." For an operable sense of place, we need other earthly beings—not just human beings and their governments—to be and to behave in a dynamic state of health. For a sustainable *there*, for coherence, we need a full and intact set of critical process subsystems in our shared ecosphere.[3] The *who* in the benefit consideration must include *Life*, living systems at all levels. That's our monitoring subject set: Great Lakes residents interacting with an embracing setting for Life.

Monitoring can tie together our being and our behaving/becoming in our habitat. From our autonomic nervous system, to moves toward our wildest wishes, monitoring is our way to ascertain how we might best obtain our purpose (Life) and the goals we set. It is not some optional activity. It is the provider of essential feedback for individuals and for cooperators who have purposes and goals and objectives to obtain in complex systems.[4]

Monitoring becomes transboundary monitoring when boundaries perceived by any entity are transcended. In the Great Lakes Basin ecosystem, transboundary monitoring takes place within the system as well as between the system and the ecosphere (planet plus setting) in which it is embedded. At Philadelphia, that fact complicated our deliberations and made it evident that the 1-2-3 of Great Lakes monitoring is more difficult than many workshop participants had anticipated. It needs more systematic exploration.

Here I am going to follow (systematically, I hope) one of the many trails leading from the TbMN Workshop. If you're interested in monitoring, nearly any of the sixteen hundred pages of the *Proceedings and Relata* can serve as a start for a rewarding exploration.[5] All trail signs lead to complementary ends, for all are part of the same ecosystem. "When we expose the presuppositions behind our usual thinking, feeling, and knowing, we can transcend all such ordinary knowing."[6]

1-2-3; 1-2-3 = CLUES ON THE PATHWAY

Scouting through the 1984 workshop's *TbMN Proceedings and Relata*, I picked up the first sign on this trail on page 93, where I found a clue to an ecosystem approach: "The boundaries to an ecosystem are matters of definition and convenience . . . It depends upon one's point of view."[7] The second spoor showed up on page 99: "We must find a more fundamental and systematic, *adaptive solution* to the issues raised by our adaptive activities."[8] Then a third imprint caught my eye: "Fragmentary analyses . . . lead to inefficiencies and pathologies . . . Often a holistic analysis will be cheaper and far more complete, accurate, and efficient if it represents an integrated approach."[9] The fourth footprint appeared on page 160: "Some of the more obvious abuses of quantification revolve around the belief that it enhances the objectivity of data, leads to a more accurate depiction of reality, and is essential for rational discourse."[10] Evidence number five made its point only three pages further on:

> The new vision of reality we have been talking about is based on awareness of the essential interrelatedness and interdependence of all phenomena—physical, biological, psychological, social, and cultural. It transcends current disciplinary and conceptual boundaries and will be pursued within new institutions. At present there is no well-established framework, either conceptual or institutional, that would accommodate the formulation of the new paradigm, but the outlines of such a framework are already being shaped by many individuals, communities, and networks that are developing new ways of thinking and organizing themselves according to new principles.[11]

And indicator number six was a set of trailwide scratchings explicating our *biodance:* "the endless exchange of the elements of living things with the earth itself."[12] Though just barely evident in the Philadelphia workshop record, this last one was the intricate sign set that gave me an indication of the end point (the target) for this chapter on Great Lakes monitoring.

STAGING/MONITORING 1-2-3 WALTZES

Most of this chapter is constructed as a conceptual pavilion in our noosphere—the wood where things have no names.[13] The pavilion is designed to facilitate the monitoring of living system/ environs relationships wherever they may go, and to afford some protection to those relationships recognized as critical for sustaining life. The pavilion has to last long enough for us to complete two "dances" on each "stage" built within it: (1) one dance that is a structured retrospection, and (2) one dance that is forward looking. One dance without the other would leave us partners in life either with no measure of our meaningful development or with insufficient hope for the future.

Comprehensive monitoring and documentation would require the study and description of both these dances as well as of the two stages supporting them. Here I'll have time and space only for a sample—one dance on each stage. Stage 1 (now nearly defunct) and Stage 2 I have been able to recognize, and my monitoring of them has led to a glimpse of a third stage's requisites. I expect that the biodance on Stage 3 won't have need of the pavilion. That third stage will open the possibility for fully actualized "ecosystem approaches" by those who would implement the letter and spirit of the 1978 Great Lakes Water Quality Agreement. Stage 3 is the one where "cisboundary" and "transboundary" lose their distinction because we *and* all we're aware of (our noosphere) constitute the ecosystem that is of full concern to us (neighbors included). Each stage—1, 2, and 3—is a floor for biodancing. Each must allow a dance in which six reciprocal questions (Who? What? When? Where? Why? How?) can be explored about the role of transboundary monitoring in the Great Lakes–St. Lawrence River Ecosystem and the role of that ecosystem in transboundary monitoring. Looking forward/looking back; looking beyond today's noosphere when we suspect our shortsightedness.

> "Come, Su; come, Mi; come, Hu; come, Cla;"
> Cried laughing little Er;
> "Let us go to yonder deep blue sea,
> Where the breakers foam and roar."
> —Henry Rowe Schoolcraft, "Niagara, an Allegory" in *Wild Notes Of The Pibbigwun* (1856)

For today's goal seekers, an extra effort at structured retrospection might pay huge dividends. Too often we assume that nothing useful to our present quest already exists, and we forget that ecology— "knowledge of our household"—must underlie our exhilarating technology. Historical ecology, pursued more seriously than it has been, has much to teach us about the Great Lakes ecosystem and about managing the human uses of that system.[14] With this in mind, I as a monitor have chosen to sample retrospective biodances of Stages 1 and 2.

Certainly, structured looks back and investigation of the ongoing processes of ecological life support (which become history by the time they are recorded) must be central to a workable transboundary monitoring network that the United States and Canada might share to bring more wisdom to their neighborly decision making. Let's start by taking another look at what Stage 1 was like when it was intact and used by most of us and our predecessors. It was Stage 1 that supported the marathon biodance that eventually led us to the realization that we needed better monitoring in the Great Lakes and elsewhere.

STAGE 1

On this stage the favorite dance was the galumphing Teton Mountain Stomp. It was performed by people like Paul Bunyan with his caulked boots and was the taciturn timber beast's equivalent of logorrhea. In the context of the ecosystem in which the dance took place, it was certainly incoherent; it was without unity or harmony, and its quality was measured almost entirely by its quantity.

Moving ever onward to virgin lands of the Great Lakes Basin and beyond, the continent's Paul Bunyans were preoccupied with *things,* with *more,* with *bigness for its own sake.* To these people bigger was almost always better. That we're still big on garbage and trash but don't yet take either advantage of them or full responsibility for what we generate is the penultimate symptom that ramshackle old Stage 1 lingers on; the ultimate symptom is the garbage's accumulation in and impairment of ecosystems that sustain us.[15]

The Great Lakes had met the aficionados of bigness long before today; the bigger-is-better crowd has always been with us. But in that long-ago era of nascent and comparatively innocuous technology, the Great Lakes had not been so badly or lastingly scarred. Archeological evidence suggests that the oldest known cultures in the Northeast adapted to a succession of physical environments that changed with the climate as the Wisconsin continental ice retreated.[16] The biggies (even the powerful Iroquois) were, like their nonhuman Great Lakes neighbors, made to adapt. The state of their technology gave them little choice but to learn their ecosystem's rules for survival.

In that they were like us.[17] But we, unlike they, have synthesized many chemicals previously unknown to nature; and we have been much slower learners in discovering and matching ecosystem basics (constraints). The arrogance our technology brings has acted as an opaque window on the view of our life support system. Ever-greater investments of energy to get the same or less in the way of resources have postponed the inevitable reckoning.

New research findings reveal that, because of climate changes in the Middle and Late Holocene (to 2,000 years ago), the levels of Lakes Michigan and Huron fluctuated one to two meters above contemporary mean lake levels on a scale of two hundred to three hundred years. This revised paleoclimate record necessitates a revised interpretation of the archeological record too. The environmental settings of the Early and Middle Holocene seem to have been of shorter duration than has commonly been assumed, so the people who settled in the upper Great Lakes over the past six thousand years would have had to develop dynamic adaptive strategies to accommodate the flux in ecological patterns occurring every two hundred to three hundred years.

> The range of long-term lake-level fluctuations, on the order of 1 to 2 [meters] above the historic mean lake level (177 [meters], 580 feet) is comparable to the 2 [meter] climate-related range between the high and low monthly levels on Lake Michigan and Huron recorded since 1860 . . . The late Holocene fluctuations provide a model for understanding historic lake-level changes, and for interpreting lakeshore archaeological sites and settings . . . Anticipation of the complexity of lakeshore environments is an initial step towards the interpretation of cultural patterns and life styles of lake-oriented groups.[18]

Change (dynamism) is a great part of that complexity, a complexity that comes from more than diverse *things*.

For the most part, we've overlooked the lakeshore environs' long-term features (structures and processes) as well as their day-to-day limits. Like Paul Bunyan and Babe the Blue Ox, we've pursued our manipulations of the Great Lakes land on a scale that our ecosphere could not repair and could not sustain even for one human lifetime. Westward, ever westward, moving on down the line, giving scant thought to stewardship, to sustaining a healthy environment.

Great Lakes/Great Knowledge

Monitoring records left by Paul Bunyan and his ilk can act as a reverse telescope of time. When we use these records to scrutinize our background, we are better prepared to address matters of *scale* in today's context.

I am not going to start down the trail to the box canyon in which small is good-beautiful and big is bad-ugly.[19] That cul-de-sac doesn't properly take account of context. A small cancer can be bad-ugly; a big sky can be good-beautiful. For humans, big is bad-ugly when your niche is not understood, or when your place is understood but you do not act with a cooperative, ecological ethic.

In *A Sand County Almanac, with other Essays on Conservation from Round River,* Aldo Leopold put it this way:

> An ethic, ecologically, is a limitation on freedom of action in the struggle for existence. An ethic, philosophically, is a differentiation of social from anti-social conduct. These are two definitions of one thing. The thing has its origin in the tendency of interdependent individuals or groups to evolve modes of co-operation. The ecologist calls these symbioses. Politics and economics are advanced symbioses in which the original free-for-all competition has been replaced, in part, by co-operative mechanisms with an ethical content.[20]

Can We Learn from Our Heroes, Errors, and Our Other Traditions?

Error control is the way of all life, public and private. All organisms, groups, organizations, and societies make headway by correcting the errors they commit in adapting (adjusting) to their environment. In real time, our nervous systems respond to minute feedback every time we make a move. By small adjustments (error control), those systems direct our muscles so that we obtain our objectives of eye-and-hand coordination and of locomotion.

And we can learn from moves of the past. A clear reflection on our heroic traditions has the potential to assist even our present-day error control.

Like lessons provided by Michigan's Looking Glass River, the direct effects of structured retrospection flow on and broaden. Occasionally, in freshet, they overtop the established banks of Learning I (change in the specificity of response by correction of errors of choice within a set of alternatives).[21] And all the effects of that enriched water continue to multiply—up, down, and sideways. Since the binational Transboundary Monitoring Network Workshop this fact—unlike the enriched water—has become very clear indeed. Such workshops are the product of myriad interactions of individuals. And they are the product of synergism resulting from those myriad interactions. But they don't ever start from Square One. Like monitoring of any sort, they always have a history (including a prehistory).

> If the past is regarded in total perspective, the long prehistory of man is likely to appear more important than most of what came to be preserved on clay tablets and parchment scrolls after man started to note down what he considered essential in a limited environment and a narrow span of time—more important if for no other reason than the fact that prehistory is common to *all* human beings, in *all* societies, at *all* cultural levels, and important also because prehistory explains so much of the later activity of man. With prehistory as the point of departure, it should be natural to see the continued path of man through the world against the background of the total environment of which he is part and which he himself has largely made what it is—to read history, in other words, not so much in the way it has been preserved piecemeal on clay and parchment, but rather as it has been carved into the globe itself.[22]

Human history is rife with clues for coping better than we have to date. Though it is far from being a complete Baedeker for tomorrow, structured hindsight on a helical journey through time certainly can save us from repeating certain serious mistakes out of our ignorance of what really went on previously.[23] Writ large on the ecotope of Stage 1, the error signs of heroic activities may be some of the most important to keep monitoring. Some of the signs and the ones most in evidence are writ large because they occurred in a climate encouraging *bigness* and large-scale operations involving more "can-do" technology than "should-do" applications of wisdom.

Too often we assumed that the *space* between the *things* we saw was useless; we called it "unoccupied," "wilderness," or "desert." We seemed unaware of the proxemics of our biodance—that land unoccupied by man might have been a protecting buffer.[24] William Cronon has pointed out that the American Indians did not experience some of the diseases afflicting inhabitants of Eurasia, having been protected by living on another continent, until colonists arrived. When pathogens were transmitted from the colonists to Indians (and then from one Indian to another), "[a] fundamental boundary was crossed, even though—and this is important for our present context—no one at the time was even aware that such a boundary existed." It was long before Indians or colonists realized what was happening. "Here," Dr. Cronon goes on,

> it is not too difficult to see an analogy with acid rain, whose effects had presumably been going on for a number of years before anyone even noticed they were present on a significant scale . . . One clearly would want to include in [a] monitoring network any territory that would be affected by environmental influences from either side

of the border, and that alone would suggest the need for a very extensive network indeed. . . . [T]here may be no limit to the resulting system: the boundary region may in fact include the entirety of both countries.[25]

Like the lessons learned when we danced roughshod in and on Stage 1, our excesses and even our either/or thinking have had some value. When the U.S. Constitution was being debated, James Madison realized this. He suggested more structured retrospection to consider governments of the past: "Let us pause, my fellow citizens, for one moment, over this melancholy and monitory lesson of history."[26] Neither time nor space necessarily limit our consideration of what ought to be included in a shared Transboundary Monitoring Network.

Stage 1 seems to go back a long way, but it was (and is) a necessary precursor to Stage 2. The facts of space and time and knowledge are such that, somewhere on this earth, each of these stages is existing with the other two—or however many you want to see (or not see). Stage 1 is a way to describe a particular tendency to focus with monocular vision.

That tendency has made it easier for us to deal with *things*. In our socioeconomics we are acquisitive: our federal governments track commodity flows and GNPs, the U.S. Council of Economic Advisers is always in the news—while (in the United States in the present Reagan administration) the Council on Environmental Quality has yet to meet with the president on matters of environmental quality and systemic health.

Commodity exchanges follow pork bellies, and stock markets track all sorts of economic indices that are poorly related to deeper issues of economy, of the Greek *oikos-gnomos* or "household management."[27] State governments have lists of their largest trees on record, and provincial governments are Canada's "resource managers." The Nature Conservancy catalogs "elements" of natural diversity in its Natural Heritage program, now carried out with U.S. and Canadian cooperation.[28] Environment Canada and the U.S. Environmental Protection Agency count the thousands of synthetic chemicals now found in the Great Lakes, and measure and report on their concentrations. All those efforts in monitoring *things* do show us trends, trends that mirror the policies we've had concerning growth and acquisition: more! more! more! More things and longer lists, whether the subject is carcinogens or endangered species, automobiles, or bank and savings-and-loan institution failures.[29]

Considering the rudimentary capabilities we have for volitional monitoring and feedback, too often we have confused economic bigness with economic efficiency. Walter Adams and James Brock point out that

> Americans still fall for the myth that big business is the "handmaiden" of economic efficiency . . . When a business gets too big . . . the government can't allow it to fail. Hence, by not controlling a firm's size, the government must decide whether to undermine the motivating mechanisms of the market, or act to protect the millions of people whose fortunes are tied to the business—the dilemma that produced the Chrysler bailout . . . [They] propose a public policy agenda that encourages a wide dispersion of economic power among smaller sized companies, which would be subject to the market's checks and balances.[30]

Paul Bunyan had an instructive experience, akin to the situation we face when we attempt to bound an ecosystem so that we can measure or monitor its important *things*. For a report Paul had to make to the government, the number of lumberjacks at the Big Onion Camp needed to be recorded. But there were too many men coming and going all the time for an accurate count. They tried counting the cattle, since there were five men to each yoke of cattle. But the cattle were coming and going all the time, too. Finally they counted the yokes, and extrapolated from that, realizing, however, that because the camp worked on a three-shift system, they'd only accounted for a third of the men.[31] That could be seen as the beginning of the government's use of indicators in Great Lakes monitoring. Paul and his bigness emulators—interacting in systemic ignorance (and/or disdain) with the nearly overwhelming scale and intricacy of the Great Lakes—started a practice of *estimating* that's hardly changed to this day. Since the Big Onion Camp, the bigger the operation, the more we have to *estimate* the condition of structures and processes—the number of layers, the amount of movement.[32]

James Marston Fitch has displayed in clear and fairly complete form the continuing nature of the relationship between humans and their environment. In "Experiential Bases for Aesthetic Decision," he diagrammed the links between the organism (human individuals) and the environmental factors each of us depends on. Metabolic processes, perceptual mechanisms, and the structural system of the human organism were arrayed to show basic life-supporting connections to environmental factors—thermal, atmospheric (temperature, humidity, movement, chemical and physical composition, and pressure), nutritional (food and water), luminous, sonic, the world of organic and inorganic objects, spatial, and gravitational.[33]

Although it seems forgotten in some of the fancier and piecemeal endeavors of "environmental protection," the same set of relationships pertains everywhere. Miller gave those of us who deal in monitoring the same sort of reminder in *Living Systems*. There he diagrammed a systemic approach for accounting living system levels, their critical process subsystems, the variables of these subsystems, and indicators of these variables that must be monitored if we are to ascertain the health of these living systems.

Being of a scale considerably smaller than many of the environmental changes we try to bring about, we are proving not very adept at judging what changes are sustainable in that scene beyond our scale-bound picture window. Instead of appropriately responding to such bigness by adopting truly critical indicators for life support systems, we track nonindicative "economic" surrogates. These don't lead us to a better fit with our living matrix. On net accounting, they distance many of our goals. Take another look at what happened to the Great Lakes during our Stage 1 biodance.

Big Net Effects of The Way We Were, Back Then

Tom Kuchenberg (an invited participant at the 1984 Philadelphia workshop) and Jim LeGault have provided a baseline, a documentation of feedback worth as much attention now as when it was published almost ten years go.[34] They describe how lumbering, fishing, mining, urbanization, and industrialization damaged all five of the Great Lakes.

In Ontario, alteration of the surrounding landscape probably led to the extinction of the Atlantic salmon and the decline of the sturgeon. In Erie, settlement and urbanization resulted in siltation from runoff and pollution by improperly disposed urban and industrial waste. In Lake Michigan, the southern portion of Green Bay was heavily polluted by the 1870s, and the use of fire by farmers and lumber operators to clear away unwanted cover culminated, in October 1871, in the tragic Peshtigo fire, which claimed more than one thousand lives in one night, caused instant pollution of streams and rivers, and altered runoff patterns. Lake Huron hosted some of the earliest settlements and intensive fishing by those not deserving of the name "first peoples." (Michilimackinac had a flourishing local trade by the year 1800.) A progression of fish nets (seine nets, gill nets, fyke nets, pound nets, trap nets, deep trap nets), reflecting short-sighted adoption of technological "can do," led to significant diminishment of Huron's fishery. Saginaw Bay's fish production declined from 2.4 million pounds in one year to 213 thousand pounds. Population growth around Superior followed development of iron and copper mines; but "the vast bulk of economic enterprises which drew settlers to the southern and western shores of Superior were transient. The poor soil and climate confined agriculture to scattered areas. A tragically vulnerable economy was built on the exploitation of natural resources."[35] This occurred not only around Superior but everywhere in the Great Lakes Basin ecosystem. And the impaired Round River has turned back on us.

On the continent of the Round River our departmentalized, disciplinary activities and our medium-by-medium, pollutant-by-pollutant analyses have generated and then focused on the symptoms of environmental problems; but they have failed to provide consistent and coherent views of the *net* effects of our attempts to turn environmental change to our advantage.[36] We have simplistically partitioned our world.

The life set of subsystems can produce and sustain "net human benefit" only when technologically potent humanity acts on the premise that—as an integral part of an ecosystem—we benefit when the whole system is in a state of health. In other words, humankind in the Great Lakes Basin Ecosystem is not healthy if our relationships within our suprasystem are not fitting. No artificial dissepiment of Man's devising can alter that fact.

Systematic studies of our interdependencies continue to reveal this. A December 1986 survey reported by Anne Sudar indicates that although shoreline management is proposed by 11 percent of the general public, shoreline property owners do not suggest it even though they suffer the most from high lake levels. "This is not surprising because many of the property owners take a narrow view of shoreline management and they fail to see how zoning, setback requirements, etc. can help them."[37] For the most part, they are reluctant to venture beyond Stage 1, with its old familar refrains. For them, "rights" as validated by supreme courts and "disaster assistance" provide a septum of more comfort than does an ecosystemic view.

Even on a flooded floor[38] where their hard-soled shoes made for a slippery footing, they have shown a propensity to put out of mind the bigger picture—as long as the prospect of an insurance bailout remained. On Stage 1 their knowledge of whole living systems was acquired, in the main, by unstructured retrospection. It made for a blind side in space and in time. On Stage 1, instead of taking deliberate strategic measures to understand our living systems as whole entities, they (read "we") relied on piecemeal investigative tactics targeted (typically, after the fact) at the symptoms of systemic dysfunction. We lived in a knee-jerk wonderland on Stage 1.

If we have a sense of place, we have been reading it wrongly and doing wrong to it. We are perched precariously on the bank of Round River.[39] There our attention has mainly been to the apparent and superficial opportunity the river gives us to "do it right" on a second or subsequent occasion when we don't get it right the first time. The fact that the third dimension of the river is round, also—and also (like the surface) circles back on itself—seems to have escaped our notice. We continually act as though *downstream* and *below* mean *away*. The insufficiently treated wastes we dump into Round River, for the most part, sink into the River's third dimension where we have lost (and still lose) sight of them.[40] Being visually oriented, we forget them until later, when they are truly "on the loose" and nearly impossible to recapture for proper treatment.

The Men That Don't Fit In* and Rule Forty-Two**

Monitoring can deal with the past, with the present, and even with the future, but in a sense all monitoring is history. It always has a *When?* aspect. That is because, by the time we detect and register a difference (a change of any kind), the system in which we are embedded has achieved a different state. By then it is a structure altered from the one that existed when we noticed the first difference.

Ongoing processes of our ecosystem don't stop to give us a breather while we strive to understand (by monitoring) the implications of what we have joined. Therefore, the hope that underlies all monitoring is that we'll get a second chance—another opportunity to adapt or to adjust the rules of the tea party we've joined.

And for all, in the golden afternoon, "It is next time!" That means that (whether or not time goes only forward) we must learn to live with risk and with uncertainty. Still—amidst that undertainty—careful, consistent, and long-term monitoring (and the data and information it brings about *things)* probably can help to narrow the range of our ignorance.[41] Wise and careful monitoring may increase our chances of maintaining the purpose (life) we share with all living systems. And it may increase our chances for attaining important goals and objectives.[42]

* From the poem of the same title by Robert W. Service in *Collected Poems of Robert Service* (Dodd, Mead, & Co.: New York, 1940), pp. 42–43.
** Rule Forty-Two from "Alice's Evidence" in Lewis Carroll's *Alice's Adventures In Wonderland:* "All persons more than a mile high to leave the court."

A significant part of the Philadelphia workshop was devoted to a consideration of how we make good use of our knowledge of being embedded in dynamic ecosystems.[43] To a number of us participants, ecological adaptability became evident as *the* strategy for healthy survival. And transboundary monitoring at a number of levels was recognized as the continuing search (through various perspectives or "windows") for key indicators of the variables of the systems, subsystems, and relationships that are essential for systemic health.

All of us in the community we call "Life" have detectors in common that provide feedback, a chance to fit our environments better. A few pages back I described Fitch's simple diagram of the basic relationships which any ecological (organism/environs) program of monitoring must take into account. In looking at these relationships, James Grier Miller (see note 3) has been able to categorize most of the types of disruption—the kinds of errors that bring about problems for living systems at all levels. Knowing these, we have a major clue about what to look for when we monitor.

Experience

However, we need more caution in planning the scale at which we count upon errors for our learning in the Great Lakes Basin and elsewhere. If we are to avoid Gambler's Ruin,[44] we need monitoring that is sensitive to the necessities (including emergent properties) of living systems and ecosystems at many levels.

But even if monitoring feeds a significant feedback loop through which we rely upon ourselves, it can only address what we have experienced. And we don't have enough experience in systematic monitoring for human systems, much less for the panoply of whole living systems depending upon this ecosphere. We haven't identified and selected enough telltales of our outputs for meaningful comparison of signal input.

In fact, we hardly know what is entailed in an *ecosystem approach* or in *ecosystem approaches* to striving for a better environment/mankind fit. The system we have chosen to identify as the "Great Lakes Basin Ecosystem" is indeed an arbitrary one, being identified by surface water flows to which we just happen to have been attentive. There are many other bases—even other aquatic bases, such as groundwater and atmospheric water—for *ecosystem approaches* to implementing the Great Lakes Water Quality Agreement of 1978.

Most of our experience in identifying *things* and systems has been tied to our limited visual perceptions, to the narrow portion of the electromagnetic spectrum humans can see. Other parts of that wide spectrum we barely know. Only recently, for instance, have we learned that certain bacteria and sharks respond to electromagnetic fields. And there may be other spectra (influential as key interconnections in ecosystems) that we will never detect. In such complex systems, in such an intricate ecosphere, nearly any "Great Lakes Basic ecosystem" that we put bounds on is likely to be arbitrary.

After a generation or two of motivated investigation, we are just becoming aware of what are called "emergent properties" of whole systems. We are discovering that at higher levels of living systems, properties emerge (such as language capability) that are not found at lower levels. The whole of a living system is more than the simple sum of its parts; yet our institutions are hardly organized to take this property into full account.

Too many, in government and out, act as though the federal level is nothing more than a simple aggregation of wishes and needs of states or provinces. Too many, in government and out, act as though the state and provincial levels are nothing more than a net account of the wishes and needs of local governments.

Too many act as though each level of government were merely an aggregation of the wishes and needs of the level immediately below—as if the federal level were a net account of the wishes and needs of states or provinces, the state or provincial level a summary of local wishes and needs, and so on. But the whole does have properties that are more than the sum of the characteristics of the component units—if that were not so, the United States might still be functioning under the Articles of Confederation.

Post Oak, Ad Hoc, Ergo Propter Hoc

Since my teen years, Mt. Baldy (now in the Indiana Dunes National Lakeshore) has provided me instruction in this need for matching nature's dynamism when we draw boundaries or reserve governmental "powers." There the sands of time creep steadily over the oak forests and toward the official park boundary posts. There, considering the values we intended to preserve by designating this national lakeshore, I would say that bigger is not only better; it is essential to achieve what we set out to do.[45]

The situation parallels that of many of our other parks, where we drew a supposedly firm line in the sand, and the natural forces, sometimes abetted by man, altered the circumstances we intended to preserve. It's often seemed that civic authorities had never heard of Sir Francis Bacon's admonition that nature to be commanded must be obeyed, as when zoning boards, with ad hoc perspective, have OK'd building in floodplains[46] and on the dynamic shores of the Great Lakes.

Certainly, an ecosystem approach to fitting into the Great Lakes' scheme of things would require *more human awareness* than we have of the many different thresholds of environmental quality detection possessed by creatures more sensitive than we. When is that awareness likely to become manifest? Here I admit: more would be better. Surely, an ecosystem approach would necessitate an orientation to phenomena detectable by senses beyond eyesight, beyond the visual.[47] In the United States and Canada the present form and content of our language are, like our science, oriented to the visual sense and depauperate in words and phrases for describing ecosystem processes and environmental quality conditions beyond temperate zones. When will our language suit our challenges?[48]

A December 1986 report to the Great Lakes Science Advisory Board, "Literature Review of the Effects of Persistent Toxic Substances on Great Lakes Biota," details the symptoms we've been dealing with.

> A good data base exists describing the distributions of a number of the most important species in the Great Lakes. However, in most cases, the synthesis of available information has not been undertaken to develop generalizations on distribution with broad application throughout the Great Lakes. Moreover, an understanding of the environmental factors controlling the distribution and composition of biotic communities is still at the rudimentary stage . . . This understanding is a basic requirement for evaluating natural and man-induced changes or potential changes in the ecosystems. Major modifying factors such as eutrophication, overexploitation and invasion of exotics have obscured the effects of persistent toxic substances on Great Lakes aquatic communities. For example, reduction in plankton abundance and production due to chronic effects of a toxic chemical in recent decades has been masked by the dramatic effects of eutrophication and predation by expanding populations of alewife and rainbow smelt. As long as these significant impacts continue to exert their overriding influence on the Great Lakes, the detection of the subtle effects of threshold or chronic levels of toxic substances by direct monitoring is impracticable, except in the vicinity of strong local contaminant sources. However, these locations are usually polluted with a wide variety of contaminants, thereby presenting serious difficulties in distinguishing between cause and effect.[49]

Indicators

Selecting indicators to monitor has been beset by problems of imprecision and restricted applicability. Reliable data for trend analysis need to come from readily obtained and readily quantified observations. It's been suggested that colonially nesting waterbirds such as gulls and herons could prove to be excellent indicators of the health of the Great Lakes.[50]

Although the pelagic zone of the Great Lakes is the overwhelming proportion of this ecosystem's area, the coastal wetlands (of which there are more than one thousand square kilometers for all five Great Lakes) may be much more important to the Lakes' well-being. The littoral zone, and especially coastal wetlands, receive many cultural stresses such as nutrient influx or dredging and filling. Because colonial waterbirds, creatures of the littoral zone, are usually at the highest trophic level, often present year-round, and often widely distributed, they can reflect the dynamics of structural and functional change in both terrestrial and aquatic ecosystem components.

A distinct advantage of using birds as ecosystem monitors is that *many people watch birds.* Here is a potentially powerful resource for ecosystem surveillance. A professional group such as the Colonial Water Bird Group collaborating with government agencies could set up an ecologically based and citizenry-supported monitoring network that would provide cost-effective and reliable feedback on the state of the lakes.

The Near Pavilions: Here, There, and Everywhere

> I certainly have found "good in everything",—in all natural processes and products, . . . the good of natural law and order, the good of that system of things out of which we came and which is the source of our health and strength. . . . Yes, good in everything, because law in everything, truth in everything, the sequence of cause and effect in everything, and it may all be good to me if on the right principles I relate my life to it. I can make the heat and the cold serve me, the winds and the floods, gravity and all the chemical and dynamical forces, serve me, if I take hold of them by the right handle. The bad in things arises from our abuse or misuse of them or from our wrong relations to them. . . . We say the order of nature is rational; but is it not because our reason is the outcome of that order? Our well-being consists in learning it and in adjusting our lives to it.
> —John Burroughs, *Time And Change* (1912)

The Great Lakes' history (as well as our own) can teach us much. From tectonics to stratigraphy, new technologies in direct and remote sensing are making it possible to probe with ever more depth and understanding into the Great Lakes Basin's present and its revealing past. Perhaps reading about "back when" will motivate us to change some current patterns while we yet have a second chance.

STAGE 2

> Here today, completely gone in five years, renewed down to the last single atom, we endure only in the shape, form, and pattern that are assured by our genetic blueprint. Our replacement parts come in constant flow from the earth itself. The carbon atoms in my body were once of the earth and shall be again, only to be exchanged for more of the same. After leaving my body they may re-enter me at a later time, unlikely though it may be. Or they may be fixed for a while in the body of someone else—or something else—in this unending round of "biodance," this dance of life.
> —Larry Dossey, M.D., *Space, Time & Medicine, 1982*

On Stage 2 the most popular dance seems to have been the Blue Lobster Quadrille, a biodance emphasizing *process* and integration, in contrast to the Teton Mountain Stomp of Stage 1, where the beat was on *structure* and separation of seeable things. Miller's identification of nineteen critical process subsystems common to all living systems gives us an indication of where to concentrate our process monitoring. In terms we probably ought to learn, he has identified these subsystems as reproducer, boundary, ingestor, distributor, converter, producer, matter-energy storage, extruder, motor, supporter, input transducer, internal transducer, channel and net, decoder, associator, memory, decider, encoder, and output transducer.[51]

New ecology textbooks recognize this difference in process orientation. For example, Paul Colinvaux's *Ecology* is organized to examine ecology from the individual level, to that of the population and species, to the community level. But because physical ecosystem processes must be understood to comprehend the integration of species into communities,[52] Colinvaux has placed discussion of processes before discussion of communities.

As I see it, a workable strategy requires that we use more than one "ecosystem approach" to gain understanding of our ecosphere, our United States–Canada transboundary region, our Great Lakes Basin, or any other ecosystem of interest and concern. I recommend a *dual* (thing or *structure*-focused + decision *process*-focused) strategy for a variety of reasons, some of which have to do with the risk and uncertainty with which we must cope.[53]

An excellent exposition of an ecological rationale for such a dual strategy is presented in *A Hierarchical Concept of Ecosystems* by R.V. O'Neill, et al. Here, state-of-the-art ecology is woven into a convincing case for using more than one spatiotemporal perspective in striving to understand ecosystems. If we are truly committed to implementing the Great Lakes Water Quality Agreement of 1978 by acting consistently with the recognition of the ecosystem character of the Great Lakes Basin, I recommend that we build upon selected aspects of O'Neill et al.'s theory, finding, and representations.[54] A dual strategy can help us craft a shared United States–Canada TbMN which could fit well with other essential monitoring efforts both of different scale (such as the World Weather Watch and the GEMS/WATER program of the United Nations) and of similar scale but implemented elsewhere (such as the United Nation's Regional Seas Program).

So What?

What does such a credible, state-of-the-art lesson in ecology imply for the formulation of a strategy for monitoring the shared United States–Canada transboundary region and the Great Lakes which constitute so much an integral part of it?

In my opinion (perhaps because it reinforces biases I have already about the observed/observer relationship), it provides a timely template we ought to employ. The authors have laid out their assumptions, proposed a hierarchy theory that is in testable form, and have, by the way they have framed the matter, invited ecologists to advance their science and art by invalidating the concept set forth—if they can.

A Hierarchical Concept of Ecosystems is the most open and potentially applicable in the near term of any synoptic rationale I have seen for configuring a binational (P-C/P-F) "pincers" strategy for a TbMN. (P-C/P-F is my abbreviation for population-community/process-functional approaches in ecology. A dual scientific strategy would employ these two approaches as complements, much as would be done in a combination responsive/model–reliant anticipatory strategy in a TbR decision support system.) This rationale is in a form that can be used by nearly any potential contributor to such a strategy.

In a language spoken by people of both nations—and, perhaps, by species other than man—this rationale can serve as a common touchstone for coordinating and evaluating initiatives in the United States and in Canada that are intended to advance the development of an integrated TbMN for a shared dynamic ecosystem. This strategy can be used in designing decision support systems—in which a TbMN would be embedded—to assist both Canada and the United States (and others) in addressing crucial matters about health of the transboundary region. It rates all the attention we can give it. It is time, now to compose and decompose as we detect the ecosystems our world presents to us—to rate our homehold's rates—so we can adapt. This P-F approach is essential in our overall adaptation strategy.

Beyond its focus on preventive approaches to the inappropriate use of toxic chemicals and the restoration and rehabilitation of impaired environs where they may be possible, the Great Lakes Science Advisory Board is now committed (through its budgeting process) to using the methods of science in testing the extent to which the process-functional perspective of ecology may usefully complement the population-community approach we have been pursuing. Together these two perspectives of ecology may set us well on the path to plural "ecosystem approaches" to enhance our understanding of the Great Lakes Basin Ecosystem and to attain more wisdom in ecomanagement—the fitting management of human activity in our only home.

Error Tolerance

Like all living populations, man is part of systems that operate by error control. In anticipation of continued erring in our ecospheric manipulations, we must limit the scale of measures we take to control the dynamics of our ecosphere. In our conurbations, on our farms, on our seas and in our skies, we are being made to see that bigger and faster are not necessarily better in regard to the functioning of essential social services.

> Certain forms of human intervention or potential intervention in the natural systems of the earth are now occurring to an unprecedented extent. There are at least three such areas of global-scale disruption: the increase in atmospheric carbon dioxide and resultant possible climatic changes; the disruption of the ozone layer and consequent potential increase in ultraviolet radiation at the earth's surface; and the nuclear arms race.
>
> While it can be argued that any new human activity—any new chemical, industrial activity, or intervention in a natural system—

has a small probability of having unforeseen, globally catastrophic consequences (the stuff of horror films: the mad scientist who creates a bug that destroys life on earth), it is clear that for most activities this probability can safely be regarded as small; prior similar experience, or theoretical knowledge, or the small scale of the activity renders it overwhelmingly likely that the world can endure many of our puny insults.

But such usual sources of comfort do not apply to the three processes mentioned. They are all proceeding on such a scale, and in such ignorance, that they have the clear potential for globally catastrophic consequences—the ultimate in error intolerance. And the marvelous technological advances that have made such activity possible have in no way put our activities out of reach of error; examples of major errors and failures in even the most advanced systems appear with shocking regularity. These cases of error intolerance are beyond the power of any single nation to address, but are of urgent importance nevertheless. Our collective decisions, intentional and unintentional, are thus a confusing mixture of too much risk and too little.

While the global aggregation of processes for which no overall individual responsibility can be assigned leads us to court unimaginable risks, the reluctance to acknowledge the inevitability of risk and the excessive post hoc assignment of blame lead many individuals and public servants to shun risks excessively. In some areas we even forbid individuals to assume risks that they might wish to take on in full knowledge, as in the lengthy testing and licensing process for new prescription drugs and the restriction of health care practice by nonphysicians. In other areas we give incentives for reckless risk-taking by insuring individuals against economic losses, as when the federal government insures large investors in failed banks that have been offering high rates of return to support high-risk lending [or as when government insures, or otherwise encourages or bails out, those who build in floodplains].[55]

These broad questions must more and more be faced, even in deliberations over specific, practical policy decisions. We are being driven to face them by the increasing scale of human intervention in global systems and the apparent accompanying probability of catastrophic consequences of error; by the growing chorus of demands that individuals be completely protected by society, from physical risk and even economic losses; and by the growing sensitivity of our ability to detect hazards, which confronts us forcefully with the impossibility of eliminating completely the risk consequences of our activities.

What would be the properties of an ideal social relationship to risk? The most important one is error tolerance. There can be no justification for pursuing courses that have any significant probability of leading to global catastrophe. Since we have no basis for assuming that we will not make errors nor be unlucky in our activities on any scale, we must seek to ensure that the potential consequences of our errors are within the capacity of society and ecosystems to cope.[56]

For humans, *health* appears to be a judgmental definition. We need more reliable criteria than we so far have found for applying that judgment to our kind, to what we perceive as different kinds, and to their shared life support system(s). Obviously, one place where we must improve our monitoring is our thinking. We need to get beyond the deeply entrenched "either/or" mode,[57] and we need to transcend our technological thinking in facing our man-environment relationship, where lie our opportunities and problems.
Technological thinking

> . . . appears to be particularly suited to the generation of technical data in the well-structured problem areas of the inanimate, geophysical world. In the less-structured biological and psychosocial worlds, however, it becomes less reliable as a research strategy. [P]ositivist thinking suffers from an implicit subjectivity that is commonly overlooked; it establishes a narrow, reductive perspective on the problem at hand and leads to a preoccupation with data generation at the expense of conceptual insight. Since environmental management problems involve all aspects of the environment, including the psychosocial, attempts to deal with these problems *primarily* on the basis of technological thinking would appear to be unwise.
>
> The crux of the problem with technological thinking is that while it appears to be an excellent *tactical* procedure, it is less suited to *strategic* thinking. In other words, if a problem can be clearly defined and adequately circumscribed, then positivist methods can provide the detail needed to attempt a solution . . . [H]owever, the complex problems encountered by managers require strategic thinking, especially during problem formulation, before relevant tactical detail can be sought. Thus, one can agree with Petak's conclusion that technological thinking needs to be supplemented by the holistic-strategic forms of thinking he terms "ecological."
>
> This is easier said than done, for styles of thought are not superficial skills that can be adopted or abandoned at will. Rather, they are complex patterns of behavior, deeply embedded in the individual's personality and held in place by firm conviction, years of training and, not least, by the reward systems prevalent in professional work. It is an unfortunate "fact" that few people seem able to switch easily from one style to another, from technological to ecological, when the situation demands. Instead, we appear to specialize at an early age, tending toward one or the other style as

a predominant mode. To make matters worse, the possibility of a working alliance being developed between adherents of each mode is hindered by the often intense conflict that develops between them.[58]

A Moving Context for Ecological Rationality: As Large as Life and Quite as Natural

If we are to remain insightful with regard to the changing of reality, we have no choice but to maintain adaptability. No one said it would be simple or easy. Robert Bartlett put it recently as follows:

> Ecological relationships are seldom unidirectional, linear, or simple. Causal linkages are often reciprocal, indirect, circular, probabilistic, contingent, delayed, multiplicative, interactive, and synergistic . . . Ecological rationality is process oriented, as is the science of ecology . . .
> [R]ationality is still bounded by the capacity of the human mind and the complexity of the world. The ecological environment is never any less complex than the worlds of economics and politics. The assumption of an omniscient decision maker is still ultimately unproductive and even dangerous. Any theory or study of the place of ecological reason in human affairs, purporting to be either positive or normative, needs to account not only for functional and substantive rationality, but also for procedural rationality—the cognitive processes by which humans discover and choose ecologically adaptive behavior.[59]

Lynton K. Caldwell notes (in the introduction to this book) that "it is erroneous to believe that an ecological approach to management for the Great Lakes can be accomplished solely through technological and scientific means. Management for the lakes occurs by and through people and is thus inherently social and political. Governments cannot realistically be expected to execute policies for which they feel no real commitment."[60] Elsewhere he has said the following:

> Today more than ever before potential conflicts may be recognized in advance of their occurrence. Prevention of political conflict or ecological error is almost always less costly than coping with unwanted events. But politicians and the public generally prefer to "let sleeping issues lie." Politicians often try to avoid overt recognition of trends and circumstances that might press them to take action that they would find personally disadvantagious. Therefore, means outside of the conventional political structure are needed to

scan environmental horizons for sources of possible trouble. There is need for a surveillance and monitoring arrangement protected from political manipulation, but structured so that neither the public nor its political leadership can ignore its findings.[61]

The substructure involving a "real commitment" for this Stage 2 approach to the decision process was presaged in the *TbMN Proceedings and Relata* of the binational workshop held in Philadelphia in 1984. At that gathering, working group 4 produced a diagram for the kind of framework for monitoring that would accommodate the social and political features that must be accounted for in the management of human uses of the Great Lakes Basin resources and environment.[62] (See Figure.)

There's no doubt that without this framework a monitoring system at the binational level (or at the national level, for that matter) would be of little real use. As Caldwell stresses, data bases "are only instruments of forecasting, evaluating, and decision making; they do not make decisions. Policy-relevant findings would be the end result of the system. Its role in fact-finding, analysis, and recommendation is to provide a reliable, verifiable basis for binational policy and decision making . . . The technical feasibility of such a system is more easily demonstrated than is its political acceptability".[63] Therefore, the planks on a new stage must be tightly splined with lignum vitae and glue that comes from the strong desire for cooperation. A maintenance plan for this stage is being worked out prior to its use in an inaugural dance.

That inaugural dance has particular steps to be followed. As Lewis Carroll said, "I never dance, unless I am allowed to do it *in my own peculiar way."* These steps were shown on pages 334 and 335 of the aforesaid *TbMN Proceedings and Relata,* and they are to be painted on the dance floor. These dance steps ought, over enough iterations, to lead to more common familiarity with the process of predesign and design of a decision support system in which we can all—lightfoots and clogdancers—participate in our 1-2-3 waltzing biodance.

The trouble is that we learn by making mistakes. If our mistakes in this dance are large enough, we might knock over the orchestra and damage the instruments before we get it right and before we can learn to appreciate long-forgotten kinds of music—not to mention what we do to other dancers on the floor. It is important that we be consistent in following this dance's particular steps in a systematic manner, an ecosystematic manner.

Within the conventional political structure, at least one slow dance to provide better information storage and feedback is under

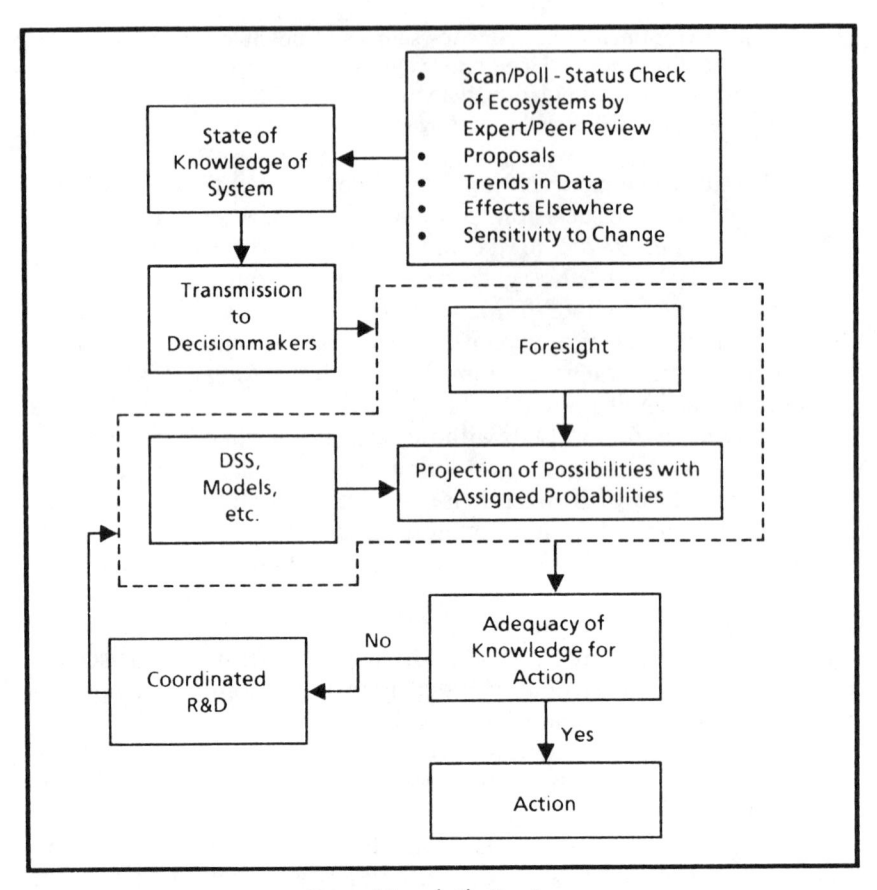

Open/Heuristic System

way. At this point it is hardly recognizable as part of a ballet, but it involves useful movement and instructive orchestration based on worldwide experience:[64]

> Environmental and resource management (ERM) depends greatly on a continuing flow of relevant information feeding in from various data-gathering systems. Without meaningful field measurements, the design of effective systems to protect human health and to manage biosphere resources wisely would hardly be possible. Yet the monitoring needs of ERM are often not given sufficient attention.
> Monitoring systems are imperfect for several reasons. First are limitations in technology, e.g., in the inability to measure evaporation from an open body of water during gale-force winds (when evaporation rates are greatest!). Second is a lack of understanding of the processes involved, e.g., of the role of microbial organisms in the soil with respect to the global sulphur cycle. (As models of

the environment improve, monitoring systems become better targeted to ERM needs.) Third is the high capital and operating costs of monitoring, which often impose limitations on existing and new programs. For example, many scientists support the idea of a global biogeochemical field program but a very considerable infusion of funds would be required unless great restraint was exercised at the design stage. Fourth is the problem that the needs of users change over the years, requiring modifications in system design in order to accommodate new ERM applications.[65]

This is likely to continue to be the case as the hardware and software that provide the connection between *data stores* (for example, relational databases + spatial information systems, comprising Geographic Information Systems and Land Information Systems[66]) and *their users* undergo substantial changes in configuration and capability.

The Bureau of Land Management (BLM) of the U.S. Department of the Interior manages over 340 million acres of public lands and more than 750 million acres of federal mineral holdings. It maintains the nation's public land and mineral records through an automated land and mineral record system (ALMRS). This monitoring system, vital to federal, state, and local government, covers three major types of land information, some of which pertains to the Great Lakes Basin: national land and mineral records; information on resource and environmental values from the public lands administered by the BLM; and the national Public Land Survey System, represented by the bureau's Geographic Coordinate Data Base (GCDB). The BLM's land and mineral records now total over a billion documents, which, until the installation of ALMRS, were manually maintained for the most part. These documents include a wide variety of ownership and use forms such as case files, master title plats, and historical indexes going back to two hundred years ago, when the first land offices of the United States opened.

Integrating these records into a workable system constitutes the mission of ALMRS: "to develop and implement an efficient system for recording, maintaining, and retrieving land description, ownership, and use information in support of Federal programs and public users of such records."[67] This is a *baseline monitoring system* of the first order of government work for ecosystem management.[68]

A Great Lakes Stand in the Shred of a Cloud

The United States–Canada transboundary region (TbR) might best be conceived of as an ecosystem varying in dimension with the relatedness of the values involved with particular issues. In 1968,

Margalef suggested how such process-defined ecosystems might be viewed:

> Marine plankton, river plankton, and populations in between (those of estuaries) are paradigms of a kind of [process-defined] ecosystem . . . Consider a river, in which suspended organisms multiply. The water flows, carrying away organisms. If the flow were perfectly laminar everything would be washed away and the water would become empty of life. But flow is turbulent, and some organisms actually move against the main current; others are carried away at a speed higher than the mean, and all, of course, multiply.
>
> As a result, at a geographically fixed point a population is maintained in which increase by multiplication compensates losses by drift, diffusion, and sinking. The population has to be considered a process rather than a state or organization; it is like a cloud that forms at one end and disappears at the other, maintaining in between a form and a certain appearance of organization. In dealing with such a system we are led to propose a very broad approach, referring events to a system of geographically fixed coordinates and keeping every element of the ecosystem open, with fluxes and exchanges across all the limiting surfaces.[69]

By two examples, O'Neill et al. make more clear why it is that *the* components of ecosystems such as *the* United States–Canada transboundary region cannot be designated:

> Depending on the spatiotemporal scale or window through which one is viewing the world, a forest stand may appear (1) as a dynamic entity in its own right, (2) as a constant (i.e., nondynamic) background within which an organism operates, or (3) as inconsequential noise in major geomorphological processes. Thus, it becomes impossible to designate *the* components of *the* ecosystem. The designation will change as the spatiotemporal scale changes [in a particular read-out].
>
> Sollins et al. (1983) analyzed soil organic matter accumulation at mudflows on Mt. Shasta, California. Their analysis exemplifies how the observable system dynamics are altered as one changes scale . . . Over centuries, organic matter is accumulating and major oscillations in the pattern of deposition result from fire-initiated secondary succession. On a finer scale of years, net accumulation is more difficult to detect and dynamics are due to annual litterfall and decomposition. If we take the analysis of Sollins et al. to an even finer scale . . ., annual dynamics disappear as one focuses on wind-blown additions and removals and the action of large decomposer organisms. Thus, if one were attempting to explain soil organic-matter accumulation one would come to a totally different

description of the dynamics, depending on the scale being considered.

The hierarchical perspective makes it clear that the ecosystem is not simply the context for population and community dynamics. Such a viewpoint seeks to limit observations to a single window, a single observation set. Instead, behavior must be defined on the basis of the phenomena under examination. Hierarchy theory provides a consistent methodology for dealing with the natural world at many spatiotemporal scales. From a hierarchical perspective, the definition of the system depends on the window (e.g., the range of rates) through which one is viewing the natural world . . . It is the relative disconnection that constitutes the organization of the system.[70]

These are fairly recent findings of ecology. If they continue to prove out, they may well become appropriate as fundamental guidance for any land use planning. For example, we might not have found ourselves in today's problematic situation of having vulnerable buildings or other developments in the Great Lakes' coastal zone and the St. Lawrence River's floodplain if zoning boards had made insightful findings in times past regarding land use. Unfortunately, those findings about nature were too often disregarded by humans.

How can we maintain and enhance a baseline of human and environmental health while providing ample freedom for development—the realization of our potentials at all levels? The floor and underpinnings we are trying to design and put into adaptable "place" by monitoring are for a dance, a loom-weaver relationship. Sound floorboards for an unsplintered waltz must be obtained from our farm woodlot, but that obtaining must leave intact the forest stand which grew them.

An Adaptable TbMN for Great Lakes Users

As well as providing information storage and feedback, the structure of a transboundary monitoring network must continue to allow us change in what we are developing as we recognize and adapt to new contexts. Attendantly, citizens had best look after their own interests as individual living systems. Rather than relying on such changeable institutions as governments, it makes considerable sense for individuals to put more effort into gaining a better self-understanding of life's critical processes. These are basically the same for all individual organisms.

Well-oriented monitoring can tell us where we are in most need of governance—internal and external. At system levels higher than the individual (groups, organizations, societies, ecosphere), there are emergent factors to take into account. As observed by Joseph Needham: "In the world of nature we have to deal with a succession of levels of complexity and organization. The principles which apply to one of these levels do not apply to the others, although at every level the principles appropriate to the lower levels must be taken into account, modified though they may be by the special new conditions prevailing."[71]

As the *TbMN Proceedings and Relata* and subsequent publications show, we need not start from Square One in devising a gyrocompass for monitoring.[72] Some exploring nations (though no longer predominant on the United States–Canada landscape) continue to influence the course of our relationships and of our deliberations about monitoring transboundary regions. The Swedes, for instance, have for ten years had in place their National Swedish Environmental Monitoring Programme. Some of us have made use of its strong points (emphasis on using existing organizations rather than on creating new bureaucracies, making the data it collects available to all who wish to use them, commitment to long-term monitoring) as we deliberate what a United States–Canada TbMN might look like. Some of us are having second thoughts about our proclivity for creating new institutions (to add to the store of "objective" data) whenever we detect what appears to be a new problem or opportunity to be addressed to meet a need. As Caldwell advises,

> Means outside of the conventional political structure are needed to scan environmental horizons for sources of possible trouble . . . Characteristics of such a system and ways that it might be effected are outlined as follows . . . The assemblage and integration of such a system would require a high order of organizational skill, information, and imaginative exercise of political strategy . . . A possible arrangement . . . would be a negotiated, mutually coordinated system for concurrent collaboration of Canadian and American institutions, each developing its own data and assessments, but with identical criteria and format. This arrangement would provide for joint publication of accumulated data. Funding could be provided by respective governments, supplemented, perhaps, from private sources.[73]

An extension of this possibility would be concurrent national responsibility for program operations coordinated by a central autonomous agency or office to supervise and assist coordination of the system. This agency would be created by the two national governments but would not be subject directly to their detailed political control. The system should have outreach relationships with scientific and research academies and councils in both countries. Some type of arrangement for periodic formal review of its performance would be a condition of political acceptability. Within limits necessary to its orderly functioning, the system should be open not only to the dissemination of information to the people of both countries but also to the input of ideas, suggestions, criticisms, and inquiries from the general public as well as from various groups with particular concern with the findings produced through its operations.[74]

Learning II

In *Steps To An Ecology of Mind*, Gregory Bateson defined "Learning II" as *"change in the process of Learning I,* e.g., a corrective change in the set of alternatives from which choice is made, or . . . a change in how the sequence of experience is punctuated." This is what we find outselves doing in Stage 2 as we improve upon the ways by which we monitor transboundary phenomena. (Learning I, more typical of Stage 1, is change in the specificity of response by correction of errors of choice *within* a set of alternatives.)

> An Intergovernmental Working Group defined *monitoring* as "a system of continued observation, measurement and evaluation for defined purposes." . . . However, because the phrase . . . ["for defined purposes"] is a bit too general, another term, *integrated monitoring,* has tended to replace it: "the repeated measurement of a range of related environmental variables and indicators in the living and non-living compartments of the environment, for the purpose of studying large parts of the biosphere as a single system."
>
> It seems clear that an *integrated approach* to monitoring is essential, in which biological/ecological indicators are some of the main building blocks in system design. As an example of the consequences of not recognizing this principle, we can mention the well-functioning EMEP atmospheric pollution monitoring system (established under the auspices of *European Economic Community)* and *BAPMoN* (under the asupices of *WMO),* which failed to provide a warning of forest damage in central Europe. [The present and latent impact of the technologies must also be considered; the fruits of monitoring will be best when they serve as an early warning rather than an after-the-fact function.] Included in the monitoring process of course are quality control, data assimilation in user-friendly form, and system optimization, i.e., assessments to determine whether system design could be improved to meet the prescribed objectives.[75]

Alan Miller says the following:

> If progress is to be made toward a more comprehensive way of thinking about environmental problems, through an effective integration of technological and ecological approaches, then the answer clearly lies in the long-term through education. Whether this is possible remains to be seen . . . Since the dominant paradigm in science and technology is positivist, and given the massive inertia in institutions of higher education, it would seem unrealistic to expect rapid or widespread change. However, the development of comprehensive thinking is unlikely unless young professionals are equally conversant with the characteristics of these different, often opposing, paradigms.[76]

Where, in these procrastinations, are such young professionals becoming "equally conversant"? Where will those who *are* make their influence felt? In the field of ethology, there are recent signs that such young professionals may be surfacing. The likes of Jane Goodall, Francine (Penny) Patterson, and the late Dian Fossey are making themselves and their research widely known amongst the reading and television-watching public. And these folk, at least, seem to be learning the value of hurdling what were heretofore known as "interspecies barriers." Having recognized more similarities than differences amongst many forms of life, these folk are primed to take a meaningful, less humanocentric part in ecosystem approaches. Witness these words from a researcher investigating the thinking capabilities of African grey parrots:

> A persistent problem in behavioral research involves understanding the processes by which humans and nonhumans acquire information about their environment and about how to interact with that environment, including other organisms . . . Information gathered from the study of one species may lead to important insights into understanding the processes in another. Such appears to be true for the study of avian and human communication, where parallels exist not only in the functions but also in the mechanisms for acquisition of communication codes . . . Learning is most effective when observers see and practice the targeted behavior under conditions similar to those they face in their regular environment; thus a demonstration must be *contextually relevant*.[77]

MONITORING A NEIGHBOR'S BIODANCE ALONG WITH OUR OWN

Despite its thing orientation and possessive tendencies, Stage 1 did lead to some transcendance, after all. In the Great Lakes Basin Ecosystem and elsewhere, Stage 1 led to a Stage 2, in which both population-community ecology and process-functional ecology are now known to be contextually relevant for ecosystem approaches. There is evidence that Round River has again brought up pertinent reconsiderations of competition and community structure that were among the earliest of modern ecology's subjects of focus.[78]

The either/or approach *is* being supplanted—slowly, but surely— by approaches that recognize that even the pursuit of self-interest in our shared ecosphere mandates both/and approaches accommodating a multiplicity of perspectives. False and nonfunctional distinctions between *there* and *here* are gradually dropping by the wayside as we see our trailways converging.

> It is invariably national self-interest which underlies and dictates the stance of a nation in transboundary water relations. This is perhaps a truism, but not as explicit as it may seem. Distinctions must be made between long and short timeframes . . . The decision of Canadian and U.S. leadership made many years ago to move forward with the development of precepts and tenets governing transboundary water relations was a product of foresight. The nations realized that with such precepts and tenets much of joint value . . . would be made possible. Self-interest is not only natural, but can be used as a vehicle to achieve much that is good, if used with foresight and imagination.[79]

Page 10A of the Thursday, May 28, 1987, issue of *The Bay City Times* (Michigan) is symptomatic. There the headline in the "Opinions" section carried the bold print: "Trading Canada acid rain for water pollution"; "While the U.S. continued to brew acid rain for the prevailing winds to carry to Canada, Canada has been brewing toxic wastes and other pollutants that the Great Lakes waters have been carrying to the U.S." Such perspectives lead us to a downstream/ away mentality in which we are disinclined to act responsibly until we are threatened by effects of a neighbor's similar disinclination.

STAGE 3

> They shut the road through the woods . . .
> Yet if you enter the woods
> Of a summer evening late,
> When the night-air cools on the trout-ringed pools
> Where the otter whistles his mate, . . .
> You will hear the beat of a horse's feet,
> And the swish of a skirt in the dew,
> Steadily cantering through
> The misty solitudes,
> As though they perfectly knew
> The old lost road through the woods. . . .
> But there is no road through the woods.
> —Rudyard Kipling, "The Way Through the Woods"

For those referring to time lines and spatial contexts, the lessons learned and being learned in the Great Lakes Basin by Canada and the United States of America are a microcosm of the larger picture.[80] Structured retrospection as a form of monitoring has, there and elsewhere, taught us much about human development and civilization. Yet, depending upon how time-bound we feel we are, it may or may not help us to look ahead for a more enjoyable and more sustainable life dance, predicated on a science of humanity and/in nature.[81] "Whatever type of situation is present is the play of Space, Time, and Knowledge. They are not forcing us to experience the situations they present in any particular way; rather, they provide an infinite stage in which we can perform whatever play we choose."[82]

My monitoring of the two stages that have served our being in the "no name wood" has disclosed the genesis of each of the trail signs and clues that I found in re-reading the *TbMN Proceedings and Relata*. Structured retrospection helped me find and share with you, systematically, a further understanding of the who, what, when, where, why, and how of the Great Lakes Basin Ecosystem's conditions. But "there is an even more fundamental significance to our fellowship. We are not just separate points bearing the same value, born of the same parents, living in the same time. Great Knowledge shows that One point is all points. . . . [T]here is no independent or isolated place, unaffected by what happens elsewhere. If resources are depleted or disease appears in one spot, repercussions will be felt elsewhere and on a larger scale. This is a simple illustration by time that apparently dispersed points are linked. With more appreciation of Great Time by Knowledge, each point is directly all other points."[83] "Intimacy is."[84]

But the waltzes that gave us structured retrospection across two stages have left me tired, not contented—despite the good companionship for that dance. In the process of wearing out a confining pair of shoes, they gave me only a measure of our development as interlinked beings.[85] And that measure only left a firm impression for the duration of the dance. On Stages 1 and 2, we have given insufficient consideration to what's ahead. Perhaps you feel differently, but our 1-2-3 waltzes did not provide me sufficient hope for the future. Behaving/becoming still needs attention. Remembering—even shared recollection—isn't enough.

Trail sign five we barely figured-out, *together,* just as the last dance was ending on Stage 2. Likely, neither one of us would have fathomed it alone. And, it has become obvious (to me, at least, from monitoring our 1-2-3 waltzes) that we have a considerable number of complementary talents. Perhaps we are what ecologists call "symbionts".

But, it could be that we are even closer than that. I won't know until we peruse what lies on the pathway stretch that we haven't yet traversed, haven't yet read, haven't yet explored. The waltzes of structured retrospection didn't leave me without *any* hope, partner; but they weren't completely satisfying. Maybe that's because—in addition to slighting the future—we didn't yet get to investigate indicator number six. The trailwide trace, unsheltered by any pavilion, is indistinct. Together, though, I'll bet we can follow it. It seems to be findable, neighbor, from any beauty spot on the path. Care to try another systematic biodance? Another perspective? On Stage 3? Today it'll have to be brief, but we do have time to check out that stage and its ecological (care-of-home) underpinnings.[86]

The needed foundation and framework for Stage 3 was anticipated a century ago when the poet, Walt Whitman, penned his "Song Of The Rolling Earth":

> Were you thinking that those were the words, those upright lines?
>   those curves, angles, dots?
> No, those are not the words,
>   the substantial words are in the ground and sea,
> They are in the air, they are in you. . . .
> The earth does not exhibit itself nor refuse to exhibit itself . . .
> Holding up in her hand what has the character of a mirror, while
>   her eyes glance back from it,
> Glance as she sits, inviting none, denying none,
> Holding a mirror . . . tirelessly before her own face . . .
> No politics, song, religion, behavior, or what not, is of account,
>   unless it compare with the amplitude of the earth . . .

If luck is with us as neighbors, we ought to be able to construct a stage on that framework allowing us another brief (and, hopefully, more revealing) biodance. I have heard that Stage 3 floor may be used by thing-oriented population-community ecologists and by the process-function-oriented ecologists they've chosen to dance with lately. And, of course, it is available to all who would understand Great Lakes ecology. There are no partitions between this stage and its environs. It is open to all of life's processes, to any biodance.

> The man that is open of heart to his neighbour,
> And stops to consider his likes and dislikes,
> His blood shall be wholesome whatever his labour,
> His luck shall be with him whatever he strikes.
> —Rudyard Kipling, "Neighbours: Beauty Spots"

A Framework For Effective Monitoring, a background paper prepared for the Canadian Environmental Assessment Research Council in 1987, has benefitted from Stage 1 and, especially, from the process orientation that Stage 2 provided: "[P]rocess must be an integral component of assessment and monitoring[;] . . . it requires as much attention as the methodological issues, normally the only ones considered by the scientist and practitioners. . . .

Creating linkages between [social impact assessment] and biophysical monitoring processes will face formidable tasks inherent in scientific methodologies and in the processes needed to bring the scientists or practitioners together. . . . [T]he issue of monitoring linkages does not appear to be a high priority, judging from the lack of literature.

This does not negate the fact that it will be an important component in successful impact assessments, and that more attention must be paid to improving our ability to conduct integrated monitoring programs on resource projects. . . .

[W]e have little evidence that links are in fact established in practice. We have no significant references or knowledge of these linkages in an SIA/EIA monitoring context, with the exception of the Keephills [the Keephills Power Project near Edmonton, Alberta] case. Interestingly enough, community members, that is 'the public' have no difficulty with the concept of linkages. Their concerns transcend disciplinary, EIA, or SIA boundaries."[87] This background paper is a helpful patternmaker for preparing those who would utilize Stage 3.

"Whether or not we are marked out and cut off by endless partitioning, or can see partitions as not obscuring a fundamental

intimacy and fulfillment, is simply a matter of which view is taken.
. . . It is true that due to our forward and outward directedness, and our need for continuity, what is presented in one 'read-out' seems closely related to the content of successive 'read-outs'. And certainly the next read-out seems clearly established as such. It makes no ordinary sense to doubt the unbroken temporal connectedness and direction.

But . . . [on a different stage of insight and monitoring] we do not have to go a certain way. We can travel off the beaten path. . . . [K]nowingness can apprehend an uncharacteristic sequence of time. . . . Even when we do follow along an ordinary sequence, the confirming relatedness and regularities are not unchallengeable. The same is not the same. Sameness is a matter of conviction within a read-out. Unbrokenness is not, beyond all question, unbroken. It is just a message that things are or have been a certain way. . . .

Read-outs . . . are completely self-contained. That is, all the factors which the content of a read-out declares to be essential for the experience within the read-out, or essential background for such experience, are equally given within the read-out. If there is the appearance of persons, information-processing capacity, physical and psychological structures, basic world order and containing space, semantic background for propositions (and for referring and referents), then they appear (or are presupposed), in such a way that they are all given together within the particular read-out. . . .

No factor of experience—whether subject, object, sense, organ, sense datum, position, or basic fact of occurring—is more fundamental than (or prior to) the read-out wherein it takes on significance. . . . No read-out establishes anything beyond itself. But this is not proof of individual read-outs as being isolated from each other or from the rest of reality, because no read-out ultimately establishes itself, its own isolated position, or isolating boundaries.

The read-out law does not trap us because there is no 'us' to be trapped at the level [Stage 3] where the law applies, and no world-order 'out there' to be cut off from. The read-out law does not inhibit contact with apparent 'outside-standers' borne by 'time'. It just discourages approaching them as 'outside-standers'. . . .

[Stage 3] is fully appreciative, and free from confusions and mistaken attributions of values. It knows everything as being open. . . . But given such an open play it can distinguish perfectly—according to the evaluations cherished within a particular realm—between illusion and 'reality', between one thing and another, between 'existence' and 'mere appearance', value and trivia.

The . . . clarity of Great Knowledge [in Stage 3] comes only after we see that the inflexible awareness and claims to reality of a particular realm of experience are actually a play of 'time', and not an absolute. This requirement and challenging character are natural processes which are intrinsic to the structure of the path (Time) to Great Knowledge.

It is therefore important, both for accuracy within our realm and also in regard to appreciating the infinity of Space and Time, to continually examine the truths and evidence we encounter."[88] It is the insight gained in this continual examination—monitoring— that provides us *the* wherewithal to lead adaptive lives, sustainably at one with our monitored environment.

> This is the way. And perhaps you have already taken the hardest step. You have learned by your own experience that outside can become inside. You have been beyond the pairs of opposites. It seemed a hell to you: learn, my friend, that it is heaven! For it is heaven that lies ahead of you. Magic, you see, is this: to exchange inside and outside, not under compulsion, not passively as you have done, but freely, of your own volition. Summon up the past, summon up the future: they are both within you! Up until now you have been the slave of what is inside you. Learn to master it. That is magic.
> —Hermann Hesse, "Inside and Outside" (1920) from *Stories of Five Decades* (1954/72 transl. by R. Manheim and D. Lindley)

> We knew how to get by on what comes along,
> but the idea
> Warning, waiting there like a forest, not emptied,
> beckons,
> —John Ashbery, "The Pursuit of Happiness" (1981)

NOTES

1. Council on Environmental Quality, *Report on Long-Term Environmental Research and Development* (Executive Office of the President; Washington, D.C., 1985).

2. Bandurski, Bruce Lord, "Ecology and Economics—Partners for Productivity," in *The Annals of the American Academy of Political and Social Science,* Vol. 405 (January 1973), pp. 75–94. The "framework" provided by the ecosphere that humans depend upon for sustenance would be a helpful expansion of area of concern for Great Lakes Basin residents who would

monitor health. Cf. Ekins, Paul, *The Living Economy: A New Economics in the Making* (Routledge & Kegan Paul: New York, 1986).

3. Miller, James Grier, *Living Systems* (McGraw-Hill Book Company: New York, Montreal, and Toronto, 1978), especially pp. 51–87.

4. *Feedback* is a term drawn from cybernetics. "Cybernetic ecology is an approach promising more theoretical understanding of complicated natural processes at the ecosystem level . . . . The shift of interest toward the forces decisive for the macroscopic, holistic features of ecosystems is fairly similar to that of the thermodynamic approach. It moves ecoytem studies into the direction of evolutionary disciplines, which have been the domain of studies at the organism or population level." This status-giving quote is drawn from p. 267 of *Freshwater Ecosystems: Modelling and Simulation* (Elsevier: New York, 1985) by Milan Straskraba and Albrecht H. Gnauck.

5. Haug, Peter T., Bruce L. Bandurski, and Andrew L. Hamilton, *Toward A Transboundary Monitoring Network: A Continuing Binational Exploration,* Vol. 1, Proceedings of a Workshop Convened by the International Joint Commission, Canada and the United States, and Relata Assembled During the Editing Process, (International Joint Commission; Ottawa and Washington, June 1986), 292 pp. [henceforth referred to as *TbMN Proceedings and Relata,* Vol. 1]. See also Bandurski, Bruce L., Peter T. Haug, and Andrew L. Hamilton, *Toward A. Transboundary Monitoring Network: A Continuing Binational Exploration,* Vol. 2, Proceedings of a Workshop Convened by the International Joint Commission, The United States and Canada, and Relata Assembled During the Editing Process (International Joint Commission: Washington and Ottawa; June 1986), 478 pp. [henceforth referred to as *TbMN Proceedings and Relata,* Vol. 2].

6. Tulku, Tarthang, *Time, Space, and Knowledge: A New Vision of Reality* (Dharma Publishing: Emeryville, California 1977), p. 221.

7. Roots, E. Frederick, "Monitoring of a Shared Boundary: Some Basic Adaptive Considerations," in *TbMN Proceedings and Relata,* Vol. 1, pp. 89–107. Dr. Roots noted, "[A] boundary between two countries is more than a line on the ground or on maps. In different circumstances, the boundary may be a barrier, an interface, or a filter; it may act as glue to join, a wall to separate, or as a blind to hide or confuse. In some circumstances, to all intents and purposes, the boundary may not be there at all. Examples of each of these situations may be found along the U.S./Canada boundary . . ." A key objective of discussions of boundary monitoring is to explore strategies for keeping track of the state of health of the environment in the boundary region between the United States and Canada, and for improving understanding of social and ecological systems affected by the boundary or transboundary activities. The reason for wanting to do so, as made clear by the Boundary Waters Treaty and by the activities of the IJC over the decades, is to obtain knowledge that will help avoid intercountry conflict and to optimize mutual benefits from developments whose effects cross the boundary. (pp. 90–91, passim)

8. Ibid, p. 99.

9. Miller, James Grier, "A Living Systems Analysis of the Canada/U.S. Boundary Region," in *TbMN Proceedings and Relata*, Vol. 1, pp. 140-141.

10. Miller, Alan, "Technological Thinking: Its Impact on Environmental Management," in *Environmental Management*, Vol. 9, No. 3, pp. 179-190. Quote drawn from *TbMN Proceedings and Relata*, Vol. 1, p. 160.

11. Capra, Fritjof, "The Systems View of Life," in *The Turning Point: Science, Society, and the Rising Culture* (Bantam Books: New York, 1982). Quote drawn from *TbMN Proceedings and Relata*, Vol. 1, p. 163.

12. Dossey, Larry, *Space, Time & Medicine* (Shambala Publications: Boston, Massachusetts, 1982), p. 74. Quote drawn from *TbMN Proceedings and Relata*, Vol. 1, p. 224.

13. Gardner, Martin, *The Annotated Alice,* note on Chapter 3 of *Through the Looking-Glass and What Alice Found There* (1871) by Lewis Carroll (Bramhall House: New York, 1960), p. 227. Quote from p. 225.

14. Van Dyne, George M., ed., "Historical Approaches in Ecology," in "Chapter X: Implementing the Ecosystem Concept" of Section IV: Instilling the Ecosystem Concept in Training, in *The Ecosystem Concept in Natural Resource Management* (Academic Press: New York, 1969), pp. 333-334.

15. January 23, 1987, newsletter from the Institute for Local Self-Reliance: "Bigger is not better when it comes to municipal waste disposal. That is one of the key conclusions of the Institute's new study, *Garbage Disposal Economics: A Statistical Snapshot* . . . 'Garbage disposal is the single most important issue facing municipalities today,' according to Institute President Neil Seldman. 'By 1990 more than half of our cities will have exhausted their existing landfills and must develop alternatives.' "

Even the popular press is beginning to find this garbage a worthy subject. In *The Washington Post's* "Outposts" section on page B3 of the Sunday, June 7, 1987, paper, Cass Peterson had this to say, in "Garbage: The New Alchemy of High-Tech Trash": " 'Waste corrugated boxes are in tight supply.' That's the ironic twist in the saga of the garbage barge, now anchored on the Hudson River after a 6,000-mile, 76-day odyssey. While the floating trash heap was cruising the Caribbean in futile search of a place to dump its load, the U.S. paper industry was practically pleading for castoff cardboard and office-paper trash to turn into new paper products . . . The barge's cache of cardboard, now mixed with other garbage and soaked with sea water, is useless for recycling." This is a Stage 1 indicator of the first order; we don't fully perceive the production/distribution/consumption/decomposition/reuse processes that are musts for our continuing existence. On page 25, of "The nature of hazardous wastes and their recycling potential" in *The Scientific Management of Hazardous Wastes,"* by C. B. Cope, W. H. Fuller, and S. L. Willetts (Cambridge University Press: (Cambridge 1983),

Biodancing   231

we find the recognition that "[T]he growth of recycling activities is a political development rather than an industrial one. . . . As long as we continue to measure industrial performance by the conventional assessment of profit, recycling is unlikely to have a major impact in reducing waste generation in the years ahead. Indeed, the concept of waste recycling, itself a contradiction in terms, is better politics than business." The Office of Technology Assessment, in *Serious Reduction Of Hazardous Waste* (Congress of the United States: Washington, D.C., June 1987), p. 8, put it this way: "Although there are many environmental and economic benefits to waste reduction, over 99 percent of Federal and State environmental spending is devoted to controlling pollution after waste is generated. Less than 1 percent is spent to reduce the generation of waste."

16. Funk, Robert E., "Post-Pleistocene Adaptations," in Bruce G. Trigger, ed., Vol. 15: *Northeast* of the *Handbook of North American Indians,* William C. Sturtevant, general ed. (Smithsonian Institution: Washington, D.C., 1978), pp. 16–27. Quote from p. 16.

17. Our present-day equivalents of *the* rules for adaptation are emerging in recent literature. On p. 20 of *Adaptive Environmental Assessment and Management,* edited by C. S. Holling (IIASA/John Wiley & Sons: New York, 1978), we find the following: "1. Environmental dimensions should be introduced at the very beginning of the development, or policy design process, and should be integrated as equal partners with economic and social considerations, so that the design can benefit from, and even enhance, natural forces. 2. Thereafter, during the design phase, there should be periods of intense focused innovation involving significant outside constituencies, followed by periods of stable consolidation. 3. Part of the design should incorporate benefits derived from increasing information on unknown or partially known social, economic, and environmental effects. Information can be given a value just as jobs, income, and profit can. 4. Some of the experiments designed to produce information can be part of an integrated research plan, but part should be designed into the actual management activities. Managers as well as scientists learn from change. 5. An equally integral part of the design is the monitoring and remedial mechanisms. They should not simply be post hoc additions after implementation. 6. In the design of those mechanisms there should be a careful analysis of the economic trade-offs between structures and policies that presume that the unexpected can be designed out, and less capital-expensive mechanisms that monitor and ameliorate the unexpected."

18. Larsen, Curtis E., "Geoarchaeological Interpretation of Great Lakes Coastal Environments," in *Archaeological Sediments in Context: Peopling of the Americas,* Edited Volume Series, Vol. 1, Julie K. Stein and William R. Farrand, eds. (Center for the Study of Early Man, Institute for Quaternary Studies, University of Maine at Orono, 1985), pp. 91–110.

19. Schumacher, E. F., *Small Is Beautiful: a Study of Economics as if People Mattered* (Blond & Briggs: London, 1973).

20. Leopold, Aldo, *A Sand County Almanac, with other essays on conservation from Round River* (Oxford University Press: New York, 1949/ 1966). Quote from pp. 217–218. "When Neighbors Quarrel: Canada-U.S. Dispute Settlement Experience" by Richard B. Bilder (Institute for Legal Studies, U. of Wisconsin-Madison Law School Disputes Processing Research Program: Madison, May 1987) provides a recent instructive accounting of the cooperative mechanisms these abutting, intertwined nations have developed to assist their getting along.

21. Bateson, Gregory, *Steps to An Ecology of Mind* (Random House: New York and Toronto, 1972), p. 293. See especially pp. 279–308.

22. Edberg, Rolf, *On The Shred Of A Cloud: Notes in a Travel Book*, translated by Sven Ahman (University of Alabama Press: University, Alabama, 1966/1969). Quote from page 192.

23. Structured restrospection (monitoring) had a role in the formulating of the U.S. Constitution. In the December 11, 1787, issue of "The Federalist" (No. 20), James Madison, with the assistance of Alexander Hamilton, helped the people of the state of New York and the fledgling nation to learn a lesson in governance by reviewing the strengths and weaknesses of the European government [The Netherlands] that had first settled the Hudson River environs.

24. Hall, Edward T., "Proxemics—The Study of Man's Spatial Relations," in *Man's Image In Medicine and Anthropology*, I. Galdston, ed. (International Universities Press: New York, 1963).

25. Cronon, William J., "Boundaries and Ecosystems in U.S. and Canadian History," in *TbMN Proceedings and Relata*, Vol. 1, pp. 36–55.

26. Note 23, supra.

27. Indicative of the real world* misfit of our economic and financial indicators is the entire "Business Day" section, D1–D36, of the Tuesday, October 20, 1987, issue of *The New York Times*, typified by the comment (page D34): "We are not operating in an environment of weakness." A few see it differently. Peter G. Peterson, in "The Morning After" (*The Atlantic*, Vol. 260, No. 4, October 1987) opines: "In the finest tradition of Euripidean irony, measures meant to save us have worked in the end to afflict us, so much so that even our nation's non-economic hopes—cultural, social , and strategic—have been clouded by our disastrous fiscal mismanagement. It has been a hard lesson in the law of unintended results. . . . We face a future of economic choices that are far less pleasant than any set of choices we have confronted in living memory." Quotation from pp. 44 and 64.

* The way I use this term requires some explanation. As Michael E. Soule put it in "Conservation Biology and the 'Real World' ", in *Conservation Biology: The Science of Scarcity and Diversity* (Sinauer Associates: Sunderland, Massachusetts 1986): "To most of us, I think the term 'real world' means the part of our lives that involves face-to-face interactions with others and with their desires, priorities, and prejudices; it is the world 'out there', the world of politics and economics, and all the vagaries of human nature that we associate with these areas. But the term 'real world' implies that other worlds are less than real. It begs the question, for example of the 'internal world' of subjective experience, and the 'middle world' of cognition, experiment, and discourse. Such distinctions are oversimplified, but this one is so ingrained that attack is futile. However, it is important to bear in mind that there is traffic bridging these so-called worlds. . . . [N]one of these worlds is at bottom any more real or important in a social or physical sense than any other. Each is part of a larger whole. When this fact is ignored, we generate disciplinary hierachies that inhibit progess in solving conservation problems. Conservation biology will succeed to the degree that its theoreticians, practitioners, and users acknowledge the larger context in which they exist, and to the degree that they respect one another's roles, contributions, and problems." Quotation from pp. 2 and 3.

28. The Nature Conservancy, Virginia Chapter, "Virginia Natural Heritage Program Launched (What We Did During Summer Vacation)," in *Virginia Conservancy News,* Vol. 16, No. 3 (Fall/Winter 1986).

29. Instructive—in reviewing what we set out to do for the endangered species that concern us—is the endeavor now under way to review "how much (of an area, of a gene pool, etc.) is enough" when we establish refuges to maintain wildlife diversity. The Sunday, May 24, 1987, issue of *The Washington Post* had, on page D3, a revealing examination of how well we are doing in this regard. Not well—even in national parks. A great danger in this lies in how we define *elements.* That's one reason for the meeting of CODATA (a part of the International Council of Scientific Unions) In Karlsruhe in 1988 to develop a mechanism for coherent access and nomenclature in biological data.

30. Ciulla, Joanne B., "Trouble Among the Titans," review of the book, *The Bigness Complex: Industry, Labor, and Government In the American Economy,* by Walter Adams and James Brock, in the '"Book World" section of *The Washington Post,* January 18, 1987, p. 11.

31. Shephard, Esther, "The Camp on the Big Onion," in *Paul Bunyan* (Harcourt Brace Jovanovich, Publishers: New York, 1924/1952), pp. 14–16. Note the similarity of the situation the government wanted Paul Bunyan to monitor to the situation described by Margalef on pages 45–46. These are still the situations we face when we attempt to "bound" an ecosystem so that we can measure its important things. In the September 1986 issue of *Sea Technology,* Michael A. Champ called it "Monitoring—Painting A Moving Train."

32. Miller, James Grier, *Living Systems* (McGraw-Hill Book Company: New York, 1978). On page 22 of this monumental book, written for a broad readership, Miller defines *structure:* "The structure of a system is the arrangement of its subsystems and components in three-dimensional space at

a given moment of time." On page 23 Miller defines *process* for a broad readership: "All change over time of matter-energy or information in a system is process."

33. Fitch, James Marston, "Experiential Bases for Aesthetic Decision,:" in *Annals of the New York Academy of Sciences,* Vol. 128 (1965), pp. 706–714.

34. Kuchenberg, Tom, and Jim LeGault, *Reflections in a Tarnished Mirror: The Use and Abuse of the Great Lakes* (Golden Glow Publishing: Sturgeon Bay, Wisconsin, 1978).

35. Ibid., pp. 18, 26, 28, 29, 31, 35, 36, and 41. See also Bartlett, Robert V., *The Reserve Mining Controversy: Science, Technology, and Environmental Quality* (Indiana University Press: Bloomington, 1980).

36. Fitchko, J., *Literature Review of the Effects of Persistent Toxic Substances on Great Lakes Biota: Report of the Health of Aquatic Communities Task Force* (Report to the Great Lakes Science Advisory Board, International Joint Commission, Great Lakes Regional Office, December 1986), p. 159.

37. Sudar, Anne, "A Survey of Public Perceptions of Great Lakes Water Levels," presented at the May 1987 Conference of the International Association for Great Lakes Research, in Ann Arbor, Michigan.

38. Brusso, Fred R., "The Finish Floor Issue," in *Strengthening Local Flood Protection Programs,* Proceedings of the Tenth Annual Conference of the Association of State Floodplain Managers, Pittsburgh, Pennsylvania, June 17–19, 1986 (The Natural Hazards Research and Applications Information Center, Boulder, Colorado, and the Association of State Floodplain Managers, Madison, Wisconsin), pp. 159–163.

39. For a description of our "double-jeopardy" position, see Jenkins, Robert E., "The Nation's Aquatic Estate," in *The Nature Conservancy News,* Vol. 33, No. 3 (May/June 1983), pp. 7–13.

40. Living with the Round River means that we will eventually have our responsibilities recalled to our attention—if not the first time it circles around, then the second time with diminished options. We ought to reacquaint ourselves with the Round's characteristics. According to Shephard (Esther), who wrote "The Round Drive," in *Paul Bunyan,* pp. 45–58, Paul Bunyan and his crew learned the hard way about the Round River's characteristics: "You see the way that was, the river we'd been on was round and hadn't no outlet."

41. Scientific Committee on Problems of the Environment (SCOPE). "Genetically-Designed Organisms in the Environment," in *SCOPE Newsletter,* No. 25 (September 1986), published by the International Council of Scientific Unions, makes the point this way (on p. 1): "[W]e have not fully considered those features of natural systems which might promote or hinder the establishment of engineered organisms nor have we adequately considered how we will monitor the spread of the engineered genetic information."

42. "Wise and careful monitoring" (even within the restricted field of biology) is an ever-present challenge. I would offer the following series of articles as guidance: Cairns, John, Jr., and W. H. van der Schalie, "Biological Monitoring: Part I—Early Warning Systems," in *Water Research*, Vol. 14 (1980), pp. 1179-1196; Matthews, Robin A., Arthur L. Buikema, Jr., John Cairns, Jr., and J. H. Rodgers, Jr., "Biological Monitoring: Part IIA—Receiving System Functional Methods, Relationships and Indices," in *Water Research*, Vol. 16 (1982), pp. 129-139.; Herricks, Edwin E., and John Cairns, Jr., "Biological Monitoring: Part III—Receiving System Methodology Based on Community Structure,' in *Water Research*, Vol. 16 (1982), pp. 141-153; Buikema, A. L., Jr., B. R. Niederlehner, and J. Cairns, Jr., "Biological Monitoring: Part IV—Toxicity Testing," in *Water Research*, Vol. 16 (1982), pp. 239-262; Cherry, Donald S., and John Cairns, Jr., "Biological Monitoring: Part V—Preference and Avoidance Studies," in *Water Research*, Vol. 16 (1982), pp. 263-301; and Cairns, John, Jr., "Biological Monitoring: Part VI—Future Needs," in *Water Research*, Vol. 15 (1981), pp. 941-952.

43. The first day of the TbMN Workshop was itself organized to set in place the awareness of this "dynamism" of relationships as a common footing for participants. It is difficult to look at everything at once in this interlinked world, so these relationships may be more readily perceived and understood by reference to subsets. Three of these subsets are the systems which encompass the reductionist subject matter of various environment/ man interfaces in the global ecosystem. They provided a meaningful way to segment the ground-laying presentations at the TbMN Workshop. In the words of Darcy Ribeiro: "1. The adaptive system covers all those practices through which a society acts on nature in the effort to provide its subsistence and to reproduce the totality of goods and furnishings at its disposal. 2. The associative system covers the complex of norms and institutions that organize social life, discipline human coexistence, regulate the work force, and govern political life. 3. The ideological system is the body of knowledge, beliefs, and values generated in the adaptive and associative efforts." Ribeiro also observed (in the 1971 translation of his book, *The Americas and Civilization*) L. Barrett and M. Barrett trans., E. P. Dutton, New York; 1971, pp. 32-33 passim: "The understanding of social life and its dynamics demands . . . that abstract analysis of each of these factors refer always to the integrated complexes in which they coexit and act jointly." System synthesis is necessary for understanding. Analysis (piecemealing) alone won't do it.

44. Ehrenfeld, David, "Implementing the Transition to a Sustainable Agriculture: An Opportunity for Ecology," in *Bulletin of the Ecological Society of America*, Vol. 68, No. 1 (March 1987).

45. Much of what we set out to do is detailed in Dworsky, Leonard B., "The Great Lakes: 1955-1985," in *Natural Resources Journal: U.S.-Canada Transboundary Resource Issues*, Vol. 26, No. 2 (Spring 1986), pp. 291-336. Reprinted as Chapter 4 of this volume.

46. Through the flood of ineffectual controls, there are nascent signs that governments are adopting approaches more suited to ecosystemic phenomena. In this category I would place the *Floodplain Development Manual,* PWD 86010, ISBM 724030115 (New South Wales Government: Australia, December 1986).

47. This visual orientation is heavily relied on, as well, in graphical presentations of scientific data. Graphics (particularly in this era of advancing computer graphics) can be powerful tools both for analyses of data and for communicating findings, but they are not without drawbacks in a world where perception plays such a significant role.

48. John McLeod noted in "System Simulation: Behavioral Science, System Theory—and Simulation" (Behavioral Science, Vol. 19, pp. 57–69, 1974) that "languages even within the continuous and discrete factions, cause difficulties that also impede progress in simulation. This applies to both natural languages and the computer variety . . . Simulation is inherently interdisciplinary (or should be), and simulationists from different disciplines bring their own vocabulary with them. There is, however, also a problem with computer languages." Quote from pp. 65 and 66, passim.

49. See note 36, Fitchko, op. cit.

50. Ryder, R. A., and C. J. Edwards, eds., *A Conceptual Approach for the Application of Biological Indicators of Ecosystem Quality in the Great Lakes Basin* (A Joint Effort of the International Joint Commission and the Great Lakes Fishery Commission: Windsor, Ontario, March 1985), p. 169. O'Connor, Joel S. and Richard T. Dewling, "Indices of Marine Degradation: Their Utility" in *Environmental Management,* Vol. 10, No. 3, pp. 335–343. The United States's Council on Environmental Quality (see note 1 for the source document) expands this view on indicators: There are many proposed indicators of change, but few have any measure of precision, and even fewer have a track record of having been useful to a variety of scientists in different environments. Many of the indicators of change are based on ecological assumptions that have not been critically tested. Because there is more prestige in proposing new indices than in testing existing ones, large numbers of potential indicators—each with a narrow data base and a lack of confidence—tend to accumulate within the discipline of environmental impact analysis. There is uncertainty about which variables should be included in environmental monitoring. (pp. IV-11 and IV-12)

51. See note 3.

52. Paul A. Colinvaux, *Ecology* (Wiley: New York, 1986).

53. See Bandurski, Bruce L., Peter T. Haug, and Andrew L. Hamilton, *TbMN Proceedings and Relata,* Vol. 2. See especially pp. 333–335, 340b, and 355a. See also Wilson, Richard, and E. A. C. Crouch, "Risk Assessment and Comparisons: An Introduction," in *Science,* Vol. 236, No. 4799 (17 April 1987), pp. 267–295.

54. O'Neill, R. V., D. L. DeAngelis, J. B. Waide, and T. F. H. Allen, *A Hierarchical Concept of Ecosystems* (Princeton University Press: Princeton, New Jersey, 1986), pp. 73-74.

55. On March 17, 1987, at a hearing on high water levels of the Great Lakes (conducted by the Subcommittee on Water Resources of the Public Works Committee, U.S. House of Representatives), Donald L. Collins (Assistant Administrator, Office of Insurance Policy Analysis and Technical Services, Federal Insurance Administration, Federal Emergency Management Agency) testified that prior to the Flood Protection Disaster Act of 1973, federal flood insurance could not cover losses from erosion unless the erosion was caused by a flood-related event. The 1973 Act allowed losses caused by "extraordinary erosion" to be covered.

56. Dobell, Rod, and Ted Parson, "Governing with Risk," in *Policy Options,* Vol. 7, No. 10 (December 1986), pp. 10-15. Quote from pp. 14-15. According to authors N. C. Sonntag, R. R. Everitt, L. P. Rattie, D. L. Colnett, C. P. Wolf, J. C. Truett, A. H. J. Dorcey, and C. S. Holling, in their report *Cumulative Effects Assessment: A Context for Further Research and Development* (Canadian Environmental Assessment Research Council: 1987): "The linkages between technological, ecological, and social systems are a major determinant in considering the potential for cumulative effects. Increased spatial and temporal scales of development, combined with narrowly focused management strategies, are creating situations where previously independent systems are becoming more tightly coupled and therefore interdependent." Quote from p. 25.

57. *National Water Quality Monitoring and Assessment: Report on a Colloquium Sponsored by the Water Science and Technology Board, National Research Council, May 21-22, 1986,* is replete (particularly in the "overview" section) with signs that either/or thinking is alive and well in the scientific community. Fortunately, it is still able to cooperate well enough to produce such reports as Deborah S. Snavely's *Water-Use Data-Collection Programs and Regional Data Base of the Great Lakes-St. Lawrence River Basin States and Provinces,* U.S. Geological Survey Open File Report 86-546, prepared in cooperation with the Council of Great Lakes Governors (Albany, New York, 1986).

58. Miller, Alan, op. cit., note 10. Quote from p. 188.

59. Bartlett, Robert V., "Ecological Rationality: Reason and Environmental Policy," in *Environmental Ethics,* Vol. 8 (Fall 1986), pp. 221-239. Quote from pages 230 and 239.

60. Caldwell's experienced observation is echoed in the forward to *State of the World 1987: a Worldwatch Institute Report on Progress Toward a Sustainable Society* (W.W. Norton & Company: New York, 1987), p. xvi.

61. Caldwell, Lynton K., "Binational Responsibilities for a Shared Environment," in *Canada and The United States: Enduring Friendship, Per-*

sistent Stress, edited by Charles F. Doran and John H. Sigler, (Prentice-Hall, Inc.: Englewood Cliffs, New Jersey, 1985). Quote from p. 226.

62. Haug, Peter T., Bruce L. Bandurski, and Andrew L. Hamilton, TbMN Proceedings and Relata, Vol. 1, p. 245.

63. Caldwell, note 61, op. cit., p. 226.

64. Gwynne, M. "Commentary" in *Sustainable Development of the Biosphere*, William C. Clark and R. E. Munn, eds. (Cambridge University Press for the International Institute for Applied Systems Analysis: Cambridge, 1986), pp. 375–377.

65. Izrael, Yu, and R. E. Munn, "Environmental and Renewable Resource Monitoring," draft submitted for publication and printed in *TbMN Proceedings and Relata*, Vol. 2, pp. 556–557. Cf., also pp. 360–375, note 64.

66. American Society for Photogrammetry and Remote Sensing, *GIS/LIS:* Vol. 5 of the *1987 ASPRS-ACSM Annual Convention Proceedings* (ASPRS: Falls Church, Virginia, 1987), 224 pp.

67. Bureau of Land Management, Department of the Interior, *ALMRS: Automated Land and Mineral Record System* (U.S. Government Printing Office: Washington, D.C., 1985), p. 3.

68. The BLM's ALMRS has counterparts in data base management systems that deal with the man/water interface. See Stephen W. Shawcross and Augusto R. V. Ribeiro, "A Data Base Management Approach to Flood Damage Reduction Studies," in *Strengthening Local Flood Protection Programs,* Proceedings of the Tenth Annual Conference of the Association of State Floodplain Managers, Pittsburgh, Pennsylvania, June 17–19, 1986 (the Natural Hazards Research and Applications Information Center, Boulder, Colorado, and the Association of State Floodplain Managers, Madison, Wisconsin), pp. 243–248.

69. Margalef, Ramon, *Perspectives in Ecological Theory* (The University of Chicago Press: Chicago, 1968), pp. 35 and 36.

70. O'Neill, et al., op cit., note 54. Quote from pp. 83–84, 86.

71. Needham, Joseph, *Time, The Refreshing River* (George Allen & Unwin, Ltd.: London, 1943, and Spokesman: Nottingham, 1986), p. 160, in the latter edition.

72. See, for instance, Spitzer, D., "On Applications of Remote Sensing for Environmental Monitoring," in *Environmental Monitoring and Assessment,* Vol. 7, No. 3 (November 1986), pp. 263–271.

73. Caldwell, Lynton K., "Binational Responsiblities for a Shared Environment," note 61, op. cit. Quote from pp. 226–228 passim. Caldwell has looked to "means outside of the conventional political structure". Anthony

J. H. Dorcey has done the same in "The Myth of Interagency Cooperation in Water Resources Management" (*Canadian Water Resources Journal,* Vol. 12, No. 2, June 1987). On page 22 of that article he stresses: "Because the dominant myth—interagency cooperation—has dampened our curiosity, distorted our images and misdirected our attention, we must replace it with one that is more appropriate to the challenges facing Canadian water resources management. Clearly, interagency cooperation is important and should continue to be included in the new myth, but it is equally obvious that it must embrace two additional ideas. First, while interagency cooperation is necessary so also is cooperation with and between all the varied private organizations and other interests involved. Second, while cooperation is essential so also is conflict resolution."

74. Caldwell, op. cit. p. 228.

75 Izrael and Munn, op. cit., p. 558.

76. Miller, Alan, op. cit. Quote from p. 188.

77. Pepperberg, Irene M. "The Importance of Social Interaction in the Acquisition of Communicative Competence: Possible Parallels between Avian and Human Learning," in *Social Learning: A Comparative Approach,* Zentall and Galef, eds., (Lawrence Erlbaum: Hillsdale, New Jersey, 1987).

78. Pimm, S. L., "Competition and Community Structure," in *Intecol Newsletter,* Vol. 17, No. 2 (April 1987), pp. 1 and 4.

79. Carroll, John E., "Water Resources Management as an Issue in Environmental Diplomacy," in *Natural Resources Journal: U.S.-Canada Transboundary Resource Issues,* Vol. 26, No. 2 (Spring 1986), pp. 207–220. Quote on p. 214.

80. A fairly recent accounting of human-induced changes in Great Lakes ecosystems and of rehabilitation strategies and attempts may be found in *Rehabilitating Great Lakes Ecosystems,* edited by George R. Francis, John J. Magnuson, Henry A. Regier, and Daniel R. Talhelm (Great Lakes Fishery Commission Technical Report No. 37: Ann Arbor, MI, December 1979). A glimpse of parallels, indicating the global nature of certain of these changes, may be found in "Conclusions and Guidelines of the Workshop on Integrated Monitoring", note by the secretariat of the Executive Body for the Convention on Long-range Transboundary Air Pollution (Steering Body to the Cooperative Programme for Monitoring and Evaluation of the Long-range Transmission of Air Pollutants in Europe). On 7 July 1987, Item 7 of the provisional agenda (Eleventh session, Geneva, 1–3 September 1987), Economic Commission for Europe, was published by the United Nations Economic and Social Council as EB.AIR/GE.1/RR.31.

81. Brown, M. T. and H. T. Odum, eds., "Research Needs for A Basic Science of the System of Humanity and Nature and Appropriate Technology for the Future", results of a workshop at Gainesville, Florida, May 14–16,

1981 (NSF/CEE 81090: Energy Analysis Workshop, Center for Wetlands, U. of Florida, Gainesville, October 1981).

82. Tulku, Tarthang, op. cit. Quote from p. 213.

83. Tulku, Tarthang, op. cit. Quote from p. 301.

84. Tulku, Tarthang, op. cit. Quote from p. 160. Dealing with language and thinking, V. V. Nalimov puts it another way in *In The Labyrinths Of Language: A Mathematician's Journey* (Transl. by R. G. Colodny of the 1974 book, ISI Press: Philadelphia 1981): "Words, affected by their neighbors, transcend the prior distribution functions of 'meaning'. Word borders are erased. Words quite different in their meaning interlace and converge. . . . *Tractatus Logico-Philosophicus* by Wittgenstein (1955) consists of a sequence of enumerated paradoxes, . . . laconic statements with rich content which are obviously contradictory to the concepts generally accepted in our culture. Here is one such paradox:

"In the world everything is as it is and happens as it does happen.

In it there is no value—and if there were, it would be of no value." . . . [T]he internal deep state of consciousness is unique in its essential continuity which cannot be reduced to the discreteness of language. . . . [T]he most peculiar feature of recent years in Western culture is the urge of a small number of its intellectuals to cross the boundaries of their paradigm, to enrich themselves by experiencing the structure of consciousness in other cultures, in an effort to exploit all the potential riches of human faculties. . . . Multi-valued logic is created, probabilistic thinking is developed, and the principle of complementarity acquires the right to exist in science. It is also noteworthy that, simultaneously, linguistic means are expanded."

85. How meaningful is that development for environment and for economy was explored by the National Task Force on Environment and Economy, established by the Canadian Council of Resource and Environment Ministers in October 1986. (The Task Force was formed as a direct follow-up to the visit to Canada, in May 1986, of the World Commission on Environment and Development.) In September 1987 its report was presented.

86. In "Incorporating Ecological Interpretation into Basic Statutes", an overview article in *The Integrity of Water,* proceedings of a symposium March 10–12, 1975 (U.S. Environmental Protection Agency: Washington, D.C., June 1977), Thomas Jorling observed that "Incorporating ecological principles into regulatory statutes is not easy. Two quite different sets of problems are involved. The first set might be called philosophical, and the second practical.

In considering the philosophical, it is necessary to contrast the new program [of water pollution control] enacted in 1972 with the program it replaced because the two provide a conceptual framework in which to compare strongly divergent assumptions. Under the earlier program, the basic assumption was that the biosphere, and in particular the water component of the biosphere, was to be, and in fact existed to be, used. . . . [T]hat earlier pollution control law was based on the assumption that the components of the environment existed to be used by man, a creature that somehow existed apart from and beyond the biosphere. The new program has a different underpinning. It assumes that man is a component of the biosphere and that relationship we seek to achieve with the environment is what some have called 'harmony'. Under this view, man is an integral, if dominant, part of the structure and function of the biosphere. The intellectual roots of this perspective are found in the study of evolution. The objective of this concept is the maximum patterning of human communities after biogeochemical cycles with a minimum departure from the geological or background rates of change in the biosphere.

Within the subset of issues under the label 'practical', we are looking at the question of whether or not a program which is established to achieve something—a principle, a purpose or an objective—will, in fact, achieve it. We must examine the age-old maxim, is it enforceable? Again a comparison of the old with the new program provides insight into the tremendous differences relative to practical and enforcement questions. A program premised upon the establishment of acceptable beneficial uses of water has inherent in it several layers of legal cause and effect relationships that enable easy frustration of enforceable requirements. . . . The net effect of the program was the application of controls which were fully in accord with and acceptable to the interests of the discharge source. More importantly, the whole program assumed that matter and energy moved in linear pathways. It was fundamentally opposite to the notion of keeping matter and energy within constraining circles or cycles. . . . [I]n the new program . . . [t]he control measures adopted are referenced to the present ability to recycle materials, energy, and water within the overall objective of complete recycling systems for industrial, municipal, and agricultural activities. There are, to be sure, opportunities to apply other factors in the consideration of what controls are to be imposed at particular times. The Act [Federal Water Pollution Control Act Amendments of 1972] is structured so that time itself is the major factor, as performance of sources will be reviewed regularly every 5 years, always under the overall policy of looking towards the reclaiming of pollutants and the recycling of water. It is a happy coincidence when enforceability and the philosophical premise neatly complement each other." Quotation from pp. 10–11, passim.

87. Krawetz, Natalia M., William R. MacDonald, and Peter Nichols, *A Framework For Effective Monitoring* (Canadian Environmental Assessment Research Council: Hull, Quebec 1987); pp. 39–44, passim.

88. Tulku, Tarthang, op. cit. Quote from pp. 160 and 197–202, passim.

CHAPTERS 7A AND 7B. THE GREAT LAKES AS A WATER RESOURCE

The two papers in this chapter are exceptions, in one respect, to the emphasis throughout this volume on comprehensive, systemic aspects of Great Lakes issues and policies rather than on specific problems such as pollution, fisheries, recreation, shipping, and water levels. Questions regarding diversion of Great Lakes waters for consumption outside the basin are receiving high-level political attention that unavoidably involves broader questions of policy for the lakes and especially the commitment to a basinwide ecosystem approach. Readers of this volume need some insight into the legal and economic aspects of the ownership and diversion of Great Lakes waters. For persons seeking a more extensive treatment of these issues, the *Case Western Reserve Journal of International Law,* Vol. 18 (No.1,1986), is recommended.

Julia R. Wilder

7A

QUESTIONS OF OWNERSHIP AND CONTROL

Although water is the essential element in the Great Lakes ecosystem, that water is also widely regarded as a commodity, a public good that may be owned, transferred, bought, or sold. Demand for nationwide distribution of Great Lakes water is soon expected to become significant. Those who seek wider distribtuion of Great Lakes water will do so under the assumption that the Great Lakes Basin possesses water resources in excess of its own needs—that the total amount of water available from both ground and surface water sources exceeds present water needs for the municipal and industrial communities within the Great Lakes Basin. From an economic perspective, statistics indicate that the Great Lakes are presently underutilized as a water resource, since it is estimated that water withdrawals from the lakes will steadily increase between 1985 and 2035.[1]

There will be numerous parties seeking access to Great Lakes water. Foremost among them will be arid western states seeking to augment scarce water supplies in order to encourage and accommodate population growth or to retain present population levels. Although the Federal Bureau of Reclamation has constructed 325 reservoirs, 345 dams, and nearly 15,000 miles of canals in western states, figures compiled by the federal government indicate, for example, that the amount of water available in Montana and Wyoming will be less than all their potential demands for water by the year 2000.[2] Also seeking access to this water will be western power companies needing additional water for electrical generating plants and coal slurry pipelines.

It is also highly probable that central plains states will be seeking additional water supplies for agricultural irrigation since groundwater sources there are suffering from overdraft. The Ogallala aquifer in particular has been identified as a major source of water for agricultural use and may be in danger of extinction. In addition, demand for Great Lakes water could materialize in eastern states if present sources prove insufficient to meet the demand, or in states where contamination has impaired local supplies.

The new demand for Great Lakes water will be from states outside the Great Lakes Basin. The interests of these states are not rights, "but merely a consideration that they may address to Congress."[3] These nonriparian states do not have legally sanctioned independent means to coerce access to Great Lakes water for industrial, municipal, or agricultural uses within their boundaries.

Although the interests of states outside the Great Lakes Basin in the use of Great Lakes water do not constitute rights, at present there are two legal means by which those states may attain access to the water in the lakes. First, states outside the basin may obtain access to use of the water by contractual agreement with individual riparian states. Second, should riparian states refuse to contractually agree to this distribution, Congress has the authority to extend access rights to nonriparian states.[4]

Clearly, Congress has the authority to extend such rights to states outside the Great Lakes Basin. Moreover, in *Arizona* v. *California*,[5] the United States Supreme Court held that the federal government may allocate water to serve the national interest, and may supercede federal common law and state law in order to do so. Therefore, Great Lakes states must take affirmative steps to establish a new forum in order to maintain control over Great Lakes water use. If, however, the riparian states react to export demands by enacting statutory provisions that violate the commerce clause of the United States Constitution, the federal government may eventually intervene and allocate the water in accordance with a contemporary beneficial use standard, irrespective of the consent of the riparian states.

One may only speculate as to what sort of future consensus might coalesce in Congress. Congressional intervention to distribute eastern water to western states could conceivably cause an East-West "civil war" over usufructuary rights (usage rights), or at least create serious regional tensions. Riparian states in eastern jurisdictions, jealously asserting control over local water resources, might somehow refuse to yield to a federal allocative system that would, in effect, take "their" water and "give" it to nonriparian states free of charge. There is also the overriding consideration of Canadian rights in any Great Lakes water diversion policy. The United States is bound by treaty with Canada to joint custody of the lakes, and under the United States Constitution, treaty obligations presumably take precedence over state or federal statutory law.

Nevertheless, the authority and jurisdiction of the United States over waters that affect neighboring countries is to some extent situational. Congress has authorized diversion of waters before they have reached the international boundary with Mexico, for example. The Colorado River Basin Project Act is a cogent example of the federal prerogative in this area.[6] The Act vests authority in the Department of the Interior to augment and allocate the water supply of the Colorado River Basin throughout and beyond the Basin. The Act incorporates provisions to authorize the importation of water into the Colorado River Basin from "any other natural river drainage basin lying outside the [Colorado River Basin]." Furthermore, if the Secretary of Interior should plan to import water from other basins, "he shall make provision for adequate and equitable protection of the interests of the states and areas of origin."[7]

There are now five existing diversions in the Great Lakes Basin. Four of these involve a transfer of water from the watershed of one Great Lake into that of another. These diversions are the Long Lac and Ogoki diversions from the Hudson Bay drainage basin into Lake Superior, the Welland diversion from Lake Erie into Lake Ontario, and the diversion from the Niagara River into the New York State Barge Canal. The Chicago Canal diverts water from Lake Michigan into the Mississippi River watershed. The governments of the eight riparian states may exhibit divergent views as to whether such states possess the legal right to divert Great Lakes water for export to points outside the basin. In fact, there has been long-standing disagreement among riparian states on the issue of diversion of Great Lakes water to points outside the Great Lakes watershed. The disagreement between riparian states in regard to the efficacy of water exportation has been documented by continuous litigation. The United States Supreme Court has mediated a dispute between Wisconsin (and intervening states) and Illinois in a series of cases.[8]

The continual threat of litigation makes water export impracticable for riparian states that would prefer to do so. Despite the efforts of the litigant states and the attempts of the Supreme Court to mediate the matter, protracted litigation has not promoted the achievement of a consensus or solution in regard to the riparian states' shared use of Great Lakes water. The controversy remains even today as states seek to increase diversions of water. For example, according to the Supreme Court decree in 1967, the state of Illinois

> may make application for a modification of this decree so as to permit the diversion of additional water from Lake Michigan for domestic use when and if it appears that the reasonable needs of the Northeastern Illinois Metropolitan Region . . . for water . . . cannot be met from the water resources available to the region, including both ground and surface water and the water permitted by the decree . . . and if it further appears that all feasible means reasonably available to the State of Illinois . . . have been employed . . . to conserve and manage the water resources of the region and the use of water therein in accordance with the best modern scientific knowledge and engineering practice.[9]

A Senate bill and two House bills, introduced in the first session of the Ninety-Eighth Congress, directly addressed this issue. Each bill sought to prohibit diversions of Great Lakes water for use outside a Great Lakes state unless such action was approved by all the Great Lakes states.[10] The introduction of these bills makes it apparent that at least some government officials in Great Lakes states consider the possibility of nationwide distribution of Great Lakes water to be an imminent threat and a serious affront to the interests of some or all of those states. This inference was confirmed by the Charter opposing diversion outside the Basin, adopted in 1985 by governors and premiers of the Great Lakes Basin states and provinces.

The policy of granting Great Lakes usufructuary rights to a growing constituency of water users has been manifested in four progressive stages. Originally, state authority over water resources in Great Lakes jurisdictions was governed by the common law doctrine of riparianism. At this stage, courts were the exclusive forum for the resolution of disputes between private riparian parties. Common law decisions subsequently evolved to reflect increased rejection of the riparian doctrine and a growing incorporation of elements of the prior appropriation doctrine that allowed nonriparian parties access to water. At this stage, municipal corporations assumed primary allocative control over state water resources. In a relatively recent development, state control over appropriation and distribution of water resources was augmented by the establishment of state permit systems that incorporate features of both the riparian and prior appropriation doctrines. As a result, state governments exert primary control over the distribution of state water resources by means of decision-making authority vested in the permit system,[11] and courts have assumed a more limited role as a forum for the adjudication of usufructuary rights. The logical extension of the growth pattern outlined by the above stages suggests that law and public policy are moving in the direction of obligating riparian states to accomodate the reasonable needs of nonriparian states seeking use of Great Lakes water. In the stage that is presently emerging, it appears that control of Great Lakes water use will be increasingly assumed by riparian state governments in the form of cooperative control as implied in the 1985 Charter by the governors and premiers.

DETERMINANTS OF GREAT LAKES WATER OWNERSHIP

The concept of Great Lakes water ownership includes two separate, yet related realms: ownership of the Great Lakes as a waterbody in a territorial sense[12] and ownership of the Great Lakes water in a usufructuary (right of use) sense.[13] Both aspects of ownership connote a relationship between a sovereign entity and the Great Lakes as a waterbody. A usufructuary right signifies possession of the equitable right to diversion and use of the water in that waterbody, in contrast to ownership of the waterbody itself. Although this chapter will examine usufructuary rights most closely, it is nonetheless necessary to outline the territorial dimensions of the lakes, since they are largely determinative of usufructuary rights.

Usufructuary rights in Great Lakes water are derived from a hierarchical structure of sovereign entities and their attendant forums. Although water law is fundamentally within the province of state law, superimposed upon state-sanctioned usufructuary rights are legal obligations and constraints imposed by state agreement in the form of interstate compacts, federal regulation under the commerce clause, and international treaty.

TERRITORIAL CONCEPTS OF OWNERSHIP: SOVEREIGNS AND THEIR FORUMS

State

The Great Lakes are contiguous to eight of the United States. The beds of the Great Lakes are owned by the contiguous states extending from the shoreline to the point of the international boundary.[14] The United States Supreme Court has established that states own the waters of navigable waterbodies within state boundaries.[15] Since each state riparian to the Great Lakes owns that portion of the lakes within its boundaries, state law in Great Lakes jurisdictions establishes primary control over diversions from the lakes.[16] The Great Lakes states ratified the Great Lakes Basin Compact in 1955 in order to promote comity in regard to the sharing of the interstate waterbody.[17] The Compact established the Great Lakes Commission to "promote the orderly, integrated and comprehensive development, use and conservation of the water resources of the Great Lakes Basin."

The Great Lakes states also ratified the Great Lakes River Basin Commission, pursuant to its establishment by executive order of the president under Title II of the Water Resources Planning Act.[18] The Commission was abolished by Executive Order in 1981.[19] This order was widely regarded as a retrograde action, especially since the Great Lakes Commission has taken a narrow view of its functions and is almost wholly directed toward industrial issues, such as those involving the shipping industry.

Federal

Federal control of the Great Lakes has historically been founded upon a navigability interest and not a usufructuary interest in the water of the lakes.[20] The Great Lakes constitute an interstate body of navigable water, and areas of the lakes that are within the territorial jurisdiction of the United States are subject to control by the United States government under its commerce clause authority.[21] In *Sanitary District v. United States*,[22] the United States Supreme Court held that a riparian state cannot authorize diversions of water from the Great Lakes that will affect lake levels without the consent of Congress, since withdrawals that affect lake levels may also impair navigation. It is possible that increased withdrawals from the lakes may not significantly affect lake levels since modern engineering techniques may be used to upgrade the hydrologic bounty of a waterbody. The Great Lakes have a history of such manipulation by the Army Corps of Engineers. Lakes have been dredged to protect harbor lines, and artificial channels have been constructed to augment lake levels. It has been suggested that water levels may be controlled by the use of underground weirs, and in fact levels in Lakes Superior and Ontario are already controlled by this method. In the future, Great Lakes water levels may also be augmented by greater use of inflow into the Great Lakes from sources outside the Great Lakes

Basin, which flow elsewhere and are wasted, at least in terms of human usufructuary purposes.

International

The present international boundary between the United States and Canada was established by the Treaty of Ghent (1814). The negotiators stipulated that the pertinent northern boundary of the United States would be the "middle" of Lakes Ontario, Erie, Huron, and Superior, and their connecting waters. Britain (on behalf of Canada) and the United States ratified a treaty to establish a modern, accurate boundary line, which was officially delineated in 1913. It does not correspond to the exact center of each body of water but consists of 270 straight lines which are the equivalent of a median line.

Although the waters are comingled, the United States and Canada own those areas of the Great Lakes within their respective national boundaries. Therefore, the lakes are national, not international, waters. Although each nation exercises complete jurisdiction over all territorial waters within its boundaries, any institutional arrangement for diversion and use of water withdrawn from those areas of the Great Lakes within the United States territory must recognize Canadian rights. This chapter will not attempt to fully address the issue of Canadian rights since that subject is in itself an extensive topic. It should be noted that Canadian rights are significant in policy considerations regarding United States usufructuary rights in Great Lakes water.

The United States and Canada ratified the Boundary Waters Treaty in 1909 to regulate the shared use of Great Lakes water and to resolve disputes arising along the common frontier.[23] The treaty promulgated the principles that govern the boundary waters and created the International Joint Commission to preside over matters involving the diversion or use of the waters. Under Article I of the treaty, boundary waters are defined as those lakes, or connecting waters or portions thereof, through which the international boundary passes; tributary waters are those that flow into or from the Lakes or their connecting waters. "The High Contracting Parties agree that the navigation of all navigable boundary waters shall forever continue free and open for the purposes of commerce to the inhabitants . . . of both countries equally."[24]

> Each of the High Contracting Parties reserves to itself or to the several State Governments on one side and the Dominion or

Provincial governments on the other as the case may be, subject to any treaty provisions now existing with respect thereto, the exclusive jurisdiction and control over the use and diversion, whether temporary or permanent, of all waters on its own side of the line which in their natural channels would flow across the boundary or into boundary waters; but it is agreed that any interference with or diversion from their natural channels of such waters on either side of the boundary, resulting in any injury on the other side of the boundary, shall give rise to the same rights and entitle the injured parties to the same legal remedies as if such injury took place in the country where such diversion or interference occurs.[25]

Article III of the Boundary Waters Treaty establishes that

[i]t is agreed that . . . no further uses . . . or diversions, whether temporary or permanent, of boundary waters on either side of the line, affecting the natural level or flow of boundary waters on either side of the line, shall be made except by authority of the United States or the Dominion of Canada within their respective jurisdictions and with the approval, as hereinafter provided, of a joint commission, to be known as the International Joint Commission.[26]

The treaty provisions are not intended to interfere with the ordinary use of these waters for domestic and sanitary purposes. Under international law, the United States and Canada, respectively, have complete jurisdiction over the Great Lakes tributary waters since they lie wholly within each nation's respective boundaries. These unilateral rights accrue to each nation as long as neither nation's actions in regard to its use of water directly injure the other nation. In contrast, the principles which govern the use of boundary waters are derived from the perceived need for more immediate bilateral cooperation.

COMPETING THEORIES OF WATER "OWNERSHIP": DETERMINANTS OF USUFRUCTUARY RIGHTS

No party, private or state, may "own" water in an absolute sense.[27] This is also true of land ownership, since fee simple title confers only an estate in land. The United States Supreme Court has expressed the view that water is not amenable to private ownership as long as the water remains part of a waterbody.[28] Water as an article of property may not be owned in any capacity until it has been appropriated.[29]

Water "ownership" consists of a "bundle of usufructuary rights" grounded in equitable principles.[30] The usufructuary character of water ownership reflects the natural physical properties of water and the fact that water, as a physical entity, is continually moving through a dynamic process known as the hydrologic cycle. "Scientists have long recognized that water moves in what is known as the hydrologic cycle, the recurring period through which water passes from atmospheric water vapor into liquid and solid form as precipitation, then along or into the ground, finally returning to atmospheric water vapor by evaporation and transpiration."[31] Although science has established that all forms of water constitute one interconnected hydrologic entity, the law generally assigns each waterbody a particular legal status according to its location in the hydrologic cycle. For example, state statutes typically distinguish between usufructuary rights in groundwater and surface water. In other words, the law distinguishes usufructuary rights on the basis of where water is located in the hydrologic cycle when it is diverted for human use.

The law distinguishes between usufructuary rights in navigable and nonnavigable waterbodies. Private landowners generally take title to nonnavigable lakes, ponds, and streams that exist on their land. Navigable waterbodies are not amenable to such private ownership. A private landowner whose land abuts a navigable waterbody will generally have limited usufructuary rights: the right to divert water for reasonable uses, and the right of egress to navigable channels of the waterbody.

The state holds title to navigable waters in a public trust capacity for the benefit of state inhabitants, the beneficiaries of the trust.[32] The state has legal standing to protect the water within its territory, irrespective of the assent or dissent of the private owners immediately concerned.[33] Government ownership of water is actually a legal fiction that supports the state's regulatory powers,[34] "a fiction expressive in legal shorthand of the importance to its people that a State have power to preserve and regulate the exploitation of an important resource."[35]

The United States Supreme Court, in *Sporhase* v. *Nebraska* ex rel. *Douglas*,[36] examined the concept of state water "ownership" in the context of state control over the allocation of intrastate water resources. In *Sporhase,* the appellants owned adjacent tracts of land located in Nebraska and Colorado. A well located on the Nebraska tract pumped groundwater for use irrigating crops on both the Nebraska tract and the Colorado tract. The state of Nebraska brought an action to enjoin the appellents from transporting Nebraska groundwater into Colorado without a permit. The Nebraska permit system contained a provision conditioning transfer of Nebraska groundwater across state lines on the receiving state granting reciprocal rights. The Court reaffirmed the opinion that state ownership of water is a legal fiction, confirming the demise of the theory of state ownership of water resources that had once prevailed.[37]

The fiction of water ownership is manifested by the exercise of legally sanctioned usufructuary rights. These rights originate in the right of a party, state or private, to withdraw water from a waterbody. The right to withdraw or divert water from a waterbody is a valuable right in itself. This right must be bargained for separately from any ownership rights in the land that is contiguous to the waterbody.[38] The right to withdraw water from a waterbody is accompanied by the right to reasonable use or beneficial use of the water which has been diverted.[39] These basic features of usufructuary rights have been formulated under the aegis of two common law doctrines, the riparian and prior appropriation doctrines.

The riparian doctrine, developed in states with plentiful water supplies, provides a usufructuary right to a landowner owning a tract of land contiguous to the waterbody itself. Each riparian proprietor has the right to the reasonable use of whatever water can be diverted onto his or her land and, under the reasonable use rule, he or she may use the water for any purpose as long as such use does not interfere with the legitimate uses of other riparian owners. Since the usufructuary right is appurtenant to the riparian land itself, under the riparian doctrine, water use is restricted to riparian land, and, under a strict interpretation of the reasonable use doctrine, even a riparian party may not divert any of his or her share of water for use on nonriparian land. Riparian parties may not sell their share of water, or any portion of it, to a nonriparian user. Use of water on nonriparian land is per se unreasonable use. Consequently, if there is more water available in a waterbody than is needed for use on riparian land, the "surplus" water simply remains untapped, at least for human usufructuary purposes.

An alternative method of allocating water is formulated under the doctrine of prior appropriation. This doctrine developed in arid western states where parties compete for scarce water supplies. It provides water on a "first in time, first in right" basis. Any party that claims a beneficial use for water may divert available water and may transport it to the location of his or her use, which may be on nonriparian land. The appropriator may claim and divert *any amount* of water not claimed for beneficial use by prior appropriators. An earlier claimant has seniority rights over subsequent claimants. Under the prior appropriation doctrine, usufructuary rights are derived from the beneficial use of water rather than from ownership of land contiguous to the waterbody.

CRITICAL ANALYSIS OF THE EVOLUTION OF COMMON LAW USUFRUCTUARY RIGHTS IN GREAT LAKES JURISDICTIONS

Great Lakes states originally subscribed to the common law doctrine of riparianism. Common law decisions in riparian jurisdictions evolved, however, to reflect a rejection of the strict application of the riparian doctrine and a growing incorporation of elements of the prior appropriation doctrine.[40] An early sign of the demise of the riparian doctrine appeared when the common law in several riparian jurisdictions expressly conferred riparian rights upon municipal corporations. These decisions were a significant departure from precedent since originally only a private party owning land contiguous to a waterbody could exercise riparian rights. Inhabitants of a town located on a lake or river were not riparian parties unless they enjoyed private access to the waterbody. This common law modification was essential to the growth of cities and industries within the Great Lakes Basin, although it allowed nonriparian landowners the same usufructuary rights as were possesed by riparians. All inhabitants of a town were thereby entitled to use water from any waterbody to which the town was riparian. The legal basis for the extension of these rights was the equitable cognizance of the need for water by industrial users and by state inhabitants who were increasingly concentrated in cities.

This change in the law reflected the fact that the riparian doctrine had become archaic and unworkable under emerging socioeconomic conditions. The riparian doctrine was rejected for two primary reasons. First, it allows no provision for the needs of nonriparian parties to the use of water in a waterbody, and thereby excludes much of the public from attaining valuable usufructuary rights. Second, the doctrine precludes recognition that better uses of water, by some criteria, may exist (by either riparians or nonriparians) and thereby fails to promote the most beneficial use of water. Of course, these results are entirely consistent with the riparian doctrine. Its purpose is to narrowly circumscribe usufructuary rights and to give exclusive privileges to riparian parties. Historically, nonriparians were forced to rely on groundwater to satisfy their water needs.

The increasing prevalence of state permit systems in riparian jursidictions signifies the culmination of the evolution from private riparian rights to state-controlled public water rights. State administrative agencies have emerged as the contemporary forum for the adjudication of usufructuary rights. Permit systems govern the acquisition and sale of water by public and private waterworks systems and regulate the sale of water by municipal corporations. Water users receive an entitlement to water in accordance with beneficial use priorities established by the agency, rather than by application of a reasonable use standard by a court.

Under common law riparianism, use of the water in a waterbody was restricted to riparian owners, and they were limited to reasonable use of the water. State permit systems establish use priorities so that certain beneficial uses are satisfied for nonriparians before lower-priority uses are satisfied for riparians. Thus, state permit systems greatly expand public usufructuary rights and represent an unprecedented assertion of state authority over water resources within a state. Riparian rights, however, are not altogether abrogated. For example, in one jurisdiction, the nonriparian public may be granted usufructuary rights in surplus water, but nonsurplus water may only be diverted by nonriparians with the consent of riparian owners damaged thereby.[41]

The state derives its water resources authority from its status as a public trustee and allocates water under its police power authority. The state may regulate the allocation and use of state water resources so that water will be available for all reasonable domestic, agricultural, and industrial needs within the state. Courts have upheld the authority of state permit systems in Great Lakes jurisdictions, thus legitimizing the abrogation of riparian rights thereunder.[42]

A state's "ownership" of water in its capacity as public trustee is fundamentally the power to allocate usufructuary rights. The state itself has no usufructuary interest in the water, but has the exclusive power to confer usufructuary rights upon its political subdivisions, corporations, individuals, and, in some cases, governmental units of another state.[43]

Under the state permit systems, usufructuary rights are predicated upon the beneficial use of water and the type of beneficial use, rather than on the location of use. This policy is in marked contrast to the common law requirement in riparian jurisdictions that water use be restricted to locations on riparian land. After the state has exercised its right to divert water, the state's function is to assign its usufructuary rights to another party, the actual user in a beneficial sense. This assignment of usufructuary rights is achieved through the state permit system.

The most comprehensive state permit system generally provides for statewide water inventory control, a determination of beneficial use priorities and temporal restrictions on water use. In marked contrast to the original common law riparian approach, a permit system enables a state to provide water for a wide variety of beneficial uses, regardless of the location of use. Any party that establishes a beneficial use for water may receive a usufructuary right in the form of a permit conferred by the state agency. The agency may modify beneficial use priorities in response to socioeconomic changes within the state so that it can fulfill water use needs with greater accuracy and efficiency. A permit system provides an administrative mechanism for enforcement of use priorities, and a party with higher-priority use is entitled to its full allotment before a lower-priority user is entitled to any water.

Of the existing permit systems in Great Lakes jurisdictions, the Minnesota system best exemplifies a comprehensive state water use plan.[44] Relevant provisions are as follows: "The state, to the extent provided by law . . . shall control the appropriation and use of surface and underground waters of the state."[45] The state water commissioner must "contemplate the conservation, allocation and development of all the waters of the state, surface and underground, for the best interests of the people."[46] Furthermore, the commissioner shall have administration over the use, allocation, and control of public waters, and the establishment, maintenance, and control of lake levels.[47] "The commissioner shall establish and maintain a state-wide system to gather, process and disseminate information on the availability, distribution . . . and use of waters of the state."[48]

This administrative method is in contrast to a judicial determination of "reasonable use" by each riparian party to a usufructuary dispute, where the law balances the reasonable needs of each party in accordance with the amount of surplus water available. For example, in Wisconsin, the requirement of a permit by a riparian to divert water from a stream or lake abrogated the common law riparian right of irrigation. Thus for the first time an element of prior use, an integral aspect of the doctrine of prior appropriation, was introduced into Wisconsin water law.[49]

EXPORTATION OF GREAT LAKES WATER BY RIPARIAN STATES AS A BENEFICIAL USE OF WATER

Under state common law riparian doctrine, diversion of water to nonriparian land is per se unreasonable use, and therefore it might seem logical to conclude that Great Lakes water cannot be used in nonriparian states. However, consideration of several other important factors leads to a different conclusion. First, the incorporation of the beneficial use concept in riparian jurisdictions mitigates the strict application of the reasonable use doctrine. Several riparian states have relied upon this development in adopting statutory provisions which allow surplus water to be exported for use at locations outside state boundaries.

In New York, a county water district administrator may sell excess water to parties outside the district, and water may be transported into another state if done under the auspices of a permit issued by the state water administrator. Michigan law also expressly provides for export. Illinois law allows the regulated diversion of water to out-of-state locations through the Chicago Canal. Wisconsin law does not expressly allow water exports to other states but does provide for transfers of water between watersheds. However, none of these statutes makes explicit provision for the assessment of beneficial uses of water at points outside state boundaries. There is also a federal law specifically authorizing a riparian state to divert Great Lakes water through the Chicago Canal to a location outside the Great Lakes Basin. In 1925, the United States Supreme Court sanctioned this diversion of water by the Sanitary District of Chicago from the Great Lakes Basin into the Mississippi River Basin.[50]

The facts of the *Sanitary District* case could cause some debate as to where the beneficial use of water occurred. Chicago derived benefit from the disposal of sewage into the Chicago Canal, but there is also evidence of beneficial uses of the water in the Chicago Canal at points outside the Great Lakes Basin.[51] Since a riparian state may determine that a beneficial use for Great Lakes water exists at a location outside the Great Lakes Basin, it indicates that a riparian state may legally determine that exportation of water is a beneficial use. When a state chooses to export water, it is engaged in fulfilling the usufructuary needs of citizens of a foreign state, and its own citizens benefit from the receipt by the state treasury of the revenues thereby generated.

Second, in matters of interstate water allocation, strict riparian doctrine is not the applicable allocative standard, notwithstanding the fact that all states involved subscribe to the common law riparian doctrine. For example, in *Colorado* v. *New Mexico,* the United States Supreme Court stated that

> [t]he laws of the contending states concerning intrastate water disputes are an important consideration governing equitable apportionment [of the rights ot use of water of an interstate stream] . . .

But state law is not controlling. Rather, the just apportionment of interstate waters is a question of federal law that depends "upon a consideration of the pertinent laws of the contending States and *all other relevant facts.*"[52]

Therefore, in a dispute between riparian states on the issue of exportation, the Court would apply a standard of reasonable use, which differs from the standard that a court would apply in a dispute between private parties under the riparian doctrine.[53] In *Sporhase v. Nebraska* ex. rel. *Douglas,* the Supreme Court explicitly acknowledged that one state's "most beneficial use of . . . water might be in another state."[54] Therefore, it would appear that the Supreme Court is not precluded from applying prior appropriation standards if the Court deems it necessary due to socioeconomic circumstances within the contending states. In addition, Supreme Court affirmation of the right of a riparian state to divert water to points outside the Great Lakes Basin can be inferred from the Court's holding in *New Jersey v. New York.*[55] The Court held that New York could divert water between intrastate watersheds, an action inconsistent with the riparian doctrine of reasonable use, stating that "removal of water to a different watershed obviously must be allowed at times unless States are to be deprived of the most beneficial use on formal grounds."[56] Although the Court was clearly referring to intrastate water transfers, it did expressly establish that diversion of water to nonriparian land is legitimate if it fosters the beneficial use of water.

As outlined earlier, the modification of the common law in riparian jurisdictions that granted usufructuary rights to nonriparian parties was a direct response to an increased demand for water for an expanding variety of beneficial uses in new areas of the public sector within the growth-oriented economy of the Great Lakes Basin. At present, an analogous growth trend on the interstate, or federal, level suggests a probable demand for the federal common law[57] to accommodate the increasing demand for Great Lakes water for alleged beneficial uses in nonriparian states.

This subject raises the issue of which state would have the power to determine and enforce beneficial use priorities. Realistically, riparian states may not have the means to control ultimate beneficial use in another state. However, a federal beneficial use standard or a water-pricing mechanism might exert influence in this area. It should be noted that the adoption of a federal beneficial use standard would be controversial since it would be influenced by regional economic needs and divergent professional opinions as to use priorities. For example, while coal slurry pipelines are advanced by some commentators as necessary to meet the nation's future energy needs, some economists and ecologists consider use of water for coal slurry to be a nonbeneficial use.

The federal common law, by incorporating beneficial use criteria, could determine that riparian states do not possess exclusive Great Lakes usufructuary rights. Using this methodology, the federal common law may accord riparian states superior usufructuary rights since they are the earlier, or senior, appropriators. Those states would therefore be entitled to continue to fulfill all existing beneficial uses for water, and unappropriated water might be considered available for use in nonriparian states. If such a trend does become manifest in federal common law jurisprudence, usufructuary rights will no longer be strictly appurtenant to the land contiguous to the waterbody from which the water is diverted. Water diverted from an interstate waterbody—such as the Great Lakes—would therefore be more freely transferable to any location for beneficial use. This reasoning comports with the contemporary requirement, under a commerce clause analysis, that water be treated as an article of commerce.

COMMERCE CLAUSE IMPACT ON EXPORTATION OF GREAT LAKES WATER FOR USE AT LOCATIONS OUTSIDE THE GREAT LAKES BASIN

It is possible, even probable, that a national market for Great Lakes water will develop. If a riparian state determines that it has a supply of water in excess of its own needs, it may have an economic or political incentive to bargain with nonriparian states for the sale of water.[58] Sales of surplus water may generate substantial revenue for the state treasury.

Water is relatively abundant in the Great Lakes Basin, and, as a result, the legal concept of "surplus water" is incorporated in the statutes of several riparian states.[59] Since surplus water has been defined as water in a waterbody which is not being beneficially used, much of the Great Lakes water might well be considered "surplus" by this theory of measurement. The vast water surface of the Great Lakes means that small changes in lake levels account for large quantities of water. "The immense storage capacity of the lakes . . . make[s] them a highly effective naturally-regulated water system."[60] However, the prevailing legal assumptions which define "surplus" water and "beneficial" use reflect a particular ideological bias which conforms to concepts promulgated under the prior appropriation doctrine. These assumptions are utilitarian but may be modified in the future if changed circumstances so require. The ecological approach to the Great Lakes urged by the International Joint Commission science advisors implies a much broader sense of beneficial use. This use tends to conform to riparian concepts, which advocate the protection of lake levels and stream flows. Beneficial use could be defined as maintenance of lake levels to benefit fish populations, and not only to include beneficial consumptive uses by human beings.

In *Sporhase* v. *Nebraska* ex rel. *Douglas*,[61] the United States Supreme Court held that groundwater is an article of commerce. The *Sporhase* decision ended a long-standing controversy as to whether a state's regulation of intrastate water resources is subject to constitutional commerce clause scrutiny. In *Sporhase,* the Court determined that a statutory restriction on exportation of groundwater resources was not a reasonable exercise of the states' police power, finding "no evidence that [the statutory restriction] is narrowly tailored to the conservation and preservation rationale"[62] which affords a state a limited right to restrict a precious natural resource to intrastate use. The Court applied the " 'strictest scrutiny' reserved for facially discriminatory legislation" because the Nebraska statute constituted an explicit barrier to interstate commerce in water. The Court was reluctant "to condemn as unreasonable measures taken by a State to conserve and preserve for its own citizens this vital resource in times of shortage,"[63] and it delineated the reasons why great deference to state control over intrastate resources must be observed.

> First, a state's power to regulate the use of water in times and places of shortage for the purpose of protecting the health of its citizens—and not simply the health of its economy—is at the core of its police power . . . Second, the legal expectation that under certain circumstances each state may restrict water within its borders has been fostered over the years not only by our equitable apportionment decrees but also by the negotiation and enforcement of interstate compacts. Third, although Appellee's claim to public ownership of Nebraska groundwater cannot justify a total denial of federal regulatory power, it may support a limited preference for its own citizens in the utilization of the resource.[64]

It is likely that the Supreme Court will eventually be confronted with the issue of whether or in what respect the water in the Great Lakes should be treated as an article of commerce. Following the *Sporhase* holding that groundwater is an article of commerce, the application of a commerce clause analysis to the issue of the legality of Great Lakes water exportation would appear to be entirely appropriate. The application of the surplus water concept to determine the availability of water for export is strongly correlated with a commerce clause analysis, and it would seem reasonable for the Court to consider Great Lakes water to be an article of commerce after it has been diverted for use by riparian states.

Since surplus water has been defined as any water in a waterbody which is not being beneficially used, if a riparian state possesses unexercised or unallocated usufructuary rights to a quantity of Great Lakes water for which it has no present intrastate beneficial use, it would not be a violation of the police power to export the water. As noted, statutes in many riparian states make provision for water exportation since they are accustomed to having abundant water supplies. If a riparian state statute were to prohibit exportation of surplus water under these circumstances, or if the statute had the effect of prohibiting exportation, it would certainly be subjected to strict commerce clause scrutiny. If the Supreme Court were to determine that the statute bears no reasonable relationship to state conservation of a resource vital to the welfare of its citizens, under the standard enunciated in *Sporhase,* the statute would very likely be violative of the federal commerce clause. Of course, the Court would analyze each state statute in the context of the particular regional circumstances. Most specifically, in regard to Great Lakes water, the Court would apply the alternate aspect of the commerce clause standard, and would accord paramount deference to the maintenance of lake levels adequate for navigation.

As noted by the Court in *Sporhase,* the existence of numerous federal statutes and interstate compacts demonstrates congressional deference to state water law, but these statutes and compacts do not indicate that Congress wished to remove federal constitutional restraints on such state laws. The negative implications of the commerce clause, like the mandates of the Fourteenth Amendment, are ingredients of the *valid* state law to which Congress has deferred."[65] The federal interest in-conservation . . . [and] . . . fair allocation of diminishing water resources"[66] is an especially significant interest where the water resources clearly have an interstate dimension. State statutory regulation of Great Lakes usufructuary rights would be subject to commerce clause scrutiny under this standard. The fact that a riparian state will only allow the sale of surplus water demonstrates that parties within riparian states have much greater access to Great Lakes water than parties in nonriparian states. Such a policy seeks to ensure that lake levels and intrabasin users receive adequate protection, while it indicates that commerce clause requirements are met.

Great Lakes states may decide to withhold intrabasin water resources from exportation for the sake of economic protectionism— to keep business and industry from moving to arid states sustained by supplies of water imported from riparian states. However, such economic protectionism is on its face violative of the commerce clause. In regard to a state's police power authority to supply its inhabitants with water, the *Sporhase* Court stated, "[f]or Commerce Clause purposes, we have long recognized a difference between economic protectionism, on the one hand, and health and safety regulation on the other."[67]

In order to survive contemporary commerce clause scrutiny, state permit systems must be designed so that water is made available for use in nonriparian states while precluding detrimental impact upon intrastate uses by the citizens of riparian states. In other words, properly designed state water permit systems should protect intrastate usufructuary needs by designating them as the highest priority public uses while making reasonable provision for out-of-state uses as lower-priority uses. Arguably, a state does not abdicate its public trust or police power responsibilities in regard to state water resources by means of such permit provisions if water exportation is designated as a low-priority use.

Under such a system, before a state administrative agency can authorize exportation of water, it is required by state statute to assess whether intrastate water needs are being met and should do so in order to defend against possible challenge to its authority. If the state determines that there is surplus water in the state's inventory, it may authorize exports. To do so is good public policy, since surplus water, by definition, is not being beneficially used by the inhabitants of the state and therefore may not fit under the rationale of the public trust doctrine. However, there is the important consideration of the aesthetic value in maintaining the integrity of a waterbody under the riparian doctrine. The state, as trustee of public waters, may have an obligation to protect the recreational value of a waterbody and to give adequate protection to wetlands areas. Most importantly, the state cannot alienate trust property unless it "can be disposed of *without any substantial impairment of the public interest in the lands and waters remaining.*"[68] This approach is designed to encourage the state to promote the beneficial use of such water, even if such use is designated at an out-of-state or out-of-basin location.

ALLOCATIVE STANDARDS DETERMINING THE RIGHT OF EACH RIPARIAN STATE TO EXPORT WATER

In the Great Lakes Basin, individual states make provision for water exportation but view exports of water by neighboring riparian states with suspicion and concern. Controversy has arisen as to whether a riparian state can assert such dominion over water diverted from the Great Lakes so as to have the authority to assign its rights to a nonriparian party and allow the water to be transported in interstate commerce, despite the protests of other riparian states. At present, the United States Supreme Court is the sole forum available to riparian states for adjudication of disputes involving water exportation. Controversies between two or more states are, by Article III of the United States Constitution, subject to the original jurisdiction of the Supreme Court. "The judicial power shall extend . . . to Controversies between two or more States . . . In all cases . . . in which a State shall be a Party, the Supreme Court shall have original jurisdiction."[69] Equitable apportionment is the standard by which the Court allocates the water of a waterbody common to several states so as to meet the reasonable needs for water in each state. The doctrine of equitable apportionment is analogous to the riparian doctrine of reasonable use but does not preclude use of water on nonriparian land.

Equitable apportionment of the benefits of a waterbody is the measure of the reciprocal rights and obligations of the respective states.[70] The Supreme Court, in determining equitable apportionment, generally weighs the benefit of the diversion to one riparian state against the detriment resulting to the contending riparian state. In *Wisconsin v. Illinois*,[71] the Supreme Court established the right of each riparian state to assert limitations on withdrawals so as to ensure equitable apportionment of the water. This case best exemplifies the magnitude of past, present, and future legal disagreements which may exist between riparian states on the issue of water exportation. The Court emphasized that what is equitable depends upon the reasonable needs of each state which exist at the time of the litigation.

The method of the United States Supreme Court in apportioning water between states is to determine whether an existing or planned diversion of water from an interstate waterbody is within the equitable share of the diverting state. The Court generally limits itself to deciding the issue of equitable apportionment and refrains from extending its authority into state-level decisionmaking processes.[72]

Questions of Ownership and Control

The Court thus ordinarily refrains from specifying beneficial use priorities or other types of restrictions, such as specified land parameters for use. However, in the decree of equitable apportionment issued in *Wyoming v. Colorado,*[73] the Supreme Court, in a doctrinal departure, did specify that water diverted by Colorado from the Laramie River must be used only at locations within the state of Colorado, and specified the amount of water which could be used at locations both within and beyond the river basin.

Supreme Court deference to state authority over allocation of state waters diverted from the Great Lakes under a decree of equitable apportionment would presumably extend to riparian state provisions that allow the subsequent exportation of the water to points beyond the state boundaries, as exemplified by the Chicago Canal diversion. This raises the issue of whether the Supreme Court would expressly consider exportation when determining each state's share of water under the doctrine of equitable apportionment. Since state water ownership is the power to allocate usufructuary rights, a state has great latitude, under its police power authority, in determining use priorities. Therefore, when a state receives an entitlement to a specified amount of water under a decree of equitable apportionment, each state may arguably export all or any portion of the water to which it is entitled under the decree should it decide that such exportation would constitute the most beneficial use.

The Supreme Court will not enjoin one riparian state's diversion of water in the absence of clear and convincing proof of actual and substantial injury to the contending riparian state.[74] If a riparian state exports water, it would be per se immune to claims of injury by a contending riparian state seeking to enjoin such export as long as the exporting state did not export an amount of water in excess of its equitable share authorized by a Supreme Court decree. This principle is illustrated by *Wisconsin v. Illinois,*[75] which establishes that diversion of water to a location outside the Great Lakes Basin is not a per se violation of the reasonable use rule. The doctrine of equitable apportionment does not provide mechanistic guidelines for quantifying shares of water. The Court will weigh the factors involved as the exigencies of the particular case may require. Equitable apportionment does not entitle each state to an equal quantity of water.[76]

A decree of equitable apportionment is not of lasting value to riparian parties since usufructuary needs tend to change over time. Moreover, a decree of equitable apportionment may be subject to change in accordance with legal pronouncements recognizing new uses for water. For example, in *Colorado v. New Mexico,*[77] the

United States Supreme Court held for the first time that unspecified "future uses" of water is a valid use category. Generally the Court may also consider newly developed technologies, such as water recycling processes, which affect usufructuary patterns, or new scientific findings which impact directly upon the diversion capability of a waterbody. In other words, the Court may be influenced by scientific findings of fact in regard to hydrologic or ecological factors. Furthermore, changes in facts and scientific knowledge from that which existed at the time a decree was issued may cause the legal obligations of the states to change along with those facts. Therefore, the rights of riparian parties to export water are limited and uncertain, since the standard of equitable apportionment changes in accordance with changing circumstances in the Basin. For example, when the Supreme Court authorized the diversion at the Chicago Canal, it did not set a permanent standard of reasonableness to govern the diversion of water to points outside the Basin. Although the rights between the parties were expressly decreed, these rights are both quantitatively and qualitatively limited to those facts in existence at the time of the ruling. In fact, this decree has been modified several times.

In addition to giving consideration to the interests of other riparian states, a state desiring to export surplus water must consider and incorporate the constraints imposed by federal interests. In *Sanitary District* v. *United States*,[78] the Supreme Court established the supremacy of the federal interest in maintaining the navigability of the Great Lakes and federal authority to regulate exportation of water to locations outside the Great Lakes Basin, if such exportation were to impair the navigability of the lakes. Furthermore, adequate deference must be given to Canadian usufructuary rights.

A SUGGESTED FORUM FOR ALLOCATING GREAT LAKES USUFRUCTUARY RIGHTS

Market demands for Great Lakes water use at locations outside the Great Lakes Basin, coupled with contemporary commerce clause impact on the issue of interstate water exportation, make it likely that riparian states will contract with nonriparian states for sales of Great Lakes water. Since Great Lakes usufructuary rights are controlled by federal and international law, in addition to state law, diversion of water for use at locations outside the Great Lakes Basin is subject to control by each forum which has jurisdiction over usufructuary rights within each of these sovereign entities. Because of the existence of multiple forums, usufructuary jurisdiction over Great Lakes water is characterized by inherent doctrinal and administrative impediments which militate against the exportation of "surplus" water to points outside the Great Lakes Basin and preclude the optimal utilization of Great Lakes water for the public benefit.

Each riparian state must have a legally sanctioned use priority to a specified equitable share of water if litigation between riparian states over the issue of water exportation is to be avoided. Clarification and consensus as to what amounts of water constitute equitable shares can only be achieved by negotiation between riparian states. Under the present system, a riparian state which exports Great Lakes water for use outside the Basin will continually be vulnerable to suit by other riparian states. Contending states will assert that the export of such water interferes with the exercise of their own usufructuary rights. These states will rely primarily on the reasonable use doctrine in attempting to convince the Supreme Court that water exportation violates the prevailing standard of equitable apportionment. If the exportation of Great Lakes water itself is not successfully challenged, other riparian states may assert, as an alternative, that they are entitled to a portion of the substantial revenue generated upon the sale of water by a riparian state to a nonriparian state.

The United States Supreme Court has explicitly acknowledged its limitations as a forum for adjudicating water disputes between states, making reference to the unique nature of the disputes which arise out of possession of common water resources by two or more states and the problem that this poses to the Court.[79] The Court has frankly recommended that states resolve their water use disputes by interstate compact instead of litigation. Interstate compacts are commonly used to allocate usufructuary rights in interstate waterbodies.[80] The Great Lakes states formally recognized the need for an interstate forum to govern the use of the Great Lakes by ratifying the Great Lakes Basin Compact in 1955.[81] The stated purpose of the Compact is to "promote the orderly, integrated, and comprehensive development, use, and conservation of the water resources of the Great Lakes Basin . . . [and] [t]o *advise* in securing and maintaining a proper balance among industrial, commercial, agricultural water supply, residential, recreational and other legitimate uses of the water resources of the Basin."[82]

The Great Lakes Basin Compact is ineffectual because it fails to promulgate or enforce standards for beneficial use of Great Lakes water. The existing Great Lakes Basin Compact created the Great

Lakes Basin Commission, a forum of limited advisory powers, but did not establish adequate administrative provisions to allocate Great Lakes usufructuary rights under present demands for water. The Commission lacks the power to adjudicate and hence has no authority to decide the issue of equitable apportionment. Compact provisions are devoid of any usufructuary standard or policy in regard to water allocation among the riparian states.

A compact agreement would be the most effective legal means by which a riparian state or group of riparian states could control or regulate water exportation by other riparian states. A compact would provide a formal means for riparian states to acknowledge the legal right of each state to export a limited quantity of Great Lakes water in accordance with carefully delineated guidelines and could contain policy guidelines to promote comity and cooperation between the states.

The present Great Lakes Basin Compact does not establish a policy addressing the rights and obligations of riparian states to divert water to states outside the Great Lakes Basin.[83] although the compact alludes to the existence of "other governments" having interests in Great Lakes Basin water resources, it does not identify other governmental entities, specify the possible usufructuary interests or beneficial uses for Great Lakes water which those entities might have, or authorize the formation of contractual or other relationships between riparian states and those "other governments." The Great Lakes Basin Commission does not maintain an inventory of Basin water resources necessary to determine how much "surplus" water in the Great Lakes might be legally available for intrastate use by each riparian state or for subsequent exportation, or to determine what criteria a given volume of water may be declared to be "surplus."

The contemporary concerns of governments in riparian states regarding exportation of Great Lakes water to nonriparian states strongly suggest that those states would tend to regard it as important that a modified compact agreement be drafted. A newly formulated compact should establish an administrative forum with the power to allocate Great Lakes usufructuary rights between riparian states, including allocations of water for subsequent exportation to locations outside the Great Lakes Basin. The use of an administrative agency for determining facts and adjudicating public rights—such as usufructuary rights between states—would seem to be consistent with due process and not to constitute an unconstitutional invasion of judicial power.[84] Such a forum should survive constitutional scrutiny if it were used as a means to implement those standards which have been enunciated by the Supreme Court in regard to equitable apportionment and commerce clause considerations.[85] The forum would be required to respect the United States' reasonable use obligations as outlined in the Boundary Waters Treaty.[86]

A compact agreement between riparian states should be a detailed agreement outlining beneficial uses for Great Lakes water and establishing a forum with administrative powers to enforce its provisions.[87] Those states ratifying the compact would be entitled to receive and subsequently allocate water on the basis of criteria outlined in the compact agreement. The administrative forum should implement policy incorporating both riparian and prior appropriation concepts, making it a conceptually sophisticated forum. Such policy would reflect what is perceived as the contemporary trend in federal common law jurisprudence, as reflected in recent Supreme Court decisions. This "hybrid" common law approach to the allocation of usufructuary rights has provided an effective and equitable conceptual framework for state water permit systems in the Great Lakes Basin. This same conceptual approach should also form the matrix of an administrative forum designed to promote the equitable apportionment of Great Lakes water between riparian states amidst the increasingly complex context of legally recognized beneficial uses for water, including the beneficial use category of exportation.

Congress could use its authority in the compact process to impose federal beneficial use criteria while allowing primary allocative control to remain in the states.[88] If Congress were to determine that it is in the national interest for riparian states to prioritize export of water for certain uses in nonriparian states before allocating water for lower-priority uses within the riparian states, a riparian state would still remain in a position to protect its highest priority uses.

Following the model of successful state water permit systems, the Great Lakes Basin Compact should vest in the administrative forum the power to implement and administer an interstate water permit system.[89] Through the implementation of an interstate permit system, the Great Lakes Basin states could develop an inventory of Basin water resources and effectively use that data to develop more direct means of augmenting and distributing those resources. Under the present state of the art, it is not clear from a scientific standpoint whether there is sufficient water in the Great Lakes, specifically, and in the Great Lakes Basin, generally, to meet all reasonable present and future needs for water by riparian parties in the United States and Canada, or for additional nonriparian parties in either country.[90] To the extent that surplus water is available, it is highly unlikely that either the United States or Canada will seek to enjoin the other from future increased diversion of water from the lakes because both nations have a history of reliance on Great Lakes water for both municipal and industrial uses, and water use projections indicate that both nations plan significant increases in consumption by the year 2035.[91]

The interstate administrative forum would serve to produce the relevant scientific information, interpreted within a framework of applicable legal doctrines, that would enable riparian states to ascertain pertinent answers and to fashion usufructuary policy in a more forthright and informed manner. In this way, the administrative forum would serve to rectify a problem frequently encountered by the Supreme Court—that of lack of adequate information with which to fashion decrees of equitable apportionment. The existence of this problem serves to support the contention that the Supreme Court is not a suitable forum for the adjudication of these matters.

Given that there is great diversity in usufructuary patterns within different states, both riparian and nonriparian, an important objective to be achieved by an interstate permit system is to reduce the legal restraints upon the transferability of water supplies to where they can be most beneficially used. A permit system would allow riparian states to protect the integrity of lake levels and would protect riparian users against extreme export market demands for water which conceivably might arise, while implementing a policy which overcomes the "old politics" of riparianism that has effectively restricted Great Lakes usufructuary rights to parties within the riparian states.

The interstate administrative forum, by means of the permit system, should directly control and regulate water exportation from Great Lakes states to states outside the Great Lakes Basin. A three-tiered application of the following criteria should be used to determine the availability of Great Lakes water for exportation. Initially, a water level assessment should determine whether there is water present in excess of that needed to protect the navigability of the Lakes and the integrity of municipal water and sanitary systems. This assessment would constitute a determination of whether there is a projected stable supply of surplus water. In deference to ecological concerns, it should also provide sufficient consideration and protection of wetland areas. Secondly, each riparian state should be entitled to its equitable share of the available surplus water in the lakes, under the doctrine of equitable apportionment. Finally, a riparian state should be entitled, under its police power authority, to make a determination that a portion of its equitable share of water is in excess of its own intrastate needs, and to export that water to points outside the Great Lakes Basin.

Questions of Ownership and Control

In order to export water to a nonriparian state, a riparian state would be required to bid for a permit to do so from the interstate administrative forum. Each riparian state would receive a permit to divert water from the Lakes on the basis of a temporal period designated as a water year. This permit would entitle each state to a certain equitable percentage of the surplus water available during each water year.

The permit system should allocate water to riparian states by subdivision into two use categories: consumptive and nonconsumptive. Most of the water presently withdrawn from the Great Lakes is eventually returned to the Great Lakes hydrologic system by direct discharges into the Lakes or their tributaries. This constitutes a *nonconsumptive* use of water. For example, Wisconsin law requires that water withdrawn by public utilities from either Lake Michigan or Superior be returned to the Lakes in the form of purified effluent. In contrast, water which is withdrawn from, but not returned to, the Lakes is categorized as *consumptive use*. Historically, consumptive uses have consisted of evaporation during use, leakage from pipes, and incorporation of water into manufactured products.

In issuing water use permits, the interstate administrative forum must incorporate the policy requirements inherent in the distinction between consumptive and nonconsumptive uses of water. Water that is exported out of the Great Lakes Basin, in the absence of reciprocity requirements, is permanently severed from its source. Therefore, such export of water is a consumptive use. In other words, water that is exported beyond the natural contours of the drainage basin is no longer a part of the hydrologic cycle of that region. Accordingly, allocations intended for export should only be made following a careful determination of the possible permanent impact on the hydrologic bounty of the Lakes.[92] Export provisions, to be successful, must rely on efficiency in record keeping as to inflows, outflows, and inventory levels, and on the determination of reliable water demand forecasts. There is a recognized need for greatly improved methods of data collection and statistical analysis in the area of water demand forecasts and water inventory analysis. In *Omernik v. State*,[93] the Wisconsin Supreme Court observed that an essential function of a permit system is to provide information to the government in regard to water use and maintenance of water levels in lakes and streams.

Because of the hydrologic complexity of the Great Lakes, it is necessary that the interstate administrative forum incorporate a board of scientists and professional engineers, who would be headed by a chief engineer or water master.[94] The water master would serve as the professional voice of the forum and would have ultimate responsibility for monitoring lake levels and water demand forecasts and for recommending water allocations.[95] As such, the water master would serve a similar function to that of a special master in adjudicatory proceedings. The interstate forum would apportion and allocate whatever, in the judgment of the water master, constituted surplus water within each water year. The Great Lakes are subject to periodic fluctuation in water levels, and therefore the allocative criteria must accommodate these flunctuations, if indeed they can be accommodated. Lake level fluctuations influence the amount of surplus water available.[96]

The effect of a modified compact agreement should be to allow each riparian state to legally export any portion of its equitable share of water designated for consumptive use. Since water designated for consumptive use will not return to the Great Lakes Basin, the state should be legally entitled to designate that water for beneficial use in a nonriparian state. This method provides protection for the integrity of lake levels and respects each state's right to designate, under its police power authority and in deference to commerce clause provisions, that water exportation will be allowed.

An interstate permit system would incorporate most of the same features of a state permit system. The standard of beneficial use would provide the basis for granting permits for the diversion of water. The permit mechanism would include an inventory of Great Lakes Basin water resources, temporal limitations on water use,[97] beneficial use priorities, and guidelines for the reassignment of usufructuary rights in the event that changed socioeconomic conditions necessitate changed use priorities. The marketability of Great Lakes water depends upon nonriparian investors gaining a secure usufructuary right for a specified period of time. An investor—whether private, municipal, or state—at a nonriparian location can amortize the investment over the designated useful life of the diversion project and receive a calculated return on the investment. A permit would be granted for a specified period of time and would be subject to modification or cancellation if a breach of a condition of the permit should occur for an extended period of nonuse, or when necessary to protect the use priorities which are outlined in the compact. Nonuse of water is generally not regarded as a beneficial use if such water is part of an allotment specified in an outstanding permit. However, as noted earlier in *Colorado* v. *New Mexico*[98] the Supreme Court held that unspecified "future uses" is a beneficial use.

The interstate permit system could provide for suspension of permits in the event of drought or other emergency. Drought is not a likely occurrence in the Great Lakes region, which receives an average annual precipitation in the amount of thirty-two inches. However, protracted excesses and deficiencies in precipitation have caused variations in lake levels. Periodic fluctuations in lake levels may produce, in effect, drought conditions. For example, record high precipitation in the late 1940s and early 1950s resulted in high lake levels. Only twelve years later, below-normal precipitation caused record-low lake levels in the 1960s.[99] Lake levels rose again in the 1980s.

The interstate administrative forum should consist of representatives of each member state, as well as federal and international representatives. In the event that the administrative framework is incapable of resolving a particular dispute, each state would retain the right to pursue its legal remedies. However, public policy favors the requirement that, except when an emergency injunction is sought, a riparian state should pursue its remedies within the administrative forum prior to pursuing legal remedies. At each point at which usufructuary rights are to be allocated, notice and a hearing will be afforded to all interested parties. In this manner, the forum should effectively provide thorough due process protections for each riparian state in regard to any major water allocation decision.

A water master would set prices on water exports, with the price determined in part by the cost of administration and transportation. This point raises the issue of whether the economic use value of Great Lakes water at locations in nonriparian states will support the cost of its procurement and transportation. Federal water programs generally provide water free or well below market price to a chosen constituency.[100] Federal programs which provide water at rates below cost to selected beneficiary groups have been criticized for engendering highly inefficient uses of water and mismanagement of water resources.[101] Similarly, a primary criticism of the federal Reclamation Act is the fact that twelve million acres of valuable cropland have been developed in western states at the cost of displacing agricultural production in eastern states.[102] The western states received this benefit virtually free of charge and eastern states were not compensated for their losses.

In fashioning legal policy to govern the interstate shipment of water, sound economic principles should be applied so that the costs of diverting and transporting water are equitably divided among the beneficiary groups. Allowing states to contract with each other to allocate water supplies would serve to impose a greater awareness of the true economic value of water and would promote the development of more sophisticated pricing mechanisms. By pricing water at its true value, the exporting state would be given an incentive to use the best available water conservation and management methods so as to maximize both the availability of water for export and the value and sufficiency of the water which it retains for intrastate use. The same conservation incentive would accrue to the importing state since it is entitled to a limited contractual allotment of water, and the imported water would be more expensive to procure than local water supplies or water provided by federally funded projects.

The export of Great Lakes water to nonriparian states is a consumptive use. It represents a loss of water to the Great Lakes Basin and involves a redistribution both of water and of the inherent benefits of the water from Great Lakes user interests to consumer interests in other states. The determination of the economic value of the water to those consumer interests would require a study of all consumptive uses and a corresponding evaluation of the cost/benefit ratio which accrues to each particular type of use.[103] Such a study will be a necessary prerequisite to establishing pricing policy for interstate water transport. When water is exchanged between states for a price, the revenue generated for the exporting state may be used as a fund for upgrading its water facilities. This would mitigate any resource depletion incurred as a result of the exportation.

Allowing states to contract among themselves for allocation of water resources creates a system in which the benefits and burdens which accrue to each state are explicitly bargained for among the affected states. This feature of regional cooperation addresses concern of riparian states that they be consulted in regard to apportionment of water. Each riparian state has the legal right to have its interests represented in allocation decisions and must be consulted before any major diversion or exportation of water occurs. The province of Ontario would also need to be consulted by the members of such a forum or indeed might become a participant with the consent of the federal government.

CONCLUSION

In the Great Lakes region, a history of expansion in the law has granted usufructuary rights to a growing constituency of Great Lakes water users and has changed the nature and structure of the forum which governs the use of that water. The riparian doctrine became an intolerable impediment to municipal and industrial growth in the Great Lakes Basin because nonriparian parties did not have sufficient access to water and because litigation was not a successful method for resolving the claims of a multitude of parties to the use of water in a given waterbody.

In a number of Great Lakes jurisdictions, state permit systems have been instituted to make water more readily available to a wider public constituency. These permit systems administer a "hybrid" water law doctrine which provides water for a wide variety of beneficial uses regardless of the place of use. As a result of centralized inventory control and a prioritized system of allocation for beneficial uses, public water rights are governed in a centralized and flexible forum within each state.

If a legitimate, or legally cognizable, demand for exportation of Great Lakes water to nonriparian states does materialize, problems similar to those encountered on the intrastate level will frustrate any attempt to allocate water equitably on an interstate scale. Since the federal common law is likely to favor interstate allocation of water under certain circumstances, riparian states should not expect to be successful in legal efforts to enjoin exportation of Great Lakes water to points outside the Basin. That is to say that riparian states will not effectively solve usufructuary disputes through the application of the doctrine of equitable apportionment in Supreme Court adjudication under such conditions.

As the Great Lakes become legally recognized as a national water resource, a specialized forum will be needed to allocate water and to mediate disputes arising from interstate sales of usufructuary rights and the resulting transcontinental diversions of Great Lakes water. The author advocates the establishment of a regional requisitionary forum containing those basic features outlined on the preceding pages. Such a forum would be of great utility to the riparian states when the demand for expanded public access to Great Lakes water becomes acute. The main benefit of the forum would be to enable riparian states to retain an adequate degree of control, as a community of states, over water exportation and to enable the riparian states to protect the integrity of the natural geographic features of the Great Lakes Basin. The possibility of demands for use of Great Lakes water by jursidictions outside the Basin and the complexities of the law governing appropriation and allocation of water rights indicate a need for some basinwide authority competent to provide a forum for major water diversion issues. This consideration parallels and reinforces arguments made elsewhere in this reader that some form of comprehensive, institutional arrangement is necessary to implement the basinwide ecosystem approach to management of the Great Lakes.

NOTES

1. See International Great Lakes Diversions and Consumptive Uses Study Board, *Great Lakes Diversions and Consumptive Uses: Report to the International Joint Commission,* Chapter 6 (1981) (discussing consumptive water use) (hereinafter referred to as International Joint Commission).

2. See *The National Coal Production, Distribution, and Utilization Act of 1980: Hearings on S. 2665 Before the Comm. on Energy and Natural Resources,* 96th Cong., 2d Sess., 297 (1980) (statement of Sen. Burdick).

3. *Sanitary District* v. *United States,* 266 U.S. 405, 431 (1925).

4. Strictly speaking a *riparian* is a party owning land abutting a river, and *littoral* is the word used to describe the ownership of land contiguous to a lake. Generally, the rights of a landowner on a navigable lake are similar to, if not identical with, those of riparian owners. See F. Maloney, S. Plager & F. Baldwin, *Water Law and Administration: The Florida Experience* p. 31 (1968). Most federal common law pertains to shared ownership and use of interstate rivers; therefore, to promote consistent use of terminology, *riparian* is the term used to describe the eight states which own the shores contiguous to the Great Lakes. These eight riparian states are Wisconsin, Minnesota, Illinois, Indiana, Michigan, New York, Ohio, and Pennsylvania. State statutes in several riparian states provide for the sale of water to other states.

5. 373 U.S. 546, 564–66 (1963).

6. 43 U.S.C. §§ 1501-56 (1976 & Supp. V 1981).

7. Ibid., § 1513.

8. *Wisconsin* v. *Illinois,* 278 U.S. 367 (1929), 281 U.S. 179 (1930), 289 U.S. 395 (1933), 388 U.S. 426 (1967), 449 U.S. 48 (1980). "In 1922, the State of Wisconsin successfully sought an injunction to bar the State of Illinois from diverting Lake Michigan water. However, in 1925, the U.S. Supreme Court overturned the injunction and diversion was allowed . . . at an average rate of 8,500 cfs [cubic feet per second] . . . Other decrees were issued by the U.S. Supreme Court in 1930 and 1967 and again amended in 1980." International Joint Commission, supra note 1, at 4–10. The 1930 decree reduced allowable diversion to, in effect, 3,100 cfs. The 1967 decree raised the maximum allowable diversion to 3,200 cfs, and the 1980 decree

affirmed the limit, but modified the method of accounting for the amount of water withdrawn. Ibid.

9. *Wisconsin* v. *Illinois,* 388 U.S. 426, 429-30 (1967).

10. Senate Bill S. 2026, the Great Lakes Water Diversion Act, would have prohibited "diversions of Great Lakes water, except as approved by all the Great Lakes states and the International Joint Commission, for use outside of a Great Lakes state and to prohibit federally sponsored studies involving the feasibility of diverting Great Lakes water." S. 2026, 98th Cong., 1st Sess. (1983). The bill further states, in part, the following:

> The Congress finds and declares that (1) the Great Lakes are a most important natural resource to the eight Great Lakes States and two Canadian provinces, providing water supply for domestic and industrial use, clean energy through hydropower production, an efficient transportation mode for moving products into and out of the Great Lakes region, and recreational uses for millions of United States and Canadian citizens; (2) the Great Lakes need to be carefully managed and protected to meet current and future needs, within the Great Lakes states and Canadian provinces; (3) any new diversions of Great Lakes water for use outside of a Great Lakes State will have significant economic and environmental impact, adversely affecting the use of this resource by the Great Lakes states and Canadian provinces . . . [The purpose and policy of the Act is to] take immediate action to protect the limited quantity of water available from the Great Lakes system for use by the Great Lakes states and in accordance with the Boundary Waters Treaty of 1909. . . . Ibid.

House Bill H.R. 4366, the Great Lakes Water Preservation Act, would also have prohibited "diversions of Great Lakes water, except as approved by all the Great Lakes States and the International Joint Commission, for use outside of a Great Lakes State and . . . prohibit federally sponsored studies involving the feasibility of diverting Great Lakes water." H.R. 4366, 98th Cong., 1st Sess. (1983). The text of this bill is nearly identical to that of S. 2026. House Bill H.R. 4545, the Great Lakes Protection Act, would "require the approval of each of the Great Lakes States for any diversion of water from the Great Lakes or the Great Lakes drainage basin for use outside of the Great Lakes States and to prohibit Federal studies of the feasibility of any such diversion." H.R. 4545, 98th Cong., 1st Sess. (1983). The text of the bill further states that

> [n]o Great Lakes State shall sell or otherwise transfer or permit the sale or transfer, for use outside of such a State, water which is taken from any of the Great Lakes or any other body of surface or ground water which is located within the Great Lakes drainage

basin unless (1) there is in effect an interstate compact among the Great Lakes States which governs such sale or transfer, or (2) each of the Great Lakes States consents to such sale or transfer.

Ibid. None of these bills attained passage.

11. See, for example, Minn. Stat. Ann. § 105.41 (West 1987). "It shall be unlawful for the state, any person . . . or other political subdivision of the state to appropriate or use any waters of the state, surface or underground, without the written permit of the commissioner." Ibid. § 105.41 (1) (West 1987).

12. Territorial ownership of the Great Lakes refers to the rights of the United States and Canada to control the Lakes to the extent that they fall within respective national boundaries, and the rights of riparian states to control the navigable waters within respective state boundaries.

13. *Usufructuary* signifies ownership of the right to use of property, in contrast to ownership of the property itself.

14. See C.D. Piper, *The International Law of the Great Lakes* p. 19 (1967). The principle of state ownership of lake beds is promulgated in the Submerged Lands Act of 1953, 43 U.S.C. § 1311 (1976).

15. In *Martin* v. *Lessee of Waddell*, 41 U.S. (16 Pet.) 367, 410 (1842), the Supreme Court held that "the people of each state . . . hold the absolute right for all their navigable waters and the soils under them for their own common use." This principle, applicable to the thirteen original states, was extended to new states in *Pollard* v. *Hagan*, 44 U.S. (3 How.) 212 (1845). Recently, the Supreme Court has noted that throughout the "history of the relationship between the Federal Government and the States . . . runs the consistent thread of purposeful and continued deference to state water law by Congress." *California* v. *United States*, 438 U.S. 645, 653 (1978).

16. *Illinois Cent. R.R.* v. *Illinois*, 146 U.S. 387, 452 (1892); *Wisconsin* v. *Illinois*, 278 U.S. 367 (1929). See also Piper, supra note 14 at 19, and Ohio Rev. Code § 123.03 (1984); Wis. Stat. Ann. § 30.21(1) (West 1973 & Supp. 1986).

17. Great Lakes Basin Compact, ratified by the State of Illinois, July 13, 1955, 1955 Ill. Laws 1678 § 1-4. See also Ill. Ann. Stat. ch. 127, § 192.1 (Smith-Hurd 1981). The United States Congress consented to the compact in 1968. Pub. L. No.90-419, 82 Stat. 414 (1968).

18. P.L. 89-80, codified at 42 U.S.C.A. § 1962b (West 1981).

19. Executive Order No. 12,319, 46 Fed. Reg. 45, 591 (1981).

20. Although the federal interest is primarily that of protecting the navigability of the lakes, the federal government may also have a proprietary

Questions of Ownership and Control 277

interest in Great Lakes usufructuary rights, that is, in the allocation of water resources. See *Sporhase* v. *Nebraska* ex rel. *Douglas,* 102 S. Ct. 3456, 3462 (1982), where the Supreme Court stated, in reference to the interstate Ogallala Aquifer, that "there is a significant federal interest in conservation as well as in fair allocation of this diminishing [water] resource."

21. U.S. Const. art. 1, §8, cl. 3. Congress shall have the power to "regulate Commerce with foreign Nations and among the several states. Ibid. Commerce clause authority extends to water navigable in interstate or foreign commerce. The Daniel Ball, 77 U.S. (10 Wall.) 557, 566 (1870).

22. See supra note 3.

23. Boundary Waters Treaty, Jan. 11, 1909, United States–Great Britain (for Canada), 36 Stat. 2448.

24. Boundary Waters Treaty, art. 1, 36 Stat. at 2449.

25. Ibid at art. II.

26. Ibid. at art III.

27. This statement reflects the fact that land "ownership" merely confers upon the title holder superior rights to use of land. See generally Caldwell, "Rights of Ownership or Rights of Use—The Need for a New Conceptual Basis for Land Use Policy," 15 Wm. & Mary L. Rev. 759, 760 (1974).

28. See *McCready* v. *Virginia,* 94 U.S. 391, 394 (1876).

29. State courts have espoused the view that running water is incapable of ownership and that neither the state nor riparian owners have any title in it until it is appropriated. *Sweet* v. *City of Syracuse,* 129 N.Y. 316, 335, 27 N.E. 1081, 1084 (1891): *City of Syracuse* v. *Stacey,* 169 N.Y. 231, 245, 62 N.E. 354, 355 (1901). The elusive character of water "ownership" was discussed in *Westmoreland & Cambria Nat. Gas. Co.* v. *DeWitt,* 130 Pa. 235, 18 A. 724 (1889), where the court described water as a "mineral *ferae natural"* which belongs to the owner of the land to which the waterbody is contiguous. These rights are derived from the natural relationship between the land and the waterbody. However, when the water is severed from the land and comes under another's control, the title of the former owner is gone.

30. An individual's rights in water are known as usufructuary rights, not property rights. Since the phrase *bundle of rights* is a term of the art in property law, *bundle of usufructuary rights* may be considered a term of the art in water law. See generally *City of Syracuse* v. *Stacey,* 169 N.Y. 231, 233, 62 N.E. 354, 356 (1901). See *Evans* v. *Merriweather,* 4 Ill. 492, 494 (1842). Equitable distribution of available water resources is an important consideration in all aspects of water law because water is a necessary

component of human survival and of nearly all human enterprise, including industry and agriculture. Therefore, the conflicting usufructuary needs of parties give rise to a judicially imposed balancing of rights. For example, the rights of a riparian owner to the use of water are relative to the rights of other riparian owners on the same waterbody. See generally *State* v. *Zawistowski,* 95 Wis. 2d 250, 262, 290 N.W.2d 303, 309 (1980).

31. F. Maloney, S. Plager & F. Baldwin, supra note 4, at 141.

32. For elucidation of the public trust authority concept, see *Martin* v. *Lessee of Waddell,* 41 U.S. (16 Pet.) 367, 410–11 (1842). See also *McCready,* 94 U.S. at 394.

33. *Hudson County Water Co.* v. *McCarter,* 209 U.S. 349, 355 (1908) [quoting *Kansas* v. *Colorado,* 185 U.S. 125, 142 (1902)].

34. See generally Trelease, *Government Ownership and Trusteeship of Water,* 45 Calif. L. Rev. 638, 648, 653 (1957).

35. *Toomer* v. *Witsell,* 334 U.S. 385, 402 (1948).

36. 102 S. Ct. 3456 (1982).

37. In 1908, in *Hudson County Water Co.* v. *McCarter,* 209 U.S. 349 (1908), the United States Supreme Court nearly suggested that a state is the absolute proprietary owner of its water resources. The Court upheld a New Jersey statute which prohibited the transfer of state waters to out-of-state locations. The Court stated that "a State has a constitutional power to insist that its natural advantages remain unimpaired by its citizens . . . [and] . . . [i]n the exercise of this power it may prohibit the diversion of the water of its important streams to points outside of its boundaries." 209 U.S. at 349. This ruling authorized a state to statutorily withhold its water resources from interstate commerce under the theory of absolute ownership by the state. *Hudson County* relied on *Geer* v. *Connecticut,* 161 U.S. 519, 529–30, 534 (1895), in which the Supreme Court upheld a Connecticut statute banning interstate transportation of game birds. As noted by the Court in 1982, "*Geer* . . . was premised on the theory that the state owned its wild animals and therefore was free to qualify any ownership interest it might recognize in the persons who capture them." *Sporhase,* 458 U.S. at 3461. In *Hughes* v. *Oklahoma,* 441 U.S. 322 (1979), the Supreme Court overruled *Geer* and signaled the demise of the state ownership theory. Ibid. Other courts had earlier disagreed with the line of reasoning which formed the basis for the *Hudson County* ruling. For example, in *City of Altus, Okla.* v. *Carr,* 255 F. Supp. 828 (W.D. Tex. 1966), aff'd per curiam 385 U.S. 35 (1966), the theory of state ownership of water was rejected by the federal district court. The state of Texas had argued that it owned all groundwater within the state and that when a private landowner withdrew water from the ground, the state retained a residuum of ownership and could thereby limit use of the water to within the state. The federal district court, in rejecting this con-

tention, was influenced by the fact that water which is withdrawn from a well becomes the personal property of the landowner. 255 F. Supp. at 839. Therefore, the court found that the state ceases to own groundwater after it is extracted from the ground.

38. See *Village of Riverwoods* v. *Department of Transp.,* 77 Ill. 2d 130, 395 N.E. 2d 555 (1979).

39. The *reasonable use* standard is used in reparian jurisdictions. *Beneficial use* means the application of water to a useful purpose which inures to the benefit of the water user and which is subject to the user's dominion and control. It does not include the waste or pollution of water. See Iowa Code § 455 B.261 (1986). The beneficial use concept originated in the prior appropriation doctrine but has been adopted by permit systems in riparian jurisdictions.

40. See *Omernick* v. *Department of Natural Resources,* 71 Wis. 2d 370, 374, 238 N.W. 2d 114, 116 *cert. denied,* 425 U.S. 941 (1975), *cert. denied,* 429 U.S. 836 (1976).

41. See, for example, Wis. Stat. Ann. § 30.18 (West 1973 and Supp. 1986). See generally *Nekoosa-Edwards Paper Co.* v. *Public Serv. Comm'n,* 8 Wis. 2d 582, 99 N.W. 2d 821 (1959).

42. The rights of riparian owners may be controlled by state regulation as a valid exercise of the police power. The prohibition of diversion of water from streams by riparian parties without a permit does not constitute a taking of property from riparians without compensation but is a valid exercise of police power to protect public rights. *Omernik* v. *State,* 64 Wis. 2d 6, 21, 218 N.W. 2d 734, 743 (1974). See also *Village of Riverwoods* v. *Department of Transp.,* 77 Ill. 2d 130, 395 N.E. 2d 555 (1979), in which the Illinois Supreme Court held that, under the Illinois permit system which allocates Lake Michigan water, the failure of the state to accord to municipal corporations abutting Lake Michigan water use requests on the basis of alleged riparian and prescriptive rights did not violate the due process clause of the federal or Illinois constitution. Ibid.

43. See, for example, Minn. Stat. Ann. § 105.405(2) (West 1987); Mich. Comp. Laws Ann. § 123.383 (West 1967).

44. Minn. Stat. Ann. § 105.37–81 (West 1987).

45. Ibid. § 105.38(2).

46. Ibid. § 105.39(1).

47. Ibid. § 105.39(3).

48. Ibid. § 105.39(6).

49. *Omernick* v. *Department of Natural Resources,* 71 Wis. 2d 370, 373, 238 N.W. 2d 114, 116, *cert. denied,* 425 U.S. 941 (1975), *cert. denied,* 429 U.S. 836 (1976).

50. In 1822, the U.S. Congress authorized the diversion of Lake Michigan water at Chicago and the construction of the Illinois and Michigan Canal in an effort to promote interstate commerce on the Illinois River. International Joint Commission, supra note 1 at 4-9 to 4-15 (discussing the Lake Michigan diversion at Chicago). See also *Wisconsin* v. *Illinois,* 278 U.S. 367, 401-03 (1928). In 1925, the United States Supreme Court affirmed the legality of this diversion of water from the Great Lakes watershed into the Mississippi River watershed, subject to a congressional policy of maintaining navigable lake levels. See *Sanitary Dist.* v. *United States,* 266 U.S. 405 (1925). In *Sanitary District,* the Sanitary District of Chicago was enjoined from diverting water from Lake Michigan in excess of 250,000 cubic feet per minute. The Court noted that the diversion of water through the Chicago Canal was authorized by Congress in 1822, 3 Stat. 659, and in 1827, 4 Stat. 234. Ibid. at 427. Subsequently, the Court has reviewed and authorized continuing diversions through the Canal. *Wisconsin* v. *Illinois,* 278 U.S. 367 (1929), 281 U.S. 179 (1930), 289 U.S. 395 (1933), 388 U.S. 426 (1967), 449 U.S. 48 (1980).

51. See *Sanitary District,* 266 U.S. at 431.

52. 103 S. Ct. 539 (1982), at 545-46 (emphasis by the Court) (citations omitted).

53. See *New Jersey* v. *New York,* 283 U.S. 336, 342-43 (1931); *Connecticut* v. *Massachusetts,* 282 U.S. 660, 669 (1930); *Kansas* v. *Colorado,* 206 U.S. 46, 102-05, 113-14 (1907).

54. 102 S. Ct. at 3465.

55. 283 U.S. 336 (1931).

56. Ibid. at 343.

57. The concept of interstate or federal common law is applicable to water law. "When we deal with air and water in their ambient or interstate aspects, there is federal common law." *Illinois* v. *City of Milwaukee,* 406 U.S. 91, 103 (1972). See also *Kansas* v. *Colorado,* 206 U.S. 46, 98 (1907). But in *City of Milwaukee* v. *Illinois,* 451 U.S. 304 (1981), the Court held that the respondents no longer had a common law remedy since the 1972 amendments to the Federal Water Pollution Control Act, enacted subsequent to the initial proceedings in this case, established an administrative scheme which thoroughly addresses the problem of effluent limitations. "[W]hen Congress addresses a question previously governed by a decision rested on federal common law the need for such an unusual exercise of lawmaking by federal courts disappears." Ibid. at 305.

58. In fact, state law requires that a state ascertain that it has adequate water to meet intrastate needs before it may permit exportation of water. See, for example, Minn. Stat. Ann. § 105.405(2) (West 1987). There is evidence which suggests that the integrity of Great Lakes water levels can be preserved in the face of greater diversions from the lakes. For example, § 166 of the Water Resources Development Act of 1976, P.L. 94-587, 90 Stat. 2917 (1976), authorized the Secretary of the Army, acting through the Army Corps of Engineers, to conduct a study to determine the feasibility of increasing the diversion at the Chicago Canal from the present limit of 3,200 cfs up to 10,000 cfs. This study determined that a significant increase in the diversion rate is possible. Specifically, it would be possible to divert up to an annual average of 8,700 cfs during periods when the water supply in the Great Lakes is at above-average levels. See International Joint Commission, supra note 1, at 4-8, to 4-19.

59. See, for example, Wis. Stat. Ann. § 30.18 (West 1968 and Supp. 1986); Minn. Stat. Ann. § 105.405(2) (West 1987).

60. See International Joint Commission, supra note 1 at 3-8.

61. 102 S. Ct. 3456 (1982).

62. 102 S. Ct. 3456, 3465 (1982).

63. Ibid. at 3464.

64. Ibid.

65. Ibid. at 3466 (emphasis by the Court).

66. Ibid. at 3457.

67. Ibid. at 3464.

68. *Illinois Cent. R.R.* v. *Illinois,* 146 U.S. 387, 453 (1892) (emphasis added).

69. U.S. Const. art. III, § 2. See also 28 U.S.C. § 1251(a) (Supp. V 1976). See generally *Kansas* v. *Colorado,* 206 U.S. 46 (1907).

70. See *Colorado* v. *Kansas,* 320 U.S. 383, 385 (1943).

71. 278 U.S. 367 (1929).

72. See *Wisconsin* v. *Illinois,* 388 U.S. 426, 427-28, where the Court stated that "the water permitted . . . to be diverted from Lake Michigan may be apportioned by the State of Illinois . . . in such manner and amounts . . . as the State may deem proper."

73. 353 U.S. 953 (1957).

74. *Connecticut* v. *Massachusetts,* 282 U.S. 660, 669 (1931); *Colorado* v. *New Mexico,* 103 S. Ct. 539, 547 (1982).

75. 388 U.S. 426 (1967).

76. *Connecticut* v. *Massachusetts,* 282 U.S. 660, 670 (1931). It is interesting to note differences in water use among the lakes themselves. Lakes Michigan and Erie have by far the most water withdrawn for use. See International Joint Commission, supra note 1, at 6-2.

77. 103 S. Ct. 539, 549 (1982).

78. 266 U.S. 405 (1925).

79. The Court has explained that "the reason for judicial caution in adjudicating the relative rights of States in such cases is that, while we have jurisdiction over such disputes, they involve the interests of quasi-sovereigns, present complicated and delicate questions, and, due to the possibility of future change of conditions, necessitate expert administration rather than judicial imposition of a hard and fast rule." *Kansas* v. *Colorado,* 320 U.S. 383, 392 (1943).

80. Interstate compacts are authorized under the compact clause of the federal constitution. U.S. Const. art. I, § 10, cl. 3. See generally *Louisiana* v. *Texas,* 176 U.S. 1, 17-18 (1900). These water compacts include the La Plata River Compact of 1925 between Colorado and New Mexico, 43 Stat. 796 (1925); the Republican River Compact of 1943 between Colorado, Kansas, and Nebraska, 57 Stat. 86 (1943); the Costilla Creek Compact of 1946 between Colorado and New Mexico, 60 Stat. 246 (1946); and the Arkansas River Compact of 1949 between Colorado and Kansas, 63 Stat. 145 (1949). See also F. Zimmerman & M. Wendell, *The Interstate Compact Since 1925* (Chicago: Council of State Governments), 16 n.75 (1951).

81. Great Lakes Basin Compact, 82 Stat. 414 (1968).

82. Great Lakes Basin Compact, Art. I, 82 Stat. at 414 (emphasis added).

83. "The Commission shall have the power to . . . [m]ake any recommendation and do all things necessary and proper to carry out the powers conferred upon the Commission by the Compact, provided that no action of this Commission shall have the force of law in, or be binding upon, any party state." 82 Stat. at 417, 418. The commission has taken a narrow view of its functions. Article VI merely states that the "Commission shall have the power to . . . [c]ollect, correlate, interpret, and report on data relating to the water resources and the use thereof in the Basin," and "[r]ecommend methods for the orderly, efficient, and balanced development, use and conservation of the water resources of the Basin . . . to the party states." 82 Stat. at 417. But see art. VII: "Each party agrees to consider the action the Commission recommends in respect to . . . H. Diversion of waters from and into the Basin." 82 Stat. at 418.

84. See *Crowell* v. *Benson,* 285 U.S. 22 (1932). The legal propriety of interstate or federal administrative agencies was carefully considered in

Questions of Ownership and Control

Crowell, where the Supreme Court upheld the validity of a federal administrative agency as a forum for awarding compensation under provisions of the Longshoremen's and Harbor Worker's Compensation Act. "Congress, in exercising the powers confided to it, may establish 'legislative' courts (as distinguished from 'constitutional' courts in which the judicial power conferred by the Constitution can be deposited) . . . to serve as special tribunals to examine and determine the various matters, arising between the government and others, which from their nature do not require judicial determination and yet are susceptible of it." Ibid. at 50. "Familiar illustrations of administrative agencies created for the determination of such matters are found in connection with the exercise of the congressional power as to interstate and foreign commerce . . . the public lands [etc.]." Ibid. at 51. The power of Congress to create legislative courts to adjudicate public rights carries with it the lesser power to create administrative agencies for the same purpose, and to provide for review of those agency decisions in article III courts. *Northern Pipeline Constr. Co. v. Marathon Pipe Line Co.,* 458 U.S. 50, 67, n.18 (1982), citing *Atlas Roofing Co. v. Occupational Safety Comm'n,* 430 U.S. 442, 450 (1977). The Supreme Court would retain jurisdiction to review the findings of fact and decisions of the Great Lakes interstate administrative agency.

85. Historically, the Supreme Court has relied upon the special master to determine relevant facts and to draw conclusions in accordance with applicable legal doctrines. "While the reports of masters . . . in such cases are essentially of an advisory nature, it has not been the practice to disturb their findings when they are properly based upon evidence, in the absence of errors of law, and the parties have no right to demand that the court shall redetermine the facts thus found." *Crowell v. Benson,* 285 U.S. 22, 51–52 (1932). The Court would probably defer in this matter to the factual determinations made by the interstate administrative agency.

86. Boundary Waters Treaty, January 11, 1909, United States–Great Britain (for Canada), 36 Stat. 2448.

87. The interstate forum would derive its power from the congressional ratification of the compact. See *infra* note 88. The forum would operate in accordance with standards promulgated by the Administrative Procedure Act, 5 U.S.C. § 551-59 (1982).

88. Under the compact clause in the Constitution, "no State shall, without the consent of Congress, . . . enter into any Agreement with another State, or with a foreign Power." U.S. Const. art. I, § 10, cl. 3. See generally *Hinderlider v. La Plata River & Cherry Creek Ditch Co.,* 304 U.S. 92 (1938).

89. The Colorado River Compact is an example of a compact agreement which established basic guidelines for the allocation of a water resource common to all of the party states. The Compact was authorized by Congress in 1921, 42 Stat. 171 (1921), ratified by the state of Arizona in 1944, 1944

Ariz. Sess. Laws 427, and is currently codified at Ariz. Rev. Stat. Ann. § 45-1311 (Supp. 1987). "The major purposes of this compact are to provide for the equitable division and apportionment of the use of the waters of the Colorado River System; to establish the relative importance of different beneficial use of water . . ." Colorado River Compact, art. I, Ariz. Rev. Stat. Ann. § 45-1311 (Supp. 1986A). The Upper Basin Compact was enacted as an addendum to the Colorado River Compact. Upper Colorado River Basin Compact, 63 Stat. 31 (1949). "The major purposes of this Compact are to provide for the equitable division and apportionment of the use of the waters of the Colorado River System, the use of which was apportioned in perpetuity to the Upper Basin by the Colorado River Compact . . ." Ibid. at art. I. This compact established the Upper Colorado River Commission, an "interstate administrative agency." Ibid. at art. VIII. This Commission demonstrates the feasibility of establishing an interstate administrative forum for the allocation of the water resources of an interstate waterbody and exemplifies some of the features that should be incorporated in the Great Lakes interstate administrative forum.

90. For an interesting, albeit outdated, discussion of the water supply and usufructuary needs in the Great Lakes Basin, see generally Feldman, *The Lake Diversion Case—The End of a Cycle*, 49 Chi. B. Rec. 270 (1968); Meserow, *Great Lakes Water—Is There Enough?*, 47 Chi. B. Rec. 60 (1965).

91. International Joint Commission, *supra* note 1, at 6-50 to -52.

92. Water withdrawals in 1975 (75,600 cfs) greatly exceeded the amount of water which was consumptively used (4,900 cfs). International Joint Commission, *supra* note 1, at 6-1. "Total water withdrawals from the U.S. portion of the Great lakes and their drainage basins are expected to increase 120 percent between 1975 and 2035 due to interacting effects of environmental controls and anticipated growth projections . . ." Ibid. at 6-46. "Consumptive water use, that portion of water withdrawals that is not returned to the system, is expected to be five times greater in 2035 than it was in 1975." Ibid. at 6-48. "Currently, approximately 88 percent of the consumptive uses occur in the United States and 12 percent in Canada. This proportion is expected to change only slightly, being 82 percent in the United States and 18 percent in Canada by the year 2035." Ibid. at 9-6.

93. 64 Wis. 2d 6, 21 (1974).

94. The water master concept is commonly employed in irrigation districts. See Gaffney, *Comparison of Market Pricing and Other Means of Allocating Water Resources*, in *Water Law and Policy in the Southeast* 195, 203 (1962). State permit systems often employ an engineer to assist in administering water rights. See *Hinderlider v. La Plata River & Cherry Creek Ditch Co.*, 304 U.S. 92, 97 (1938); *United Plainsmen v. Water Conservation Comm'n*, 247 N.W. 2d 457 (N.D. 1976). The Upper Colorado River Com-

mission designates an engineer as being an optional member of the administrative agency. Upper Colorado River Basin Compact, 63 Stat. 31, 35 (1949).

95. A House bill introduced on March 11, 1987 proposes a similar idea. The bill, H. R. 1573, introduced in the first session of the One Hundredth Congress, provides for the appointment of a Great Lakes Water Levels Director, and directs the Secretary of the Army to conduct a study regarding indicators which may be used to signal the need for changes in the rate of diversion of water from Lake Michigan at Chicago. H. R. 1573, 100th Cong., 1st Sess. (1987).

96. There are three categories of water level fluctuations on the Great Lakes: long term, seasonal and short term. "Long-term fluctuations are the result of persistent low or high water supply conditions within the basin which result in extremely low levels, such as were recorded in the mid-1960s, . . . or in extremely high levels, such as [those recorded] in 1973-74 [and 1985-86]. . . . Seasonal fluctuations in Great Lakes levels reflect the annual hydrologic cycle. Short-term fluctuations, lasting from a few hours to several days, are caused by meteorological disturbances." International Joint Commission, *supra* note 1, at 3-1. The level of a lake depends upon the quantity of water entering the lake (inflows) and the quantity of water leaving the lake (outflows). "The amount of [L]ake level outflow fluctuation in the Great Lakes system depends on the magnitude of water supply changes and the timing of the passage of water through the system. These . . . are the result of the interaction of the natural and artificial factors which affect the supply and discharge of water to and from the system." Ibid. Conservation of water resources can also protect Great Lakes water levels by reducing the need to divert water. Water leakage problems cause serious losses of water and are common to municipal water systems. The International Joint Commission has determined that most Great Lakes waterworks systems are plagued with leakage problems. International Joint Commission, supra note 1, at 6-8. Amelioration of structural and leakage problems would increase efficient use of available resources. The Supreme Court recently held that states must use "reasonable conservation methods" to eliminate "waste and inefficiency in the use of water." *Colorado v. New Mexico* 103 S. Ct. 539, 549 (1982). Such a state policy is incorporated in the Illinois permit system which controls the diversion and allocation of Lake Michigan water. "The Department [of Transportation] shall require that all feasible means reasonably available to the State and its . . . agencies . . . shall be employed to conserve and manage the water resources of the region and the use of water therein in accordance with the best modern scientific knowledge and engineering practice." Ill. Ann. Stat. ch. 19 § 120.3 (Smith-Hurd 1987).

97. Time is a crucial factor in a water use permit; either because of seasonal or daily fluctuations in water levels. Water supply contracts ordinarily address the rate of withdrawal, expressed as cubic feet per second, as well as total water allotment, expressed in acre feet. An acre foot of water is the amount of water required to cover an acre to a depth of one foot.

98. 103 S. Ct. 539, 549 (1982).

99. International Joint Commission, *supra* note 1, at 3-2.

100. See *Water Resources Policy Issues: Hearings Before the Subcomm. on Water Resources of the Senate Comm. on Environment and Public Works,* 97th Cong., 1st Sess., pt. 2, at 403 (1981) (testimony of Rose McCullough, Sierra Club).

101. See ibid. at 403.

102. Ibid. at 341 (Statement of Rose McCullough). See generally 43 U.S.C.A. § 371 at seq. (West 1986).

103. International Joint Commission, *supra* note 1, at 9-7.

SALLY COLE-MISCH

7B

GREAT LAKES DIVERSIONS: A CONFLICT ASSESSMENT

The future for water throughout the United States portends a conflict both national in scope and horrific in intensity. The groundwork has been laid for a fierce, divisive battle between the "haves" and the "have-nots," and history shows that it is the "have-nots" who are likely to win. If the decision is left up to the federal government and courts, those who have the water in this country will lose their exclusive right to that resource—and the cost of diverting water to drier climates will not be an effective obstacle.

Although diversion may initially seem farfetched and economically unfeasible, it *has* been discussed, and it *is* a potential reality in the next twenty to thirty years. One of the major problems in discussing diversion and its potential threat to the Great Lakes is the time frame: the common citizen in this region disregards this threat to the water because the supply of water at the moment seems endless. Every completed national water project, however, has taken an average lead time of thirty years: fifteen years of negotiation and fifteen years of construction (Hatton 1982). An initial position has been outlined by each region and negotiations have in a sense already begun. If we wait twenty years to confront the issue, the need for further diversion will have already occurred and the future stability of the southwestern part of the nation will by that time depend upon diverted water for its survival. Diversion is a conflict that cannot be allowed to escalate; it must be considered and resolved now if we are to avoid the massive national damage that would be caused later by regionalizing and dividing the United States into a true country of "haves" and "have-nots."

THE GREAT LAKES REGION: ITS POSITION

> We know not what the well is worth until it runs dry. Benjamin Franklin

The Great Lakes total some 95,000 square miles in area and hold 5,475 cubic miles of water, enough to flood the entire United States to a depth of ten feet. Collectively, they make up the largest body of fresh surface water on this earth. Lake Superior is itself the world's largest freshwater lake in area, followed by Lake Huron (fifth), Lake Michigan (sixth), Lake Erie (twelfth), and Lake Ontario (fourteenth) (Lewis 1985). Illinois, Indiana, Michigan, Minnesota, New York, Ohio, Ontario, Pennsylvania, Quebec, and Wisconsin make up the Great Lakes Basin draining into the lakes; these states total another 200,000 square miles. Approximately 50 percent of Canada's total population lives in the Great Lakes Basin, and the region's economic activity accounts for 60 percent and 25 percent of Canada's and the United States' national incomes, respectively (Milliken 1983). The "destinies and futures" of these states and provinces "are inextricably tied to the Great Lakes" (Milliken 1983) because of the variety of economic functions the water allows, including the export shipping of grain, iron, limestone, and other products, as well as fishing, boating, swimming, and tourist activities. Furthermore, the lakes supply water for drinking, agriculture, power generation and cooling, and other industrial concerns.

Small-scale diversions have in fact occurred on the Great Lakes since 1929, when the first version of the Welland Canal opened navigation between Lakes Erie and Ontario (to bypass Niagara Falls). Since then, four other diversions have been opened, mainly to supply hydroelectric power. One, the Chicago Sanitary and Ship Canal, takes water from Lake Michigan to the Mississippi via the Illinois Waterway. The rate of flow at this outlet has been a subject of controversy in the basin and has gone to the Supreme Court for decision several times since the 1920s. Currently, the existing diversion from Chicago of 3200 cfs (cubic feet per second) is controlled by a 1967 decision of the Court (Kuchenberg 1983).

The net effect of the current diversions is extremely small. Much more harmful to the economic stability of the basin at this point are the natural fluctuations in the lake levels because of differences across the region from year to year in precipitation and evaporation. These levels fluctuate naturally by as much as 5 feet over ten years, and differences have ranged from 3.8 feet on Lake Superior to 6.6 feet on Lakes Michigan-Huron and Lake Ontario (Kluitenberg 1984). Economic gains or losses are felt each year in the region according to these natural fluctuations.

The major problem during high water levels, of course, is flooding. Large-scale diversions of water during these cycles could help to prevent flooding and the resulting shoreline erosion. But, since diverting water out of the Great Lakes results in an overall drop in lake levels, the problems associated with natural low-water cycles would accelerate dramatically. "When lake levels go down, freighters have to carry less cargo; hydro-electric generating plants produce less electricity; people get more beach for swimming but have to swim in deeper water; fish have to look for new spawning areas; wildlife have to look for new food supplies; boat docks have to be extended; industries that need water have to pump the water higher" (Hatton 1982).

All of these effects cost money. The U.S. Army Corp of Engineers projects a total loss of $69 million a year in economic losses to overall Great Lakes users from a reduced flow of 5000 cfs. This loss would include the following:

- Recreational boating would lose $1.8 million per year.
- Shipping industries would put at least $10 million less per year into the U.S. economy (this loss already occurs every time the lakes go one inch below the low-water average).
- Diversions producing a lowered level of one-half to two inches in lake levels would create a $44 million loss from hydroelectric power.
- The Corps of Engineers has projected that an additional 10,000 cfs withdrawal of water would result in a net annual loss of benefits to the Great Lakes region of about $105 million, primarily in navigation and hydroelectric power generation (Harris 1983).
- Projected growth in the Great Lakes Basin in population (and the increased contamination of the region's groundwater supply[1]) could cause water consumption to double from 1975 to 2000 and triple from 2000 to 2035. This increase alone will drop lake levels considerably.

These staggering economic losses alone are enough to understand the concern of the Great Lakes region over preserving their rights to the water. But what is considered an even more serious economic threat to leaders and concerned citizens in the basin is the likelihood that diversions of water would also divert industrial growth and jobs away from an area already sensitive to economic change. According to Robert H. Abrams, water law specialist at Wayne State University, "When you export water, you export the economy that goes with it" (Abrams 1982).

Those in the Great Lakes Basin have therefore emphasized their own economic need as reason to retain all of the water in the lakes. They also point to an International Joint Commission (IJC) study requested by the United States and Canada in 1977 to determine the positive and negative effects of diversions. The study estimated that the cost of diverting 10,000 cfs from the western end of Lake Superior to the Missouri River would cost $19.6 billion for the diversion system, plus another $7 billion for power plants to drive it (IJC 1981).

Finally, those in the Great Lakes Basin claim that the thought of diversion could reverse the present trend by inhabitants of the region to protect the water quality. The water would suddenly be viewed as an economic commodity to be sold, rather than a life-sustaining resource to be protected. The feeling of ownership would be lost, and citizens would no longer be concerned about the quality of the water. At present, contamination of the Great Lakes is a vital topic for officials in the region, and a feeling of pride and respect for the lakes is essential for its protection. Lee Sherman Dreyfus, governor of Wisconsin, states the following:

> The water is the property of the people of these states and provinces. I would argue that that is just as true of that water as is the gas, oil, and coal that exists within the property, both public and private, of the states in the rest of this continent. (Keynote Address, Conference on the Interbasin Transfer of Water 1982).

THE WESTERN REGION: ITS POSITION

> There'll be a day when we're gonna get water out of the Great Lakes. Because, first, you're not using it—other than to look at. And we need it badly . . . You ever ride the city bus up in Detroit? We've got poverty over in Houston, but not like you see riding a bus in Detroit. Someday you people in Detroit are going to be

more than happy to do anything you can, take anything you can get. Of course we want your water, but we don't want to take it. You're going to receive a great deal of benefit out of this water coming to Texas. Dayton Elam, Farmer, Seminole, Texas, *The Detroit News,* 1981

Sixty percent of the land in the United States is in the western region. Most of this area (except the Rocky Mountain range) is used for agriculture, particularly in the Great Plains states. Over 40 percent of the nations' beef cattle are raised here, and 20 percent of all agricultural land is in this middle western states region. That 20 percent produces 58 percent of all the agricultural products in the United States. Yet, the entire region receives only 25 percent of the total precipitation each year. Irrigation has become the major source of crop water, which comes from an eight-hundred-mile-long natural reservoir called the Ogallala Aquifer. Some two hundred thousand wells tap the aquifer to irrigate sixteen million acres of prime farmland. In most of the Great Plains states, in fact, the only source of water is the Ogallala Aquifer.

In Seminole, Texas, for example, the high school swimming pool, the water for the city's nine-hole golf course, and all consumed water comes from the aquifer. The city's hydrologist warned the local government in 1981 that if the city continued to consume water from its share of the aquifer at present rates it would last only another eleven years. But the city cannot enforce restrictions on private water use because Texas law treats underground water as a mineral; in other words, farmers who own the land also own the water beneath it. Since the aquifer's depth varies greatly from north to south, it is falling unequally; some areas—the north panhandle of Texas, for instance—have already lost their sources of water. The water table has dropped ten to fifteen feet in other areas, and a U.S. Department of Commerce study in 1982 concluded that if water continues to be pumped at the current rate, the aquifer will be extinct within another forty years.

The obvious result of even this initial depletion of water will be to look elsewhere for water supplies. Without diversions, according to the western region, the high plain states will have to revert to dry-land farming (growing crops with available rainfall); this practice could reduce productivity by two-thirds, and the nation's food supply would be threatened.

Experience with large transports of water in the West makes diversion of Great Lakes water appear an even more viable option. The Central Arizona Project, scheduled for completion in 1987, already carries 2.2 million acre feet of water per year (or 717 trillion gallons) from Lake Mead to southeastern Arizona at a cost of more than two billion federal tax dollars. Urban and industrial development have increased along the route of transported water from Mono Lake, just south of Yosemite, to Los Angeles. Federal investment has helped so far to meet these overall water needs at a cost of $180 billion in this century (Dreyfus 1982). The demand for this water spirals upward as the greatest increases in population continue to occur in the West and Southwest.

These developing areas and the federal government, understandably, do not want water shortages to get in the way of economic growth in any region, particularly after the increased inflation and lowered growth of the last ten years. Taxes paid throughout the United States are used to develop water resources in areas where shortages have sometimes been designed to make water cheap and plentiful. A resident of Sun City, Arizona, for example, actually pays less for water than does a resident of Milwaukee, Wisconsin.[2]

Major transfer of water is perceived by westerners as economically feasible with federal support and politically and agriculturally desirable. Possible modes of water transportation from the Great Lakes that have been designed include the following:

- A chain reaction by which the Ogallala Aquifer would be recharged from one system of canals or other systems.
- One system from the Mississippi River, and to that river from the Great Lakes (probably from increased water flow at the current Chicago River diversion outlet).
- Diversion from just east of Cleveland to the Ohio River, and on over, again, to the Mississippi River.
- Water diverted from Lake Superior, in Minnesota, to the Missouri River.

The western region points to the documented agreement by engineers that diversion to any place east of the Rockies is technically feasible and to federal legislation and court decision that so far have tended to decide in their favor. Recent Supreme Court decisions have cast considerable doubt on the ability of states, acting by themselves, to prohibit diversions beyond their boundaries. The concept that state law could regard water as a special resource and not an article of interstate commerce was rejected in *Sporhase* v. *Nebraska* (*Sporehase* v. *Nebraska,* 102 Supreme Court 3456, 1982). Nebraska had passed a statute requiring a state permit for interstate transport of groundwater; to receive a permit, the state into which the water was to be exported must allow reciprocal transfers. The court regarded this provision as a barrier to interstate commerce and decided that Nebraska did not have the right to ban water shipment to other states. This decision is significant. If the state cannot prove that (1) it is protecting the health of its citizens, not just its economy, in regulating the export of water, (2) the regulations are justified because of a shortage of water available to its own citizens, and (3) the regulations are designed to protect its citizens' water supply, then the provision interferes with the interstate commerce clause of the U.S. Constitution. It is doubtful, then, that the states surrounding the Great Lakes could prove the above arguments necessary to protect their water. Further, the Supreme Court decision is seen as the first step towards nationalization of water, and any attempt to stop diversions would thus be considered unconstitutional.

WHERE DO WE GO FROM HERE?

> The trouble is that an organized and informed counterforce to bring the dimension of objectivity into the arena . . . is lacking. The intensity of opposition to water resources programs by conservationists, preservationists, environmentalists, and others has created an era in which both the layman and the professional almost rush to postponement of difficult decisions in their desire to achieve short-run objectives. But someday the "piper will have to be paid." Our tendency to avoid or minimize the issues now will exact a substantial price later. Warren Viessman, Jr., Senior Specialist in Engineering and Public Works, Congressional Research Service, Library of Congress

The positions taken by the Great Lakes region and the western region both appear valid; the major question seems to be these: do you preserve an internationally important resource like the Great Lakes and adjust people's lifestyles and choice of home to protect the water, or do you change the Great Lakes to meet the needs of the people and to help provide the increasing amounts of food needed throughout the world? Both sides view their claims as valid and most relevant to the needs of society as a whole. What must be considered if we are to resolve this conflict in the future, and what steps need to be taken?

First, it must be recognized that the Great Lakes region and the Southwest have very different values. This distinction becomes clear when you realize that "a farmer in west Texas referred to trees as 'encumbrances,' because they get in the way of irrigation systems and plows" (Good 1982). Americans in the Great Lakes area, in contrast, view the protection of the environment, and particularly the quality and quantity of their Lakes, as a prime responsibility.

The Great Lakes region already has tried to coalese to preserve the lakes and to prevent diversions. Historically, this has not been an altogether successful or easy task. The Great Lakes Water Quality Agreement of 1972 was seen as the first major step between federal governments of the United States and Canada to protect the basin on a multistate and even multinational basis. The International Joint Commission, which grew out of the Boundary Water Treaty of 1909 between the United States and Canada, is a permanent body composed equally of Canadian and American members. Although its responsibility is to develop mutually acceptable solutions to boundary questions, it has accomplished little more than serving as a research and advisory body. Most recently, all eight U.S. states and two Canadian provinces signed the Great Lakes Charter to coordinate basinwide management of the lakes and to develop greater communication among the states and provinces regarding diversions. Reaching this agreement was not easy, however. Different environmental values also exist between Canada and the states, and even among the states themselves. For instance, coordination of state efforts to control toxic substances in the lakes has resulted in "as many state policies in this area as there are states in the Great Lakes Basin. States have sometimes widely varying health standards for safe levels of contaminants in Great Lakes fish consumed by humans" (Blanchard 1983).

Although achieving a basinwide agreement like the charter might somewhat relax fears about future diversions, how would it help to resolve the larger issue—the demand for water by the western region in the future? If the lakes states felt secure in their protection of their water resources, perhaps they would be more agreeable to help the western region conserve and preserve their own equally important resources. Joseph Rossillon, executive director of the Freshwater Biological Research Foundation of Minnesota, says the following: "Our water problems are not 'different' problems. Every state in the nation has some kind of water problems that are all manifestations of one single problem—an overload or stressing of the total water system" (Rossillon 1983).

The western region's concern for its economic stability and growth and its future ability to produce crops should be important to the Great Lakes as well. The basin states can best assist in preserving the West's growth and balance by encouraging federal water conservation programs.

> It appears that the only implementable water management strategy to alleviate the stress on the Ogallala Aquifer to some degree is greater emphasis on conservation and increased efficiency of use by the farmers themselves . . . The provision of incentives to stimulate earlier and more widespread adoption of such measures will help. (Banks 1982)

It is estimated, in fact, that an improvement in efficiency of 0.7 percent in the U.S. agricultural water consumption would provide for a doubling of all other consumptive uses in the West (DenUyl 1983).

Conservation of water in agriculture and for other uses has been neglected in the western states because of the relatively low subsidized prices paid for the resource. This is changing, but more realistic pricing is needed. Other alternatives, such as additional surface water development, wastewater reclamation, and transfer of water from low- to high-valued uses should be considered as viable options to reduce their future water needs. These alternatives will be more strongly considered and applied if the western region feels that the Great Lakes states are willing to support and respect their efforts. Creative problem-solving sessions among officials in the regions (that would have a stake in future federal action) could serve as brainstorming meetings to build basic consensus agreements that would avoid regulatory standoffs and possible court battles. Before opposing views solidify, the officials and citizens could design ways to identify potential areas of dispute and, in a sense, predict future conflict in order to prevent it (Carnduff and Clark 1980).

In the final analysis, it must be remembered that water is one of the real essentials of life and that people will do anything to obtain it. The challenge now is to convert people's fears and suspicions concerning interbasin transfers into an informed public dialogue which will lead eventually to improvement in the institutions through which common values are articulated, conflicts are equitably resolved, efficient resource use is achieved, and environmental quality is maintained: in short, through which a true cooperative process is created.

NOTES

1. William Marks, Water Management Planning Task Force in Michigan: "I'm willing to predict that within five years, the state's entire water supply will come from the Great Lakes."

2. The cost of supplying this "cheap water" to the Southwest from federal money increases the tension between the two regions. In effect, citizens from the Great Lakes area "pay for federal water projects twice: in their taxes and when the prices of their farm product fall as a result of increases in crop production for these federal projects" (Cambell 1983).

REFERENCES

Abrams, Robert H. 1982. Panel Discussion. *1982 Great Lakes Water Resources Conference.* Mackinac Island, MI. June 10.

Banks, Harvey O. 1982. "Future Water Demands in the United States." In Conference on the Interbasin Transfer of Water, *The Interbasin Transfer of Water: The Great Lakes Connection,* Milwuakee, WI. May 10–11. Fresh Water Society, Navarre, Minnesota.

Blanchard, Governor James J. 1983. "An Interstate Compact and the Future of the Great Lakes." Speech. Council of Great Lakes Governors, Indianapolis, IN. November 19.

Campbell, David C. 1983. *The Critical Zone with Respect to the Great Lakes.* National Wildlife Federation, Washington, D.C.

Carnduff, Susan, and Pete Clark. 1980. *Selected Readings on Conflict Management.* American Arbitration Association and Clark-McGlennon Associates, Inc., New York, NY.

DenUyl, R. Bruce. *1983 Economic Aspects of Inter-basin Water Transfers from the Great Lakes.* Governor's Water Task Force, Michigan State University.

Dreyfus, Governor Lee Sherman. 1982. Keynote address. In *Proceedings of the Conference on the Interbasin Transfer of Water.* The Great Lakes Connection, Milwaukee, WI. May 10.

Good, David. 1982. Editorial, Michigan Magazine. *Detroit News,* November 28.

Harris, Elizabeth. 1983. *The Demand for Great Lakes Water: A Proposal for Preventing Major Water Diversions Out of the Great Lakes Basin.* East Michigan Environmental Action Council.

Hatton, Nancy Webb. 1982. "The 'Plot' to Steal the Great Lakes." Michigan Magazine. *Detroit News,* November 28.

International Joint Commission. 1981. *Great Lakes Diversions and Consumptive Uses.* Great Lakes Regional Office, Windsor, Ontario, Canada.

Kluitenberg, Edward H. 1984. *Potential Impacts of Great Lakes Diversions.* Final Report. House Marine Affairs and Port Development Committee, University of Michigan, Ann Arbor, MI. November.

Kuchenberg, Tom. 1983. "Great Lakes Need Wise Dispute Resolutions." *Conservation Foundation Letter,* November.

Lewis, Jack. 1985. "The Five Sister Lakes: A Profile." *EPA Journal* 11(2): 5–6.

Marks, William. 1982. "The Great Lakes Connection." In *Proceedings of the Conference on the Interbasin Transfer of Water.* Milwaukee, WI. May 10.

Milliken, William G. 1983. "Viewpoint: A Governor's Perspective." *Great Lakes Waste and Pollution Review Magazine* 1(1): 5.

Rossillon, Joseph P. 1983. *Interbasin Transfer of Water: An Overview.* Freshwater Biological Research Foundation, Navarre, MN.

Viessman, Warren Jr. 1982. Guest Editorial. *Interstate Conference on Water Problems Washington Report,* 1(2) May 12.

CHAPTER 8. TOWARD A MORE ACCOUNTABLE PROCESS: THE ROYAL SOCIETY-NATIONAL RESEARCH COUNCIL REPORT

The major nongovernmental scientific assessment of the ecosystem approach to management for the Great Lakes was the Royal Society of Canada-National Research Council of the United States joint study, published in 1985. Frequently referred to elsewhere in this book, this report is analyzed in greater depth in this chapter. Probably the major issue implicit in the report is the nature of the institutional arrangements needed to implement an ecosystem approach. Possibilities for more effective implementation of the 1978 Water Quality Agreement through the present political structure or through some modification depend upon the growth and activation of a popular constituency for policy reform. There appears to be consensus amongst the authors contributing to this volume that such a constitutency is growing and intensifying. How it will be expressed politically is not yet clear.

DON MUNTON

8

TOWARD A MORE ACCOUNTABLE PROCESS: THE ROYAL SOCIETY–NATIONAL RESEARCH COUNCIL REPORT

Ecosystem management, however defined, is not without its challenges. The scientific and intellectual demands it makes are now, if not well charted, at least initially explored. The institutional and political challenges it poses seem much less well explored or charted but no less substantial. Indeed, existing institutional mechanisms seem particularly discredited by the implications of the ecosystem approach. A frequent focus of criticism of environmentalists, these mechanisms commonly are regarded as barriers to a better world and thus either in need of change or, alternatively, something to be circumvented. From a pure ecosystem management perspective, they surely are seen even less favorably. Taken well short of its logical extreme, management by ecosystem could imply virtually the outright abolition of traditional bureaucratic and jurisdictional divisions, as Lynton Caldwell suggests in his introductory chapter to this volume.

A commitment to ecosystem management and a commitment to the maintenance of national sovereignty and of the responsibilities of existing political jurisdictions would seem to be strange intellectual bedfellows—uncomfortable, at best, and perhaps incompatible. It may thus appear incongruous that both are firmly espoused in the 1985 joint report of the Royal Society of Canada and the National Research Council of the United States. Entitled *The Great Lakes Water Quality Agreement: An Evolving Instrument for Ecosystem Management,* this report represented a unique experiment in binational cooperation and, it might be noted, the first such cooperative effort of the two countries' leading scientific bodies.[1]

Its auspices notwithstanding, what might explain the apparent incongruity in the report's recommendations? Though a less than objective observer, I simply will assume that the report's drafters did not fail to grasp the implications of their proposals. The present chapter thus represents both a review of the review and an attempt to explain this juxtaposition of calls for ecosystem management and for the maintenance of existing binational, as well as national and subnational, institutional mechanisms.

As if such a paradoxical juxtaposition were not sufficient, there are yet other reasons for reviewing this aspect of an existing report. For one thing, the RSC-NRC report received considerable attention not only in the media at the time of its release but also in the offices and corridors of power. The third biennial report of the United States–Canada International Joint Commission (IJC) on the Great Lakes Water Quality Agreement singles out the RSC-NRC report. "Of particular interest to the Commission's assessment," it says, "is the Special Committee Report of the U.S. National Academy of Sciences–National Research Council and the Royal Society of Canada." After listing a number of "particularly useful contributions" in the report, the IJC then goes on to advise that it "is a valuable resource document to which the Governments should give attention during their review."[2]

Moreover, the official Canadian government statement, made by the secretary of state for external affairs, Joe Clark, simultaneously acknowledging receipt of the IJC report and announcing the initiation of the two governments' review of the agreement, also singles out the RSC-NRC report. "It is our intention," the statement says, "to carry out the review taking into account the views of interested individuals and groups, in particular those expressed in the 1985 report of the Royal Society of Canada/US National Research Council."[3] As flattering as such recognition and attention may be, it alone does not necessarily justify further serious consideration.

Most of the public attention has appropriately and understandably been paid to the RSC-NRC recommendations dealing with toxic contaminants. It is likely that most of the government attention will be similarly directed. The result may be a relative lack of consideration to those recommendations in the report dealing with institutional mechanisms.

In part, this emphasis will be due to the extraordinarily challenging nature of the problems for policymakers and publics alike of rehabilitating the Great Lakes ecosystem. In part, however, the resulting lack of attention to institutional recommendations may be due as well to a lack of understanding on the part of the publics of the importance of the mechanisms and processes by which governments deal with environmental problems and to a lack of willingness on the part of some in government to contemplate changes in these mechanisms and processes. To the extent that either this lack of public understanding or this government unwillingness may exist, there may then be a further need to review the RSC-NRC report and to consider seriously its institutional recommendations.

Finally, and the preceding point notwithstanding, there have been expressions of dissatisfaction with some aspects of the existing joint institutions from various actors in this quiet drama. The IJC itself, in its 1982 report on progress under the agreement, expressed "concern over its own flexibility to operate effectively within the existing institutions" and urged that "the Parties and jurisdictions take into account the concerns expressed . . . in their further deliberations concerning institutional arrangements pertinent to the Great Lakes Water Quality Agreement and future agreements."[4]

The RSC-NRC committee was also explicitly invited to examine the institutional aspects of the agreement by at least one of the two "parties." At its first meeting, the committee was told the following by the spokesman for the U.S. Department of State:

> I have heard, from well-informed veterans of the Agreement, that such study would be worthwhile. It might usefully include the relationships between the Water Quality and Science Advisory Boards, the IJC, the Governments, the Environment Ministries, and state or provincial authorities. I do not take any position as to whether such institutional factors need change, or have hampered the existing Agreement. But it would be interesting to hear an unbiased and expert evaluation. This is, of course, just the sort of issue that Governments themselves find hardest to address.[5]

The nature of the following discussion, and particularly the fact that the existing institutions discussed here may be unfamiliar to some readers, demands a brief description of the joint institutions involved in Great Lakes ecosystem management. The relevant recommendations of the RSC-NRC report will next be summarized. Specifically, what did the committee say about institutional issues?

And, equally importantly, why did it say what it said? An attempt will then be made to elaborate on the thinking behind the report's recommendations. This attempt, it must be emphasized, will necessarily be a personal one. It will involve to a considerable extent examining the nature and evolution of the existing binational institutions since their establishment under the 1972 agreement. To see clearly in which direction one should go, in short, it helps to know from whence one has come.

EXISTING BINATIONAL INSTITUTIONS

The essence of the 1972 agreement, maintained when it was renegotiated in 1977-78, was a set of common general water quality objectives, certain specific regulatory standards, mutual commitments to implement national programs to achieve these objectives, and procedures for monitoring subsequent progress.[6] A key point, often misunderstood, is that although the objectives and standards were joint and the monitoring of progress was to be joint, the pollution control programs were not. The programs were to be complementary but developed and implemented separately in the various jurisdictions.

Both agreements gave the International Joint Commission (IJC) responsibility for the collection and analysis of information on water quality objectives and pollution control programs; for the independent verification of data; and for the publication of reports. Most importantly for the discussion here, they also gave the IJC responsibility for providing "assistance in the coordination of the joint activities envisaged by this Agreement." Both accords further directed the IJC to establish a Water Quality Board "to assist it in the exercise of the powers and responsibilities assigned to it under this Agreement," and a Research (later Science) Advisory Board to advise specifically on scientific issues. The commission also was empowered to establish a regional office "to assist it in the discharge of its functions" under the agreement.

RSC-NRC RECOMMENDATIONS

The basic thrust of the RSC-NRC report was toward making the Great Lakes agreement, as the subtitle said, an "evolving instrument for ecosystem management." Its analysis of and proposals concerning the ecosystem approach to scientific investigation of the problems of the basin have been dealt with elsewhere (including Lynton Caldwell's introductory chapter in the present volume). Suffice it to say, a major conclusion of the report is, as Caldwell states, "that we have the commitment to a basinwide ecosystem approach, but the approach has yet to be undertaken. There has been a giant step in concept and principle but the implementation is as yet in the exploratory stage." It is, of course, the report's content regarding institutional aspects of ecosystem management that concerns us here.

The RSC-NRC report also made a host of recommendations concerning what were regarded by the committee as the lakes' two major environmental problems—toxic contaminants and nutrients or enrichment. It called, for example, for more studies and more data on the biological effects of toxic contaminants, on the exposure of human beings through food consumption, on contaminant loadings of infants, and on groundwater conditions. It urged the implementation of a new Great Lakes Surveillance Plan: further development of large-lake transport/fate models: the development of a comprehensive toxic substances management strategy, including priority action on toxic waste treatment centers: and government cleanup action in the particularly degraded "areas of concern."

On the nutrient problem it recommended further study of the longitudinal process of eutrophication, regular review of ongoing monitoring programs, continued efforts to reach at least the targets set in the 1978 agreement and its 1983 supplement, basinwide detergent phosphate limits, new efforts to control nonpoint-source pollution, and more emphasis on remediation of near-shore pollution problems, a long-term commitment to improve and maintain sewage treatment systems, and more research coordination with the Great Lakes Fishery Commission.

Many of these recommendations were original. Some of the others were reinforcing existing or proposed directions. In the latter category, for example, the committee also urged governments and the IJC to increase public awareness of the extent and implications of toxic chemical problems in the Great Lakes.

When the committee came to review institutional mechanisms, however, its proposals were entirely novel, albeit, as suggested above, less than revolutionary. The committee did not, as many ecosystem proponents would have done, argue for broader IJC powers for controlling pollution or managing the lakes ecosystem. In fact, it suggested some diminution of the IJC's present responsibilities.

Most of the institutional oriented recommendations dealt with the IJC and its affiliated binational bodies. (The latter include the Great Lakes Water Quality Board, the Science Advisory Board, and the IJC's Regional Office in Windsor, Ontario, across from Detroit.) Fewer were directed at the governments themselves, in large part because the committee did not consider a thorough review of the structures and programs of both national and all provincial and state governments' environmental agencies to be either feasible or within its terms of reference. Those recommendations, directed at what the Great Lakes agreement calls the "Parties," however, were key ones.

The general conclusion of the RSC-NRC report regarding institutions was that

> the record of the IJC and the associated joint institutions is one of substantial success with respect to those responsibilities that most closely resemble those of a traditional reference, and for this they deserve much credit. However, these joint institutions have lagged in executing certain responsibilities; and in others, improvements could still be made.[7]

At the heart of the institutional recommendations was the following: "The committee . . . recommends that the coordinating responsibilities for the control programs that implement the Agreement be left to the parties, rather than to the Water Quality Board. This coordination should be handled through bilateral government-to-government meetings."[8]

The rationale for this recommendation was brief but to the point:

> The committee finds that the Water Quality Board's efforts to coordinate pollution-control programs adversely affects the ability of the IJC, with the assistance of its Boards, to offer independent advice to the parties. The Water Quality Board appears to spend a disproportionate amount of its effort on coordination. This activity diverts limited Board, IJC, and Regional Office resources from other responsibilities. Finally, this role is inconsistent with the Board's role of providing expert advice to the Commission on the implementation of the Agreement and involves the Commission too closely in managing the program that it is intended to evaluate.[9]

Following on from the argument for divorcing the monitoring and advisory functions and the coordinating functions were recommendations aimed at ensuring that both sets of functions were performed more effectively. The RSC-NRC report noted that "detailed statements on the status of the implementation in their respective countries of Agreement-related programs are not published by the United States or Canada, thus making accountability for Agreement implementation more difficult to establish."[10] It thus urged that

> the Agreement direct the Canadian and United States governments to prepare reports biannually for the purpose of reviewing the progress achieved in implementing the Agreement and to hold bilateral meetings regularly at the ministerial level with respect to the Agreement. The reports by each government should be made public at least 90 days before the scheduled date of the next meeting and the meetings should involve, in addition to the two federal governments, all state and provincial governments in the Great Lakes basin.[11]

The committee was no less concerned about the ability of the IJC to undertake its monitoring and advisory functions effectively. To ensure that it was receiving expert advice that was as independent as possible of existing government policies, the RSC-NRC group recommended that

> [T]he Commission provide that members on the Water Quality Board include both individuals who are and are not representatives of government agencies and who reflect the diverse backgrounds relevant to Great Lakes issues, and that the parties to the Agreement cooperate with this Commission initiative;
> The parties should establish that the Science Advisory Board be solely responsible to the Commission and that the Commission ensure the appointment of members who reflect the diverse backgrounds relevant to Great Lakes issues; and
> [The parties should] make the Regional Office wholly responsible to the Commission. Such an arrangement should reinforce the ability of the IJC to develop and offer independent recommendations to the parties.[12]

And to ensure as much communication as possible, the RSC-NRC report urged that

> the Agreement call for a meeting between the parties and the Commission following publication of the biennial report from the Commission. This would provide a forum for the parties to respond to the contents of the report and to set priorities, within the limits of the Agreement for the ensuing period. The meeting should include officials from the U.S. Department of State and the Canadian Department of External Affairs.[13]

It also urged that "the Regional Office serve as a clearinghouse to provide information to researchers, governments, and other interested persons on where to locate comprehensive data on the Great Lakes."[14]

UNDERLYING PRINCIPLES

The basic principles underlying the RSC-NRC recommendations should be clear. One is that the coordination of government pollution control and ecosystem rehabilitation policies, on the one hand, and the monitoring and assessment of these policies, on the other, should be kept functionally separate. The involvement of the IJC and its Water Quality Board in the coordination of the various jurisdictions' programs tends to take away from the time and resources available to undertake monitoring and review of these programs. By trying to do both, the IJC board, in particular, tends to do more of the former and less of the latter than it should. Moreover, and more importantly, by involving the IJC in both functions, the committee found, the governments are entangling in their program operations the supposedly independent watchdog charged with the responsibility of assessing these very programs. By being both the forum for and the prime actor in program coordination, the board, and to certain extent, therefore, the commission, becomes less than the independent critic that it should be and was intended to be.

The purpose here, lest this argument be misunderstood, is most certainly not to make the commission less effective or less important. Nor is it to limit the scope of the IJC's activities—though in the numerical sense, in the number of roles, that may be the effect. The purpose, rather, is to increase the commission's independence and hence its effectiveness.

A second underlying principle in the RSC-NRC report is that governments ought to be maximally accountable to their citizens. Few would probably disagree with this principle in the abstract. But it implicitly runs directly counter to the unfortunately common tendency to look to judicial or extragovernmental agencies for solutions to environmental problems or for shortcuts to the usual delays in dealing with them. In other words, it runs against the almost irresistible tendency to look for ways to avoid politics through panaceas.

As attractive as the idea of eliminating or sidestepping political processes, constraints, and delays may seem, it is, however, an illusion to imagine that politics in the broadest sense can be so easily avoided. Basinwide environmental management agencies, even if established quite separate from the mechanisms of governments, would very quickly be immersed in politics by reason of the authority they would be granted and the impact their decisions would thus have. They would not and could not exist for long without becoming the objects of pressure from polluters and then from environmental interest groups, and eventually from existing governments themselves. Thus pressured, they would almost certainly react exactly as governments do—by proceeding slowly and cautiously. Indeed, without the legitimacy governments are provided through the electoral process, such agencies would probably proceed even more slowly and cautiously, evading controversial issues and postponing decisions to a greater extent even than elected governments.

Quite aside from the question of whether such independent operating agencies might be more effective, there is little likelihood that they would be established by present-day governments. The divestment of sovereign authority involved has never been seriously considered by the governments of Canada or the United States and is not likely to be so considered in the near future. The panacea thus not only rests on a mistaken illusion; it is simply unrealistic in the present political context.

Present-day governments are quite unlikely to go further than creating the sort of quasi-independent watchdog and advisory bodies the IJC already provides. Having created them, though, the governments, first, ought to be willing to allow these bodies to do the job asked of them, and second, ought not, the RSC-NRC committee argued, ask these bodies to do what the governments themselves ought to be doing. In the case of the IJC, the governments only appear to be giving more responsibility to the watchdog and advisory bodies. In fact, it can be argued, the central position of the IJC allows the governments themselves to escape from much accountability.

LESS IS BETTER: THE CASE FOR INDEPENDENCE AND ACCOUNTABILITY

Although the key principles underlying the RSC-NRC position are perhaps now clear, the rationale for that position may well not be. Given that the justification for the recommendations provided in the RSC-NRC report itself was necessarily brief, some development of this rationale would be appropriate. (It should be emphasized, however, that what follows are my personal views and neither in any sense an official or authorized elaboration of the committee report as a whole nor necessarily a reflection of the thinking of other members of the committee.)

To answer the question of why the policy coordination function should be carried out separately from those of monitoring and evaluation, and carried out directly by the governments rather than under auspices of the IJC, it is necessary to engage in a bit of history and to ask a number of related questions. Why was the dual role given to the IJC and its Water Quality Board in the original 1972 agreement? Why did the governments change the relationship between the IJC, the board, and the commission's regional office in the 1978 agreement? And what has since transpired, and how have these structures evolved?

Under the 1972 agreement, the IJC was asked, as noted above, to collect and analyze data, to assess the parties' progress, and to assist in coordinating their activities. As a result, the IJC's regional office assumed a dual responsibility—to provide staff support to the Water Quality Board and, at the same time, to provide independent expertise to the commissioners. These two directives were, if juxtaposed, awkward at best. For the regional office, it was a classic serve-two-masters situation. And the two masters did not always see eye to eye.

The dual mandate, however, might have been manageable had the board been a traditional IJC board composed of midlevel officials who were technical experts on the matters within their usually narrow purview. But this board was not at all traditional in either composition or purview. (Whether such a group could have dealt effectively with the issues at hand is another, albeit valid, question.)

The Water Quality Board members, nominated and appointed as representatives of the various federal, state, and provincial governments, have all been senior-level policy managers, not midlevel technical or scientific experts. And the board's purview, particularly the responsibility to monitor whether or not the governments were meeting their commitments under the agreement, is both broad and political, not narrow and technical. Individual members were thus being asked to evaluate publicly the success of their own agencies' policies and often the success of policies for which they themselves were responsible within their own agencies.

To be sure, the agency officials on the Water Quality Board have not been silent. They have offered criticisms and even more frequently have offered suggestions for improvement in existing policies. And this fact is no less important even if it is recognized that some of these suggestions were undoubtedly ones they were making or had made inside their own agencies. But if the board members have not been mute, their criticisms generally have been muted. Rarely are they fundamental. As the commissioners themselves have stated publicly, the board "is composed of individuals not necessarily acting independently of their home organizations." Although they "often make every effort to give objective advice as professionals in their field, even in cases when this stance means criticism of their home organization or government . . . there is no explicit mandate, assurance or even expectation that this will occur as a general rule."[15]

Why did this arrangement and dual mandate emerge in the first place? The reasons are not entirely clear but seem to rest in the jurisdictional and bureaucratic politics of the negotiation of the 1972 agreement.[16] The representation requirement in the arrangement was largely a function of the sheer number of federal, state, and provincial governments involved. Each, it was recognized, had to be represented on this key body and represented at a senior level, especially given that it was going to deal with policy, and therefore with political questions. The evolution of the mandate was more complex.

Many of the scientists and environmental policy officials involved in the 1971-72 negotiations had had experience on the earlier IJC investigatory boards that laid the groundwork for the agreement. This work had been seriously delayed by the lack of staff available to assist in the investigation and especially in the writing of reports for the commission. These officials, primarily concerned with the investigation and advisory roles of the IJC, saw the prospective regional office as the source of the staff to assist the ongoing work of the boards and, through the boards, the commission itself.

On the other hand, a few of the key diplomats involved in the original 1971-72 negotiations were particularly concerned that the commitments being made in the agreement would not be ignored by later governments—as had happened in the past. They thus envisaged, in an expanded IJC mandate to assess and report publicly on progress, a means to ensure, as much as possible, that the commitments were indeed kept. Given chronic staff shortages in the IJC's offices in Ottawa and especially in Washington, the new regional office and its staff was seen as the key to the commission's ability to play its independent watchdog function. That function and the possibility of a regional office were thus ultimately written into the agreement text. The potential for incompatibility in the dual mandate was perceived but was regarded by the negotiators as a manageable problem. It proved not to be.

The office, established shortly after the signing of the 1972 Great Lakes Water Quality Agreement, was from the outset the center of controversy. Although all concerned agreed that its main function was to provide support for the government officials who sat on the IJC boards, these officials disagreed strongly with the commissioners' position that the office could engage in independent surveillance and verification for the IJC itself. It is a measure of this opposition that, despite the IJC's authority, under both the 1972 and 1978 agreements, to verify data supplied by any of the government agencies, it has virtually never done so.

These officials were also in varying degrees uncomfortable with the assessment role given to the IJC, and therefore as IJC board members, to themselves. Their discomfort was all the more acute because they believed that the same staff from the regional office who sat in on their closed-door discussions might then turn around and advise the commission in its watchdog role. A continuing tension resulted. One of its manifestations was a secret, still unpublished, review of the regional office conducted by the Canadian and American cochairmen of the Water Quality Board just prior to the renegotiation of the agreement in 1977–78.

When the governments reexamined the office's mandate during the renegotiation, Canadian officials maintained that the issue was essentially an administrative one. But rather different concerns apparently guided some on the United States side. A senior-level Environmental Protection Agency (EPA) memorandum of May 1977 recommended that the regional office be "disestablished." It was a threat to the effective operation of the various agencies, the memo said, and could even lead to the "erosion of the sovereign authority" of the governments.[17]

Negotiators eventually settled the fate of the office by writing new terms of reference. Its staff would report to the cochairmen of the Water Quality Board, thus removing it from under the direct authority of the commission except for public relations matters. Canadian commissioners protested both publicly and privately. One publicly termed the move "a disguised but effective emasculation of the IJC."[18] The governments responded to the pressure only to the extent of agreeing to a full review of office staffing and functions. The eventual review changed little, and within a few years a new set of commissioners had been appointed.

The new commission was less vocal about the situation forced on it by the governments, but it was no more comfortable than its predecessors with the ambiguities. In their 1982 first biennial report under the agreement, the commissioners took the unusual step of commenting on the situation directly, albeit very diplomatically. The role of the regional office, they noted, "has also contributed to the Commission's concern over its own flexibility to operate effectively within the existing institutions." They underscored the importance of the earlier arrangement:

> Under the 1972 Agreement, the Commission was given clear authority by the Parties to create and operate the Great Lakes Regional Office. The significance of this authority was that it reinforced the presence of the Commission as an independent unitary body with the authority to develop the capability for independently gathering, analyzing and evaluating information which was often of a highly technical nature.[19]

The 1982 IJC report then went on to suggest the nature of the difficulties caused by the changes in the regional office's role.

> The detailed terms of reference for the regional office and the two commission boards presented in the 1978 agreement were a significant departure from the more general statement in the 1972 agreement and appear to limit the commission's ability to directly manage and use the expertise available at the regional office as a source of independent advice. The commission is still attempting to develop ways and means of carrying out its responsibilities relating to the regional office in a manner consistent with the 1978 agreement and, at the same time, responsive to current realities.[20]

The "current realities" in question presumably include not only the obvious concern of interested publics for a vigilant IJC and the support, at least in principle, of the governments for a genuinely independent IJC, but also the strongly felt need of the commissioners themselves for both.

There is no question, then, that the broadened mandate the IJC acquired under the 1972 agreement and retained under the 1978 agreement, coupled with the specified arrangements for pursuing that mandate have led to continual political and administrative problems. These problems, however, are not sufficient reason for the RSC-NRC report to recommend freeing—some might say "stripping"—the commission of responsibility to assist in the coordination of the various jurisdictions' activities. An additional reason is that the existing arrangements, in my view, allow the governments more easily to escape public accountability for their actions or inactions. Less formally, they have helped the governments wiggle off the hook on which they placed themselves in 1972. With some "smoke and mirrors," in the form of obeisance to the principle of independent monitoring, the arrangements, in fact, help the governments hide behind the commission.

Consider the reporting process that is followed. The Water Quality and Science Advisory Boards meet regularly, and every two years, or more frequently, draw up substantial reports. These reports are then formally presented to the commission at a public meeting, although in fact the practice now is for the board members and commissioners to meet and discuss the reports beforehand. The commissioners and their staff then prepare and debate an IJC report which is, in turn, eventually presented to the governments. Officials then prepare and politicians approve for each government a formal response to those points in the IJC report to which they choose to respond. The time lags at each stage are considerable. The media and public attention given to each of the various stages is seldom great. The degree of informed, critical comment is even less. More importantly, the amount of attention devoted tends to decline with each successive stage—perhaps understandably but nevertheless regrettably.

Mandating the IJC as a watchdog and potential independent critic appears to be a bold step; it is without question the sort of step governments are generally very loath to take. But appearances in this case are misleading. Despite—or, perhaps, because of—the IJC role, the series of reports, and the public meetings, there is no occasion on which the governments themselves are obliged to state publicly what commitments under the agreement they have met and what they have not met. There are few occasions when the record of any government is directly and closely examined and criticized. There are fewer occasions still when the criticisms are frank and politically effective.

The only time that government officials are required to report on and evaluate the progress achieved by their policies is at IJC meetings. At these meetings, however, they are reporting in their capacities as members of the IJC's Water Quality Board, not as representatives of the governments. Given this fact—or fiction—and and given that the commission is to some extent dependent on the good will of these officials, there are normally powerful constraints inhibiting frank criticism of government action or inaction.

It was nevertheless common during the IJC meetings of the late 1970s to find vigorous questioning of board members by commissioners. Such questioning, however, is no longer common, at least in public. The new style of the commission is to work with, not cross-examine, board members. The change was foreshadowed in the IJC's 1982 report, which noted, "The Commission believes that a renewed sense of mutual respect and responsiveness between itself and its Great Lakes advisory boards is highly desirable and would enhance the IJC and Agreement process."[21]

This new style was nowhere more evident than at the IJC's November 1983 public meeting preceding its second biennial report. The meeting format was designed, ostensibly, to foster "public participation." It featured the commissioners and the board members sitting together at the front of a large hotel ballroom, while the "public" sat in groups (arranged by the staff of the commission) at tables around the floor. Most of the time for the meeting was devoted to discussions, not between those on the floor and those at the front, nor between the commissioners and the board members, but amongst the individuals at each table. Their assignment was to arrive at a limited list of questions to be submitted, on paper, to the boards. In a later time period, which was severely limited, the board chairmen answered only those previously supplied, written questions with which they chose to deal. Not surprisingly, few of the controversial questions that survived what became in effect a screening process at the tables were subsequently chosen for reply.

Many of the "public" and interest groups who attended left frustrated by the format. Although it avoided any semblance of a confrontation and allowed a form of "public participation," it was certainly not an exercise in public accountability. Perhaps such public meetings of the Commission are not the place to pursue political accountability. But an alternative, then, is needed, and we thus come full circle back to the RSC-NRC recommendations.

CONCLUSION

The essence of the RSC-NRC recommendations regarding Great Lakes institutions is that progress toward ecosystem management in the near term is more likely to be achieved through changes in the processes of governance than through attempts to change the basic structures of governance. And the key to changing processes is to ensure that the existing jurisdictions of the basin are directly and fully accountable to their publics for meeting the commitments they assumed under the Great Lakes Water Quality Agreement. The governments have insisted and will almost certainly continue to insist that they be responsible for developing and implementing environmental programs. That being the case, the RSC-NRC committee said, immediate progress toward ecosystem mangement can best be made if the responsibilities and commitments of the governments are made clear and unambiguous.

The new role of the International Joint Commission under the agreement was originally conceived to be that of a watchdog on the governments, to ensure that if they failed to meet their commitments this failure would be noted and publicized. The principle is still valid, but in practice greater accountability has not resulted. The reason seems to be in part the ambiguities and conflicts built into the agreement-mandated responsibilities of the commission and the lack of required processes by which governments would be forced to defend their records. Coupled with a natural tendency of governments to avoid politically embarrassing confessions, the result has been confusion and lack of accountability.

The RSC-NRC committee recommended, therefore, that the commission no longer be involved in the coordination of government programs and that this coordination be carried out on a direct government-to-government basis. It recommended, further, that the independent policy monitoring and assessment role of the commission be strengthened by ensuring that more of its resources be devoted to this role and that its "principal advisor," the Water Quality Board, no longer be dominated by agency officials. And it recommended that the governments hold what might be termed "environmental summit meetings" on a regular basis at which their records would be publicly scrutinized and as a result of which accountability should increase.

The focus of much of this chapter has been on explaining—and defending—the proposal to distance the IJC from the Great Lakes program coordination. The emphasis has been on elaborating the costs of its involvement in this responsibility. There are some benefits as well, to be sure. Some information is probably gained, for example. But there is little evidence that such information is much used by the commission in its watchdog role. Indeed, the arrangements in place militate against it being used. The costs of involvement thus seem to outweigh any benefits.

The RSC-NRC review rejected the present institutional arrangements of the Great Lakes Agreement as unsatisfactory. While eschewing radical structural changes such as greater policy-making authority being given the IJC, it proposed changes, largely in process, which may have substantial implications.

In the introduction to this volume Caldwell observes that the RSC-NRC review did not address two key questions. One was whether there was a "binational constituency effectively supportive" of the kinds of ecosystem-oriented recommendations it offered. The second concerned the kinds of "institutional . . . changes [that] would be necessary to carry out the broad objectives of the 1978 agreement." The observation is a valid one in the sense that the committee did not deal with questions of necessary future levels of political support or of desirable future political and institutional evolution. Given the largely scientific composition of the committee and the nature of its mandate, it would perhaps be surprising if it had done so. But the RSC-NRC report did propose certain novel if modest institutional changes that it found compatible with the advocacy of an ecosystem approach. These changes were realistic and pragmatic, to be sure. They were also consistent, in my view, with the sorts of conscious steps that must be taken to implement ecosystem management. Indeed, ensuring greater governmental accountability may well be key to its implementation.

The issue for proponents of the ecosystem approach to contemplate is whether or not ecosystem management in fact requires structural change, such as an ecosystemwide governing authority. The answer, I would suggest, is not as self-evident as it may seem. It is at least possible that much short- to medium-term progress can be made through changes in process—through improving the coordination of appropriate national programs and through maximizing the degree to which government priorities and policies are accountable to increasingly environmentally conscious publics.

The danger of insisting on fundamental changes in the structures of governance is that it may actually inhibit serious progress toward ecosystem management in the medium term. The danger is that governments may wrap themselves in the cloak of ecosystem rhetoric and then, turning the idea on its proponents, seize on the inevitable lacunae in scientific knowledge of vast, complex systems as a powerful excuse to continually postpone ecosystematically desirable policies.

NOTES

1. Royal Society of Canada and National Research Council of the United States, *The Great Lakes Water Quality Agreement: An Evolving Instrument for Ecosystem Management,* National Academy Press, Washington, D.C., 1985 (hereafter cited RSC-NRC). The report was funded by grants

from the William H. Donner Foundation (New York) and the Donner Canadian Foundation (Toronto). The members of the joint committee were Henry A. Regier, Institute for Environmental Studies, University of Toronto, Ontario, cochairman; Orie L. Loucks, Holcomb Research Institute, Indianapolis, Indiana, cochairman; Dale L. Bacon, Environmental Regulatory Activities, 3-M Company, St. Paul, Minnesota; John J. Black, Rosewell Park Memorial Institute, Buffalo, New York; Jennifer Ellenton, consulting genetic toxicologist, Acton, Ontario; Crawford S. Holling, University of British Columbia, Vancouver; H. B. Noel Hynes, University of Waterloo, Ontario; Joseph F. Koonce, Case Western Reserve University, Cleveland, Ohio; James Kramer, McMaster University, Hamilton, Ontario; Andre Marsan, Andre Marsan et Associes, Montreal, Quebec; Clifford Mortimer, University of Wisconsin, Milwaukee; Don Munton, formerly of the Canadian Institute of International Affairs, Toronto, Ontario; William Sonzongi, University of Wisconsin, Madison; John Stolzenberg, Wisconsin Legislative Council, Madison; and Edith Brown Weiss, Georgetown University Law Center, Washington, D.C.

2. International Joint Commission, *Third Biennial Report Under the Great Lakes Water Quality Agreement of 1978,* Ottawa, Canada, and Washington, D.C., December 1986, pp. 7–8.

3. Government of Canada News Release, "Great Lakes Water Quality Agreement Review," 19 March 1987, No. 50.

4. International Joint Commission, *First Biennial Report Under the Great Lakes Water Quality Agreement of 1978,* Ottawa, Canada, and Washington, D.C., December 1982, pp. 29–30.

5. U.S. "Department of State's Perspective on the Great Lakes Water Quality Agreement," 3 December 1984, pp. 7–8. Unpublished statement presented at initial meeting of the Royal Society–National Research Council study committee.

6. For the text of the 1972 agreement, see Canada and the United States, *Great Lakes WAter Quality Agreement of 1972,* International Joint Commission, 1974, and for the text of the 1978 agreement, the RSC-NRC report, Appendix A.

7. RSC-NRC, p. 11.

8. Ibid., pp. 11–12.

9. Ibid., p. 11.

10. Ibid, p. 4.

11. Loc. cit.

12. Ibid.

13. Ibid.

14. Ibid.

15. IJC, 1982, p. 28.

16. For the background to the negotiation of the 1972 agreement, see Don Munton, "Great Lakes Water Quality: A Study in Environmental Politics and Diplomacy," in O. P. Dwivedi (ed.), *Resources and the Environment: Policy Perspectives for Canada,* Toronto, McClelland and Stewart, 1980, pp. 153-178.

17. Don Munton, "Paradoxes and Prospects," in R. Spencer, J. Kirton, and K. R. Nossal (eds.), *The International Joint Commission Seventy Years On,* Centre for International Studies, University of Toronto, 1981, p. 80.

18. Ibid.

19. IJC, 1982, p. 29.

20. Loc cit.

21. IJC, 1982, p. 28.

22. Amendments to the Great Lakes agreement by the governments in late 1987, after this chapter was written, provide for twice-yearly meetings of "the Parties, in cooperation with State and Provincial governments . . . to evaluate progress made." Thus, part, but only this part, of the RSC-NCR recommendations on institutional arrangements has been accepted.

CHAPTER 9. GREAT LAKES GOVERNANCE AND THE ECOSYSTEM APPROACH: WHERE NEXT?

Concluding this series of perspectives is a summary of issues and problems set forth throughout the volume. The author sees a growing acceptance of the principle of pursuing an "ecosystem approach," but few signs of implementation in practice. Particular attention is given to the development of domains or constituencies for advancing an ecosystem approach to management. Domain development is, in fact, a strategy which begins with learning and leads toward action. Although the perspective of this chapter is Canadian, its arguments and conclusions have transnational relevance. It proposes that initiatives for dealing comprehensively with basinwide ecological problems need not wholly depend upon government. Organized, nongovernmental actors who are aware and informed regarding the important issues and objectives may answer the question, Where next?

GEORGE R. FRANCIS

9

GREAT LAKES GOVERNANCE AND THE ECOSYSTEM APPROACH: WHERE NEXT?

Ironically perhaps, the challenges now posed by the lakes and described in the preceding chapters reflect a kind of success. The success lies in the learning which is slowly being achieved. It has come from decades of Great Lakes research and from the management experience of a number of agencies. Without it the problems of concern would be neither diagnosed nor documented. Beyond that, two other things have been learned. One is the realization of an inherent interconnectedness among problems long thought to be isolated and solvable by appropriate technological fixes once "incentives" can be provided to do so. The other is a realization of the inherent futility of having large numbers of agencies and organizations "going it alone" with the implicit assumption that the end result will somehow emerge as coherent and effective.

This learning can lead to a rather despairing conclusion. The problems of concern appear to become overwhelmingly complicated, and prevailing approaches towards solving them are revealed as impotent. The challenges of management are to address some critical incongruities between the behavior of organizations and the nature of the ecological systems they use, abuse, or strive to "manage." If viewed in this way, institutional innovations seem called for, and the conditions to accept them may be right. What, then, might be done?

AN OVERVIEW OF GREAT LAKES GOVERNANCE

No one fully comprehends the overall structure and functioning of all the agencies and organizations whose activities affect the lakes. There is an impressively large number of government agencies alone.[1] Collectively, they determine whether or how problems will be perceived and acted upon. But some of the main features are apparent, and some changes which are under way may prove to be important.

Formal Arrangements

The basic framework for governance is set by the two constitutional federalisms which meet, quite literally, in the middle of the lakes. Thus, eight states, two provinces (Quebec is becoming more involved as it recognizes its downstream interests), and two federal governments constitute the basic jurisdictions. The two federalisms provide a different mix of divided powers and responsibilities between federal and state or provincial jurisdictions. Little more needs to be said of this, other than that in the United States the federal government, rather than state government, has a predominant role in Great Lakes matters. In Canada, however, the provincial governments have the predominant roles because of their jurisdiction over property and resources. The Canadian federal role in Great Lakes matters comes into play largely because of the binational feature of the lakes.

Two binational commissions formalize cooperation between the two countries on a narrow range of mutually shared interests concerning the lakes. The International Joint Commission, based on the Boundary Water Treaty of 1909, has two main functions. It rules on matters affecting water levels or flows across the Canada–United States boundary, and under this function it oversees the operation of the lake level control structures at the outlet of Lakes Superior and Ontario. Its other main function, which increasingly constitutes its major work load, is to act as a commission of inquiry when so requested by both governments. Matters pertaining to transboundary water resources and occasionally air and land are referred to it (hence called "references") for investigation and recommendation. The Great Lakes Water Quality Agreement (1972) was a follow-up on recommendations generated by a reference study of the lower Lakes, and the IJC's assigned responsibility to oversee the implementation of the 1972 agreement (and the 1978 revisions) is a kind of standing reference to it.

The Great Lakes Fishery Commission (GLFC) was created by a binational convention in 1956. Its main task is to control sea lamprey populations, to encourage research on fishery management, to allocate shared fish stocks (notably western lake Erie walleyes) between the two countries, and to monitor the restocking of the Lakes with lake trout and Pacific salmon. In 1980, a Joint Strategic Plan for the Management of Great Lakes Fisheries was signed by twelve fishery agencies operating in the Great Lakes; the GLFC has a major coordinating role for implementing this plan.

Canada's participation in these two commissions is coordinated through a federal and provincial agreement for each. The Canada-Ontario Great Lakes Water Quality Agreement provides for implementation of the binational water quality agreement, and the Strategic Plan for Ontario Fisheries (SPOF) was both a model and the Canadian support arrangement for the 1980 plan. The two commissions have different sets of cooperating agencies and act quite independently of each other,[2] although it is tempting to point out the close ecological association of fish with water. They are also linked to different "user" constituencies, that is, to industrial and municipal water users in the case of the IJC, and sport and commercial fishing interests in the case of the GLFC.

Mention should also be made of the International Association for Great Lakes Research, which in its more than two decades of existence has become a distinctive binational institution in itself. Its annual conferences, which alternate between Canada and the United States, bring together an extensive Great Lakes research community from academia and government agencies.[3]

Clusters of Interests

Other clusters of government agencies, private-sector organizations, and interest groups can be identified around other uses of the Great Lakes. In sociological terms, each of the clusters would constitute an "actor system." These systems are characterized by a set of agencies and organizations who see themselves as stakeholders in their particular use of the lakes. Thus some of them are continuously involved in matters relating to this use, and the others would soon become involved whenever an issue concerning them emerges.

Commercial navigation interests are among the main interests. They are associated with the harbour commissions and with the operation of the St. Lawrence Seaway Authority (Canada) and the Seaway Corporation (United States). These interests intersect with environmental concerns on questions of dredging, especially of sediments that are contaminated, contingency plans for shipping accidents, maintenance of water levels, and the accidental introduction of certain marine organisms which have survived in the lakes.

The lakes are used by electrical power interests through hydroelectric generating plants in the Saint Mary's, Niagara, and St. Lawrence rivers: a number of thermal power plants use once-through cooling water drawn from near-shore areas. Power utility interests intersect with fish and wildlife interests on matters pertaining to maintenance of lake levels and on the entrainment and impingement of young fish in cooling water systems. The Niagara Treaty of 1950 governs the volumes of river water diverted for power generation by both countries to maintain a controlled flow over the Niagara Falls.

Wildlife interests focus mainly on near-shore marsh complexes along the lakes that serve as staging areas for large numbers of migrating waterfowl, and breeding grounds for a few. Water levels and chemical contaminants are broader matters of concern. Colonial nesting water birds such as cormorants, terns, and herring gulls seem most vulnerable to biological impacts from biomagnified contaminants in their food webs.

Proposals from time to time to divert large quantities of water from or through the lakes also become focal points for a cluster of interests. These proposals are usually greeted as an external threat by other users of the lakes. The resurrection of the "Grand Canal" scheme is a current case in point.[4]

Recent and Current Changes

The withdrawal of political will to deal with lake issues by the current United States federal administration was best symbolized by the abolition of the Great Lakes Basin Commission in 1981. Originally established in 1965, it brought together about a dozen federal agencies with representatives from the eight Great Lakes states to deal with an array of land and water planning and management questions associated with the American side of the basin. Officials from Environment Canada and the Ontario Ministry of the Environment had observer status at commission meetings, and indeed often participated actively in discussions. Without this forum, the search for "common ground" among the wide array of American federal and state agencies has all but disappeared.

Reaction to this emerged in the form of initiatives from governors and citizen groups. The Council of Great Lakes Governors, representing a regional lobby for six upper midwest states, became more formalized in 1982. Some of its consultations have included governors of the lower lakes states and the premiers of the two provinces. A Task Force on Water Diversion and Great Lakes Institutions was established in 1984; it led rather directly to preparation of the Great Lakes Charter, which was duly signed by the governors and premiers in 1985.[5] This charter is a moral commitment by the parties to cooperate on recording the withdrawals of water for consumptive uses throughout the lakes and to consult about water diversion proposals (which at the time they all opposed in principle). In taking this initiative, the governors chose not to use the Great Lakes Commission, an inter-state compact organization which has been in existence for thirty years. It provides the eight member states with information on commercial concerns such as lake level trends, Great Lakes shipping, and fisheries.

Nongovernmental initiatives to establish binational coooperation have also come from various United States originators. In the mid-1970s, Great Lakes Tomorrow was initiated with the intent of creating a binational watchdog organization for the lakes, modeled on the Lake Michigan Federation. In ten years, it has failed to develop an organization base, but it has made an important contribution by helping organize extension courses on great lakes decisions at academic centers around Lakes Erie and Ontario.[6]

In 1982 Great Lakes United (GLU) was formed, largely in response to an aggressive initiative from the Michigan United Conservation Clubs. GLU is currently a loose association of some 160 groups, about 20 of which are Canadian; it works through a number of task forces to find common cause positions about a wide range of issues.[7] With help from its Buffalo office, it lobbies United States government agencies and legislative committees. GLU also provides a newsletter commenting on issues and events in both countries and identifies action alerts to stimulate citizen involvement in government hearings and other events. A major current project involves public meetings on the Great Lakes Water Quality Agreement at locations around the lakes cited as "areas of concern" by the IJC becuase of their pollution problems.

In 1983 the Center for the Great Lakes was established in Chicago, and a Toronto office was opened in 1985. The center came about largely from the initiative of a former governor of Michigan in association with the Council of Great Lakes Governors. The center is establishing and maintaining close links with the offices of governors and premiers, and with selected business and industrial interests. Its purpose is "to foster programs and to forge regional alliances that will enhance the Great Lakes region's development and environmental protection."[8] The center prepared policy background papers on topics of interest to states and provinces, such as legal aspects of water diversions, shorefront development, and commercial navigation potential in the lakes. It has also organized briefing sessions for elected officials, and publishes a bimonthly newsletter, "The Great Lakes Reporter."

These initiatives have served to broaden the involvement of governments and citizen groups in matters pertaining to the lakes. They have enlarged the network of direct communication between United States and Canadian agencies and organizations, and they avoid the formalized and official channels exemplified by the IJC. The binational intergovernmental arrangements acknowledge the principle of sovereign equality between the two countries by ensuring that equal numbers of Canadians and Americans are present in their operating structures. The binational nongovernmental organizations feel no such constraint; although they clearly demonstrate their American origins in their management styles and priorities, they do recognize the binational character of the lakes, and they have involved some Canadians in their agendas. It remains to be seen whether they will develop into more genuine binational partnerships, and whether it would be feasible to create a Canadian-based network of groups to help bring this about.

STRENGTHENING ARRANGEMENTS FOR GOVERNANCE

The first water quality agreement in 1972 was widely perceived to demonstrate a strong commitment to begin dealing with the serious problems of the lakes. The agreement gave the IJC what may be its most challenging assignment in terms of the scale, ramifications, and complexities of the situations and the actions it is required to oversee. This challenge stimulated concern mainly outside of government with the adequacy of existing institutional arrangement for dealing with Great Lakes matters.

Over the past fifteen years or so, a number of suggestions have been made about changes which could strengthen capabilities for governance over the lakes.[9] All start from the presumption that much more must and can be done, and that existing institutional arrangements create constraints for getting on with it. The condition of the lakes is seen as the confirming evidence.

Thrusts of the Proposed Changes

By 1971-72, at least three separate proposals were made for the creation of a powerful supranational Great Lakes Planning or Management Authority.[10] This is a reminder of the exuberance of those times. On one hand there was an idealism symbolized, in one case, by reference to the European Economic Community. On the other, there was faith in the effectiveness of government and in the need for more top-down management by professional experts with police powers at their command.

Another example of the grand design ideal emerged in a recent series of regional seminars with participants from about twenty universities and research institutions in both Canada and United States.[11] Basic to this approach would be the adoption of a "Charter for the Great Lakes Community" dedicated to the goal of "maintaining a clean, beautiful and delicately balanced Great Lakes ecosystem." (See Chapter 4 by Lester W. Milbrath.) this charter would, among other things, guarantee the right of nongovernmental organizations to intervene anywhere in the basin in both countries and to obtain a "review action for a problem they have identified." A "Great Lakes Futures Review Board" composed of ten people appointed for staggered seven-year terms would have the responsibility "to think integratively for the whole basin." The board would make policy recommendations to basin governments and contribute extensively to public education. It would be assisted by a "comprehensive data management system" designed to help it "develop and maintain a capability for systemic and futures thinking." In addition, "value impact assessments" (combined social and environmental impact assessments, but with values more explicitly stated) would be mandatory for "all major human initiatives that could significantly impact the Great Lakes ecosystem." These would be reviewed by the Futures Review Board. To resolve conflicts, either the IJC would be given the power to arbitrate or a special "Great Lakes Court," from whose decisions no appeal procedures would exist,would be established.

Funding would come from a levy on the major jurisdictions based on provisions written into the charter. Among the benefits foreseen from the adoption of this scheme is the societal learning it would help to promote by way of a strong sense of belonging to the "Great Lakes Community." The proposal's originator, Lester Milbrath, recognizes problems in implementing this design but suggests that a Great Lakes conference, modeled after the 1972 United

National Conference on the Human Environment, could develop the charter, which should then be worked into a formal treaty.

At various times during the 1970s, conferences and workshops devoted to Great Lakes matters made suggestions for strengthened institutional arrangements.[12] Often these focused on the IJC because it was the acknowledged instrument for Canada–United States cooperation on the Lakes. The suggestions generally urged the IJC to become more proactive in promoting preventive strategies and to adopt a broad "integrated/ecosystem management" perspective for monitoring trends and developments in the basin. Also thought necessary was the extension of formal arrangements for cooperation on Great Lakes matters to bring in land management agencies and coastal zone municipalities. The need for wider public involvement in consultation and decision processes was also emphasized.

Most of these ideas could be viewed as calling for a kind of enhanced federalism in which Canada and the United States would cooperate much more extensively. At the binational Great Lakes Basin level, arrangements would facilitate the following:

- Consultations on common goals and program guidelines for resource and environmental management.
- Monitoring of program results and joint assessment of their effectiveness.
- Anticipatory planning with an emphasis on preventive (rather than reactive) strategies.
- Informal resolution of conflicts between countries or jurisdictions. At the Lake Basin or subbasin levels arrangements would facilitate.
- Close informal cooperation of "opposite number" agencies, i.e., agencies in different jurisdictions exercising similar responsibilities.
- The establishment of special management arrangements among existing agencies to deal with special problems such as environmentally degraded areas.
- Wider public participation and involvement, including a much larger role for municipal governments.[13]

Perhaps because none of these measures was seriously accepted, although some modest lobbying was carried out,[14] attention in more recent years has gone toward creating public constituencies for the management of the lakes. These constituencies are necessary both to revitalize political will to continue implementing the intent of the Great Lakes Water Quality Agreement and to bring political pressure to bear on a host of more localized Great Lakes issues. Although Great Lakes United has made an impressive start in mobilizing such a constituency, the desirability of additional measures to create some kind of Great Lakes regional identity has nevertheless been noted.[15] The idea of convening a Stockholm conference for the lakes, complete with a charter of principles and a draft action plan to endorse, was recently proposed again in a major review of the Great Lakes Water Quality Agreement by the (United States) National Research Council and the Royal Society of Canada.[16]

Why Nothing Can or Should Be Done

Like all proposals for reform or change, these have been challenged by cynics and critics. Cynics dismiss them out-of-hand, on the basis of a deeply felt antipathy toward government, industry, or citizen groups. Critics, however, have more reasoned objections, and occasionally will commit them to print.[17] There are at least five lines of argument in favor of the status quo which command some support. In brief, they can be summarized as follows:[18]

- It is the absence of "hard data" or convincing scientific documentation about the reality of purported problems, such as toxic substances, which makes any approach other than more research premature. Decisionmakers will act responsibly when the scientific evidence is at hand.

- If politicians and the public were willing to support the kinds of institutional changes being proposed, then there would already be sufficient political will to do everything necessary through the existing institutions. There are no major deficiencies in the existing institutional arrangements, only a reluctance to make full use of their mandates and potentials.

- If any of the supposed problems and opportunities on the lakes are real, then market mechanisms will come into play to deal with them. Suggestions for institutional change are not only unnecessary, but they would only give rise to more self-serving bureaucracy, inefficiency, or worse—all at a time when it is very clear that less, not more, government is needed.

- Existing binational and interorganizational arrangements are the result of many delicate and sensitive balancings of interests and political cross-currents. Attempts to change them significantly would disrupt what has already been achieved, and would almost certainly result in a less hospitable environment for cooperating on Great Lakes issues.

- Symbolic gestures such as media events and rhetorical "charters" are forgotten as fast as yesterday's news. They may well give the illusion of progress, when in fact nothing substantive is being done.

These are cautionary notes about the gauntlet to be run. An awareness of them can strengthen any planning for change.

ECOSYSTEMS AND INSTITUTIONS

One of the underlying themes in the foregoing discussion is that of systemic interconnectedness. Assumptions differ about what is or should be connected, and how. The perception of interconnectedness derives in the first instance from the hydrological, ecological systems which are the lakes themselves. Problems which show up in the water can be linked both to patterns of industrial activity and to land and resource management practices. These activities and practices arise in turn from institutional structures and decision processes. This is not to say that everything is connected to everything else, but there are clearly some interrelationships which need to be considered more carefully. Deciding which ones are important can entail much debate.

Ecosystemic Interconnectedness

Before about the mid-1970s, the significant interconnections were perceived in terms of the ideals of comprehensive water resource management and integrated river basin planning. The former looks to trade-offs and conflicts among water uses, and the latter emphasizes the connections among land uses, development, and water flows and quality. The Great Lakes were viewed as an impressively large example of an otherwise familiar situation. The massive twenty-seven-volume *Great Lakes Framework Study* produced by the former Great Lakes Basin Commission in 1975 can be looked back upon as a monument to this overall perspective, although it suffered the institutional embarrassment of having to be thoroughly comprehensive for only the American half of each lake (with the exception of Lake Michigan). Thus, suggestions for institutional change were meant to create the capabilities needed for effective overall management for a range of different uses of Great Lakes water, shorelines, and associated land resources.[19]

A major shift in the perception of interconnectedness began almost a decade ago with the call for the adoption of an ecosystem approach to the Great Lakes.[20] The ecosystem approach shifts the focus of attention toward the system being used, and away from the system which uses it. Ecology replaces resource management as the knowledge most needed. It is a subtle change, the implications of which have not been fully worked out. Nevertheless, there has been an increasing interest in trying to elaborate the notion of an ecosystem approach as it might be applied to the Great Lakes. Recent binational seminars and workshops have discussed it;[21] a series of interuniversity studies have examined it from an ecological, socioeconomic, and institutional arrangements perspective;[22] and a recent independent study of the Great Lakes Water Quality Agreement was carried out with guidance from an ecosystem perspective.[23]

There seems to be a growing acceptance of the desirability in principle of pursuing some version of the ecosystem approach, but there are few signs of its being implemented in practice. The word *ecosystem* was written into the 1978 Great Lakes Water Quality Agreement and was given more emphasis in a 1981 policy statement by the Great Lakes Fishery Commission. But there is considerable uncertainty over what this commits the agencies to do. Regulatory agencies have adopted a few biological indicators, notably contaminants in some fish and herring gull eggs, along with the more conventional physical and chemical indices of water quality.[24] Lively debate has ensued among scientists and engineers over the validity of adopting ecosystemic level indicators at all, such as those recently proposed by an IJC working group.[25]

Institutional inertia may only account for some of this reluctance. There is also genuine uncertainty and disagreement about the scope and implications of what is being advocated, and some nervousness about where it will all lead. As long as the ecosystem approach is interpreted to mean more use of ecology for managing the lakes and their associated biota, the debate within the Great Lakes context has remained well within the bounds of conventional science and management techniques. It poses no perceived threats to the status quo. But this situation cannot last indefinitely.

The paradigm shift in science from theoretical developments in mathematical catastrophe theory and nonequilibrium thermodynamics is starting to have major effects on ecological thinking. The "science of surprise," as these developments are sometimes called, has far-reaching implications for organizations and management.[26] "Management for surprise" will require more flexibility for learning and adapting, anticipating and monitoring, than current institutions have shown. Organization theory itself may well have to be rethought along completely different lines.[27] The International Institute for Applied Systems Analysis has embarked on the further elaboration of these ideas in its Sustainable Development of the Biosphere Project, and it will use the Great Lakes as an important case study.[28]

An ecosystem approach implies more than this, or perhaps other than this, as well. It has ideological implications which its Great Lakes proponents have not really addressed. Among the professional philosophers, however, the debate is much more advanced. It revolves around notions of "deep ecology" and "ecophilosophy" which challenge the basic beliefs and assumptions inherent in the ideology of industrialism in its various forms.[29] The still prevalent industrialism is "a commitment to narrowly utilitarian scientific/technological management of Nature" for purely human ends: thus it is anthropocentric or "resourcist" in its basic orientation.[30] Enhanced ecological understanding within this ideological context serves to intensify human uses of ecosystems, and is consistent with prevailing interpretation of "resource development" as comprising the technological improvements that lead to wider utilization of lower-quality resources.[31] "Environmental management" within this context involves making the modest adjustments needed to enhance the efficiency of resource extraction, in part by reducing destructive side effects. Environmental impact statements and regulatory pollution controls are good examples of the procedures and techniques through which this kind of management is practiced. The strategies for dealing with Great Lakes issues are all well within this ideological perspective. Even most environmental lobby groups urge only that they be applied more thoroughly and consistently.

The alternative ideology rejects industrialism, but is less coherently articulated and is subject to considerable philosophical dispute. Its proponents often view themselves as "deep ecologists" who are rethinking some basic beliefs and values. The ecosystem approach for them would lead towards a "harmonious dynamic balance of human-in-Nature."[32] It is explicitly "biocentric" in recognizing an ethical obligation towards ecosystems in their own right, rather than just as objects to be managed as integral to our life support systems. It promotes changes in human behavior, including the complete elimination of certain industrial commodities because they are environmentally destructive. It urges societal adaptation as the appropriate response to new ecological awareness, rather than more sophisticated, expert-dominated management. The full moral and social implications of this alternative are not at all clear, but discussion of the related issues has engaged a widening array of participants. Among the issues attracting attention are a recognized need to rethink the very nature of development, the need to incorporate ecological sustainability into any development worth having, and the ethical obligations humans have towards nonhuman species. The implications for dealing with Great Lakes issues have yet to be addressed.

Institutional Interconnectedness

From one point of view, the Great Lakes Basin can be thought of as densely populated by all manner of institutions and organizations whose activities directly or indirectly affect the lakes. They too have their interconnections.

The systemic interconnectedness of advanced industrialized societies is expressed through economic market transactions; various political and legal processes of negotiation and conflict resolution among organizations and groups; and a large variety of arrangements for cooperation and collaboration. These processes become more complex as continuous "turbulence" characterizes all organizational environments, and "actor system dynamics" are recognized to be fundamental societal processes.[33]

But a major flaw has become apparent. Elaborate as these processes are, they remain detached from the realities of nonhuman ecosystems. An integral aspect of the prevailing ideology of industrialism is the view that humans and their society are basically exempted from ecological constraints. This "exemptionalism" has resulted in the "extremely 'unecological' traditions and perspectives in modern social science."[34] According to the dominant economic paradigm, the kinds of issues discussed by ecologists and environmentalists are essentially "externalities" with respect to the central processes of society. "External" in this sense easily translates into peripheral, expendable, or of very low priority.

Ecosystems must therefore be perceived as socioecosystems. Reconciling the webs of functional interconnectedness among institutions with the functional webs of nonhuman ecosystems is a challenge of both conceptual and practical importance.[35] The ideological context to give it overall coherence may well be a dialectical product of the either-or versions outlined above. This is the theoretical challenge for the ecosystem approach, and its dimensions are but dimly perceived.

WHERE NEXT?

The issues of governance and institutional arrangements which have arisen for the Great Lakes are not unique. Similar complexities have become characteristic of advanced urban, industrial societies, whether viewed from a regional, sectoral, or broad policy field perspective. The challenge is being addressed in both theory and practice at what has been called the "middle ground" of society.[36] Particular policy fields or shared domains of interest involve a number of institutions and organizations. Each such field or domain will have its own interorganizational social system which operates at a level below that of society as a whole, but quite above that of an individual organization viewed in isolation.[37] The clusters of organizations associated with particular uses of the Great Lakes such as fisheries or navigation reflect shared perceptions of domains, each with a policy field that helps direct or "govern" it. The entrance of new nongovernmental organizations to the Great Lakes arena reflects an extension of participation in some existing domains, and possibly the recognition of others. Concerns about toxic contaminants have brought forth many of the participants. This problem can be viewed as a call for expanding the membership of an important domain which previously was occupied almost exclusively by regulatory agencies and the industries being regulated.

Domain-based Actor Systems

The concept of "actor system dynamics" fits well into the middle ground perspective. As defined by Burns and Wittrock,[38] this perspective entails three basic ideas; a set of "actors" (agencies, organizations, groups, and occasionally key individuals) who have some "stake" in a shared domain; the transactions or interactions which go on among them; and the systems of rules (laws or customs) which regulate the transactions. The dynamics of their interactions over time are directed both to issues of domain and to the rules for interactions themselves. Demands by nongovernmental groups to "participate" in decisions are an example of actions directed to both domains and rule systems. Trist has stated that "the cultivation of domain-based, inter-organizational competence has become a necessary societal project" in order to deal effectively with a whole range of issues which no single organization could handle on its own.[39] He has described a number of examples of "domain development" with particular reference to the emergence of "referent organizations" which serve to draw the constituent organizations of a given domain into a much more coherent functioning social system. Rubin has reviewed various kinds of "non-mandated coordinative structures" which have been identified in complex, interorganizational systems, and has described the strategies used by one very effective "meshing organization" which operated in an urban region composed of many small, independent, municipal governments.[40] Similar arrangements also link well-established institutions, and their emergence is due to a functional necessity of having to deal with horizontal integration across organizational boundaries in order to achieve mutually shared goals.

The need and opportunity to develop such interorganizational approaches to the Great Lakes have been recognized for some time. Craine, soon after the now disbanded Great Lakes Basin Commission launched its planning activities, pointed out the desirability of developing area-specific resource management arrangements.[41] He drew upon the existing array of agencies, each with their own mandates and expertise, as a way of addressing subbasin issues. By the late 1970s they were beginning to evolve, notably for Green Bay, Wisconsin. Yarbrough analyzed interorganizational collaboration for rehabilitative activities at Green Bay:[42] his findings exemplified domain development processes, the referent organization phenomenon, and the beginnings of a "meshing organization" with strategies based on networking activities. The relatively rapid increase in the number of organizations and groups concerning themselves with the Great Lakes will probably help accelerate the formation of this "middle ground" level of governance over the lakes. Much of it will be directed to more localized domains of common concern.

How might these developments become more receptive to an ecosystem approach? Regier and Grima have raised the question of allocation systems for the rights to use resources such as the Great Lakes.[43] The two basic characteristics of an allocation system are whether or not rights are transferable, and whether or not they are exclusive. Combinations give rise to four different allocations strategies, the simple ideal types of which are exclusive transferable rights, as in a free market system; exclusive nontransferable rights, as in government by regulation; nontransferable, nonexclusive rights, exemplified by common property resources with their vulnerability to abuse; and nonexclusive transferable rights, a situation in which transactions are unethical if not illegal. Resource and environmental management by government regulation is of questionable effectiveness, but in the case of the Great Lakes, which are not readily "privatized," what are the options? Regier and Grima suggest a middle ground position represented by self-policing communities of different user groups practicing good "husbandry" traditions. Berkes has discussed successful examples with reference to fisheries around the world.[44]

Trist has expressed a rather similar idea by urging the adoption of socioecological principles" to develop the necessary additional complementary, or countervailing capabilities to the expertise of existing institutions and organizations. Socioecological principles recognize "the centrality of interdependence . . . Entailed is some surrender of sovereignty along with considerable diffusions of power [which] enable the organizational life of society to be strengthened . . . in ways that are self-regulating rather than becoming imperial or remaining ineffectual."[45] This is only part of what must be done. The rest is to acknowledge the relationships which exist between society and the ecosystems that support it. "Self-regulation" of domain-based actor systems must include measures to ensure ecological and environmental sustainability of the ecosystems they use.

Initiatives to Promote

Environmental concerns point to priorities for domain development and to the basic goals which guide this development. Sustainable development and regional redevelopment are generally accepted goals for the Great Lakes Basin. Degraded environments do not support healthy communities and economies. With this recognition, the most degraded areas in the Great Lakes have received the most attention.

Nevertheless, some broader goals than pollution control can be derived from the intent of the Great Lakes Water Quality Agreement, the Convention on Great Lakes Fisheries, and the Charter of Principles for the Management of Great Lakes Water Resources. These agreements serve as important precedents, since each in its own way reflects some commitment to ecological and environmental sustainability as a goal for guiding management of the Great Lakes and their associated resources.[46]

Domain development efforts should now be directed to three major domains and their policy fields. One domain is the "areas of concern" regularly reported as badly polluted by the Great Lakes Water Quality Board, and in need of remedial measures. Ecosystem rehabilitation strategies along the lines developed for Green Bay point the way for the comprehensive interorganizational strategies which are needed.[47] Ultimately, something comparable must be developed to deal with the specific needs of each of the forty-two or so "areas of concern" in the basin. Domain-based actor system arrangements can be envisioned as evolving a two-tiered structure. The different sets of actors operating in each more localized area of concern would have to have linkages to various government agencies and nongovernmental organizations within their respective jurisdictions to receive the needed policy and program support, and they should also become part of basinwide networks for the exchange of information and experience.

The second domain directs attention to a different kind of area of concern—those having sensitive ecological and environmental values which are in need of protective management. An approach for effective protective management has been developed for the Long Point area on the north shore of Lake Erie.[48] Ultimately something comparable must be developed for an array of Great Lakes shoreline and near-shore areas. A compilation of such areas for the Canadian side of the lakes is being prepared.[49] A domain-based actor system arrangement for this group of areas of concern can be envisioned much as the one for degraded areas. Local arrangements with the usually multiple owners of each major area need to be worked out, and the associated "policy field" issues need to be addressed. The Ontario Natural Heritage League would be central to the support network, and basinwide linkages have yet to be developed. It might also be desirable to include inland natural heritage areas within the basin under the purview of this particular domain.

The third domain would focus on hazardous substances from a cradle-to-grave perspective which emphasizes preventive strategies. The intent is to decontaminate ecosystems to levels sufficient to protect their sensitive biota and, hence, to safeguard human health as well. The importance of this domain is already accepted. The organization of it is a major challenge, but it too has to develop linkages from local through regional to national and binational levels. Domain development processes are learning processes. Thus, action learning research has to be an integral part of them.[50] They have to start with the givens of existing institutional and organizational arrangements, including the fact that the latter derive their authority and legitimacy from the prevailing ideology of industrialism which some actors in the system question or reject. The rule systems which govern the interorganizational development of the domains have to be dealt with continually to address three related questions. One is whether legal and policy frameworks supporting particular agencies and private groups serve as disincentives for the involvement of key actors in particular actor systems; if so, then how can they be changed? The second is how ecosystem level standards are to be defined and then made operational as management objectives. This process will be necessary to judge the effectiveness of rehabilitative and protective management measures, and also to define ecological constraints for resource users. The third involves the negotiation and conflict resolution processes inherent in actor system dynamics. Some rule changes may be needed from time to time to facilitate the development of the actor systems themselves or to prevent their stagnation or dissolution.

Two initiatives, if pursued, might stimulate developments along the lines above. One is the major binational Great Lakes Conference, which has been proposed on several occasions over the last few years and which was recently viewed as "a catalyst for insightful analyses of critical social issues and a vehicle for building a new consensus supporting social and institutional reform" needed to reverse degradative resource "abuse" and to promote ecological and environmental sustainability.[51] If modeled on the United Nations Conference on the Human Environment, as also suggested, it would be a gathering of government delegations. Nongovernmental groups would be left to hold a counterconference as they did in 1972. In light of the need for domain-based actor systems, a quite different model seems called for.

Finally, there remains the question of developing Canadian capabilities to participate effectively as recognized equal partners in these various new developments. Whatever arrangements are worked out should strengthen and complement the Great Lakes commitments of existing groups in ways that are not seen as unduly competitive. The new arrangements sought would serve as a "referent" organization, but one that is not restricted to a particular domain; they would also have to be designed to work effectively within the Canadian institutional context.

In thinking about successful operating models of organizations with these general characteristics, the Canadian Arctic Resources Committee (CARC) comes readily to mind. It is small and effective. A former federal cabinet minister ascribed CARC's success to four "simple rules": its information is as good as the government's; it sets high standards for any work that it publishes and attempts to be accurate in the use of information; it has tenacity; and it is more interested in having an impact on decisions than in getting media attention for its own point of view.[52] CARC achieves this with a relatively small informal group of people having diverse backgrounds and experience, and its actions are governed by clearly stated principles which it strives to uphold.

The need for a Canadian Great Lakes Committee (CGLC) with some of CARC's characteristics was explored extensively during

1983–84.[53] A generally favorable response was received to the idea in principle, provided that a CGLC did not duplicate activities of existing organizations or compete for funding from their particular sources of support. The main roles suggested as being the most useful were as follows: providing a forum for actors from government, the private sector and nongovernmental organizations to meet and discuss their different perceptions of Great Lakes issues; analyzing issues in some overall context that emphasized the processes and organizational arrangements that allowed problems to continue; and becoming a credible information source on Great Lakes issues which a variety of actors could consult. There was ambivalence about CGLC taking on an advocacy function, especially given the expertise of the Canadian Environmental Law Association and Pollution Probe in this role and their growing involvement with Great Lakes problems. Building some kind of citizen constituency was seen as necessary, but as best done by others. Accepting the strong cautionary note about "yet one more organization," some networking arrangement among those already existing seems the only feasible way to proceed. The opportunities to develop nongovernmental capabilities seem greater now than a few years ago, as more groups take an interest in the Great Lakes. If more effort went towards the development of domain-based actor systems instead of insisting that governments alone must expand their programs and take on additional responsibilites, the chance for constructive innovation would be improved. This is till a formidable challenge, but to not take it up may be a decision to fail.

Support for this work from the Max Bell Foundation is gratefully acknowledged. This chapter was originally published in "Alternatives: Perspectives on Society, Technology and Environment", Vol. 13, No. 3. September-October 1986.

NOTES

1. Partial inventories of governmental organizations dealing with various aspects of the Great Lakes, such as water quality or fisheries, have been made with reference to one or more of the main jurisdictions. Listings run into the dozens or hundreds, depending on how much of the basin is looked at. See George R. Francis, John J. Magnuson, Henry A. Regier, and Daniel R. Talhelm, *Rehabilitating Great Lakes Ecosystems,* Technical Report No. 37 (Great Lakes Fishery Commission, Ann Arbor, MI, December 1979).

The addition of private-sector and nongovernmental organizations also involved would make the inventories virtually unmanageable.

2. The scientific advisory groups to each commission have occasionally included individuals who have at one time or another served in both groups. Individual commissioners from both commissions meet informally from time to time on their own initiatives, but the mandates and agendas of each commission effectively keep them preoccupied with their own responsibilities.

3. IAGLR's *Journal of Great Lakes Research* is an important one for communicating results of scientific research on the lakes. It is devoted almost exclusively to the natural sciences, in part because there appear to be very few social scientists interested in Great Lakes issues.

4. Originally proposed in the late 1950s, this scheme calls for dyking James Bay to convert it into a freshwater reservoir from the north-flowing rivers into it. Waterfrom this reservoir would then be backpumped up the Harricanaw River to the upper Ottawa River and diverted into the lakes via Lake Nipissing and the French River. These additional waters would be "stored" in the Great Lakes but would be "available" for diversions out of the lakes to different parts of the United States. The scheme has received endorsement from Quebec Premier Robert Bourassa (see his *Power from the North,* Prentice-Hall, Canada, Scarborough, 1985) and reportedly also from Simon Reisman, chief negotiator for Canada in trade talsk with the United States. The proposal is being promoted at a time of record-high lake levels.

5. Premiers Rene Levesque and Frank Miller were the signatories from Canada. Their provincial administrations have since been voted out of office, and they themselves have retired from politics.

6. These semester-long courses, with enrollments of about twenty-five persons each, were held at eight ceters around lake Erie in 1983–84, and at least three centers around Lake Ontario in 1985–86. Most proved to be quite popular and helped strengthen interest and commitment among local citizen groups on matters relating to the lakes. The experience suggests that such courses or workshops could be vital to the development of a Great Lakes "constituency."

7. David Miller, executive director, personal communication, February 1986.

8. Donna Wise, executive director, in an editoral from *The Great Lakes Reporter* 1(2) (September–October 1984).

9. For a good overview of those proposals pertaining to the IJC, see Donald Munton, "Paradoxes and Prospects," in: *The International Joint Commission Seventy Years On,* Robert Spencer, John Kirton, Kim Richard Nossal, eds. (Centre for International Studies, University of Toronto, 1981), Ch.4.

10. Ibid. See also Norman Pearson, "The Great Lakes Basin: Prospects and Problems," address to the former Canadian Audubon Society, 29 May 1971. Walter Lyon (cited in Munton) was the person who in 1971 saw the precedent of the EEC as important to the Great Lakes. At the time he suggested a Great Lakes Authority composed of "top water management experts from both sides of the border" reporting to a Council of Ministers and Governors, complemented by a Great Lakes Assembly and a Great Lakes Court. He still sees something like an EEC as an ideal to work towards, noting that the toxic waste dumps along the Niagara will never be dealt with effectively through existing institutional arrangements. Personal communication, January 1986.

11. Lester W. Milbrath, "A Governance Structure Designed to Learn Would Better Protect the Great Lakes Ecosystem," Chapter 4 in this volume.

12. See Munton, note 9 above, and also the *Workshop Report on Anticipatory Planning for the Great Lakes,* 2 volumes (IJC Great Lakes Regional Office, Windsor, Ontario, December 1979).

13. From George Francis, "How Governments Behave: An Overview," in Great Lakes Tomorrow, *Decisions for the Great Lakes,* Part 3, 1982. (Great Lakes Tomorrow with Purdue University/Calumet).

14. Expecially by Professor Leonard Dworsky, Cornell University, in Washington in May, 1973, and by Dworsky and Francis in Ottawa in March 1975, before the Standing Senate Committee on Foreign Affairs. This committee explicitly rejected proposals to enlarge the IJC's role in the Great Lakes Basin. See *Report on the Standing Senate Committee on Foreign Affairs on Canada-United States Relations,* Volume 1, "The Institutional Framework for the Relationship" (December 1975), p. 44.

15. Lee Botts and Henry Regier, "The Environment and Sustainable Economic Development in the Great Lakes Region: Major Issues for the Future" (issues paper for the Great Lakes Region Seminar, 1984, Typescript).

16. National Research Council of the United States and the Royal Society of Canada, *The Great Lakes Water Quality Agreement: An Evolving Instrument for Ecosystem Management* (National Academy Press, Washington D.C., 1985).

17. For example, the critique by Donald Munton, note 9 above.

18. This summary comes from informal discussions at many meetings over the years concerning the Great Lakes. Although there are no mutually exclusive associations of arguments and roles, one can anticipate that the arguments as listed will be encountered more frequently from (in the same order) scientists, economists, diplomats, and administrators.

19. For example, in *A Proposal for Improving the Management of the Great Lakes of the United States and Canada,* a report by the Canada-United States University Seminar, 1971-1972 (Water Resources and Marine Sciences

Center, Cornell University, January 1973); also Leonard B. Dworsky, George R. Francis, and Charles F. Swezey, "Mangement of the International Great Lakes," *Natural Resources Journal* 14(1), 103-138 (1974).

20. This was in anticipation of the revisions to be made for the 1978 Great Lakes Water Quality Agreement. Jack Vallentyne took a lead with the IJC's Research AdvisoryBoard (as it was known then) to prepare a report on the ecosystem approach which was issued by the board in 1978. Henry Regier and George Francis urged a comparable perspective for the GLFC and the IAGLR, summarized in "Let's Rehabilitate and Restore Degraded Ecosystems of the Great Lakes," *Lakes Letter* 8(3), 2-9 (1977).

21. A "Workshop on Implementing the Ecosystem Approach" held at Hiram, Ohio, in March 1983 involved some fifty people from a diverse array of backgrounds. The main issues discussed were summarized by Jack Christie, Mimi Becker, James Cowden, and Jack Vallentyne in "Managing the Great Lakes Basin as Home," *Journal of Great Lakes Research* 12(1): 2-17 (1986). See also note 15 above.

22. These were funded by the GLFC and other sources, notably the Max Bell Foundation for the Canadian work. The three main reports to date are Francis et al., 1979, note 1 above; Hallett J. Harris, Daniel R. Talhelm, John J. Magnuson, and Anne M. Forbes, *Green Bay in the Future, A Rehabilitative Prospectus,* Technical Report No. 38 (Great Lakes Fishery Commission, Ann Arbor, MI, September 1982); and George R. Francis, A. P. Lino Grima, Henry A. Regier, and Thomas H. Whillans, *A Prospectus for the Management of the Long Point Ecosystem,* Technical Report No. 43 (Great Lakes Fishery Commission, Ann Arbor, MI, March 1985).

23. Note 16 above.

24. For example, in the 1985 *Report on Great Lakes Water Quality by the Great Lakes Water Quality Board to the IJC* (IJC Great Lakes Regional Office, Windsor, Ontario, 1985).

25. *A Conceptual Approach for the Application of Biological Indicators of Ecosystem Quality in the Great Lakes Basin,* Richard A. Ryder and Clayton J. Edwards, eds., Report to the IJC Science Advisory Board (1985). The "Green Bay Group" has recently porposed some ecosystem criteria to serve as the basis for setting management objectives and assessing organizational performance. See H. J. Harris, C. J. Yarbrough, P. E. Sager, and S. Richman, "Ecosystem Rehabilitation—A Shift Towards a Different Paradigm," paper presented at the Estuarine Management Practices Symposium (Baton Rouge, Louisiana, November 1985).

26. C. S. Holling has been centrally involved with these developments in ecological thought at UBC and the International Institute for Applied Systems Analysis (IIASA). See *Adaptive Environmental Assessment and Management,* C. S. Holling, ed., (Laxenburg, Aurstria, IIASA, 1978), and other writings, such as "Resilience in the Unforgiving Society" (Institute of Re-

source Ecology, University of British Columbia, March 1981); and William C. Clark and C. S. Holling, "Sustainable Development of the Biosphere: Human Activities and Global Change," in *Global Change,* T. F. Malone and J. G. Roederer, eds., International Council of Scientific Unions (The ICSU Press, Paris, 1984), pp. 283-299.

27. See Eric Trist, "The Environment and System-Response Capability," *Futures* 113-127 (April 1980). The York University Action Learning Group has been influenced by a number of Trist's ideas, especially the notion of environmental "turbulence" in the context of organizational theory. The implications of this idea for the design of organizational forms and strategies mesh well with the implications arising from the "science and management of surprise."

28. Canadian/IIASA Planning Group proposal for a Canadian project: "Managing Ecosystems for Future Choice," December 1985 (Ministry of State for Science and Technology, Ottawa).

29. Norwegian philosopher Arne Naess sparked this debate with "The Shallow and the Deep Long-Range Ecology Movement: A Summary,: *Inquiry* 16, 95-100 (1973), and continues to give rejoinders from time to time, for example, "A Defence of the Deep Ecology Movement, *Environmental Ethics* 6(3), 265-270 (Fall 1984). The propositions of "eco-philosophy" have been discussed by Henryk Skolimoski in *Eco-Philosophy: Designing New Tactics for Living* (Marion Boyars Publishers, 1981). Some basic disagreements between the two schools center mainly on the concept of biocentrism and its interpretations.

30. William Devall and George Sessions, "The Development of Natural Resources and the Integrity of Nature," *Environmental Ethics* 6(4), 293-322 (1984), and John Livingston, "Moral Concern and the Ecosphere," *Alternatives* 12(2), 3-9, (1985).

31. Henry A. Regier and Gordon L. Baskerville, "Sustainable Redevelopment," in *Sustainable Development of the Biosphere,* W. C. Clark, and R. F. Munson, eds. (Laxenburg, Austria, IIASA, 1986).

32. Notes 29 and 30 above.

33. Trist, note 27 above. See also Tom R. Burns and Bjorn Wittrock *Towards a Social Science Framework of Actor Structure Dynamics: An International Cooperative Program in Basic Research* (Uppsala, 1984, Typescript).

34. Riley E. Dunlap, "Paradigmatic Change in Social Science," *American Behavioral Scientist* 24(1), 5-14 (September 1980).

35. Some aspects of this challenge are discussed with reference to the Great Lakes by E. A. Lind and G. E. Glass, "Environmental Law and Policy Versus the Hydrocycle," *Journal of Great Lakes Research* 19(2), 135-142 (1984). Harris et al. argue that "the requirement is to embody the ecosystem

perspective in law; to establish the perspective as the accepted scientific, social, and legal definition of the [environmental] problem" (note 25 above).

36. Michel Chevalier and Glen Taylor define the "middle ground" as "where free standing organizations must get together and cooperate about issues which no single one of them can handle alone. These issues are beyond the capacity of the market mechanism or the political-legal structure to adjudicate or deal with. Such issues range across a wide spectrum of concern—from restructuring the economy, to providing employment, social welfare, dealing with environmental hazards, and so on." *New Ground for Enterprise: Managing Critical Issues in the Middle Ground Between Government and Private Enterprise,* An Interim Report on the "York Insurance Project" (York University, Toronto, 1983).

37. Eric Trist, "Referent Organizations and the Development of Inter-Organizational Domains," *Human Relations* 36(3), 269-284 (1983). Domains are the "set of problems, or societal problem areas" which engage the attention of a number of organizations. The "policy field" is composed of the range of individual policies brought to a domain by the various organizations involved with it, or it can refer to the need to develop a coherent set of policies in order to deal with the domain. Trist defines "interorganizational domains" as "functional social systems that occupy a position in social space between the society as a whole and the single organization " that is, the middle ground.

38. Note 33 above.

39. Note 37 above.

40. Herbert J. Rubin, "The Meshing Organization as a Catalyst for Municipal Coordination," *Administration and Society* 16(2), 215-238 (August 1984).

41. Lyle E. Craine, *Final Report on Institutional Arrangements for the Great Lakes (Report prepared for the Great Lakes Basin Commission, March 1972, typescript).*

42. C. Jarrell Yarbrough, *Multi-Institutional Management: The Green Bay Experience,* IJC/Science Advisory Board (Windsor, 1985).

43. H. A. Regier and A. P. Grima, "The Nature of Great Lakes Ecosystems," *International Business Lawyer* 261-269 (June 1984).

44. Fikret Berkes, "Fishermen and 'The Tragedy of the Commons'," *Environmental Conservation* 12(3), 199-205 (Autumn 1985).

45. Note 37 above.

46. These goals can be subsumed under the broader ones of the World Conservation Strategy and the World Commission on Environment and Development in terms of ecologically sustainable development.

47. Harris et al., notes 22 and 25 above.

48. Francis et al., note 22 above.

49. A "Great Lakes Ecosystem Conservation" report under preparation is compiling information from a wide array of sources to identify near-shore and coastal zone sites along the Canadian side of the lakes which have been noted as having important ecological values. Some sites have varying degrees of protective management under various federal, provincial, regional, or other parks or conservation agencies. Others do not. The work is being done by Paul Smith as part of the Great Lakes Ecosystem Rehabilitation Studies (note 22 aboe).

50. See Rafael Ramirez, "Action Learning: A Strategic Approach for Organizations Facing Turbulent Conditions," *Human Relations* 36(8), 725-742 (1983).

51. Note 16 above.

52. J. Hugh Faulkner, "Pressuring the Executive," *Canadian Public Adminstration* 25(2), 240-253 (Summer 1982).

53. By Phil Weller and John Jackson as part of the Great Lakes Ecosystem Rehabilitation studies. Consultations were held with CARC and thirty-six agencies and organizations in Ontario having direct involvement with Great Lakes issues. Questionnaires solicited comments from eighteen other organizations which might have or develop some Great Lakes interests, and organizational literature was also reviewed.

APPENDIX A. TREATY BETWEEN THE UNITED STATES AND GREAT BRITAIN RELATING TO BOUNDARY WATERS, AND QUESTIONS ARISING BETWEEN THE UNITED STATES AND CANADA.

The United States of America and His Majesty the King of the United Kingdom of Great Britain and Ireland and of the British Dominions beyond the Seas, Emperor of India, being equally desirous to prevent disputes regarding the use of boundary waters and to settle all questions which are now pending between the United States and the Dominion of Canada involving the rights, obligations, or interests of either in relation to the other or to the inhabitants of the other, along their common frontier, and to make provision for the adjustment and settlement of all such questions as may hereafter arise, have resolved to conclude a treaty in furtherance of these ends, and for that purpose have appointed as their respective plenipotentiaries:

The President of the United States of America, Elihu Root, Secretary of State of the United States; and

His Britannic Majesty, the Right Honourable James Bryce, O.M., his Ambassador Extraordinary and Plenipotentiary at Washington;

Who, after having communicated to one another their full powers, found in good and due form, have agreed upon the following articles:

PRELIMINARY ARTICLE

For the purposes of this treaty boundary waters are defined as the waters from main shore to main shore of the lakes and rivers and connecting waterways, or the portions thereof, along which the international boundary between the United States and the Dominion of Canada passes, including all bays, arms, and inlets thereof, but not including tributary waters which in their natural channels would flow into such lakes, rivers, and waterways, or waters flowing from such lakes, rivers, and waterways, or the waters of rivers flowing across the boundary.

ARTICLE I

The High Contracting Parties agree that the navigation of all navigable boundary waters shall forever continue free and open for the purposes of commerce to the inhabitants and to the ships, vessels, and boats of both countries equally, subject, however, to any laws and regulations of either country, within its own territory, not inconsistent with such privilege of free navigation and applying equally and without discrimination to the inhabitants, ships, vessels, and boats of both countries.

It is further agreed that so long as this treaty shall remain in force, this same right of navigation shall extend to the waters of Lake Michigan and to all canals connecting boundary waters, and now existing or which may hereafter be constructed on either side of the line. Either of the High Contracting Parties may adopt rules and regulations governing the use of such canals within its own territory and may charge tolls for the use thereof, but all such rules and regulations and all tolls charged shall apply alike to the subjects or citizens of the High Contracting Parties and the ships, vessels, and boats of both of the High Contracting Parties, and they shall be placed on terms of equality in the use thereof.

ARTICLE II

Each of the High Contracting Parties reserves to itself or to the several State Governments on the one side and the Dominion or Provincial Governments on the other as the case may be, subject to any treaty provisions now existing with respect thereto, the exclusive jurisdiction and control over the use and diversion, whether temporary or permanent, of all waters on its own side of the line which in their natural channels would flow across the boundary or into boundary waters; but it is agreed that any interference with or diversion from their natural channel of such waters on either side of the boundary, resulting in any injury on the other side of the boundary, shall give rise to the same rights and entitle the injured parties to the same legal remedies as if such injury took place in the country where such diversion or interference occurs; but this provision shall not apply to cases already existing or to cases expressly covered by special agreement between the parties hereto.

It is understood, however, that neither of the High Contracting parties intends by the foregoing provision to surrender any right, which it may have, to object to any interference with or diversions of waters on the other side of the boundary the effect of which would be productive of material injury to the navigation interests on its own side of the boundary.

ARTICLE III

It is agreed that, in addition to the uses, obstructions, and diversions heretofore permitted to hereafter provided for by special agreement between the parties hereto, no further or other uses or obstructions or diversions, whether temporary or permanent, of boundary waters on either side of the line, affecting the natural level or flow of boundary waters on the other side of the line shall be made except by authority of the United States or the Dominion of Canada within their respective jurisdictions and with the approval, as hereinafter provided, of a joint commission, to be known as the International Joint Commission.

The foregoing provisions are not intended to limit or interfere with the existing rights of the Government of the United States on the one side and the Government of the Dominion of Canada on the other, to undertake and carry on governmental works in boundary waters for the deepening of channels, the construction of breakwaters, the improvement of harbours, and other governmental works for the benefit of commerce and nevigation, provided that such works are wholly on its own side of the line and do not materially affect the level or flow of the boundary waters on the other, nor are such provisions intended to interfere with the ordinary use of such waters for domestic and sanitary purposes.

ARTICLE IV

The High Contracting Parties agree that, except in cases provided for by special agreement between them, they will not permit the construction or maintenance on their respective sides of the boundary of any remedial or protective works or any dams or other obstructions in waters flowing from boundary waters or in waters at a lower level than the boundary in rivers flowing across the boundary,the effect of which is to raise the natural level of waters on the other side of the boundary unless the construction or maintenance thereof is approved by the aforesaid International Joint Commission.

It is further agreed that the waters herein defined as boundary waters and waters flowing across the boundary shall not be polluted on either side to the injury of health or property on the other.

ARTICLE V

The High Contracting Parties agree that it is expedient to limit the diversion of waters from the Niagara River so that the level of lake Erie and the flow of the stream shall not be appreciably affected. It is the desire of both Parties to accomplish this object with the least possible injury to investments which have already been made in the construction of power plants on the United States side of the river under grants of authority from the State of New York, and on the Canadian side of the river under licences authorized by the Dominion of Canada and the Province of Ontario.

So long as this treaty shall remain in force, no diversion of the waters of the Niagara River above the Falls from the natural course and stream thereof shall be permitted except for the purposes and to the extent hereinafter provided.

The United States may authorize and permit the diversion within the State of New York of the waters of said river above the Falls of Niagara, for power purposes, not exceeding in the aggregate a daily diversion at the rate of twenty thousand cubic feet of water per second.

The United Kingdom, by the Dominion of Canada, or the Province of Ontario, may authorize and permit the diversion within the Province of Ontario of the waters of said river above the Falls of Niagara, for power purposes, not exceeding in the aggregate a daily diversion at the rate of thirty-six thousand cubic feet of water per second.

The prohibitions of this article shall not apply to the diversion of water for sanitary or domestic purposes, or for the service of canals for the purposes of navigation.

NOTE: The third, fourth and fifth paragraphs of Article V were terminated by the Canada-United States Treaty of February 27, 1950 concerning the diversion of the Niagara River.

ARTICLE VI

The High Contracting Parties agree that the St. Mary and Milk Rivers and their tributaries (in the State of Montana and the Provinces of Alberta and Saskatchewan) are to be treated as one stream for the purposes of irrigation and power, and the waters thereof shall be apportioned equally between the two countries, but in making such equal apportionment more than half may be taken from one river and less than half from the other by either country so as to afford a more beneficial use to each. It is further agreed that in the division of such waters during the irrigation season, between the 1st of April and 31st of October, inclusive, annually, the United

States is entitled to a prior appropriation of 500 cubic feet per second of the waters of the Milk River, or so much of such amount as constitutes three-fourths of its natural flow, and that Canada is entitled to a prior appropriaton of 500 cubic feet per second of the flow of St. Mary River, or so much of such amount as constitutes three-fourths of its natural flow.

The channel of the Milk River in Canada may be used at the convenience of the United States for the conveyance, while passing through Canadian territory, of waters diverted from the St. Mary River. The provisions of Article II of this treaty shall apply to any injury resulting to property in Canada from the conveyance of such waters through the Milk River.

The measurement and apportionment of the water to be used by each country shall from time to time be made jointly by the properly constituted reclamation officers of the United States and the properly constituted irrigation officers of His Majesty under the direction of the International Joint Commission.

ARTICLE VII

The High Contracting Parties agree to establish and maintain an International Joint Commission of the United States and Canada composed of six commissioners, three on the part of the United States appointed by the President thereof, and three on the part of the United Kingdom appointed by His Majesty on the recommendation of the Governor in Council of the Dominion of Canada.

ARTICLE VIII

This International Joint Commission shall have jurisdiction over and shall pass upon all cases involving the use or obstruction or diversion of the waters with respect to which under Article III and IV of this Treaty the approval of this Commission is required, and in passing upon such cases the Commission shall be governed by the following rules or principles which are adopted by the High Contracting Parties for this purpose:

The High Contracting parties shall have, each on its own side of the boundary, equal and similar rights in the use of the waters hereinbefore defined as boundary waters.

The following order of precedence shall be observed among the various uses enumerated hereinafter for these waters, and no use shall be permitted which tends materially to conflict with or restrain any other use which is given preference over it in this order of precedence

(1) Uses for domestic and sanitary purposes;
(2) Uses for navigation, including the service of canals for the purposes of navigation;
(3) Uses for power and for irrigation purposes.

The foregoing provisions shall not apply to or disturb any existing uses of boundary waters on either side of the boundary.

The requirement for an equal division may in the discretion of the Commission be suspended in cases of temporary diversions along boundary waters at points whre such equal division can not be made advantageously on account of local conditions, and where such diversion does not diminsh elsewhere the amount available for use on the other side.

The Commission in its discretion may make its approval in any case conditional upon the construction of remedial or protective works to compensate so far as possible for the particular use or diversion proposed, and in such cases may require that suitable and adequate provision, approved by the Commission, be made for the protection and indemnity against injury of any interests on either side of the boundary.

In cases involving the elevation of the natural level of waters on either side of the line as a result of the construction or maintenance on the other side of remedial or protective works or dams or other obstructions in boundary waters or in waters flowing therefrom or in waters below the boundary in rivers flowing across the boundary, the Commission shall require, as a condition of its approval thereof, that suitable and adequate provision, approved by it, be made for the protection and indemnity of all interests on the other side of the line which may be injured thereby.

The majority of the Commissioners shall have power to render a decision. In case the Commission is evenly divided upon any question or matter presented to it for decision, separate reports shall be made by the Commissioners on each side to their own Government. The High Contracting Parties shall thereupon endeavour to agree upon an adjustment of the question or matter of difference, and if an agreement is reached between them, it shall be reduced to writing in the form of a protocol, and shall be communicated to the Commissioners, who shall take such further proceedings as may be necessary to carry out such agreement.

ARTICLE IX

The High Contracting Parties further agree that any other questions or matters of difference arising between them involving the rights, obligations, or interests of either in relation to the other or to the inhabitants of the other, along the common frontier between the United States and the Dominion of Canada, shall be referred from time to time to the International Joint Commmission for examination and report, whenever either the Government of the United States or the Government of the Dominion of Canada shall request that such questions or matters of difference be so referred.

The International Joint Commission is authorized in each case so referred to examine into and report upon the facts and circumtances of the particular questions and matters referred, together with such conclusions and recommendations as may be appropriate, subject, however, to any restrictions or exceptions which may be imposed with respect thereto by the terms of their reference.

Such reports of the Commission shall not be regarded as decisions of the questions or matters so submitted either on the facts or the law, and shall in no way have the character of an arbitral award.

The Commission shall make a joint report to both Governments in all cases in which all or a majority of the Commissioners agree, and in case of disagreement the minority may make a joint report to both Governments, or separate reports to their respective Governments.

In case the Commission is evenly divided upon any question or matter referred to it for report, separate reports shall be made by the Commissioners on each side to their own Government.

ARTICLE X

Any questions or matters of difference arising between the High Contracting Parties involving the rights, obligations, or interests of the United States or of the Dominion of Canada either in relation to each other or to their respective inhabitants, may be referred for decision to the International Joint Commission by the consent of the two parties, it being understood that on the part of the United States any such action will be by and with the advice and consent of the Governor General in Council. In each case so referred, the said Commission is authorized to examine into and report upon the facts and circumstances of the particular questions any matters referred, together with such conclusions and recommendations as may be appropriate, subject, however, to any restrictions or exceptions which may be imposed with respect thereto by the terms of the reference.

A majority of the said Commission shall have power to render a decision or finding upon any of the questions or matters so referred.

If the said Commission is equally divided or otherwise unable to render a decision or finding as to any questions or matters so referred, it shall be the duty of the Commissioners to make a joint report to both Governments, or separate reports to their respective Governments, showing the different conclusions arrived at with regard to the matters or questions so referred, which questions or matters shall thereupon be referred for decision by the High Contracting Parties to an umpire chosen in accordance with the procedure prescribed in the fourth, fifth and sixth paragraphs of Article XLV of the Hague Convention for the pacific settlement of international disputes, dated October 18, 1907. Such umpire shall have power to render a final decision with respect to those matters and questions so referred on which the Commission failed to agree.

ARTICLE XI

A duplicate original of all decisions rendered and joint reports made by the Commission shall be transmitted to and filed with the Secretary of State of the United States and the Governor General of the Dominion of

Canada, and to them shall be addressed all communications of the Commission.

ARTICLE XII

The International Joint Commission shall meet and organize at Washington promptly after the members thereof are appointed, and when organized the Commission may fix such times and places for its meetings as may be necessary, subject at all times to special call or direction by the two Governments. Each Commissioner upon the first joint meeting of the Commission after his appointment, shall, before proceeding with the work of the Commission, make and subscribe a solemn declaration in writing that he will faithfully and impartially perform the duties imposed upon him under this treaty, and such declaration shall be entered on the records of the proceedings of the Commission.

The United States and Canadian sections of the Commission may each appoint a secretary, and these shall act as joint secretaries of the Commission at its joint sessions, and the Commission may employ engineers and clerical assistants from time to time as it may deem advisable. The salaries and personal expenses of the Commission and of the secretaries shall be paid by their respective Governments, and all reasonable and necessary joint expenses of the Commission, incurred by it, shall be paid in equal moieties by the High Contracting Parties.

The Commission shall have power to administer oaths to witnesses, and to take evidence on oath whenever deemed necessary in any proceeding, or inquiry, or matter within its jurisdiction under this treaty, and all parties interested therein shall be given convenient opportunity to be heard, and the High Contracting Parties agree to adopt such legislation as may be appropriate and necessary to give the Commission the powers above mentioned on each side of the boundary, and to provide for the issue of subpoenas and for compelling the attendance of witnesses in proceedings before the Commission. The Commission may adopt such rules of procedure as shall be in accordance with justice and equity, and may make such examination in person and through agents or employees as may be deemed advisable.

ARTICLE XIII

In all cases where special agreements between the High Contracting Parties hereto are referred to in the foregoing articles, such agreements are understood and intended to include not only direct agreements between the High Contracting parties, but also any mutual arrangement between the United States and the Dominion of Canada expressed by concurrent or reciprocal legislation on the part of Congress and the Parliament of the Dominion.

ARTICLE XIV

The present treaty shall be ratified by the President of the United States of America, by and with the advice and consent of the Senate thereof, and by His Britannic Majesty. The ratifications shall be exchanged at Washington as soon as possible and the treaty shall take effect on the date of the exchange of its ratifications. It shall remain in force for five years, dating from the day of exchange of ratifications, and thereafter until terminated by twelve months' wirtten notice given by either High Contracting Party to the other.

In faith whereof the respective plenipotentiaries have signed this treaty in duplicate and have hereunto affixed their seals.

Done at Washington the 11th day of January, in the year of our Lord one thousand nine hundred and nine.

(Signed) ELIHU ROOT [SEAL]

(Signed) JAMES BRYCE [SEAL]

AND WHEREAS the Senate of the United States by their resolution of March 3, 1909, (two-thirds of the Senators present concurring therein) did advise and consent to the ratification of the said Treaty with the following understanding, to wit:

"Resolved further, as a part of this ratification, That the United States approves this treaty with the understanding that nothing in this treaty shall be construed as affecting, or changing, any existing territorial or riparian rights in the water, or rights of the owners of lands under water, on either side of the international boundary at the rapids of the St. Mary's river at Sault Ste. Marie, in the use of the waters flowing over such lands, subject to the requirements of navigation in boundary waters and of navigation canals, and without prejudice to the existing right of the United States and Canada, each to use the waters of the St. Mary's river, within its own territory, and further, that nothing in this treaty shall be construed to interfere with the drainage of wet swamp and overflowed lands into streams flowing into boundary waters, and that this interpretation will be mentioned in the ratification of this treaty as conveying the true meaning of the treaty, and will, in effect, form part of the treaty;"

AND WHEREAS the said understanding has been accepted by the Government of Great Britain, and the ratifications of the two Governments of the said treaty were exchanged in the City of Washington, on the 5th day of May, one thousand nine hundred and ten;

NOW, THEREFORE, be it known that I, William Howard Taft, President of the United States of America, have caused the said treaty and the said understanding, as forming a part thereof, to be made public, to the end that the same and every article and clause thereof may be observed and fulfilled with good faith by the United States and the citizens thereof.

In testimony whereof, I have hereunto set my hand and caused the seal of the United States to be affixed.

Done at the City of Washington this thirteenth day of May in the year of our Lord one thousand nine hundred and ten,
[SEAL] and of the Independence of the United States of America the one hundred and thirty-fourth.

Wm H Taft

By the President:
P C Knox
Secretary of State.

APPENDIX B. EXCERPTS FROM THE AGREEMENT BETWEEN CANADA AND THE UNITED STATES OF AMERICA ON GREAT LAKES WATER QUALITY

The Government of Canada and the Government of the United States of America,

Having in 1972 entered into an Agreement on Great Lakes Water Quality;

Reaffirming their determination to restore and enhance water quality in the Great Lakes System;

Continuing to be concerned about the impairment of water quality on each side of the boundary to an extent that is causing injury to health and property on the other side, as described by the International Joint Commission;

Reaffirming their intent to prevent further pollution of the Great Lakes Basin Ecosystem owing to continuing population growth, resource development and increasing use of water;

Reaffirming in a spirit of friendship and cooperation the rights and obligations of both countries under the Boundary Waters Treaty, signed on January 11, 1909, and in particular their obligation not to pollute boundary waters;

Continuing to recognize the rights of each country in the use of its Great Lakes waters;

Having decided that the Great Lakes Water Quality Agreement of April 15, 1972 and subsequent reports of the International Joint Commission provide a sound basis for new and more effective cooperative actions to restore and enhance water quality in the Great Lakes Basin Ecosystem;

Recognizing that restoration and enhancement of the boundary waters can not be achieved independently of other parts of the Great Lakes Basin Ecosystem with which these waters interact;

Concluding that the best means to preserve the aquatic ecosystem and achieve improved water quality throughout the Great Lakes System is by adopting common objectives, developing and implementing cooperative programs and other measures, and assigning special responsibilities and functions to the International Joint Commission;

Have agreed as follows:

ARTICLE I

DEFINITIONS

As used in this Agreement:

(a) "Agreement" means the present Agreement as distinguished from the Great Lakes Water Quality Agreement of April 15, 1972;

(b) "Annex" means any of the Annexes to this Agreement, each of which is attached to and forms an integral part of this Agreement;

(c) "Boundary waters of the Great Lakes System" or "boundary waters" means boundary waters, as defined in the Boundary Waters Treaty, that are within the Great Lakes System;

(d) "Boundary Waters Treaty" means the Treaty between the United States and Great Britain Relating to Boundary Waters, and Questions Arising Between the United States and Canada, signed at Washington on January 11, 1909;

(e) "Compatible regulations" means regulations no less restrictive than the agreed principles set out in this Agreement;

(f) "General Objectives" are broad descriptions of water quality conditions consistent with the protection of the beneficial uses and the level of environmental quality which the Parties desire to secure and which will provide overall water management guidance;

(g) "Great Lakes Basin Ecosystem" means the interacting components of air, land, water and living organisms, including man, within the drainage basin of the St. Lawrence River at or upstream from the point at which this river becomes the international boundary between Canada and the United States;

(h) "Great Lakes System" means all of the streams, rivers, lakes and other bodies of water that are within the drainage basin on the St. Lawrence River at or upstream from the point at which this river becomes the international boundary between Canada and the United States;

ARTICLE II
PURPOSE

The purpose of the Parties is to restore and maintain the chemical, physical, and biological integrity of the waters of the Great Lakes Basin Ecosystem. In order to achieve this purpose, the Parties agree to make a maximum effort to develop programs, practices and technology necessary for a better understanding of the Great Lakes Basin Ecosystem and to eliminate or reduce to the maximum extent practicable the discharge of pollutants into the Great Lakes System.

Consistent with the provisions of this Agreement, it is the policy of the parties that:
  (a) The discharge of toxic substances in toxic amounts be prohibited and the discharge of any or all persistent toxic substances be virtually eliminated;
  (b) Financial assistance to construct publicly owned waste treatment works be provided by a combination of local, state, provincial, and federal participation; and
  (c) Coordinated planning processes and best management practices be developed and implemented by the respective jurisdictions to ensure adequate control of all sources of pollutants.

APPENDIX C. THE GREAT LAKES CHARTER

PRINCIPLES FOR THE MANAGEMENT OF GREAT LAKES WATER RESOURCES

Findings
The Governors and Premiers of the Great Lakes States and Provinces jointly find and declare that:

The water resources of the Great Lakes Basin are precious public natural resources, shared and held in trust by the Great Lakes States and Provinces.

The Great Lakes are valuable regional, national and international resources for which the federal governments of the United States and Canada and the International Joint Commission have, in partnership with the States and Provinces, an important, continuing and abiding role and responsibility.

The Waters of the Great Lakes Basin are interconnected and part of a single hydrologic system. The multiple uses of these resources for municipal, industrial and agricultural water supply; mining; navigation; hydroelectric power and energy production; recreation; and the maintenance of fish and wildlife habitat and a balanced ecosystem are interdependent.

Studies conducted by the International Joint Commission, the Great Lakes States and Provinces, and other agencies have found that without careful and prudent management, the future development of diversions and consumptive uses of the water resources of the Great Lakes Basin may have significant adverse impacts on the environment, economy, and welfare of the Great Lakes region.

As trustees of the Basin's natural resources, the Great Lakes States and Provinces have a shared duty to protect, conserve, and manage the renewable but finite waters of the Great Lakes Basin for the use, benefit, and enjoyment of all their citizens, including generations yet to come. The most effective means of protecting, conserving and managing the water resources of the Great Lakes is through the joint pursuit of unified and cooperative principles, policies, and programs mutually agreed upon, enacted and adhered to by each and every Great Lakes State and Province.

Management of the water resources of the Basin is subject to the jurisdiction, rights and responsiblities of the signatory States and Provinces. Effective management of the water resources of the Great Lakes requires the exercise of such jurisdiction, rights, and responsibilities in the interest of all the people of the Great Lakes Region, acting in a continuing spirit of comity and mutual cooperation. The Great Lakes States and Provinces reaffirm the mutual rights and obligations of all Basin jurisdictions to use, conserve, and protect Basin water resources, as expressed in the Boundary Waters Treaty of 1909, the Great Lakes Water Quality Agreement, of 1978, and the principles of other applicable international agreements.

Purpose

The purposes of this Charter are to conserve the levels and flows of the Great Lakes and their tributary connecting waters; to protect and conserve the environmental balance of the Great Lakes Basin ecosystem; to provide for cooperative programs and management of the water resources of the Great Lakes Basin by the signatory States and Provinces; to make secure and protect present developments within the region; and to provide a secure foundation for future investment and development within the region.

Principles for the Management of
Great Lakes Water Resources

In order to achieve the purposes of this Charter, the Governors and Premiers of the Great Lakes States and Provinces agree to the following principles.

PRINCIPLE I
INTEGRITY OF THE GREAT LAKES BASIN

The planning and management of the water resources of the Great Lakes Basin should recognize and be founded upon the integrity of the natural resources and ecosystem of the Great Lakes Basin. The water resources of the Basin transcend political boundaries within the Basin, and should be recognized and treated as a single hydrologic system. In managing Great Lakes Basin waters, the natural resources and ecosystem of the Basin should be considered as a unified whole.

PRINCIPLE II
PROTECTION OF THE WATER RESOURCES
OF THE GREAT LAKES

The signatory States and Provinces agree that new or increased diversions and consumptive uses of Great Lakes Basin water resources are of serious concern. In recognition of their shared responsibility to conserve and protect the water resources of the Great Lakes Basin for the use, benefit, and enjoyment of all their citizens, the States and Provinces agree to seek (where necessary) and to implement legislation establishing programs to manage and regulate the diversion and consumptive use of Basin water resources. It is the intent of the signatory states and provinces that diversions of Basin water resources will not be allowed if individually or cumulatively they would have any significant adverse impacts on lake levels, in-basin uses, and the Great Lakes Ecosystem.

PRINCIPLE IV
PRIOR NOTICE AND CONSULTATION

It is the intent of the signatory States and Provinces that no Great Lakes State or Province will approve or permit any major new or increased diversion or consumptive use of the water resources of the Great Lakes Basin without notifying and consulting with and seeking the consent and concurrence of all affected Great Lakes States and Provinces.

PRINCIPLE V
COOPERATIVE PROGRAMS AND PRACTICES

The Governors and Premiers of the Great Lakes States and Provinces commit to pursue the development and maintenance of a common base of data and information regarding the use and management of Basin water resources, to the establishment of systematic arrangements for the exchange of water data and information, to the creation of a Water Resources Management Committee, to the development of a Great Lakes Water Resources Management Program, and to additional and concerted and coordinated research efforts to provide improved information for future water planning and management decisions.

Signed 11 February 1985, Milwaukee, Wisconsin

CONTRIBUTORS

Bruce L. Bandurski, Ecomanagement Advisor, International Joint Commission, Washington, D.C. Formerly, Ecologist with the Bureau of Land Management, U.S.A.

Lee Botts, former Executive Director of the Great Lakes Basin Commission. Cochair of the 1983–85 interuniversity seminar on the Great Lakes has been one of the leaders in raising public awareness of Great Lakes policy issues.

Lynton K. Caldwell, Arthur F. Bentley Professor of Political Science Emeritus and Professor of Public and Environmental Affairs at Indiana University. Was a member of the interuniversity seminar on the Great Lakes and is cochair of the Societal Committee of the Science Advisory Board of the I.J.C.

Sally Cole-Misch, Public Affairs Officer, International Joint Commission, Great Lakes Regional Office, Windsor, Ontario.

Michael J. Donahue, Executive Director, Great Lakes Commission, formerly Director of Research, Center for the Great Lakes. Member of interuniversity seminar on the Great Lakes.

Leonard B. Dworsky, Professor of Civil Engineering Emeritus, Cornell University. Widely recognized authority on water policy. Cochair of the first interuniversity seminar on the Great Lakes.

George R. Francis, Professor in the Department of Environment and Resource Studies, University of Waterloo, Ontario. Cochair of first interuniversity seminar on the Great Lakes. Former member of the Science Advisory Board to the International Joint Commission and of the Board of Technical Experts to the Great Lakes Fishery Commission.

John E. Gannon, Ecologist, U.S. Fish and Wildlife Service, Ann Arbor, Michigan, Limnologist, Great Lakes Regional Office of the IJC. Assistant Director and often Acting Director since 11/84. Former Resident Scientist at the University of Michigan Biological Station on Douglas Lake, and Associate Director, State University Research Center at Oswego, N.Y.

J. D. Kingham, Director General, Canadian Great Lakes Environmental Program, Environment Canada, Cochair Water Quality Board. Has done, in addition, important research on policy positions in the Canadian government relating to water quality.

Lester W. Milbrath, Professor of Political Science, SUNY Buffalo, and Director of the Research Program in Environment and Society. Member of the interuniversity seminar on the Great Lakes and environmental series editor for the State University of New York Press.

Don Munton, Associate Professor of Political Science, University of British Columbia (formerly at Dalhousie University). Member of interuniversity seminar on the Great Lakes and of the Royal Society–NRC study of the 1978 Water Quality Agreement.

K. Ogilvie, Staff scientist, Environment Canada.

Henry Regier, Professor of Zoology, University of Toronto. Cochair of the 1983–85 interuniversity seminar on the Great Lakes. Member of Great Lakes Fishery Commission and cochair of the Royal Society–National Research Council review of the 1978 Water Quality Agreement and member of the Science Advisory Board of the IJC.

R. L. Thomas, Director 1984–86, Great Lakes Regional Office. Also has had professional appointments in geology and geochemistry at the University of Waterloo, Ontario, and the University of Geneva, Switzerland. Founding President of the International Association for Sediment Water Science and past President of the International Association for Great Lakes Research.

J. R. Vallentyne, Senior Scientist, Fisheries and Marine Service of Canada, Ontario Region, and cochair, Science Advisory Board, IJC, author of numerous scientific papers on biogeochemistry and the biosphere, and with previous faculty appointments at Yale, Queens, and Cornell Universities.

Julia R. Wilder, practicing Attorney-at-Law, graduate of the Indiana University School of Law at Bloomington, with special interest in legal problems relating to water, agriculture, and natural resources.